PERTH COLLEGE STUDY CENTRE

07710

07710
ACCA
657-45

ACCA
STUDY TEXT

Professional Paper 10

Accounting and Audit Practice (Auditing)

New in this June 1998 edition

- Year 2000

- Recent developments in reporting on internal control

- SAS 480

- Recent developments in auditor liability

FOR DECEMBER 1998 AND JUNE 1999 EXAMS

BPP Publishing
June 1998

First edition 1993
Sixth edition June 1998

ISBN 0 7517 0135 1 (Previous edition 0 7517 0075 4)

British Library Cataloguing-in-Publication Data
A catalogue record for this book is available from the British Library

Published by

BPP Publishing Limited
Aldine House, Aldine Place
London W12 8AW
http://www.bpp.co.uk

Printed and bound by Progressive Printing (U.K.) Limited, Leigh-on-Sea, Essex.

All rights reserved. No part of this publication may be reproduced, stored in a retrieval system or transmitted, in any form or by any means, electronic, mechanical, photocopying, recording or otherwise, without the prior written permission of BPP Publishing Limited.

We are grateful to the Association of Chartered Certified Accountants for permission to reproduce in this text the syllabus and teaching guide of which the Association holds the copyright.

We are grateful to the Auditing Practices Board for permission to reproduce the glossary of auditing terms.

We are also grateful to the Association of Chartered Certified Accountants and the Institute of Chartered Accountants in England and Wales for permission to reproduce past examination questions in our Exam Question Bank. The Exam Answer Bank has been prepared by BPP Publishing Limited.

©
BPP Publishing Limited
1998

HOW TO USE THIS STUDY TEXT

Aims of this Study Text

To provide you with the knowledge and understanding, skills and applied techniques required for passing the exam °

The Study Text has been written around the ACCA's Official Syllabus and the ACCA's Official 1998-9 Teaching Guide (reproduced below, and cross-referenced to where in the text each topic is covered).

- It is **comprehensive**. We do not omit sections of the syllabus as the examiner is liable to examine any angle of any part of the syllabus - and you do not want to be left high and dry.

- It is **up-to-date as at 1 June 1998**, which means that it fulfils the requirement for the December 1998 exams that students should be up-to-date as at 1 June 1998.

- And it is **on-target** - we do not include any material which is not examinable. You can therefore rely on the BPP Study Text as the stand-alone source of all your information for the exam, without worrying that any of the material is irrelevant.

To allow you to study in the way that best suits your learning style and the time you have available, by following your personal Study Plan (see below)

You may be studying at home on your own until the date of the exam, or you may be attending a full-time course. You may like to (and have time to) read every word, or you may prefer to (or only have time to) skim-read and devote the remainder of your time to question practice. Wherever you fall in the spectrum, you will find the BPP Study Text meets your needs in designing and following your personal Study Plan.

To tie in with the other components of the BPP Effective Study Package to ensure you have the best possible chance of passing the exam

Recommended period of use	Elements of BPP Effective Study Package
3-12 months before exam	**Study Text** Acquisition of knowledge, understanding, skills and applied techniques
1-6 months before exam	**Practice and Revision Kit** Tutorial Questions and helpful checklists of the key points lead you into each area. There are then numerous exam questions to try, graded by topic area, along with realistic suggested solutions prepared by BPP's own authors in the light of the Examiner's Reports. June 1999 examinees will find the 1999 edition of the Kit invaluable for bringing them up-to-date as at 1 December 1998, the cut-off date for the June 1999 examinable material
last minute - 3 months before exam	**Passcards** Short, memorable notes focused on what is most likely to come up in the exam you will be sitting

Settling down to study

By this stage in your career you are probably a very experienced learner and taker of exams. But have you ever thought about *how* you learn? Let's have a quick look at the key elements required for effective learning. You can then identify your learning style and go on to design your own approach to how you are going to study this text - your personal Study Plan.

Key element of learning	Using the BPP Study Text
Motivation	You can rely on the comprehensiveness and technical quality of BPP. You've chosen the right Study Text - so you're in pole position to pass your exam!
Clear objectives and standards	Do you want to be a prizewinner or simply achieve a moderate pass? Decide.
Feedback	Follow through the examples in this text and do the questions and the Quick Quizzes. Evaluate your efforts critically - how are you doing?
Study plan	You need to be honest about your progress to yourself - do not be over-confident, but don't be negative either. Make your Study Plan (see below) and try to stick to it. Focus on the short-term objectives - completing two chapters a night, say - but beware of losing sight of your study objectives
Practice	Use the Quick Quizzes and Chapter Roundups to refresh your memory regularly after you have completed your initial study of each chapter

These introductory pages let you see exactly what you are up against. However you study, you should:

- **read through the syllabus and teaching guide** - this will help you to identify areas you have already covered, perhaps at a lower level of detail, and areas that are totally new to you

- **study the examination paper section**, where we show you the format of the exam (how many and what kind of questions etc) and analyse all the papers set so far under the syllabus.

Key study steps

The following steps are, in our experience, the ideal way to study for professional exams. You can of course adapt it for your particular learning style (see below).

Tackle the chapters in the order you find them in the Study Text. Taking into account your individual learning style, follow these key study steps for each chapter.

Key study steps	Activity
Step 1 *Chapter topic list*	Study the list. Each numbered topic denotes a numbered section in the chapter
Step 2 *Introduction*	Read it through. It is designed to show you *why* the topics in the chapter need to be studied - how they lead on from previous topics, and how they lead into subsequent ones
Step 3 *Knowledge brought forward boxes*	In these we highlight information and techniques that it is assumed you have 'brought forward' with you from your earlier studies. If there are matters which have changed recently due to legislation etc then these topics are explained in full. Do not panic if you do not feel instantly comfortable with the content - it should come back to you as we develop the subject for this paper. If you are really unsure, we advise you to go back to your previous notes
Step 4 *Explanations*	Proceed methodically through the chapter, reading each section thoroughly and making sure you understand. Where a topic has been examined, we state the month and year of examination against the appropriate heading. You should pay particular attention to these topics.
Step 5 *Key terms* and *Exam focus points*	• **Key terms** can often earn you *easy marks* if you state them clearly and correctly in an appropriate exam answer (and they are indexed at the back of the text so you can check easily that you are on top of all of them when you come to revise) • **Exam focus points** give you a good idea of how the examiner tends to examine certain topics - and also pinpoint *easy marks*
Step 6 *Note taking*	Take brief notes if you wish, avoiding the temptation to copy out too much
Step 7 *Examples*	Follow each through to its solution very carefully
Step 8 *Case examples*	Study each one, and try if you can to add flesh to them from your own experience - they are designed to show how the topics you are studying come alive (and often come unstuck) in the real world
Step 9 *Questions*	Make a very good attempt at each one
Step 10 *Answers*	Check yours against ours, and make sure you understand any discrepancies
Step 11 *Chapter roundup*	Check through it very carefully, to make sure you have grasped the major points it is highlighting

 BPP Publishing

Key study steps	Activity
Step 12 *Quick quiz*	When you are happy that you have covered the chapter, use the **Quick quiz** to check your recall of the topics covered. The answers are in the paragraphs in the chapter that we refer you to
Step 13 *Examination question(s)*	Either at this point, or later when you are thinking about revising, make a full attempt at the **Examination question(s)** suggested at the very end of the chapter. You can find these at the end of the Study Text, along with the **Answers** so you can see how you did. We highlight for you which ones are introductory, and which are of the full standard you would expect to find in an exam

Developing your personal Study Plan

Preparing a Study Plan (and sticking closely to it) is one of the key elements in learning success.

First you need to be aware of your style of learning. There are four typical learning styles. Consider yourself in the light of the following descriptions. and work out which you fit most closely. You can then plan to follow the key study steps in the sequence suggested.

Learning styles	Characteristics	Sequence of key study steps in the BPP Study Text
Theorist	Seeks to understand principles before applying them in practice	1, 2, 3, 4, 7, 8, 5, 9/10, 11, 12, 13 (6 continuous)
Reflector	Seeks to observe phenomena, thinks about them and then chooses to act	
Activist	Prefers to deal with practical, active problems; does not have much patience with theory	1, 2, 9/10 (read through), 7, 8, 5, 11, 3, 4, 9/10 (full attempt), 12, 13 (6 continuous)
Pragmatist	Prefers to study only if a direct link to practical problems can be seen; not interested in theory for its own sake	9/10 (read through), 2, 5, 7, 8, 11, 1, 3, 4, 9/10 (full attempt), 12, 13 (6 continuous)

Next you should complete the following checklist.

Am I motivated? (a) [   ]

Do I have an objective and a standard that I want to achieve? (b) [   ]

Am I a theorist, a reflector, an activist or a pragmatist? (c) [   ]

How much time do I have available per week, given: (d) [   ]

- the standard I have set myself

- the time I need to set aside later for work on the Practice and Revision Kit and Passcards

- the other exam(s) I am sitting, and (of course)

- practical matters such as work, travel, exercise, sleep and social life?

Now:

- take the time you have available per week for this Study Text (d), and multiply it by the number of weeks available to give (e).

(e) [ ]

- divide (e) by the number of chapters to give (f)

(f) [ ]

- set about studying each chapter in the time represented by (f), following the key study steps in the order suggested by your particular learning style.

This is your personal **Study Plan**.

Short of time?

Whatever your objectives, standards or style, you may find you simply do not have the time available to follow all the key study steps for each chapter, however you adapt them for your particular learning style. If this is the case, follow the Skim Study technique below (the icons in the Study Text will help you to do this).

Skim Study technique

Study the chapters in the order you find them in the Study Text. For each chapter, follow the key study steps 1-3, and then skim-read through step 4. Jump to step 11, and then go back to step 5. Follow through steps 7 and 8, and prepare outline Answers to Questions (steps 9/10). Try the Quick Quiz (step 12), following up any items you can't answer, then do a plan for the Examination Question (step 13), comparing it against our answers. You should probably still follow step 6 (note-taking), although you may decide simply to rely on the BPP Passcards for this.

Moving on...

However you study, when you are ready to embark on the practice and revision phase of the BPP Effective Study Package, you should still refer back to this study text:

- as a source of **reference** (you should find the list of key terms and the index particularly helpful for this)

- as a **refresher** (the Chapter Roundups and Quick Quizzes help you here)

And remember to keep careful hold of this Study Text when you move onto the next level of your exams - you will find it invaluable.

ACCA OFFICIAL SYLLABUS

Paper 10 *Accounting and Audit Practice* covers two related topics; accounting and financial accounting (approximately 65% of exam marks) and auditing (approximately 35% of exam marks).

*Covered in
Chapter*

1   The theoretical and regulatory accounting framework   *See Note*

(a)   The interpretation and application of the following theories and principles:

    (i)   theories of accounting in relation to the measurement of:
- income
- capital maintenance
- valuation of assets and liabilities

    (ii)   principles of accounting for price level changes

    (iii)   accounting conventions

    (iv)   the recognition of revenue

    (v)   the recognition of assets and liabilities.

(b)   The objectives of financial statements

    (i)   criteria of useful information
    (ii)   usefulness for particular purposes.

(c)   The interpretation and application of all extant SSAPs and FRSs.

(d)   The appreciation of the role of the legal and regulatory framework of accounting.

2   Preparing financial statements   *See Note*

(a)   The preparation and presentation of financial statements, under conditions of stable prices, for:

    (i)   partnerships, including conversion of partnership to a limited company

    (ii)   branches

    (iii)   limited companies, within the legal and regulatory requirements including the application of all extant SSAPs and FRSs
- profit and loss accounts
- balance sheets
- cash flow statements
- directors' reports.

(b)   Calculation and accounting treatment of:

    (i)   pre-incorporation profits
    (ii)   distributable profits
    (iii)   purchase of own shares

2   Preparing financial statements - continued   *See Note*

(c)   Groups of companies

  (i)   explaining statutory and professional requirements relating
        to the preparation for publication of consolidated accounts

  (ii) accounting for the following organisational situations
        - joint ventures
        - associated undertakings
        - simple groups

  (iii) evaluating the following alternative group accounting
        methods
        - equity accounting
        - proportional consolidation
        - acquisition accounting
        - merger accounting.

3   Analysing and appraising financial and related information   *See Note*

(a)   Interpreting and appraising financial statements for indications of
       business performance, using inter-firm and inter-temporal
       methods.

(b)   Assessing information weaknesses in the financial statements.

4   Communicating to users   *See Note*

(a)   Producing reports as specified to meet the needs of internal and
       external users, supported by appropriate accounts and financial
       statements, which include information on, and where necessary
       explanations of:

  (i)   the results of operations and the state of affairs
  (ii) projected results
  (iii) accounting policies and practices used
  (iv) main assumptions on which the reports are based
  (v)   significant departures from accounting standards, concepts
        and conventions
  (vi) any other material considerations

5   Advanced auditing practices and procedures

(a)   Controlling the audit including advanced aspects of audit   6, 7, 10
       planning, audit programme design and testing, statistical sampling
       and sampling methods, evaluation of audit risk and test results.

(b)   Organising and planning complex audit situations including group   3, 8, 10
       audits, joint audits, working with specialists, utilisation of CAATs

(c)   Reviewing financial statements for their compliance with GAAP.   9

**Covered in
Chapter**

5   Advanced auditing practices and procedures - continued

(d)   Evaluating other critical areas - going concern status, related party   9, 11
transactions, pending legal action, illegal acts by clients.

(e)   Reviewing the auditor's responsibility for preceding year amounts.   9

(f)   Reviewing unaudited information included with audited financial   9
statements.

(g)   Managing the audit client, including compiling and reviewing   6, 7, 9, 10
information on clients throughout the year.

(h)   Managing the audit relationship   12

6   The audit framework

(a)   Monitoring and evaluating important developments in   All

    (i)   auditing concepts and principles
    (ii)   auditing standards and guidelines
    (iii)   auditing methods and techniques
    (iv)   Companies Act requirements and case law
    (v)   Financial Services Act.

(b)   Monitoring the impact of information systems development on the   8
audit process including the impact of computers on the auditing
process, monitoring best practice in systems design, operation and
the management of information systems development, and the
resource implications of IT systems.

Note. This Study Text covers Sections 5-6 of the syllabus. Sections 1-4 of the syllabus are
covered in the companion Study Text *Accounting and Audit Practice (Accounting)*.

ACCA OFFICIAL 1998-1999 TEACHING GUIDE

This is the official 1998-1999 Teaching Guide, for the December 1998 and June 1999 exam.

Syllabus reference

Session 23   Risk and Audit Sampling

5(a), (g)

- explain the logic of assessing audit risk and risk based audits
- describe how the auditor assesses inherent risk and control risk in establishing the detection risk for a particular audit test
- explain how the audit programme reflects the application of audit objectives
- explain the use of audit sampling in the conduct of an audit

Self Study

- explain the nature, purpose and scope of an audit
- explain the regulatory framework of auditing
- identify the fundamental principles and concepts which affect auditing
- outline the nature of the audit process
- outline the importance of audit evidence

Session 24   Substantive Testing and Analytical Review

5(a)

- discuss the nature of substantive testing and substantive analysis
- discuss the use of substantive testing in the verification of financial statements
- formulate conclusions on substantive tests in line with critical audit objectives, risk evaluation and materiality levels
- explain the relationship between substantive analysis and analytical review
- describe the major analytical review techniques
- describe how analytical review techniques can be used in audit planning and risk assessment
- describe the uses of analytical review in the review of the financial statements

Session 25   Computer Auditing

5(a), 6(b)

- discuss the use of computers in the audit process (including the use of microcomputers for audit purposes)
- discuss the audit implications of the computerisation of a client's records
- describe the use of CAATs (computer assisted auditing techniques) including the use of expert systems and audit enquiry programs
- evaluate the usefulness of CAATs in the audit process
- describe the importance of the audit procedures relating to systems development, acquisition and maintenance, and their resource implications
- describe the trends in Information Technology and their impact on auditors

Session 26   The Final Audit

5(c), (d), (e), (f)

- explain the importance of the review of audit working papers
- explain the ways in which the auditor reviews the financial statements
- explain the importance of representations by management, audit completion checklists and other final audit matters
- explain the audit responsibility for opening balances and comparatives
- describe the auditors' role to consider client compliance with Law and regulations
- explain the audit implications of other information in documents containing audited financial statements
- describe the tests conducted to discover pending legal action and other post balance sheet events and contingencies
- describe the auditor's responsibilities for establishing the going concern status of the client

Self Study
- describe any recent changes in legislation or case law which may affect the auditor
- describe the changing role of the auditor

Session 27   Group Audits

5(b), (d)

- explain the organisation, planning and managing of complex audit situations
- explain the special considerations of the planning and controlling of a group audit
- discuss the regulatory requirements of accounting for groups of companies and the auditing implications thereof
- explain the relationship between principal and other auditors, and using the work of an expert
- explain the problems of auditing a foreign subsidiary
- describe the audit implications of related party transactions

Self Study
- explain the auditors' duties regarding directors' remunerations and transactions involving directors

Session 28   Audit Reporting, Auditor's Liability and Current Issues   5(c), 6(a)

- describe the content and meaning of unqualified and qualified audit reports as specified in SAS 600 'The auditors' report on financial statements'. (Students would not be expected to reproduce an audit report in full)

- prepare and audit reports to meet different specified situations

- describe the extent to which users understand the audit report

- discuss the ways in which the audit report could be improved

- discuss how audit qualifications may be avoided by negotiations with management

- describe and apply the ACCA rules of professional conduct and ethical responsibilities

- describe the current position on the legal liability of the auditor and the relationship with indemnity insurers

- describe the implications and principles involved when undertaking common forms of non-audit and related services engagements eg consultancy work, reporting on forecast information

Self Study

- describe any recent changes in legislation which affect the auditor

THE EXAMINATION PAPER

Format of the paper

		Number of marks
Section A:	2 (out of 3) questions on financial accounting	50
Section B:	Compulsory integrated accounting and auditing question	30
	Compulsory auditing question	20
		100

Time allowed: 3 hours

The financial accounting content will account for approximately 65% of the marks and will be examined in Section A and part of Section B. The auditing content will account for the remaining 35% of the marks and will be examined in Section B.

Analysis of pilot paper

The examiner for Paper 10 changed from the June 1997 exam onwards. To reflect the change in style that this caused (although the paper format remained the same), the ACCA produced a pilot paper. The contents are as follows.

Section A (2 out of 3)
1 Published accounts from trial balance
2 Cash flow statement
3 Creative accounting

Section B (compulsory)
4 Audit of group accounts; equity and acquisition methods
5 Audit risk

Analysis of past papers

The analysis below shows the topics which have been examined in the eight sittings of the new syllabus.

December 1997

Section A (2 out of 3)
1 Branch accounts; SSAP 21
2 Fixed assets - SSAPs 4 and 21; FRS 3
3 Revenue recognition; *Statement of Principles*

Section B (compulsory)
4 Consolidated profit and loss account (merger and acquisition accounting); procedures on taking over an audit
5 Audit of newly computerised system; impact of developments in IT on audit

June 1997

Section A (2 out of 3)
1 Consolidated balance sheet; discussion of its usefulness
2 Earnings per share: calculations and disclosure
3 Critical discussion of FRS 3

Section B (compulsory)
4 Report on financial performance and its value to auditors; going concern
5 Non-audit services; weaknesses of audit procedures; liability of auditors

December 1996

Section A (2 out of 3)
1   Consolidated accounts; fair values
2   SSAP 25 segmental report
3   Treatment of goodwill and its effect on realised profits

Section B (compulsory)
4   Redraft foreign accounts under UK standards; principal and other auditors
5   Auditing and the Internet

June 1996

Section A (2 out of 3)
1   Consolidated balance sheet; dividend by subsidiary out of pre-acquisition profits
2   Partnership: conversion to limited company; exemptions from statutory disclosure requirements
3   FRS 3 explanations; effect of transactions on various FRS 3 statements

Section B (compulsory)
4   Long term contracts: accounting and audit aspects
5   Audit risk; cash management confidentiality of client's information

December 1995

Section A (2 out of 3)
1   Redrafting group financial statement to comply with CA 85 and accounting standards
2   Published accounts with branch
3   Agency theory; positive accounting terms, *Statement of Principles*

Section B (compulsory)
4   Audit of group accounts; equity and acquisition methods
5   Audit tests to detect fraud; confidentiality; negligence

June 1995

Section A (2 out of 3)
1   Cash flow statement and notes; advantages of cash flow forecasts
2   Earnings per share calculation: effect on EPS of rights issue; importance of EPS
3   Current cost accounting with ratios

Section B (compulsory)
4   Reconstructing accounts of holding company from consolidated accounts and accounts of subsidiary; controls and audit approach
5   Inherent risk; audit evidence; restrictions of time budgets

December 1994

Section A (2 out of 3)
1   Consolidated P & L account per FRS 3 and CA 1985; group reserves
2   Partnership: new partners P & L a/c and balance sheet; WIP in an audit firm's accounts
3   FRS 5: explanation, discussion; treatment of two items

Section B (compulsory)
4   Private company redeeming shares; use of 'expert systems' in audit work; small company audit
5   New client: risk; ethical problems; opinion shopping; reducing risk of litigation

June 1994

Section A (2 out of 3)

1   Exclusion of subsidiaries from consolidation; consolidated balance sheet; effect of subsidiary's losses
2   Need for accounting standards; criticisms of ASC vs new standard-setting regime; effect of FRS 1 on uniformity
3   Prepare FRS 3 statements; explain effect of closure of subsidiary under FRS 3

Section B (compulsory)

4   Reliance on work of secondary auditor; suitability of stock accounting policies; stock valuation; policy note
5   Computer network: audit risk; control problems with micros; auditor's use of a micro; quality control in an IT environment

Further guidance from the ACCA

The ACCA provides the following further guidance on the examination paper for Paper 10 *Accounting and Audit Practice*.

The objective of the Professional Stage

The main aim of the Professional Stage is to establish evidence of competence to practise as a professional accountant in public practice, public sector or in industry and commerce. This requires candidates to demonstrate not only that they have mastered the range of required knowledge, skills and techniques, but also that they are able to apply them in a managerial context.

By this stage, knowledge has to be fully integrated in the way it is used by professionals with a recognition of how the different subjects contribute to dealing with problems. This stage will present students with problems which test their skills and sensitivity in dealing with new contexts and unforeseen circumstances. In dealing with such situations, students will be expected to tailor situations to previous problems appropriately and in a way which demonstrates their grasp of managerial skills.

Although emphasis will be given to practical issues, students will also be expected to criticise current practice and express views on developments in accounting. They will also be expected to show evidence of the necessary personal qualities and interpersonal skills required of the professional accountant.

Skills to be tested in the Professional Stage

Students should be able to demonstrate the ability to:

- draw on knowledge across all earlier papers studied;
- integrate that knowledge effectively and use it creatively in applying concepts and techniques;
- analyse and interpret data and information and present reasoned conclusions;
- diagnose and formulate appropriate solutions to problems which indicate commercial awareness;
- exercise judgement based on technical, political and commercial factors in developing and evaluating alternatives and in proposing solutions;
- adapt to new systems and circumstances;

- communicate analyses and conclusions effectively and with sensitivity for differing purposes and to contrasting audiences with due emphasis on social expectations.

While the skills identified above will be tested directly by the questions set, in assessing the answers weight will be given to the student's ability to demonstrate a grasp of the following personal skills and attributes:

Interpersonal skills

Tact, sensitivity to political tensions and cultural differences, awareness of social, economic and political pressure, ability to influence.

Management skills

Resource management: people, material, time and money, management of the client, management of change, in particular in technology, and contingency planning.

Personal qualities

Persistence to pursue inquiries and probe responses, integrity, objectivity, independence and public responsibility.

Aim of paper 10

To ensure students have developed a thorough knowledge and understanding of accounting and auditing principles and concepts and can begin to apply this grounding to the situations that they will typically meet at work.

On completion of this paper students should be able to:

- prepare financial statements in a form appropriate for use by various interested parties - partnerships, branches, joint ventures, single and group companies;
- appraise the theoretical and regulatory accounting framework, including all extant SSAPs and FRSs;
- analyse and interpret financial and related information and produce reports to meet the needs of internal and external users;
- understand and implement advanced auditing practice and procedures;
- evaluate current issues relating to auditing and the regulation of audits;
- demonstrate the skills expected at the Professional Stage.

Prerequisite knowledge

Students will be expected to have a thorough understanding of the content of Paper 1 Accounting Framework and Paper 6 Audit Framework.

Paper 10 develops the coverage of financial accounting in Paper 1 by:

- examining the preparation of accounts for partnerships and branches in more complex situations
- introducing further SSAPs and FRSs to be applied in the preparation of accounts for single companies and, in addition, for groups
- introducing the measurement issues involved in accounting
- giving more emphasis to the analysis and interpretation of financial statements

Paper 10 develops the coverage of auditing from Paper 6 by:

- examining advanced audit situations – group audits, joint audits, working with specialists etc
- testing, in more depth, computer auditing issues
- evaluating critical areas – going concern status, audit risk, fraud and error, related party transactions etc
- monitoring and appraising changes to the audit framework
- ethical issues
- managing audit relationships call on negotiations with management

The Examiner wants to ensure that students understand the basic principles and have a firm footing for Paper 13. Paper 10 is the last substantive auditing paper, therefore, the Examiner will test the more complex areas of auditing as the basic principles will have been covered in Paper 6. Students will not be asked to calculate complicated numbers just for the sake of it. Questions will concentrate on practical and up to date techniques. Students will be required to apply information within a regulatory framework of accounting and auditing.

The Examiner will not examine frequently areas which have been examined in a previous paper, however, where such topics are examined a greater depth will be expected. The main areas of interest will be recent FRSs and those Standards not examined at Paper 1. Many of the Standards are very detailed; however, at Paper 10 these will be examined at a basic/summary level. Students should be aware of the key elements of the Standards, and why they were introduced.

Key areas of the syllabus

Accounting

- Concepts of accounting
- Regulatory framework
- Revenue recognition
- Distributable profits

Accounting standards

- Cash flow (FRS 1)
- Reporting financial performance including segmental information (FRS 3 and SSAP 25)
- Capital instruments (FRS 4)
- Reporting the substance of transactions (FRS 5)
- Earnings per share (SSAP 3)
- Accounting for taxation (SSAP 8 and 15)
- Accounting for leases and hire purchase contracts (SSAP 21)

Group accounting

- Simple groups including associates and joint ventures, the use of acquisition, merger and equity accounting and proportional consolidation simple fair value adjustments (SSAP 1, FRS 2, 6 and 7)

Accounting theory

- Interpretation of financial statements

Auditing

- Concepts of auditing
- Statements of auditing standards
- Analytical review and audit risk
- Auditing computerised accounting systems
- Group audits, working with another auditor
- Ethical issues
- Audit reports
- Fraud and error

The following areas of the syllabus are not as important although they will be examined occasionally or may form part of a question

- Accounting standards that have been examined at Papers 1 and 6:
  2, 9 (other than long-term contracts), 12, 13, 17 and 18
- Other accounting standards
  4, 5, 19, 20 and 24
- Basic audit principles examined at paper 6

Examining approach

The examining approach will be in line with the information given above, ie the Examiner will not set large computational questions for the sake of it. Questions will be in a practical context and students will be required to apply information within the regulatory framework of accounting and auditing. The emphasis of this paper will be on up to date practices in the real world and to ensure that students understand basic principles and have a sound foundation for Paper 13.

The approach of the paper will be:

Questions 1 and 2 - a computation basis often followed by a related written element

Question 3   - a discursive basis with the possibility of some simple calculations for explanatory purposes

Question 4   - a computational element with a mix of accounting and auditing issues

Question 5   - an auditing question, probably based on a case study or a scenario format

Articles are regularly published in the Students' Newsletter which are relevant to Paper 10. It is important that students read this.

Extent of integration

Paper 10 makes reference to information technology by considering its impact on the audit process and the utilisation of computer assisted audit techniques. Students will also need to draw upon their techniques in the context of statistical sampling methods used in auditing.

Paper 10 is a combined paper – financial accounting will account for approximately 65% of the marks and auditing the remainder. The questions may draw on both disciplines as indicated above in the section on assessment methods. It is important that lecturers link the two subjects so that students are prepared for the integrated accounting and auditing question. The teaching guide demonstrates the areas where accounting and auditing may be merged in the same question.

Development of paper 10 topics in subsequent papers

Paper 10 provides the technical background in financial accounting and auditing for Paper 13 Financial Reporting Environment.

Paper 13 builds upon the technical knowledge gained in Paper 10 by examining the topics in a managerial context, giving more emphasis to analysis and interpretation and making reference to the audit implications of different activities.

Part A
Basic auditing concepts

Chapter 1

THE NATURE, PURPOSE AND SCOPE OF AUDITING

Chapter topic list	Syllabus reference
1 The purpose of external audit	Revision
2 True and fair	Revision
3 The scope of external audit	Revision
4 The chronology of an audit	Revision

Introduction

The first four chapters in this Study Text are, on the whole, revision of the most important general practices and procedures of auditing with which you should already be familiar from Paper 6 *The Audit Framework*.

Use the questions in Part A and illustrative questions 1 to 4 as revision. If you have any difficulty with these questions, you should go back to your Paper 6 material and revise where necessary.

Remember that you will be expected to demonstrate a much greater knowledge of financial accounting than you were in Paper 6 because *all* extant SSAPs and FRSs are examinable in Paper 10.

Part B of this Study Text goes on to reflect the syllabus and teaching guide in its coverage of more advanced auditing practices and procedures.

1   THE PURPOSE OF EXTERNAL AUDIT

Definition of an audit

1.1 The Auditing Practices Board's *Glossary of Terms* defines an audit of financial statements as follows.

KEY TERM

An **audit** is an exercise whose objective is to enable auditors to express an opinion whether the financial statements give a true and fair view (or equivalent) of the entity's affairs at the period end and of its profit and loss (or income and expenditure) for the period then ended and have been properly prepared in accordance with the applicable reporting framework (for example relevant legislation and applicable accounting standards) or, where statutory or other specific requirements prescribe the term, whether the financial statements "present fairly".

1.2 This wording follows very closely that of the auditors' report on financial statements, which we will look at later.

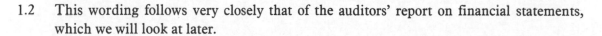

1.3 We will also look at some definitions of terms used here, in particular 'true and fair view', later on.

1.4 The APB's Statement of Auditing Standards SAS 100 *Objective and general principles governing an audit of financial statements* summarises what audits are all about.

> **SAS 100.1**
>
> In undertaking an audit of financial statements auditors should:
>
> (a) carry out procedures designed to obtain sufficient appropriate audit evidence, in accordance with Auditing Standards contained in SASs, to determine with reasonable confidence whether the financial statements are free of material misstatement;
>
> (b) evaluate the overall presentation of the financial statements, in order to ascertain whether they have been prepared in accordance with relevant legislation and accounting standards; and
>
> (c) issue a report containing a clear expression of their opinion on the financial statements.

1.5 The SAS's explanatory material highlights the credibility given to financial statements by the auditors' opinion; it provides 'reasonable assurance from an independent source that they present a true and fair view'.

Limitations of audit

1.6 There are provisos, of course. First of all, the auditors' opinion is *not:*

(a) a guarantee of the future viability of the entity; or
(b) an assurance of the management's effectiveness and efficiency.

Responsibility of directors

1.7 Most importantly, the standard makes clear that the auditors do not bear any responsibility for the preparation and presentation of the financial statements.

> The responsibility for the preparation and presentation of the financial statements is that of the directors of the entity. Auditors are responsible for forming and expressing an opinion on the financial statements. The audit of the financial statements does not relieve the directors of any of their responsibilities.

Use of auditor judgement

1.8 **'Reasonable assurance'** lies at the heart of what a user of financial statements can and should expect from an auditors' report. SAS 100 attempts to close the **'expectations gap'** between what people think auditors do, and what auditors really do in practice. First of all, it is pointed out that financial statements are *not* 'absolute' or 'correct' as they represent a combination of fact and judgement.

1.9 The standard then discusses the use of the auditors' judgement.

The work undertaken by auditors to form an opinion is permeated by the exercise of judgement, in particular regarding:

(a) the gathering of evidence: for example, in deciding the nature, timing and extent of audit procedures; and

(b) the drawing of conclusions based on the evidence gathered: for example, assessing the reasonableness of the estimates made by the directors in preparing the financial statements.

1.10   In other words, the auditors are expressing an opinion, not certifying whether a set of accounts is completely correct or not. This would be impossible, because of the inherent (ie existing and permanent characteristic or attribute) limitations of any audit. These limitations restrict the extent to which *audit risk* (that auditors may give an inappropriate opinion on financial statements) can be reduced.

Such limitations include those resulting from:

(a) the impracticality of examining all items within an account balance or class of transactions;

(b) the inherent limitations of any accounting and control system;

(c) the possibility of collusion or misrepresentation for fraudulent purposes; and

(d) most audit evidence being persuasive rather than conclusive.

1.11   Material misstatements may exist in financial statements and auditors will plan their work on this basis, ie with **professional scepticism**. SAS 100 makes it clear that, even where auditors assess the risk of litigation or adverse publicity as very low, they must still perform sufficient procedures according to auditing standards, ie there can never be a reason for carrying out an audit of a lower quality than that demanded by the auditing standards

The role of the auditors

1.12   In the modern commercial environment, the owners of the business need an **independent examination** of the accounts so that they can assess how well management have discharged their stewardship.

1.13   The work of auditors today is regulated mainly by two sources:

(a)   **statutes,** of which the Companies Act 1985 is the most important; and
(b)   **professional pronouncements on auditing,** (including SASs, Practice Notes and Bulletins) which are issued by the Auditing Practices Board.

Professional pronouncements include the rules of professional conduct issued by the professional bodies to which auditors belong. The most important professional pronouncements on the practice of auditing in the UK are the auditing standards which are issued by the Auditing Practices Board (APB).

1.14   The statutory framework of auditing is discussed in Chapter 2, and the rules of professional conduct in Chapter 5.

> **SAS 100.2**
>
> In the conduct of any audit of financial statements auditors should comply with the ethical guidance issued by their relevant professional bodies.

1.15 Per SAS 100 the ethical principles which govern auditors' responsibilities include:

- Integrity
- Objectivity
- Independence
- Professional competence and due care
- Professional behaviour
- Confidentiality

These matters are discussed in Chapter 5.

The expectations gap

1.16 There are some common misconceptions in relation to the role of the auditors, even among 'financially aware' people, including the following examples.

(a) Many people think that the auditors report to the directors of a company, rather than the members.

(b) Some think that a qualified audit report is more favourable than an unqualified audit report, whereas the converse is true (see Chapter 12).

(c) There is a perception that it is the auditors' duty to detect fraud, when in fact the detection of fraud is the responsibility of the directors (see Chapter 12).

1.17 These findings highlight the 'expectations gap' between what auditors do and what people in general think that they do. Add the fact that many 'financially aware' people do not look at the report and accounts of a company they are considering investing in, and you have some sobering facts for the auditors to contemplate!

1.18 Some of the recent large company collapses have emphasised the need to reduce the expectations gap. For this reason, reports such as that of the Cadbury Committee on *The Financial Aspects of Corporate Governance* have been published. The *Cadbury Report* aims to reduce the expectation gap (at least in relation to quoted companies) by laying out a 19 point code of conduct for directors, as well as making suggestions for the content of company reports (and in particular the directors' and auditors' reports).

2 TRUE AND FAIR

2.1 The accounts of a limited company are required by s 226(2) of the Companies Act 1985 to show a **true and fair view** of the company's financial position as at the balance sheet date and of its profit or loss for the year ending on that date. The auditors are required to state in their report whether, in their opinion, the accounts satisfy that requirement.

2.2 The requirement to present a true and fair view is stated in the Act to override any other requirement with which it might conflict, although surprisingly the Act does not define truth and fairness.

2.3 Most commentators give definitions of truth and fairness along the following lines.

KEY TERM

True: Information is factual and conforms with reality, not false. In addition the information conforms with required standards and law. The accounts have been correctly extracted from the books and records.

Fair: Information is free from discrimination and bias and in compliance with expected standards and rules. The accounts should reflect the commercial substance of the company's underlying transactions.

2.4 The Accounting Standards Committee (ASC), the predecessor to the Accounting Standards Board, obtained the following opinion.

> 'A SSAP is a declaration by the ASC, on behalf of its constituent professional bodies, that save in exceptional circumstances accounts which do not comply with the standard will not give a true and fair view.'

2.5 This opinion also made these points:

(a) 'Accounts will not be true and fair unless the information they contain is **sufficient** in **quantity** and **quality** to satisfy the reasonable expectations of readers to whom they are addressed.'

(b) The expectations of readers will have been influenced by the **normal practices** of accountants.

(c) **SSAPs** serve the following purposes.

  (i) They **crystallise professional opinion** about what may be expected in accounts that are true and fair.

  (ii) Because accounts are obliged to comply with SSAPs, **readers** will thus **expect accounts to conform** with SSAPs.

(d) SSAPs therefore have an indirect but important effect on truth and fairness. 'The courts will treat compliance with accepted accounting principles as prima facie evidence that the accounts are true and fair. Equally the deviation from accounting principles will be prima facie evidence that they are not.'

2.6 This opinion was reinforced by an opinion given to the Accounting Standards Board by the Honourable Mrs Justice Arden QC.

2.7 She pointed out that the Companies Act 1989 gave further statutory backing to accounting standards in that:

(a) S 256 indicates statutory policy favours the issue of, and compliance with, accounting standards; s 256(3) provides for public funding to be given to investigate departures.

(b) Sch 4 s 36A of the Companies Act requires disclosure of non-compliance with accounting standards; therefore, accounts which meet the true and fair requirement will in general follow rather than depart from standards and their departure is sufficiently abnormal to require to be justified. 'The courts are likely to hold that compliance with accounting standards is generally necessary to meet the true and fair requirement.'

2.8 Mrs Justice Arden made the following other points:

(a) The changes in the standard setting process since 1989 had in her opinion enhanced the status of standards.

(b) The courts would also be likely to take the view that compliance with UITF requirements was necessary for truth and fairness.

(c) Truth and fairness is a dynamic (constantly-changing) concept.

2.9 You should particularly note that the main thrust of recent developments in company law and standard setting have considerably strengthened the previous opinion that compliance with accounting standards indicates that a true and fair view is being shown. The implication is that companies which do *not* follow accounting standards are presumed 'guilty', ie their accounts do *not* show a true and fair view.

3   THE SCOPE OF EXTERNAL AUDIT

Statutory and non-statutory audits

3.1 Audits are required under statute in the case of a large number of undertakings, including the following.

Undertaking	*Principal Act*
Limited companies	Companies Act 1985
Building societies	Building Societies Act 1965
Trade unions and employer associations	Trade Union and Labour Relations Act 1974
Housing Associations	Various acts depending on the legal constitution of the housing association, including: Industrial and Provident Societies Act 1965; Friendly and Industrial and Provident Societies Act 1968; Housing Act 1980; Companies Act 1985; Housing Association Act 1985.
Certain charities	Various acts depending on the status of the charity, including special Acts of Parliament.
Unincorporated investment businesses	Regulations made under the Financial Services Act 1986.

3.2 Non-statutory audits are performed by independent auditors because the owners, partners, members, trustees, professional and governing bodies or other interested parties want them, rather than because the law requires them.

3.3 Auditors may also give an audit opinion on statements other than annual accounts, including:

• summaries of sales in support of a statement of royalties;

• statements of expenditure in support of applications for regional development grants;

• the circulation figures of a newspaper or magazine.

3.4 In all such audits the auditors must take into account any regulations contained in the internal rules or constitution of the undertaking. Examples of the regulations which the auditors would need to refer to in such assignments would include:

• the rules of clubs, societies and charities;

- partnership agreements.

External and internal audit

3.5 We have discussed auditing in particular in the context of the APB definition quoted at the start of Section 1 of this chapter. The definition relates to the work of *external* auditors, independent persons brought in from outside an organisation to review the accounts prepared by management. **Internal auditors** perform a different role, which we will discuss briefly here, and in depth in Chapter 6.

3.6 The management of an organisation will wish to establish systems to ensure that business activities are carried out efficiently. They will institute clerical, administrative and financial controls. Even in very small businesses with informal accounting systems it will be found that some limited checks and controls are present.

3.7 Larger organisations may appoint full-time staff whose function is to monitor and report on the running of the company's operations. **Internal** audit staff members are one type of control. Although some of the work carried out by internal auditors is similar to that performed by external auditors, there are important distinctions between the nature of the two functions.

(a) **External** auditors are **independent** of the organisation, whereas **internal auditors** (as employees) are **responsible** to the management.

(b) The **responsibilities** of **external** auditors are fixed by **statute**, but **internal** auditors' responsibilities are decided by **management**.

(c) **External** auditors **report** to the **members**, **internal** auditors **report** to the **management** (directors).

(d) **External** auditors perform work to enable them to express an **opinion** on the **truth** and **fairness** of the **accounts**. **Internal** auditors' work may range over many **operational** and **financial** areas and activities, as determined by management.

Staffing of external audits

3.8 Some external audits will be carried out by sole practitioners who hold a valid practising certificate. Alternatively a partnership will be appointed. The reporting partner will take overall responsibility for the conduct of the audit assignment, and will sign the audit report. Although overall responsibility rests with the reporting or engagement partner, he may delegate aspects of the audit work to staff of the firm.

3.9 The usual hierarchy of staff on a typical company audit assignment is illustrated in the diagram below.

Reporting partner
|
Audit manager
|
Supervisors/audit seniors
|
Audit assistants

4   THE CHRONOLOGY OF AN AUDIT

4.1   The chart on the next page outlines the main stages of an audit that are *normally* followed.

4.2   Before examining each stage in detail it is worth stating the more important duties of the auditors of a limited company. They must satisfy themselves that:

- **proper accounting records** have been **kept**;
- the **accounts** are in **agreement** with the **accounting records**;
- the **accounts** have been **prepared** in accordance with the **Companies Act**, and relevant **accounting standards**;
- the **balance sheet** shows a **true and fair view** of the **state of the company's affairs** and the **profit and loss account** shows a **true and fair view** of the **results for the period**.

The objects of most other audits will be broadly similar.

4.3   Thus a major part of the auditors' work will involve:

(a)   **making such tests** and **enquiries** as they consider necessary to form an opinion as to the reliability of the accounting records as a basis for the preparation of accounts;

(b)   **checking** the **accounts** against the underlying records; and

(c)   **reviewing** the **accounts** for compliance with the Companies Act and accounting standards.

4.4   We will now look at the various stages identified in the diagram.

Determine audit approach

Stage 1

4.5   The first stage in any audit should be to determine its scope and the auditors' general approach. For statutory audits the scope is clearly laid down in the Companies Act as expanded by the standards of current best practice. A letter of engagement will be submitted or confirmed before the start of each annual audit.

4.6   In addition to the letter of engagement auditors should prepare an audit plan to be placed on the audit file. The purpose of this memorandum is to provide a record of the major areas to which the auditors attach special significance and to highlight any particular difficulties or points of concern peculiar to the audit client.

4.7   The detailed audit planning which arises from the determination of the scope of work is discussed further in Chapter 3.

Ascertain the system and internal controls

Stage 2

4.8   The objective at this stage is to determine the **flow of documents** and **extent of controls** in existence. This is achieved by discussing the accounting system and document flow with all the relevant departments, including typically, sales, purchases, cash, stock and accounts personnel. A rough record of the system should be made during this fact finding stage, which will be converted to a formal record at Stage 3 below.

A DIAGRAMMATIC REPRESENTATION OF THE SYSTEMS AUDIT

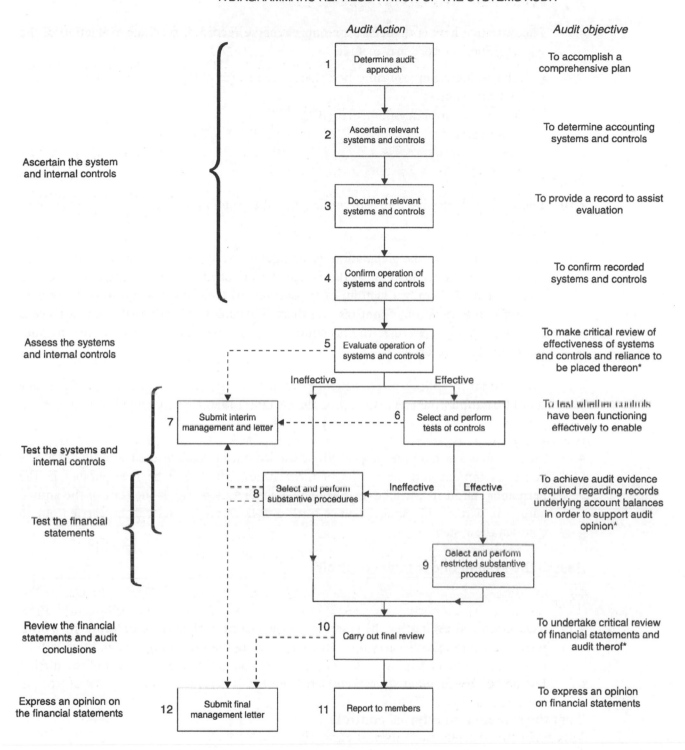

Audit Action   *Audit objective*

Ascertain the system and internal controls

1 Determine audit approach — To accomplish a comprehensive plan

2 Ascertain relevant systems and controls — To determine accounting systems and controls

3 Document relevant systems and controls — To provide a record to assist evaluation

4 Confirm operation of systems and controls — To confirm recorded systems and controls

Assess the systems and internal controls

5 Evaluate operation of systems and controls — To make critical review of effectiveness of systems and controls and reliance to be placed thereon*

Ineffective / Effective

Test the systems and internal controls

7 Submit interim management and letter

6 Select and perform tests of controls — To test whether controls have been functioning effectively to enable

Test the financial statements

8 Select and perform substantive procedures   Ineffective / Effective — To achieve audit evidence required regarding records underlying account balances in order to support audit opinion*

9 Select and perform restricted substantive procedures

Review the financial statements and audit conclusions

10 Carry out final review — To undertake critical review of financial statements and audit therof*

Express an opinion on the financial statements

12 Submit final management letter

11 Report to members — To express an opinion on financial statements

- - - - - - - - - - →   Stages in audit procedures

─────────────→   Contact with management

*   A secondary objective of this audit action is to recommend to management improvements in systems controls and in accounting procedures and practices

Stage 3

4.9   The objective here is to prepare a **comprehensive record** to facilitate evaluation of the systems. Such a record may include:

- charts, for example organisation charts and records of the books of account;
- narrative notes;
- internal control questionnaires (ICQs);
- flowcharts.

Stage 4

4.10   The auditors' objective here is to confirm that the **system recorded** is the same as that in operation.

4.11   After completion of the preparation (or update) of the systems records the auditors will confirm their understanding of the system by performing **walk-through** tests. These involve tracing literally a handful of transactions of each type through the system and observing the operation of controls over them. This procedure will establish that there is no reason to suppose that the accounting system does not operate in the manner ascertained and recorded.

4.12   The need for this check arises as client's staff will occasionally tell the auditors what they should be doing (the established procedures) rather than what is actually being done in practice.

4.13   Stages 2 and 3 as described above will be carried out in detail at the beginning of a new audit assignment and the results of these stages, which will be incorporated in the permanent audit file, will be reviewed and amended each year at the start of the annual audit. As part of this annual review further walk-through tests will be carried out to confirm the system.

Assess the system and internal controls

Stage 5

4.14   The purpose of **evaluating** the **systems** is to gauge their reliability and formulate a basis for testing their effectiveness in practice. Following the evaluation, the auditors will be able to recommend improvements to the system and determine the extent of the further tests to be carried out at Stages 6 and 8 below.

Test the system and internal controls

Stage 6

4.15   If the controls are strong, the records should be reliable and consequently the amount of detailed testing can be reduced.

4.16   Auditors should however check that the controls are as effective in practice as they are on paper. They will therefore carry out **tests of controls**. These are like walk through checks in so far as they are concerned with the workings of the system. They differ in that they:

(a)   are concerned only with those areas subject to effective control;
(b)   cover a representative sample of transactions throughout the period.
(c)   are likely to cover a larger number of items than walkthrough tests.

4.17 The conclusion drawn from the results of a test of controls may be either:

 (a) that the **controls** are **effective,** in which case the auditors will only need to carry out restricted substantive procedures; or

 (b) that the **controls** are **ineffective** in practice, although they had appeared strong on paper, in which case the auditors will need to carry out more extensive substantive procedures.

4.18 Stage 6 should only be carried out if the controls are evaluated at Stage 5 as being effective. If the auditors know that the controls are ineffective then there is no point in carrying out tests of controls which will merely confirm what is already known. Instead the auditors should go straight on to carry out full substantive procedures. Many small companies do not have satisfactory evidence of operation of controls, therefore their audits are largely substantive.

Stage 7

4.19 After evaluating the systems and carrying out tests of controls, it is normal practice to send management an **interim management letter** identifying weaknesses and recommending improvements.

Test the financial statements

Stages 8 and 9

4.20 These tests are not concerned with the workings of the system, but with substantiating the figures in the books of account, and eventually, in the final accounts themselves. Substantive tests are also designed to assess the extent of errors should errors exist.

4.21 Before designing a substantive procedure it is essential to consider whether any errors produced by weak systems could lead to material differences. If the answer is 'NO' there is no point in performing a test.

Review the financial statements

Stage 10

4.22 The aim of the overall review (including analytical procedures) is to determine the overall reliability of the accounts by making a critical analysis of content and presentation.

Express an opinion

Stage 11

4.23 The report to the members is the end product of the audit in which the auditors express their opinion of the accounts.

Stage 12

4.24 The final letter to management is an important non-statutory end product of the audit. Its purpose is to make further suggestions for improvements in the systems and to place on record specific points in connection with the audit and accounts.

Examples of tests	
Walkthrough tests	Taking a few transactions and following them through every stage of the system, from material requisition to settlement of supplier's invoice.
Tests of controls	Taking a representative sample of transactions, and testing certain significant controls. For purchases, test controls over payments by checking purchase invoices have been authorised before payment.
Substantive procedures	Taking a large sample of balances, and testing for completeness and accuracy. For creditors, compare suppliers' statements with purchase ledger to ensure creditors are stated at their correct amount.

These tests are discussed later in the text in turn.

Risk-based audits

4.25 In recent years there has been a shift towards risk-based auditing.

4.26 Risk-based auditing refers to the development of auditing techniques which are responsive to risk factors in an audit. The auditors apply judgement to determine what level of risk pertains to different areas of a client's system and devise appropriate audit tests. This approach should ensure that the greatest audit effort is directed at the riskiest areas.

Exam focus point
We will consider risk-based auditing further in Chapter 6. Audit risk is an important topic for this paper.

4.27 The stages of the audit shown in the diagram will still be followed in a risk-based audit.

Question

(a) 'Auditors are only interested in having more and more controls in any accounting system.'

(b) 'There is no point in issuing an audit report on a proprietary company (that is, an owner-controlled company).'

Required

Discuss both the above statements giving reasoned arguments as to why you agree or disagree with them.

Answer

(a) *Auditors are only interested in having more and more controls in any accounting system*

It would be wrong to suggest that auditors seek to have controls for their own sake. Auditors would recognise the need for any client's system to be cost effective and one would have to query the benefit of any controls which cost more to institute and maintain then the loss that would be suffered in the absence of that control.

Having said this, however, one must concede that the existence of a sound system of controls within any client organisation is of interest and benefit to both the organisation and the auditors. The existence of a satisfactory system of controls can reduce the amount of detailed work and required in order for the auditors to arrive at their opinion and this will be of benefit to the client in helping to keep down the cost of the audit. If the auditors are of the opinion that the control systems established by a client are inadequate, given the nature and size of the client's business, or that systems evaluated as being sound in theory are not operating satisfactorily in practice, they should point out the weaknesses to the client and at the same time offer their recommendations as to how those weaknesses might be eliminated.

(b)   *There is no point in issuing an audit report on a proprietary company*

It is often claimed that, because in the small or 'proprietary' company both shareholders' funds and day-to-day management are provided by the same people, the requirement for independent auditors to review and report on the company's financial statements is super-fluous and an unnecessary expense. The small size of such enterprises normally means a limited and simple organisational structure compensated for by close managerial supervision of staff and detailed involvement in the day-to-day routine of transacting and recording business. It is maintained that the owners of such enterprises are therefore better equipped to evaluate the progress and financial position of their company than independent auditors whose work is concerned solely with reporting on historical performance.

Such arguments, however, fail to recognise a number of important considerations. First, the provision of funds by proprietors is not the only requirement for the business entity to exist. The social and economic environment in which an enterprise operates (for example, the provision and maintenance of roads, law and order) must be paid for, and the revenue for such services is raised by the fiscal system. A large proportion of this revenue is raised by taxing the profits of the business unit. The accuracy and honesty of the financial statements used as the basis for tax assessments is relied upon by the Inland Revenue and Customs & Excise authorities and the credibility of such statements derives from the opinion of the independent auditors.

Secondly, there are interested parties other than the ultimate proprietors who place reliance on the financial statements. Trade and loan creditors, bankers and potential investors, for example, may be approached by small companies to provide credit or finance. Such users rely on the accuracy of financial statements in making decisions, and receive assurance from the independent opinion of the auditors. The importance to these other interested parties, or users, of the auditors cannot be overstressed.

Chapter roundup

- An audit is essentially an **independent knowledgeable** scrutiny and review.

- In this text we shall be concentrating on **audits** of **accounts**. The aim of this type of audit is for auditors to report on whether a **true** and **fair view** is shown by the accounts.

- Auditors are regulated by statute, professional bodies and the **Auditing Practices Board** (APB).

- The APB defines the key stages of an audit as being:
  - Carry out procedures to obtain **sufficient appropriate audit evidence**
  - **Evaluate** the **presentation** of accounts
  - Issue a report containing a **clear expression** of **opinion**.

- The APB also points out that audits at best give **reasonable assurance** that the accounts are free from material misstatement.

- The Companies Act does not define **truth and fairness**.

- Most commentators take truth and fairness to mean accounts are **factual, free from bias** and **comply with legislation and standards**. The information contained must be **sufficient** in **quality** and **quantity**.

- **Compliance with accountancy standards** (SSAPs and FRSs) has an important influence on whether accounts are true and fair.

- As well as audits of accounts, there are various other types of audit, statutory and non-statutory.

- **Internal auditors** are employed as part of an organisation's system of controls. Their responsibilities are determined by management and may be wide-ranging.

- The **key** stages of the audit process are:
  - Determine audit approach
  - Ascertain the accounting system and internal controls
  - Assess the accounting system and internal controls
  - Test the accounting system and internal controls
  - Test the financial statements (substantive testing)
  - Review the financial statements
  - Express an opinion

Quick quiz

1   Define an audit of financial statements. (see para 1.1)

2   What procedures should auditors carry out when undertaking an audit? (1.4)

3   What is the main reason why an audit is considered to be necessary? (1.12)

4   Who is responsible for issuing auditing standards? (1.13)

5   What does SAS 100 say about ethical matters? (1.14, 1.15)

6   CA 1985 defines 'true and fair'. True or false? (2.2)

7   How, according to Mrs Justice Arden, does the Companies Act give statutory backing to accounting standards? (2.7)

8   List four types of undertaking for which audits are a statutory obligation. (3.1)

9   What are the main differences between external and internal audit? (3.7)

10   Briefly sketch the typical stages of an audit defined in terms of the audit action required. (*Audit diagram*, 4)

11   What Is a 'walk through test'? (4.11)

12   Distinguish a test of control and a walk through test. (4.16)

The question indicated below acts as a refresher of certain terms which you met at Paper 6, and which remain important for Paper 10

Question to try	Level	Marks	Time
1	Revision	n/a	30 mins

Chapter 2

THE REGULATORY FRAMEWORK OF AUDITING

Chapter topic list	Syllabus reference
1 The structure of the UK accounting and auditing profession	Revision
2 Auditing standards	Revision
3 The role of government and international auditing bodies	Revision
4 Appointment of auditors	Revision
5 Resignation and removal of auditors	Revision
6 Duties and rights of auditors	Revision

Introduction

This chapter describes the main bodies and the major factors which govern auditing. Of great importance here is the auditing standard-setting process, described in Section 2. The Auditing Practices Board (APB) has produced a set of auditing standards (SASs).

The more secondary role of the government and European influences are discussed briefly in Section 3.

The Companies Act provisions relating to auditors are extremely important. They enforce the regulatory framework discussed in Sections 1 to 3. They aim to protect the rights of auditors as well as laying out their duties. Without such legal backing, the auditors would be in a very weak position.

The contents of this chapter are quite dry, but you must learn everything there. Any question involving a dispute between auditors and client may call for knowledge of the rights and duties of the auditors. A number of questions in recent exams have involved situations where the relationship with an audit client is delicate.

1   THE STRUCTURE OF THE UK ACCOUNTING AND AUDITING PROFESSION

1.1   In the UK there are a large number of different accountancy, or accountancy-related, institutes and associations.

- Association of Chartered Certified Accountants (ACCA)
- Institute of Chartered Accountants in England and Wales (ICAEW)
- Chartered Institute of Management Accountants (CIMA)
- Association of Accounting Technicians (AAT)
- Chartered Institute of Public Finance and Accounting (CIPFA)

1.2   All these bodies vary from each other, either moderately or radically, depending on the nature of their aims and the specialisms their members wish to attain. They are all, however, characterised by various attributes common across the accounting profession.

- Stringent entrance requirements (examinations and practical experience)
- Strict codes of ethics
- Technical updating of members

1.3 The membership of all these bodies is scattered through practice, industry, government and public bodies.

Eligibility as auditor

1.4 The Companies Act 1985 also requires an auditor to hold an 'appropriate qualification'. A person holds an 'appropriate qualification' if he or she:

   (a) has satisfied existing criteria for appointment as an auditor under CA 1985; or
   (b) holds a recognised qualification obtained in the UK; or
   (c) holds an approved overseas qualification.

1.5 Membership of an RSB (discussed below) is the main prerequisite for eligibility as an auditor. The Companies Act 1989 allows a 'firm' to be appointed as a company auditor. A firm may be either a body corporate (such as a company) or a partnership.

Ineligibility as auditor

1.6 Under the Companies Act 1985, a person is *ineligible* for appointment as a company auditor if he or she is:

   (a) an **officer** or **employee** of the company;

   (b) a **partner** or **employee** of such a person;

   (c) a **partnership** in which such a person is a partner;

   (d) **ineligible** by virtue of (a), (b) or (c) for appointment as auditor of any parent or subsidiary undertaking or a subsidiary undertaking of any parent undertaking of the company; or

   (e) there exists between him or her or any associate (of his or hers) and the company (or company as referred to in (d) above) a **connection** of any description as may be specified in regulations laid down by Secretary of State.

1.7 The legislation does *not* disqualify the following from being an auditor of a limited company:

   (a) a shareholder of the company;

   (b) a debtor or creditor of the company;

   (c) a close relative (such as a husband, wife, son or daughter) of an officer or employee of the company.

1.8 However, the regulations of the accountancy bodies applying to their own members are stricter than statute in this respect.

1.9 Under the Companies Act 1985, a person may also be ineligible on the grounds of 'lack of independence'; the definition of lack of independence is to be determined by statutory instrument following consultation with the professional bodies.

1.10 Under s 389 CA 1985, if during their term of office a company auditor becomes ineligible for appointment to the office, he must vacate office and give notice in writing to the company.

Recognised Supervisory Bodies

1.11 CA 1989 brought UK legislation into line with the EC 8th Directive on company law. This Directive requires that persons carrying out statutory audits must be approved by the authorities of EU member states. The authority to give this approval in the UK is delegated to Recognised Supervisory Bodies (RSBs). The new legislation introduced certain rules and procedures which RSBs must embody in their own rules. Under the new Act, an auditor must be a member of an RSB and be eligible under its own rules. Registers of individuals and firms eligible to act as auditors have also been set up.

1.12 ACCA is a recognised supervisory body; there are a number of others.

1.13 The RSBs are required to have rules to ensure that persons eligible for appointment as a company auditor are either (4(1), Sch 11, CA 1989):

(a) individuals holding an appropriate qualification; or
(b) firms controlled by qualified persons.

1.14 A number of other requirements concern the procedures which RSBs must follow to maintain the competence of members.

1.15 Professional qualifications, which will be prerequisites for membership of an RSB, will be offered by Recognised Qualifying Bodies ('RQBs') approved by the Secretary of State.

Question 1

Outline the role of the Recognised Supervisory Bodies (RSBs).

Answer

See Paragraphs 1.11 - 1.15.

Supervisory and monitoring roles

1.16 RSBs must implement procedures for inspecting their registered auditors on a regular basis. A Monitoring Unit was set up for this purpose by the ACCA.

1.17 The frequency of inspection will depend on the number of partners, number of offices and number of listed company audits (these factors are also reflected in the size of annual registration fees payable). The inspections depend in length on the size of the firm.

1.18 The following features should be apparent in each practice visited by the monitoring unit.

(a) **A properly structured audit approach**, suitable for the range of clients served and work undertaken by the practice.

(b) Carefully instituted **quality control procedures**, revised and updated constantly, to which the practice as a whole is committed. This will include:

    (i)   staff recruitment;

    (ii)   staff training;

    (iii) continuing professional development;

    (iv) frequent quality control review.

(c) **Commitment to ethical guidelines**, with an emphasis on independence issues.

(d) An emphasis on **technical excellence**.

(e) Adherence to the **'fit and proper'** criteria by checking personnel records and references.

(f) Use of internal and, if necessary, external **peer reviews**, consultations etc.

(g) **Appropriate fee** charging per audit assignment.

1.19   Each inspection ends with an interview at which detailed findings are discussed and any necessary recommendations are issued. Notes are taken and subsequently copied to the monitoring units who, once satisfied that they adequately reflect what was agreed, will retain them as its record. If necessary, these notes can be passed to the registration authorities for consideration of any further action.

2   AUDITING STANDARDS

2.1   On 1 April 1991, a new Auditing Practices Board (APB) was set up to replace the old standard setting body, the Auditing Practices Committee (APC). The APB:

(a) can issue auditing standards in its own right without having to obtain the approval of all the professional accounting bodies;

(b) has strong representation from outside the accounting profession;

(c) has a larger budget than the APC;

(d) has a commitment to openness, with agenda papers being circulated to interested parties, and an annual report being published.

2.2   The APB issued a document in May 1993 entitled *The scope and authority of APB pronouncements*. The APB makes three categories of pronouncement.

- Statements of Auditing Standards (SASs)
- Practice Notes
- Bulletins

2.3   The scope of **SASs** is given as follows.

'SASs contain basic principles and essential procedures ('Auditing Standards') which are indicated by bold type and with which auditors are required to comply, except where otherwise stated in the SAS concerned, in the conduct of any audit of financial statements. SASs are also published containing Auditing Standards which apply, as stated therein, to other audits and related services, provided by auditors.

In addition to SASs of general application the APB issues SASs containing additional Auditing Standards applicable to the conduct of audits of certain types of entities, such as those within specialised industries.

SASs also include explanatory and other material which, rather than being prescriptive, is designed to assist auditors in interpreting and applying Auditing Standards. Auditing Standards need not be applied to matters whose effect is in the auditors' judgement not material.'

We have already seen this 'in action' in SAS 100 in Chapter 1.

2.4 The authority of SASs is given in the document.

'Auditors who do not comply with Auditing Standards when performing company or other audits in Great Britain make themselves liable to regulatory action by the RSB with whom they are registered and which may include the withdrawal of registration and hence of eligibility to perform company audits.'

2.5 **Practice Notes** are issued 'to assist auditors in applying Auditing Standards of general application to particular circumstances and industries'.

2.6 **Bulletins** are issued 'to provide auditors with timely guidance on new or emerging issues'.

2.7 Practice Notes and Bulletins are persuasive rather than prescriptive, but they indicate good practice and have a similar status to the explanatory material in SASs. Both Practice Notes and Bulletins may be included in later SASs.

2.8 The APB standards which are examinable for Paper 10 are listed below, along with some old APC standards and guidelines which are also examinable as they have yet to be replaced by the APB.

Statements of Auditing Standards (SASs): APB		*Issue date*
Series 001/099	*Introductory matters*	
010	Scope and authority of APB pronouncements	May 93
Series 100/199	*Responsibility*	
100	Objective and general principles governing an audit of financial statements	Mar 95
110	Fraud and error	Jan 95
120	Consideration of law and regulations	Jan 95
130	The going concern basis in financial statements	Nov 94
140	Engagement letters	Mar 95
150	Subsequent events	Mar 95
160	Other information in documents containing audited financial statements	Mar 95
Series 200/299	*Planning, controlling and recording*	
200	Planning	Mar 95
210	Knowledge of the business	Mar 95
220	Materiality and the audit	Mar 95
230	Working papers	Mar 95
240	Quality control for audit work	Mar 95
Series 300/399	*Accounting systems and internal control*	
300	Accounting and internal control systems and audit risk assessments	Mar 95
Series 400/499	*Evidence*	
400	Audit evidence	Mar 95
410	Analytical procedures	Mar 95
420	Audit of accounting estimates	Mar 95
430	Audit sampling	Mar 95
440	Management representations	Mar 95
450	Opening balances and comparatives	Mar 95
460	Related parties	Nov 95
470	Overall review of financial statements	Mar 95

Series 500/599	*Using the work of others*	
500	Considering the work of internal audit	Mar 95
510	The relationship between principal auditors and other auditors	Mar 95
520	Using the work of an expert	Mar 95
Series 600/699	*Reporting*	
600	Auditors' report on financial statements	May 93
610	·Reports to directors or management	Mar 95
620	The auditors' rights and duties to report to regulators in the financial sector	Mar 94
	Glossary of terms	Mar 95

Notes

1   You should be aware of the nature and meaning of the audit report and should be able to discuss the contents and wording of the report. You would not be asked to reproduce the audit report in full in an exam question, but you may be requested to prepare the explanatory paragraph, qualification and opinion paragraphs for unqualified and qualified audit reports.

2   Questions will be based on the principles and good practice set out in the Statements of Auditing Standards.

Auditing Guidelines: APC   *Issue date*

308	Guidance for internal auditors	Jun 90
401	Bank reports for audit purposes	Jun 82
405	Attendance stocktaking	Oct 83
407	Auditing in a computer environment	Jun 84

2.9   Each SAS is discussed in this Study Text in the relevant chapter. The old APC guidelines which are still extant are indicative of best practice as they have not yet been replaced by SASs. These are also covered in the text where applicable.

2.10   Note that, in the exam, you *must* answer in accordance with the new SAS where there is one, not on the basis of the old APC standards and guidelines (if you happen to have studied these in the past).

APC *The auditor's operational standard*

2.11   The matters dealt with in *The auditor's operational standard* were the cornerstones of auditing until the new auditing standards were produced. Although it is not examinable itself it is used as the basis for some of the old auditing guidelines which are still relevant (see above). Here is the full text.

'The auditor's operational standard

This Auditing Standard should be read in conjunction with the Explanatory Foreword to Auditing Standards and Guidelines. General guidance on procedures by which this auditing standard may be complied with are given in auditing guidelines:

Planning, controlling and recording
Accounting systems
Audit evidence
Internal controls
Review of financial statements

1   This auditing standard applies whenever an audit is carried out.

Planning, controlling and recording
2   The auditor should adequately plan, control and record his work.

Accounting systems

3   The auditor should ascertain the enterprise's system of recording and processing trans-
     actions and assess its adequacy as a basis for the preparation of financial statements.

Audit evidence

4   The auditor should obtain relevant and reliable audit evidence sufficient to enable him to
     draw reasonable conclusions therefrom.

Internal controls

5   If the auditor wishes to place reliance on any internal controls, he should ascertain and
     evaluate those controls and perform compliance tests on their operation.

Review of financial statements

6   The auditor should carry out such a review of the financial statements as is sufficient, in
     conjunction with the conclusions drawn from the other audit evidence obtained, to give him
     a reasonable basis for his opinion on the financial statements.

Effective date

7   This auditing standard is effective for the audit of financial statements relating to
     accounting periods starting on or after 1 April 1980.'

2.12   Each of the key paragraphs 2 to 6 had an associated guideline, as indicated in the
       introduction to the standard. These have now been replaced by SASs.

3   THE ROLE OF GOVERNMENT AND INTERNATIONAL AUDITING BODIES

3.1   As we have already seen, auditing is a self-regulating profession. The current regime was,
       however, instituted by statute (CA 1989), and in such instances the government has most
       effect on the auditing profession.

3.2   The CA 1989 was an instance where the UK government was choosing the best way to
       implement European Union policy, in this case the 8th Directive.

3.3   The government will also introduce legislation on its own behalf, for example the
       legislation that requires external auditors to report to an external regulator under certain
       circumstances. Legislation was required in this kind of situation to give the auditors
       protection for their breach of confidentiality. The government has been involved in
       other aspects of auditing.

3.4   It is not unusual to find government officials sitting as observers at meetings, such as
       those of the APB.

3.5   The Department of Trade and Industry will appoint inspectors to investigate company
       collapses or frauds and the auditors have often been criticised after such investigations,
       although never prosecuted.

The European Commission and International Auditing Bodies

3.6   We have already discussed the role of the EC itself on auditing. This has mainly been
       through the 8th Directive, the provisions of which were implemented through the CA
       1989 in the UK.

3.7   The European Commission has some impact on European auditing. For example, it has
       adopted a proposal for a regulation for a voluntary Community environmental auditing
       scheme (known as the eco-audit scheme).

International Auditing Practices Committee (IAPC)

3.8   Similar in nature to the International Accounting Standards Committee (IASC), the IAPC issues International Standards on Auditing (ISAs). In general terms these standards have not been as detailed or stringent as UK auditing standards and guidelines.

3.9   Recently, however, the International Organisation of Securities Commissions (IOSCO) approved ISAs, so that multi-national accounts which are audited in compliance with ISAs are now acceptable to securities regulatory authorities around the world. It will also make transactions, such as cross border offerings, much easier and less costly than before. The ISA project took IOSCO five years to complete. It involved examining basic auditing principles and essential procedures. A joint task force identified a number of areas in which changes were needed and most of the resulting recommendations have been incorporated into the ISAs.

3.10   This development has been seen as important as it will provide an incentive for countries to bring their standards into line with international ones. The APB will be paying great attention to ISAs in its review of existing UK auditing pronouncements, to ensure that these reflect all the basic precepts of the international standards.

4   APPOINTMENT OF AUDITORS

4.1   The Companies Act 1985 requires that the auditors should be **appointed** by and therefore be **answerable** to the **shareholders**.

4.2   The basic rule is that every company shall at each general meeting at which accounts are laid, appoint an auditor. He or she will hold office from the conclusion of that meeting until the conclusion of the next general meeting at which accounts are laid (s 385 CA 1985). The retiring auditor may be reappointed at the general meeting, but by positive resolution only. Re-appointment is not automatic.

4.3   The following are exceptions to the basic rule.

(a)   The directors may appoint the auditor:

(i)   at any time before the first general meeting at which accounts are presented, such auditor to hold office until the conclusion of that meeting (s 385(3) CA 1985);

(ii)   to fill any casual vacancy in the office of auditor (s 388 CA 1985).

(b)   If the directors fail to appoint the first auditor, these powers may be exercised by the members in general meeting.

The surviving or continuing auditor will continue to act while a casual vacancy continues.

4.4   Where no auditors are appointed or re-appointed at any general meeting of a company at which accounts are laid before the members, the Secretary of State may appoint a person to fill the vacancy (s 387 CA 1985). The company must inform the Secretary of State within one week of his power under this subsection becoming exercisable. Failure to give such notice makes the company and its officers who are in default liable to a daily fine.

Special notice of appointment

4.5   In certain cases relating to appointment of an auditor special notice (28 days) is required for the appropriate resolutions at a general meeting (ss 388(3) and 391 A(1)(b) CA 1985). Such resolutions are those proposing:

(a)   to **appoint** as **auditor** a person **other than the retiring auditor;**

(b)   to fill **a casual vacancy** in the office of auditor; or

(c)   to **re-appoint as auditor** a retiring auditor who was appointed by the directors to fill a **casual vacancy.**

4.6   On receipt of notice of one of these resolutions the company must immediately send a copy thereof (ss 388(4) and 391 A(2) CA 1985) to:

(a)   the **person** whom it is intended to **appoint;**

(b)   the **retiring auditor,** if applicable;

(c)   the **auditor who resigned,** if applicable, where a casual vacancy was caused by a resignation.

Elective regime for private companies

4.7   The Companies Act 1989 introduced a regime whereby a private company may elect not to comply with some of the statutory requirements of the Companies Act. Such an election is called an elective resolution.

4.8   A private company may by elective resolution elect not to be required to appoint auditors annually (s 386 CA 1985). In such a case, the auditors in office will be deemed to be re-appointed annually. While the election is in force, any member may give notice in writing proposing that the auditor be removed, and the directors must convene a general meeting to decide the issue within 28 days of the notice. (Remember an elective resolution requires agreement by all members entitled to vote at or attend the meeting.)

4.9   A private company may also elect not to lay accounts before the members in general meeting (although under s 253 members and auditors may require a general meeting to be held for the laying of accounts). If the company makes such an election without making an election not to reappoint auditors annually, it must hold a general meeting annually to re-elect the auditors (s 385A CA 1985). This meeting must be held within 28 days of dispatching the accounts to members, and an auditor so appointed will hold office until the corresponding time for appointing auditors for the next financial year.

4.10   The elective regime is likely to result in many private companies not holding annual general meetings, but instead dealing with AGM business in written resolutions which are signed by the directors.

Remuneration

4.11   The remuneration of the auditors, which will include any sums paid by the company in respect of the auditors' expenses, will be fixed (s 390A CA 1985) either by:

(a)   **whoever made** the **appointment** which could be:

(i)   the members;

(ii)   the directors;

(iii)   the Secretary of State; or

(b)   in **such manner** as the **company in general** meeting may determine.

4.12   However the auditors' remuneration is fixed, it must be disclosed in the annual accounts of the company (s 390A(3) CA 1985). S 390A(5) CA 1985 requires the disclosure in the company's accounts to include the value and nature of benefits in kind provided to the auditors. The Act also gives the Secretary of State the right to introduce regulations to require the disclosure of the remuneration of auditors and their associates in other capacities.

Appointment procedures and ethical guidance

4.13   Under the ACCA's *Rules of Professional Conduct* in Statement 5: *Changes in Professional Appointment*, auditors must undertake certain procedures to ensure their appointment is valid and they are free to act.

Before accepting nomination

4.14   Before a new audit client is accepted, the auditors must ensure that there are **no independence** or **other ethical problems** likely to cause conflict with the ethical code. Furthermore, new auditors should ensure that they have been appointed in a proper and legal manner, especially since one auditor's appointment is normally another's removal or resignation.

4.15   The potential new auditors must carry out the following procedures:

(a)   Ensure that they are **professionally qualified** to act, not disqualified on any of the legal or ethical grounds set out in earlier chapters.

(b)   Ensure that the firm's **existing resources are adequate** to service the needs of the new client: this will raise questions of staff and time availability and the firm's technical expertise.

(c)   **Seek references** in respect of the new client company. It may be that the directors of the company are already personally known to the firm; if not, independent enquiries should be made concerning the status of the company and its directors. We will consider how firms obtain more information in Section 3.

(d)   **Communicate** with the **present auditors.**

   (i)   Strict rules of conduct are laid down in *Statement 5 Changes in Professional Appointment*s, regarding the purpose and the nature of such a communication. The purpose is primarily to protect the shareholders.

      (1)   The proposed auditors should not accept nomination without first enquiring from the existing auditors whether there is any reason for or circumstances behind the proposed change of which they should be aware.

      (2)   Communication is also important from the viewpoint of professional courtesy.

   (ii)   The statement requires the following actions on the part of the **proposed auditor.**

      (1)   They should request the prospective client's permission to communicate with the auditors last appointed. If such **permission** is **refused** they should **decline nomination**.

(2) On receipt of permission, they should **request in writing** of the auditors last appointed **all information** which ought to be made available to them to enable them to decide whether they are prepared to accept nomination. (*Note.* If no reply is received, a further letter may be sent which states that if no answer is received by a specified date, it will be assumed that there are no reasons not to accept nomination.)

(iii) The current auditors receiving the request in (ii)(2) above should perform the following actions.

(1) They should **request the permission** of the **client** to **discuss** the **client's affairs** freely with the proposed auditors. If this request is not granted the auditors should report that fact to the proposed auditors, who should not accept nomination.

(2) They should **discuss freely** with the **proposed auditors** all matters relevant to the appointment of which the latter should be aware, and disclose fully all information which appears to them to be relevant to the client's affairs or which may be reasonably requested of them by the proposed nominees.

Example letters

4.16 This is an example of a initial communication.

To: Retiring & Co
         Certified Accountants

Dear Sirs

Re: New Client Co Ltd

We have been asked to allow our name to go forward for nomination as auditors of the above company, and we should therefore be grateful if you would please let us know whether there are any professional reasons why we should not accept nomination...... .

Acquiring & Co

Certified Accountants

4.17 The following letter would be sent if the nominee has not received a reply to the letter above within a reasonable time.

To: Retiring & Co
     Certified Accountants

Dear Sirs

Re: New Client Co Ltd

As we have been unable to obtain a reply to our letters of the 1 and 14 September we would inform you that, unless we hear from you by 30 September, we shall assume that there are no professional reasons preventing our acceptance of nomination as auditors of the above company and we shall allow our name to go forward. We ourselves are not aware of any reasons why we should not consent to act for this company.... .

Acquiring & Co

Certified Accountants

4.18 Having negotiated these steps the auditors will be in a position to accept the nomination, or not, as the case may be.

Procedures after accepting nomination

4.19   The following procedures should be carried out after accepting nomination.

(a)   **Ensure** that the **outgoing auditors' removal** or **resignation** has been **properly conducted** in accordance with the Companies Act 1985.

The new auditors should see a valid notice of the outgoing auditors' resignation (under s 392 CA 1985), or confirm that the outgoing auditors were properly removed (under s 391 CA 1985).

(b)   **Ensure** that the **new auditors' appointment is valid.** The new auditors should obtain a copy of the resolution passed at the general meeting appointing them as the company's auditors.

(c)   Set up and **submit a letter of engagement** to the directors of the company (see Section 4 of this chapter).

Other matters

4.20   Where the previous auditors have **fees still owing** by the client, the new auditors need not decline appointment solely for this reason. They should decide how far they may go in helping the former auditors to obtain their fees, as well as whether they should accept the appointment.

4.21   Once a new appointment has taken place, the new auditors should obtain **all books and papers** which belong to the client from the old auditors. The former accountants should ensure that all such documents are transferred, *unless* they have a lien over the books because of unpaid fees. The old auditors should also pass any useful information to the new auditors if it will be of help, without charge, unless a lot of work is involved.

4.22   Where accountants are appointed to a **non-audit engagement** at a client which has different auditors or accountants performing work, the new accountants should inform the existing auditors/accountants of their appointment as a matter of courtesy. This requirement may be waived in certain circumstances.

5   RESIGNATION AND REMOVAL OF AUDITORS

Resignation

5.1   Certain provisions of the Companies Act 1985 are designed to ensure that auditors do not resign without an explanation of their action. If the auditors wish to resign part-way through their term of office they must carry out the following procedures.

Step 1   The auditors must deposit **written notice** of their resignation at the registered office of the company. Resignation is effective on the day the notice is received, unless the auditors have specified some later date.

The auditors must accompany such notice with a **statement** (s 394 CA 1985) that either:

(a)   there were no circumstances connected with this resignation which they consider should be brought to the notice of the members or creditors of the company; or

(b)   a statement detailing any such 'surrounding circumstances'.

Note. Unless there is a statement as required by s 394, the auditors' resignation will not be effective.

Step 2   The **company** must send a copy of the auditors' **resignation** to the **Registrar of Companies** within 14 days. The **auditors** must send a copy of the **statement of circumstances** to the **registrar of companies** within 28 days.

Step 3   Should the statement of circumstances so dictate, then further copies must be sent to all members and all debenture holders of the company.

Step 4   The auditors *may* attach a signed requisition for the directors to convene an **extraordinary general meeting**, in order that the circumstances surrounding his resignation can be brought to the attention of the members. S 392A(5) requires that this meeting takes place within 28 days of the notice convening the meeting.

Step 5   Before the general meeting is convened, the auditors *may* request the company to circulate to its members a **written statement of circumstances**. This need not necessarily be the same statement mentioned in Step 1. The company must circulate this statement to all members to whom notice of the meeting is being sent. If for any reason this fails to happen, the statement can be read out at the meeting.

Step 6   The auditors who have resigned may also exercise their other rights:

(a)   They are entitled to receive all **notices** relating to:

(i)   the general meeting at which their term of office would have expired;

(ii)   any general meeting at which it is proposed to fill the casual vacancy caused by their removal.

(b)   They are entitled to **attend** such meetings and to speak at them on any part of the business which concerns them as former auditors. Prior to the meeting they can also have circulated a statement of circumstances as in Step 5.

Removal of an auditor

5.2   The detailed provisions relating to the removal of the auditors, set out in ss 391 and 391A CA 1985, place the authority for removal of the auditors with the **members** in general meeting. The auditors *cannot* be removed by board resolution; if the directors are unhappy with the auditors, they can only try and have the auditors removed by exercising any rights they have as members.

5.3   The objects of these provisions are:

(a)   to **preserve the right of the members** to **appoint** the auditors of their choice; and

(b)   to **preserve the auditors' independence** of the directors by not permitting directors, who may be in disagreement with the auditors, to dismiss them.

5.4   If a private company has dispensed with the annual appointment of auditors under the elective regime, any member may deposit a written notice at the company's registered office proposing that the auditors' appointment be terminated. The directors must convene a general meeting at which the matter must be discussed within 28 days of such a notice (s 393 CA 1985).

Step 1   The initial notice to remove the auditors *before* the expiration of their term of office can come about in two ways:

(a)   by giving **special notice** (28 days) of an ordinary resolution to the company: s 391(2) CA 1985. The auditors are entitled to receive a copy of this resolution; or

(b) if the annual appointment of auditors has been dispensed with under the elective regime, any member may deposit **a written resolution** at the company's registered office proposing that the auditors' appointment be terminated. The directors must convene a general meeting to discuss the matter within 28 days of the notice being received: s 393 CA 1985.

Step 2   The auditors may make **representations** as to why they think they ought to stay in office. Provided they are not received too late and are of reasonable length, they may require the company (s 391A(4)):

(a) to state in any notice of the resolution given to the members that representations have been made; and

(b) to send a copy of the representations to the members.

If the representations are not sent out either because they were received too late or because of the company's default, the auditors may require that they are read out at the meeting. This will not prejudice their normal right to speak at the meeting (s 391A(5) CA 1985).

Step 3   If the resolution is passed at the general meeting:

(a) the company must **notify the registrar** within 14 days of the date of the meeting: s 391(2) CA 1985; and

(b) the auditor must deposit a **s 394 statement of circumstances** with the company within 14 days of ceasing to hold office. The auditor must then send a copy to the Registrar of Companies within 28 days of depositing the statement with the company.

Step 4   Auditors who are being **removed** are given two further rights by s 391(4) CA 1985..

(a) They are entitled to receive all **notices** relating to:

(i) the general meeting at which their term of office would have expired;

(ii) any general meeting at which it is proposed to fill the casual vacancy caused by their removal.

(b) They are entitled to **attend** such meetings and to speak at them on any part of the business which concerns them as former auditors.

Other types of departure from office

5.5   Auditors may be removed from office by a resolution at the annual general meeting to appoint new auditors. Special notice is required of such a resolution, and the auditors are able, prior to the AGM, to make representations as to why they think they should stay in office.

5.6   Alternatively auditors may merely decline to offer themselves for re-election at the AGM.

Exam focus point

The duty to make a statement of circumstances is very important since it allows auditors to inform members and creditors of problems they have found.

Statement of circumstances

5.7   Whatever way the auditors depart from office, a s 394 statement of circumstances must be deposited at the company's registered office and sent to all those entitled to receive a copy of the accounts.

5.8   The exception to this rule is that if the company or any other person feels aggrieved by the statement, they may apply to the court for an order that the statement need not be sent out. The application must be made within 14 days of the statement being deposited.

5.9   If the court feels that the auditors are using the statement to secure needless publicity for defamatory matters:

(a)   it will direct that copies of the statement need not be sent to everyone entitled to receive a copy of the accounts; and

(b)   it may order the company's costs to be paid in whole or part by the auditors.

5.10 The company has similar rights to apply to the court in relation to a written statement of circumstances made by the resigning auditors prior to the auditor-convened general meeting (Step 5 under resignation of auditors), or in relation to representations made by auditors who have received notice of a proposed resolution to remove them from office (Step 2 removal of auditors).

Exam focus point

You may be asked to apply the statutory rules to a real-life situation, for example considering how the directors can try to have auditors they dislike removed.

6   DUTIES AND RIGHTS OF AUDITORS

Duties

6.1   The principal statutory duties of auditors in respect of the audit of a limited company are set out in ss 235 and 237 CA 1985. The auditors are required to report on every balance sheet and profit and loss account laid before the company in general meeting.

6.2   The auditors must consider the following provisions.

s 235(2)	*Compliance with legislation*	Whether the accounts have been prepared in accordance with the Act.
s 235(2)	*Truth and fairness of accounts*	Whether the balance sheet shows a true and fair view of the company's (or the group's) affairs at the end of the period and the profit and loss account shows a true and fair view of the results for the period.

s 237(2)	Proper records and returns	Whether proper accounting records have been kept and proper returns adequate for the audit received from branches not visited by the auditor.
s 237(2)	Agreement of accounts to records	Whether the accounts are in agreement with the accounting records.
s 235(3)	Consistency of directors' report	Whether the directors' report is consistent with the accounts.

6.3   Only compliance with legislation and truth and fairness of accounts need to be explicitly referred to in the audit report; the other matters can be reported *by exception only*.

Duties in relation to fraud

6.4   As we will see in Chapter 11 later, SAS 110 *Fraud and error* states that:

SAS 110.1

Auditors should plan and perform their audit procedures and evaluate and report the results thereof, recognising that fraud or error may materially affect the financial statements.

6.5   It is the duty of the *directors* to prevent, detect and correct fraud. The auditors are only concerned with fraud as it affects the truth and fairness of the financial statements of the entity.

Rights

6.6   The Companies Act provides statutory rights for auditors to enable them to carry out their duties.

6.7   The principal rights, excepting those dealing with resignation or removal, are set out in the table below, and the following are notes on more detailed points.

s 389A(1)	Access to records	A right of access at all times to the books, accounts and vouchers of the company.
s 389A(1)	Information and explanations	A right to require from the company's officers such information and explanations as they think necessary for the performance of their duties as auditors.
s 390(1)(a) and (b)	Attendance at/notices of general meetings	A right to attend any general meetings of the company and to receive all notices of and communications relating to such meetings which any member of the company is entitled to receive.
s 390(1)(c)	Right to speak at general meetings	A right to be heard at general meetings which they attend on any part of the business that concerns them as auditors.
s 381B(2)-(4)	Rights in relation to written resolutions	A right to receive a copy of any written resolution proposed.
s 253	Right to require laying of accounts	A right to give notice in writing requiring that a general meeting be held for the purpose of laying the accounts and reports before the company.

Rights to information

6.8   Ss 389A and 390 CA 1985 states the auditors' rights to information as indicated above, and also provide specifically for a holding company auditor's right of access to information regarding and subsidiaries companies whether incorporated in the United Kingdom or not. If auditors have not received all the information and explanations they consider necessary, they should state this fact in their report.

6.9   The Act makes it an offence for a company's officer knowingly or recklessly to make a statement in any form to an auditor which:

(a)   purports to convey any information or explanation required by the auditor; and

(b)   is materially misleading, false or deceptive.

The penalty is a maximum of two years' imprisonment, a fine or both (s 389A(2)).

Rights to require laying of accounts

6.10   The right to require a general meeting for the laying of accounts applies where, under the elective regime for private companies, an election to dispense with the laying of accounts is in force. The same right is extended to members of the company.

Question 2

The Companies Act includes provisions regarding the appointment, duties and powers of a company's auditor.

Required

(a)   State the ways in which an auditor can be appointed.
(b)   Detail the statutory duties imposed on an auditor.
(c)   Specify the statutory powers given to the auditor to enable him to carry out his work.

Answer

(a)   The 1985 Act requires that the auditor should be appointed by (and he will therefore be ultimately answerable to) the members of the company. The basic rule is that every company shall at each general meeting at which accounts are laid, appoint an auditor. He will hold office from the conclusion of that meeting until the conclusion of the next general meeting at which accounts are laid (s 385). The retiring auditor may be reappointed at the general meeting, but by positive resolution only. Re-appointment is not automatic.

The following are exceptions to the basic rule.

(i)   The directors may appoint the auditor:

(1)   at any time before the first general meeting at which accounts are presented, such auditor to hold office until the conclusion of that meeting (s 385(3) CA 1985);

(2)   to fill any casual vacancy in the office of auditor (s 388 CA 1985).

(ii)   If the directors fail to appoint the first auditor, these powers may be exercised by the members in general meeting.

(iii)   A dormant private company need not necessarily appoint an auditor (ss 250 and 388A CA 1985).

The surviving or continuing auditor will continue to act while a casual vacancy continues.

Where no auditors are appointed or re-appointed at any general meeting of a company at which accounts are laid before the members, the Secretary of State may appoint a person to fill the vacancy (s 387 CA 1985). The company must inform the Secretary of State within one week of his power under this subsection becoming exercisable. Failure to give such notice makes the company and its officers who are in default liable to a daily fine.

In certain cases relating to appointment of an auditor special notice (28 days) is required for the appropriate resolutions at a general meeting (ss 388(3) & 391A(1)(b) CA 1985). Such resolutions are those proposing:

(i)   to appoint as auditor a person other than the retiring auditor;

(ii)   to fill a casual vacancy in the office of auditor; or

(iii)   to re-appoint as auditor a retiring auditor who was appointed by the directors to fill a casual vacancy.

On receipt of notice of one of these resolutions the company must immediately send a copy thereof (ss 388(4) & 391A(2) CA 1985) to:

(i)   the person whom it is intended to appoint;
(ii)   if applicable, the retiring auditor;
(iii) if applicable, the auditor who resigned, where a casual vacancy was caused by a resignation.

(b)   Under CA 1985 the auditor is required to perform an independent examination of the financial statements of a company and express an opinion thereon.

The auditor will state whether, in this opinion, the financial statements (balance sheet, profit and loss account and statement of recognised gains and losses:

(i)   show a true and fair view of the state of the company's affairs at the balance sheet date and the results for the period then ended; and

(ii)   have been properly prepared in accordance with the Companies Act 1985.

The auditor must also report by *exception* on whether:

(i)   proper accounting records have been maintained;
(ii)   adequate returns have been received in respect of any branches not visited;
(iii) the financial statements are in agreement with the underlying records;
(iv)   all information and explanations considered necessary have been received;
(v)   the directors' report is consistent with the financial statements.

The auditor's report must also detail statutory disclosure provisions if they have not been given elsewhere in the financial statements, namely:

(i)   details of directors' emoluments;
(ii)   details of directors' emoluments waived;
(iii) details of loans to officers;
(iv)   details of directors' interests in material transactions with the company;
(v)   details of higher paid employees.

(c)   The auditor has various statutory rights, including:

(i)   right of access to all books, accounts and vouchers of the company;
(ii)   right to all such information and explanations as he considers necessary for the performance of his duties;
(iii) right to attend any general meeting and to receive all notices and communications relating thereto which any member of the company is entitled to receive;
(iv)   right to speak at general meetings on any part of the business which concerns him as auditor.

Chapter roundup

- The Companies Act requires auditors to hold an **appropriate qualification** and to be a member of a **recognised supervisory body.**

- A person is **ineligible** to act as auditor if he is an **employee** or officer or has various other close connections with the company.

- The Auditing Practices Board issues:

    o SASs
    o Practice Notes
    o Bulletins

- SASs contain **basic principles** and **procedures** with which auditors must comply as well as other material designed to help auditors.

- Legislation affecting auditors is introduced by the government on its own initiative or in response to European Commission **directives.**

- The Auditing Practices Board takes account of standards set by the **International Auditing Practices Committee** when setting auditing standards.

- The most significant aim of the legislation relating to the **appointment** and **removal** of auditors is to ensure that auditors are ultimately answerable to the **members, not** the **directors.**

- Auditors are generally **appointed** annually at the general meeting at which accounts are laid (except when there is an elective resolution in force).

- Auditors can leave office by one of the following means:

    o   resignation;
    o   not seeking reappointment;
    o   being removed at a general meeting before their term of office would have expired;
    o   being removed at a general meeting at which their term of office expires.

- Auditors **cannot** be removed by board resolution alone.

- Auditors leaving office for any reason have a duty to make a statement either:

    o   to state that there are **no circumstances** connected with their departure about which members and creditors should know; or

    o   to **list those circumstances.**

- Auditors leaving office have other rights depending on the manner of their departure.

- Auditor **duties** include the duties to report explicitly on the **truth** and **fairness** of the accounts audited and their **compliance** with legislation.

- Auditors have a duty to **report** on other matters, such as whether proper accounting records have been kept, by **exception.**

- Auditor rights include the rights of **access** to **records** and to receive **information** and **explanations**, also rights relating to **attendance** and **speaking** at **general meetings**.

Quick quiz

1   How is an auditor's 'appropriate qualification' defined? (see paras 1.4, 1.5)

2   When is a person ineligible for appointment under CA 1985? (1.6)

3   What features will the monitoring unit expect to see when it visits an auditing firm? (1.18)

4   What type of documents does the APB produce? (2.2)

5   State the scope of Statements of Auditing Standards. (2.3)

6   What are the five measures outlined as necessary in an audit by *The auditor's operational standard*? (2.11)

7   For what period do the auditors hold office? (4.2, 4.3)

8   In what circumstances is 'special notice' required in the context of the auditors' appointment? (4.5)

9   What formal steps should the auditors take before accepting a new client? (4.15)

10 What procedures should the auditors undertake after accepting nomination? (4.19)

11 How may the auditors resign part way through their term of office? (5.1)

12 Where an attempt is made to remove the auditors during their term of office, what rights do the auditors have? (5.4)

13 What are the main statutory duties of the auditors? (6.1, 6.2)

14 What are the statutory rights of the auditors? (6.6 - 6.10)

The question indicated below is designed to highlight what you need to know about statutory rights and duties

Question to try	Level	Marks	Time
2	Revision	n/a	25 mins

Chapter 3

AUDIT PLANNING

Chapter topic list	Syllabus reference
1 Client screening	Revision
2 The engagement letter	Revision
3 Aims of planning	Revision
4 Knowledge of the business	Revision
5 Materiality	Revision
6 Experts, audit staffing and service organisations	Revision
7 The overall audit plan	Revision
8 The audit programme	Revision

Introduction

This chapter firstly revises the practical matters that auditors need to consider when deciding whether to **accept** a new client, including risks and supervisory controls. These matters are possible Paper 10 topics, examined as part of a question also involving ethical situations.

This chapter also covers the aspects of the audit which will be considered during **planning**.

The planning aspects of auditing are extremely important. At this stage, the extent and type of audit work to be performed are decided. Any misjudgement may therefore be crucial.

The assessment of audit risk is connected to audit planning. You should already be familiar with audit risk from your Paper 6 studies, but in this Study Text audit risk is examined with internal controls and audit sampling in Chapter 6.

The SASs discussed in this chapter are important and they should be read carefully.

1 CLIENT SCREENING

1.1 Many firms, particularly larger firms, carry out stringent checks on potential audit (and other) client companies and their management. There are a number of reasons for this, as we will see shortly.

1.2 The procedures laid out here are tailored to the extreme case of a large audit firm and a large (probably public) company audit, but the procedures may be adapted for smaller audit firms and smaller audits.

1.3 Auditors are likely to be concerned with the following matters in relation to client screening:

- the factors to consider in determining whether to accept a prospective audit client;
- the approvals required before accepting a prospective client;
- additional procedures for special cases, for example financial services companies;
- acceptance procedures for other types of work;

- the documentation of client acceptance.

Basic factors for consideration

1.4   Considerations of whether to accept a client will fall under these or similar headings.

- Management integrity
- Risk
- Economics of the engagement
- Mutual satisfaction from the professional relationships
- Ability to perform the work

Management integrity

1.5   The integrity of those managing a company will be of great importance. One has only to mention 'Maxwell' to see why!

Risk

1.6   In this context, 'risk' means the danger of damaging the audit firm's reputation. A low risk client is one which:

(a)   has a **viable business** with good long-range prospects;

(b)   is **well financed** with strong internal controls;

(c)   applies **conservative, prudent accounting principles,** rather than those which are aggressive or dubious;

(d)   has **competent, honest management,** particularly a good finance director, well qualified with a close relationship to the rest of the board.

1.7   It is assumed that higher risk will be indicated by the following factors or events.

(a)   **prospective litigation** about the company's reporting practices;

(b)   **qualification** of its previous audit report;

(c)   **significant related party transactions** with a sister company which has different auditors;

(d)   **significant weaknesses** in the **internal control** structure;

(e)   they are **unable to prepare financial statements**;

(f)   they follow **aggressive,** rather than prudent or conservative **accounting policies.**

Audit risk is considered in more detail in Chapter 6.

1.8   Audit firms may have standard forms for analysing potential risk, particularly in specialist areas (banking, pensions, and so on) which will highlight industry-specific risk factors which must be addressed.

1.9   Other factors to be addressed would include such matters as whether the potential client intends to apply for a full listing on the Stock Exchange in the near future, in which case the client should be treated as if it was already fully listed.

1.10   Where the risk level of a company's audit is determined as anything other than low, then the specific risks should be identified and documented. It might be necessary to assign specialists in response to these risks, particularly industry specialists, as independent reviewers. Some audit firms have procedures for closely monitoring audits which have been accepted, but which are considered high risk.

1.11 If possible, the most recent reports on the company's internal controls, by the external *or* internal auditors, should be examined to determine whether any material weakness exists. Any such weakness would need to be closely monitored if such a client was accepted.

Engagement economics

1.12 Generally, the expected fees from a new client should reflect the **level of risk** expected. They should also offer the same sort of return expected of clients of this nature and reflect the overall financial strategy of the audit firm. Occasionally, the audit firm will want the work to gain entry into the client's particular industry, or to establish better contacts within that industry. These factors will all contribute to a total expected economic return.

Relationship

1.13 The audit firm will generally want the relationship with a client to be long term. This is not only to enjoy receiving fees year after year; it is also to allow the audit work to be enhanced by better knowledge of the client and thereby offer a better service.

1.14 Conflict of interest problems are significant here; the firm should establish that no existing clients will cause difficulties as competitors of the new client. Other services to other clients may have an impact here, not just audit.

Ability to perform the work

1.15 The audit firm must have the resources to perform the work properly, as well as any relevant specialist knowledge or skills. The impact on existing engagements must be estimated, in terms of staff time and the timing of the audit.

Investigations

1.16 Certain types of client normally require a thorough investigation before acceptance. Each audit firm will have different criteria for deciding which clients should be investigated using an external agency, but examples would be:

(a) financial services companies (eg banks, brokers, insurance, credit or leasing companies);

(b) businesses whose receipts are mainly in cash (eg turf accountants, casinos, bingo halls and parking lots);

(c) other industries perceived as high risk for a variety of reasons, such as builders, contractors, waste management services and so on.

1.17 With some firms all potential clients are investigated unless the firm has knowledge gained over time of the company's reputation and the reputation of its managers and directors. These firms believe that investigations are cost effective in avoiding embarrassing or damaging situations.

1.18 Where it is decided that an investigation is not necessary, this fact must be documented, along with the relevant reasons and authorisation obtained (probably from the managing or technical partner).

1.19 An investigation request should be documented and a standard form may be available.

1.20 Where an investigation uncovers suspicious, unresolved allegations and questions or concerns about the reputation, ethics or business practices of a prospective client, it will be usual to consult the managing partner, and possibly the opinion of Counsel will be sought. Any such procedures must be fully documented.

1.21 The investigative report must be timely. If it is received too long before the client is accepted, then an update might be necessary. On the other hand, delay of acceptance of a client because the investigative report was still awaited would be extremely bad practice.

Inquiries of other sources

1.22 Confidential enquiries might be made of the prospective client's bankers, solicitors, underwriters or other relevant connection.

Review of documents

1.23 The prospective client's most recent annual accounts should be examined, along with any interim statements. Other similar documents worth examination might include the company's original 'placing' documents when it obtained a listing. For private companies it may be advisable to obtain a Dun & Bradstreet (credit rating) or similar report.

Previous accountants/auditors

1.24 The prospective client will be asked for permission for the firm to contact the outgoing auditors, to enquire whether there are any reasons why the firm should not take up the appointment. A refusal or limitation by the company will normally lead to a refusal as an audit client. These contacts are discussed further in Section 2 of this chapter.

1.25 The firm should ask both the company and its former auditors whether there have been any **fundamental disagreements** or any events which have led to a report to the Stock Exchange or the relevant regulatory authority (for example the Bank of England). Where such a disagreement did arise, the matter should be referred to the regional managing partner. He or she should also be consulted if a prospective audit client expects the firm to accept an accounting policy that the previous auditors did not accept.

Review of rules and standards

1.26 SAS 210 emphasises the importance of understanding the regulatory environment in which the prospective client operates, in particular:

- specific rules and regulations pertaining to the industry; and
- accounting standards applicable to the industry.

We will discuss this SAS further later in this chapter.

Request for Prospective Client Investigation

Regular Service ☐
Urgent service ☐

To :

_____

_____

_____

Name and address of investigative agency

Legal form of prospective client

☐ Private company
☐ Public company
☐ Partnership
☐ Association
☐ Proprietorship
☐ Individual
☐ Government or Government Agency

1   Name and address of prospective client (attach current Dun & Bradstreet Report.)

2   Type of service to be provided.   Audit ☐   Tax ☐   Consultancy ☐

Other ☐ _____

(Describe)

3   Identify prospective client's bankers and/or solicitors.

4   Information regarding key individuals to be investigated (list key owners and members of management; directors, officers, shareholders, partners, managers).

		If known		
Name and title	Approximate age	Home address	National Insurance number	Other business interests

5   Add any additional information that may reduce investigative time and expense (eg other names used and locations for this business; current or known litigation; identity of suppliers, customers, and current auditors/accountants).

_____

Date

_____

Signature of Partner or Senior Manager

_____

Office

Copy 1 - Send to investigative agency
Copy 2 - Attach to Client Acceptance Form
Copy 3 - Send to security partner, National Office

Approval

1.27 Once all the relevant procedures and information gathering has taken place, the company can be put forward for approval. The engagement partner will have completed a client acceptance form and this, along with any other relevant documentations, will be submitted to the managing partner, or whichever partner is in overall charge of accepting clients. There may be formal procedures in place for collaboration to reach a decision over approval for certain situations:

- companies about to go public;
- derogatory information in the investigative report;
- financial services companies;
- companies with perceived problems requiring close monitoring;
- disagreements with previous auditors over accounting policies.

1.28 No audit work whatsoever should take place before the approval is given and documented, and probable not until the change of auditors has been notified to the Registrar (see Section 3).

Documentation

1.29 The managing partner will maintain files relating to the consideration of prospective clients. When a decision is made not to accept a prospective client based on the results of an investigation or other information that raises questions about the prospective client's integrity, then a brief summary memorandum should be prepared. This should summarise the procedures undertaken, the problems which arose, and the reasons for refusal.

1.30 An example of a client acceptance form is given on the next few pages. These will obviously vary from firm to firm and many firms will not have a standard form.

Exam focus point
In the exam you may be given a 'real-life' client situation and asked what factors you would consider in deciding whether to accept appointment.

Client Acceptance Form - Audit clients   Form A1.1

We perform our client acceptance procedures, and in particular the investigation procedures, as early in the proposal process as possible to avoid incurring significant time and effort on a prospective client that we might later decide not to accept.

Background Information

Prospective client_____   Accounting period _____

Address_____

Nature of business (eg industry, products or services, major customers, major suppliers)_____

_____

_____

_____

If the business was started within the past 5 years, indicate the year: 19 ___   Company reg. no. _____

Type of service(s) to be rendered_____

Does the prospective client meet the definition of a "Stock Exchange engagement"? Yes _____ No_____

Is the prospective client considering "going public" in the next year? Yes _____ No_____ N/A _____

Anticipated person in charge _____

Anticipated independent reviewer, if identified _____

Total estimated fee (if available):

Year 1   £_____   recurring   £_____   non-recurring

Year 2   £_____   recurring   £_____   non-recurring

Billing and payment agreement and any special fee arrangements_____

_____

Financial information (for last two years):

Year end	Total assets	Total debt	Shareholders' funds	Total turnover	Profit/(loss)
_____	_____	_____	_____	_____	_____
_____	_____	_____	_____	_____	_____

Has the prospective client been investigated? Yes _____ No_____ If not, document in an attached memorandum the reasons for not requesting an investigation.

Was there any information in the investigative agency's (oral or attached written) report that indicates we should question whether to accept the prospective client? Yes _____ No_____ If yes, discuss in an attached memorandum along with any mitigating factors.

Key officers, directors, and major shareholders	Officer	Director	Own%	Other businesses/comments
_____	_____	_____	_____	_____
_____	_____	_____	_____	_____
_____	_____	_____	_____	_____
_____	_____	_____	_____	_____

Client Acceptance Form - Audit clients   Form A1.2

List the principal solicitors, commercial bankers, and investment bankers with whom the prospective client has a relationship (indicate with an asterisk those individuals who are contacted as part of our client acceptance procedures) and other individuals contacted:

Individual   Firm or Bank

_____   _____

_____   _____

_____   _____

_____   _____

_____   _____

Did any matters arise in our contacts with the solicitors, commercial bankers, investment bankers, or others that need further consideration in deciding whether to accept the prospective client?   Yes _____   No _____

If yes, describe the matters in an attached memorandum.

Predecessor Auditors/Accountants

Inquiries of prospective client regarding predecessor auditors/accountants:

Firm name and office _____

Length of firm's relationship with the prospective client _____

Services rendered to the prospective client _____

_____

Type of opinion issued last year _____

Prospective client's reason(s) for changing auditors/accountants _____

_____

Were there any disagreements with the predecessor auditors/accountants over accounting principles, audit, review, or compilation procedures, or other significant matters during the entity's two most recent fiscal years and any other subsequent interim period? Yes _____ No _____ If yes, describe the disagreements in an attached memorandum.

Any reportable conditions/material weaknesses in the internal control structure?   Yes _____   No _____

If yes, describe the conditions/weaknesses in an attached memorandum.

Enquiries of predecessor auditors/accountants:

Date of inquiries _____

Names and titles of individuals who responded to our enquiries (should include the partner in charge) _____

_____

Predecessor's understanding of the reason(s) for changing auditors/accountants _____

_____

Any facts that might bear on the integrity of management _____

_____

_____

Have the predecessor's fees been paid in full? Yes _____ No _____ If not, indicate the reasons _____

Were there any disparities between the prospective client's replies and the preceding auditor's replies?

Yes _____   No _____   If yes, describe the differences in an attached memorandum.

Client Acceptance Form - Audit clients   Form A1.3

Other significant considerations (Explain answers with an asterisk in an attached memorandum)

<table>
<tr><td></td><td></td><td>Yes</td><td>No</td><td></td><td></td><td>Yes</td><td>No</td></tr>
<tr><td>1</td><td>Are there possible conflicts of interest with concerns of existing clients (eg conflicts with litigation services engagements)?</td><td>—*</td><td>—</td><td>6</td><td>Will we be auditing all entities under common control?</td><td>—</td><td>—</td></tr>
<tr><td>2</td><td>Are there any independence issues, including family relationships, that need to be considered before we could accept the prospective client?</td><td>—*</td><td>—</td><td>7</td><td>Are there significant related party transactions with consolidated or other entities that we will not be auditing?</td><td>—*</td><td>—</td></tr>
<tr><td>3</td><td>Will the engagement require specialised (eg industry specific) knowledge and experience not now available in the local or area office?</td><td>—</td><td>—</td><td>8</td><td>Does management have a proven track record in this or other businesses?</td><td>—</td><td>—</td></tr>
<tr><td></td><td>If yes describe in an attached memorandum the plan to obtain the neccessary expertise from other offices and/or to develop it within the office and obtain the concurrence of the national regional director of industry services.</td><td></td><td></td><td>9</td><td>Does the prospective client have a high likelihood of (continued) business success?</td><td>—</td><td>—</td></tr>
<tr><td></td><td>Will the addition of the client adversely affect the ability of the office to staff any of its other engagements requiring similar expertise?</td><td>—*</td><td>—</td><td>10</td><td>Are there any conditions or events that indicate there could be substantial doubt about the prospective client's ability to continue as a going concern?</td><td>—*</td><td>—</td></tr>
<tr><td>4</td><td>Have any significant accounting or auditing issues been identified?</td><td>—*</td><td>—</td><td>11</td><td>For non-public entities, are there third parties (eg lenders or investors) whom we know would be receiving copies of our reports on the client's financial statements?</td><td>—*</td><td>—</td></tr>
<tr><td>5</td><td>Does the prospective client expect the firm to accept an accounting policy the predecessor auditors did not accept?</td><td>—*</td><td>—</td><td>12</td><td>Will the firm be assuming more than a low level of risk if this prospective client is accepted?</td><td>—*</td><td>—</td></tr>
<tr><td></td><td></td><td></td><td></td><td>13</td><td>Are there any other factors that should be considered in evaluating the prospective client?</td><td>—*</td><td>—</td></tr>
</table>

Other procedures

1   Seek information and advice from others in the firm who are likely to have significant information bearing on a decision to accept the prospective client, including other partners in the office, in other offices in the area, and where applicable, in other offices in cities where the entity has significant operations or where we have performed other services.

2   For a prospective client in a specialised industry, consult with the partner of industry services with regard to industry specific factors that should be addressed in considering the prospective client for acceptance.

3   For public and significant non-public prospective audit clients, contact the partner in charge of litigation services to determine if there are any conflicts or potential conflicts that need to be evaluated.

4   In the space below, list any head office personnel consulted when performing the client acceptance proceedures. If there are any unresolved issues remaining from those consultations, describe them in an attached memorandum.

Client Acceptance Form - Audit clients   Form A1.4

Attachments (attach the following, where applicable, to this form)

- Memoranda, as required, to document considerations described elsewhere on this form
- Investigation report or memorandum documenting the reasons for not requesting an investigation

Accompanying information

- Public companies - the most recent annual shareholders' report, the form reporting the change in auditors and the predecessor auditors' letter. Any recent placing or other documents.

- Private companies - the most recent annual financial statements, and if available, the latest interim financial statements.

Conclusions

I have considered the professional, business, and economic factors regarding this engagement and recommend the acceptance of this prospective client.

Client will be ___ /will not be ___ designated for close-monitoring.

Evaluating Person_____   Date _____

Approvals

I am satisfied that this recommendation is in compliance with our policy on client acceptance of this prospective client. Acceptance of this client does ___ /does not ___ require the concurrence of the National

Office Managing Partner _____   Date _____

I concur with the acceptance of this prospective client.

National Managing Partner_____   Date _____

2   THE ENGAGEMENT LETTER

2.1   An engagement letter should:

(a)   define clearly the **extent** of the **auditors' responsibilities** and so minimise the possibility of any misunderstanding between the client and the auditors;

(b)   provide **written confirmation** of the **auditors' acceptance** of the appointment, the scope of the audit, the form of their report and the scope of any non-audit services.

2.2   If an engagement letter is not sent to clients, both new and existing, there is scope for argument about the precise extent of the respective obligations of the client and its directors and the auditors. The contents of an engagement letter should be discussed and agreed with management before it is sent and preferably prior to the audit appointment.

2.3   Guidance is available in the form of the SAS 140 *Engagement letters*, which applies to *audit* engagements. The statements made by the standard are as follows.

SAS 140.1

The auditors and the client should agree on the terms of the engagement, which should be recorded in writing.

SAS 140.2

Auditors should agree the terms of their engagement with new clients in writing. Thereafter auditors should regularly review the terms of engagement and if appropriate agree any updating in writing.

SAS 140.3

Auditors who, before the completion of the audit, are requested to change the engagement to one which provides a different level of assurance, should consider the appropriateness of so doing. If auditors consider that it is appropriate to change the terms of engagement, they should obtain written agreement to the revised terms.

SAS 140.4

Auditors should ensure that the engagement letter documents and confirms their acceptance of the appointment, and includes a summary of the responsibilities of the directors and of the auditors, the scope of the engagement and the form of any reports.

Timing

2.4   The auditors should send an engagement letter to all new clients soon after their appointment as auditors and, in any event, before the commencement of the first audit assignment. They should also consider sending an engagement letter to existing clients to whom no letter has previously been sent as soon as a suitable opportunity presents itself.

Content of letter

2.5   This is shown in the example given in an Appendix to the SAS, which is reproduced below. The main emphasis is on the 'principal relevant responsibilities of the directors and the auditors and the scope of the audit.'

Form of reports

2.6 The letter should identify any reports which the auditors will submit *in addition to* the statutory audit report, such as reports to the directors/managers on material internal control weaknesses etc. Confidentiality aspects of such reports should be mentioned.

Other matters

2.7 The other matters which the SAS highlights for possible inclusion in the engagement letter are as follows.

(a) Fees and billing arrangements

(b) Procedures where the client has a complaint about the service

(c) Where appropriate, arrangements concerning the involvement of:
   (i) other auditors and experts in some aspect of the audit;
   (ii) internal auditors and other staff of the entity

(d) Arrangements, if any, to be made with the predecessor auditors, in the case of an initial audit

(e) Any restriction of the auditors' liabilities to the client (when such possibility exists)

(f) Where appropriate, the country by whose laws the engagement is to be governed (not possible with limited companies)

(g) A reference to any further agreements between the auditors and the client

(h) A proposed timetable for the engagement

2.8 The following example of an engagement letter for a UK limited company client. Remember that it is not necessarily comprehensive or appropriate to every audit as each client is different; it must be tailored to meet the specific requirements of the engagement.

AN EXAMPLE OF AN ENGAGEMENT LETTER

To the directors of...

The purpose of this letter is to set out the basis on which we (are to) act as auditors of the company (and its subsidiaries) and the respective areas of responsibility of the directors and of ourselves.

Responsibility of directors and auditors

1   As directors of the above company, you are responsible for ensuring that the company maintains proper accounting records and for preparing financial statements which give a true and fair view and have been prepared in accordance with the Companies Act 1985. You are also responsible for making available to us, as and when required, all the company's accounting records and all other relevant records and related information, including minutes of all management and shareholders' meetings.

2   We have a statutory responsibility to report to the members whether in our opinion the financial statements give a true and fair view of the state of the company's affairs and of the profit or loss for the year and whether they have been properly prepared in accordance with the Companies Act 1985 (or other relevant legislation). In arriving at our opinion, we are required to consider the following matters, and to report on any in respect of which we are not satisfied:

(a)   whether proper accounting records have been kept by the company and proper returns adequate for our audit have been received from branches not visited by us;

(b)   whether the company's balance sheet and profit and loss account are in agreement with the accounting records and returns;

(c)   whether we have obtained all the information and explanations which we think necessary for the purposes of our audit; and

(d)   whether the information in the directors' report is consistent with the financial statements.

In addition, there are certain other matters which, according to the circumstances, may need to be dealt with in our report. For example, where the financial statements do not give full details of directors' remuneration or of their transactions with the company, the Companies Act requires us to disclose such matters in our report.

3   We have a professional responsibility to report if the financial statements do not comply in any material respect with applicable accounting standards, unless in our opinion the non-compliance is justified in the circumstances. In determining whether the departure is justified we consider:

(a)   whether the departure is required in order for the financial statements to give a true and fair view; and

(b)   whether adequate disclosure has been made concerning the departure

Our professional responsibilities also include:

(a)   including in our report a description of the directors' responsibilities for the financial statements where the financial statements or accompanying information do not include such a description; and

(b)   considering whether other information in documents containing audited financial statements is consistent with those financial statements.

4   Our audit will be conducted in accordance with the Auditing Standards issued by the Auditing Practices Board, and will include such tests of transactions and of the existence, ownership and valuation of assets and liabilities as we consider necessary. We shall obtain an understanding of the accounting and internal control systems in order to assess their adequacy as a basis for the preparation of the financial statements and to establish whether proper accounting records have been maintained by the company. We shall expect to obtain such appropriate evidence as we consider sufficient to enable us to draw reasonable conclusions therefrom

5   The nature and extent of our procedures will vary according to our assessment of the company's accounting system and, where we wish to place reliance on it, the internal control system, and may cover any aspect of the business's operations. Our audit is not designed to identify all significant weaknesses in the company's systems but, if such weaknesses come to our notice during the course of our audit which we think should be brought to your attention, we shall report them to you. Any such report may not be provided to third parties without our prior written consent. Such consent will be granted only on the basis that such reports are not prepared with the interests of anyone other than the company in mind and that we accept no duty or responsibility to any other party as concerns the reports.

6   As part of our normal audit procedures, we may request you to provide written confirmation of oral representations which we have received from you during the course of the audit on matters having a material effect on the financial statements. In connection with representations and the supply of information to us generally, we draw your attention to section 389A of the Companies Act 1985 under which it is an offence for an officer of the company to mislead the auditors.

7   In order to assist us with the examination of your financial statements, we shall request sight of all documents or statements, including the chairman's statement, operating and financial review and the directors' report, which are due to be issued with the financial statements. We are also entitled to attend all general meetings of the company and to receive notice of all such meetings.

8   The responsibility for safeguarding the assets of the company and for the prevention and detection of fraud, error and non-compliance with law or regulations rests with yourselves. However, we shall endeavour to plan our audit so that we have a reasonable expectation of detecting material misstatements in the financial statements or accounting records (including those resulting from fraud, error or non-compliance with law or regulations), but our examination should not be relied upon to disclose all such material misstatements or frauds, errors or instances of non-compliance as may exist.

9   (Where appropriate). We shall not be treated as having notice, for the purposes of our audit responsibilities, of information provided to members of our firm other than those engaged on the audit (for example information provided in connection with accounting, taxation and other services).

10   Once we have issued our report we have no further direct responsibility in relation to the financial statements for that financial year. However, we expect that you will inform us of any material event occurring between the date of our report and that of the Annual General Meeting which may affect the financial statements.

Other services

11   You have requested that we provide other services in respect of ... . The terms under which we provide these other services are dealt with in a separate letter. We will also agree in a separate letter of engagement the provision of any services relating to investment business advice as defined by the Financial Services Act 1986.

Fees

12   Our fees are computed on the basis of the time spent on your affairs by the partners and our staff and on the levels of skill and responsibility involved. Unless otherwise agreed, our fees will be billed at appropriate intervals during the course of the year and will be due on presentation.

Applicable law

13   This (engagement letter) shall be governed by, and construed in accordance with, (English) law. The Courts of (England) shall have exclusive jurisdiction in relation to any claim, dispute or difference concerning the (engagement letter) and any matter arising from it. Each party irrevocably waives any right it may have to object to an action being brought in those Courts, to claim that the action has been brought in an inconvenient forum, or to claim that those Courts do not have jurisdiction.

14   Once it has been agreed, this letter will remain effective, from one audit appointment to another, until it is replaced. We shall be grateful if you could confirm in writing your agreement to these terms by signing and returning the enclosed copy of this letter, or let us know if they are not in accordance with your understanding of our terms of engagement.

Yours faithfully

Certified Accountants

Notes to the example letter

1   *Other services.* When a firm provides accounting, taxation or other services for an audit client, information may be provided to members of the audit firm other than those engaged on the audit. In such cases, the audit engagement letter should include this or a similar paragraph to indicate that the auditors are not to be treated as having notice, for the purposes of their audit responsibilities, of such information. This emphasises that a company would not be absolved from informing the auditors directly of a material matter.

2   *Additional paragraph: complaints procedures.* Certain professional bodies require members to notify clients of their own complaints procedures and of the clients' right to make complaints to those professional bodies. This might appropriately be included in the engagement letter in a form such as the following.

> 'We aim to provide you with a fully satisfactory service and (name) as engagement partner will seek to ensure that this is so. If, however, you are unable to deal with any difficulty through (him/her) and (his/her) team please contact (name). We undertake to look into any complaints promptly and to do what we can to resolve the position. If you are still not satisfied you may of course take up the matter with (professional body) by whom we are regulated for audit purposes.'

Recipient of letter

2.9   The letter should be addressed to the board of directors or audit committee of the organisation to be audited. The terms of the letter should be evidenced as accepted by the organisation by the signature of an appropriate senior person.

Changes in terms or nature of an engagement

2.10   Once it has been agreed by the client, an engagement letter will, if it so provides, remain effective from one audit appointment to another until it is replaced. However, the engagement letter should be reviewed annually to ensure that it continues to reflect the client's circumstances. The SAS suggests that the following factors may make the agreement of a new letter appropriate.

(a)   Any indication that the client **misunderstands** the objective and scope of the audit
(b)   A **recent change of management**, board of directors or audit committee
(c)   A **significant change in ownership**, such as a new holding company
(d)   A **significant change in the nature or size** of the client's business
(e)   Any **relevant change in legal or professional requirements**

2.11   It may be appropriate to remind the client of the original letter when the auditors decide a new engagement letter is unnecessary for any period.

2.12   In the case of a change in the terms of engagement prior to completion, this may result from:

(a)   a **change in circumstances** affecting the need for the service;

(b)   a **misunderstanding** as to the nature of an audit or of the related service originally requested; or

(c)   a **restriction on the scope** of the engagement, whether imposed by management or caused by circumstances.

2.13   The auditors should consider such a request for change, and the reason for it, very seriously, particularly in terms of any restriction in the scope of the engagement. The SAS then goes on:

> 'If auditors consider that it is not appropriate to change the terms of engagement, they consider their position and may need to take legal advice, or, if appropriate, consult a regulatory body. If auditors are unable to agree to a change of engagement and are not permitted to continue the original engagement, they withdraw and consider whether there is any obligation, contractual or otherwise, to report to other parties, such as the board of directors or shareholders, the circumstances necessitating the withdrawal.'

2.14   The SAS also mentions the statement on ceasing to hold office required by s 394 CA 1985, mentioned in Chapter 2.

Question 1

Explain why a letter of engagement is desirable for the auditors.

Answer

Reasons why it is desirable for the auditors to send a letter of engagement include the following.

(a) It defines the extent of the auditors' responsibilities and so minimises the possibility of any misunderstanding between the management of the enterprise and the auditors.

(b) It documents and confirms the auditors' acceptance of the appointment, the objective and scope of the audit, the extent of his responsibilities, and the form of their report(s).

3   AIMS OF PLANNING

3.1   An effective and efficient audit relies on proper planning procedures. The planning process is covered in general terms by SAS 200 *Planning*.

3.2   Other more detailed areas are covered in SAS 210 *Knowledge of the business* and the other SASs covered in this chapter.

SAS 200.1
Auditors should plan the audit work so as to perform the audit in an effective manner.

3.3   The SAS distinguishes between the general strategy and the detailed approach which must be formulated.

KEY TERMS

An **audit plan** is the formulation of the general strategy for the audit, which sets the direction for the audit, describes the expected scope and conduct of the audit and provides guidance for the development of the audit programme.

An **audit programme** is a set of instructions to the audit team that sets out the audit procedures the auditors intend to adopt and may include references to other matters such as the audit objectives, timing, sample size and basis of selection for each area. It also serves as a means to control and record the proper execution of the work.

3.4   The objectives of planning work involve:

(a) ensuring that **appropriate attention is devoted** to the different areas of the audit;
(b) ensuring that **potential problems** are **identified**; and
(c) **facilitating review**.
(d) **helping** to **assign** the proper tasks to the members of the audit team, co-ordinating outside experts, etc.

3.5   Planning procedures will depend on the size of the entity. Audit procedures should be discussed with the client's management, staff and/or audit committee in order to co-ordinate audit work, including that of internal audit. However, all audit procedures remain the responsibility of the external auditors.

3.6   A structured approach to planning will include the following stages:

(a) **Updating knowledge of the client** by:

(i) reviewing engagement letters

(ii) reviewing the client's business

(iii) reviewing current operations

(iv) preliminary client meeting

(b) **Preparing** the **detailed audit approach** considering risk, materiality, analytical procedures.

(c) Making **administrative decisions** such as staffing and budgets.

These stages are considered in more detail in the next sections.

4 KNOWLEDGE OF THE BUSINESS

4.1 SAS 210 *Knowledge of the business* covers this area.

SAS 210.1

Auditors should have or obtain a knowledge of the business of the entity to be audited which is sufficient to enable them to identify and understand the events, transactions and practices that may have a significant effect on the financial statements or the audit thereof.

4.2 The detailed matters which auditors should consider in relation to knowledge of the business are given in an appendix to the SAS and are discussed below. The SAS gives the following, more general guidance.

Obtaining the knowledge

4.3 This is discussed in three stages:

(a) prior to acceptance of an engagement;

(b) following acceptance of an engagement; and

(c) updating knowledge for succeeding periods.

The SAS then looks at the sources of such knowledge.

Prior to acceptance of the engagement

4.4 The auditors must, at this stage, obtain a 'preliminary knowledge' of the industry and of the ownership, directors, management and operations of the entity to be audited.

Following acceptance of the engagement

4.5 Obviously, the auditors can obtain more detailed knowledge after they have accepted the appointment. As much knowledge should be acquired as early as possible, at the start of the engagement. However, the process should be seen as being 'continuous and cumulative', allowing reassessment at all stages of the audit.

Updating knowledge for succeeding periods

4.6 Auditors should consider the information gathered previously and perform procedures designed to identify any significant changes since the last audit.

Sources of knowledge

4.7 The sources mentioned by the SAS are as follows.

(a) **Previous experience** of the client and its industry

(b) **Visits** to the client's premises and plant facilities

(c) **Discussion with** the client's **staff** and **directors**

(d) **Discussion with other auditors** and with legal and other advisors who have provided services to the client or within the industry

(e) **Discussion with knowledgeable people outside the client** (eg economists, industry regulators)

(f) **Publications** related to the industry (eg government statistics, surveys, texts, trade journals, reports prepared by banks and securities dealers, financial newspapers)

(g) **Legislation and regulations** that significantly affect the client

(h) **Documents produced** by the client (eg minutes of meetings, material sent to shareholders or filed with regulatory authorities, promotional literature, prior years' annual and financial reports, budgets, internal management reports, interim financial reports, management policy manuals, manuals of accounting and internal control systems, charts of accounts, job descriptions, marketing and sales plans)

(i) **Professional literature** giving industry-specific guidance

Matters to consider in relation to knowledge of the business

4.8 This appendix to the SAS provides a useful list of matters to consider. However, the SAS points out that the list is 'not exhaustive, not is it intended that all matters listed will be relevant to every engagement'.

4.9 The following list is given in the appendix to the SAS.

Knowledge of the business	
General economic factors	General level of economic activity (eg recession, growth)
	Interest rates and availability of financing
	Inflation
	Government policies
	Foreign currency rates and controls
The industry: conditions affecting the client's business	The market and competition
	Cyclical or seasonal activity
	Changes in product technology
	Business risk (eg high technology, high fashion, ease of entry for competition)
	Declining or expanding operations
	Adverse conditions (eg declining demand, excess capacity, serious price competition)
	Key ratios and operating statistics
	Specific accounting practices and problems
	Environmental requirements and problems
	Regulatory framework
	Specific or unique practices (eg relating to labour contracts, financing methods, accounting methods)

The entity: directors, management and ownership

Corporate structure: private, public, government (including any recent or planned changes)

Beneficial owners, important stakeholders and related parties (local, foreign, business reputation and experience) and any impact on the entity's transactions

The relationships between owners, directors and management

Attitudes and policies of owners

Capital structure (including any recent or planned changes)

Organisational structure

Group structure

Subsidiaries' audit arrangements

Directors' objectives, philosophy, strategic plans

Acquisitions, mergers or disposals of business activities (planned or recently executed)

Sources and methods of financing (current, historical)

Board of directors:

(a) Composition

(b) Business reputation and experience of individuals

(c) Independence from and control over operating management

(d) Frequency of meetings

(e) Existence and membership of audit committee and scope of its activities

(f) Existence of policy on corporate conduct

(g) Changes in professional advisors (eg lawyers)

Operating management:

(a) Experience and reputation

(b) Turnover

(c) Key financial personnel and their status in the organisation

(d) Staffing of accounting department

(e) Incentive or bonus plans as part of remuneration (eg based on profit)

(f) Use of forecasts and budgets

(g) Pressures on management (eg over-extended, dominance by one individual, support for share price, unreasonable deadlines for announcing results)

(h) Management information systems

Internal audit function (existence, quality)

Attitude to internal control environment

The entity's business: products, markets, suppliers, expenses, operations	Nature of business(es) (eg manufacturer, wholesaler, financial services, import/export)
	Location of production facilities, warehouses, offices
	Employment (eg by location, supply, wage levels, union contracts, pension commitments, government regulations)
	Products or services and markets (eg major customers and contracts, terms of payment, profit margins, market share, competitors, exports, pricing policies, reputation of products, warranties, order book, trends, marketing strategy and objectives, manufacturing processes)
	Important suppliers of goods and services (eg long-term contracts, stability of supply, terms of payment, imports, methods of delivery such as 'just in time')
	Stocks (eg locations, quantities)
	Franchises, licences, patents
	Important expense categories
	Research and development
	Foreign currency assets, liabilities and transactions by currency, hedging
	Legislation and regulations that significantly affect the entity
	Information systems: current, plans to change
	Debt structure, including covenants and restrictions
Financial performance: factors concerning the entity's financial condition and profitability	Accounting policies
	Earnings and cash flow trends and forecasts
	Leasing and other financial commitments
	Availability of lines of credit
	Off balance sheet finance issues
	Foreign exchange and interest rate exposures
	Comparison with industry trends
Information technology	The significance and complexity of computer processing in each significant accounting application (consider the volume of transactions, complexity of computations, electronic data interchange).
Reporting environment: external influences which affect the directors in the preparation of the financial statements	Legislation
	Regulatory environment and requirements
	Taxation
	Accounting requirements

> Measurement and disclosure issues peculiar to the business
>
> Audit reporting requirements
>
> Users of the financial statements

Using the knowledge

4.10 Having obtained knowledge relating to the entity discussed above (and below in the appendix to the SAS), the auditors must use it:

(a) to **assess risks** and **identify problems**;
(b) to **plan** and perform the audit **effectively** and **efficiently**; and
(c) to **evaluate audit evidence**.

4.11 The audit areas subject to judgement which may be affected by knowledge of the business are given by the SAS as follows.

(a) **Developing the overall audit plan** and the **audit programme**

(b) **Considering risks** pertaining to the entity's business activities and the directors' response thereto

(c) Assessing **inherent risk** and **control risk**

(d) Determining a **materiality** level and assessing whether the materiality level chosen remains appropriate

(e) Considering the complexity of the entity's **information systems** and any effect on the audit approach

(f) Identifying areas where **special audit considerations and skills** may be necessary

(g) Assessing **audit evidence** to establish its appropriateness and the validity of the related financial statement assertions

(h) Evaluating **accounting estimates** and **representations** by the directors or management

(i) **Recognising conflicting information** (eg contradictory representations)

(j) **Recognising unusual circumstances** (eg undisclosed related party transactions, possible fraud or non-compliance with law or regulations, or unexpected relationships of satisfied operating data with reported financial results)

(k) **Making informed enquiries** and assessing the reasonableness of answers

(l) **Considering the appropriateness of accounting policies** and financial statement disclosures

Communication of knowledge

4.12 Knowledge of the entity can only be used effectively if it is communicated to members of the audit team.

SAS 210.2

The audit engagement partner should ensure that the audit team obtains such knowledge of the business of the entity being audited as may reasonably be expected to be sufficient to enable it to carry out the audit work effectively.

4.13 Such information will usually be provided in the planning documentation, but the partner should ensure that staff regularly share any subsequent knowledge they have gained with the rest of the team.

5 MATERIALITY

5.1 The concept of 'true and fair' is linked with the concept of materiality, which is fundamental to the whole process of financial accounting. The auditors' task is to decide whether accounts show a true and fair view, not to establish that they are correct in every particular. It can take a great deal of time and trouble to check the correctness of even a very small transaction and the resulting benefit may not justify the effort. Furthermore, financial accounting inevitably involves a degree of estimation which means that financial statements can never be completely precise.

KEY TERM

Materiality is an expression of the relative significance or importance of a particular matter in the context of financial statements as a whole.

A matter is material if its omission or misstatement would reasonably influence the decisions of an addressee of the auditors' report.

Materiality may also be considered in the context of any individual primary statement within the financial statements or of individual items included in them.

Materiality is not capable of general mathematical definition as it has both qualitative and quantitative aspects.

5.2 Materiality is the subject of the APB's SAS 220 *Materiality and the audit*, which begins by stating the following.

SAS 220.1

Auditors should consider materiality and its relationship with audit risk when conducting an audit.

5.3 The SAS goes on:

'Auditors plan and perform the audit to be able to provide reasonable assurance that the financial statements are free of material misstatement and give a true and fair view. The assessment of what is material is a matter of professional judgement and includes consideration of both the amount (quantity), and the nature (quality) of misstatements.'

5.4 Small amounts should be considered if there is a risk that they could occur more than once and create a cumulatively material amount. Also, qualitative aspects must be considered, for example in the inaccurate and therefore misleading description of an accounting policy.

5.5   Materiality consideration will differ depending on the aspect of the financial statements being considered.

> 'Materiality is considered at both the overall financial statement level and in relation to individual account balances, classes of transactions and disclosures.'

The standard example given is of directors' emoluments which make normal materiality considerations irrelevant, because they *must* be disclosed by the auditors if they are not disclosed correctly by the directors in the financial statements.

Materiality during audit planning

SAS 220.2

Auditors should consider materiality when determining the nature, timing and extent of audit procedures.

5.6   Materiality considerations during **audit planning** are extremely important. The assessment of materiality at this stage should be based on the most recent and reliable financial information and will help to determine an effective and efficient audit approach. Materiality assessment will help the auditors to decide:

(a)   **how many** and **what items** to **examine**;

(b)   whether to use **sampling techniques**;

(c)   what **level of error** is likely to lead to a qualified audit opinion

and other such matters.

5.7   The resulting combination of audit procedures should help to reduce audit risk to an appropriately low level.

5.8   Materiality assessment when **evaluating the results of audit procedures** may differ from that during audit planning because of:

(a)   a change in circumstances; or

(b)   a change in the auditors' knowledge as a result of the audit (ie actual results are different from expected results).

5.9   If any factors arise which cause the auditors to revise their initial assessment of materiality, then the nature, timing and extent of all audit procedures may be modified.

Practical implications

5.10   To set the materiality level the auditors need to decide the level of error which would distort the view given by the accounts. Because many users of accounts are primarily interested in the profitability of the company, the level is often expressed as a proportion of its profits.

5.11   Some argue, however, that materiality should be thought of in terms of the size of the business. Hence, if the company remains a fairly constant size, the materiality level should not change; similarly if the business is growing, the level of materiality will increase from year to year.

5.12   The size of a company can be measured in terms of turnover and total assets before deducting any liabilities (sometimes referred to in legislation as 'the balance sheet total') both of which tend not to be subject to the fluctuations which may affect profit. As a guide, between ½% and 1% of turnover and between 1% and 2% of total assets are often taken as a measure of what is material.

5.13 These figures form the basis of the materiality levels set and evidenced in the planning memorandum. Note that the auditors will often calculate a range of values, such as those shown below, and then take an average or weighted average of all the figures produced as the materiality level.

Value	%
Profit before tax	5
Gross profit	½ - 1
Turnover	½ - 1
Total assets	1 - 2
Net assets	2 - 5
Profit after tax	5 - 10

5.14 The effect of planning materiality on the audit process is shown in the diagram below.

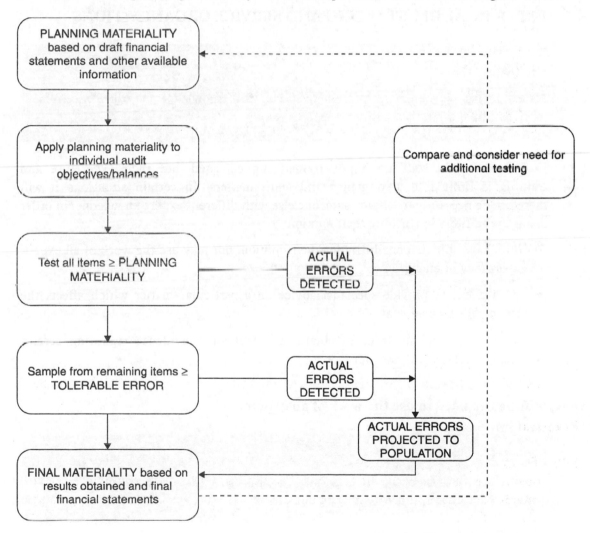

5.15 **Tolerable error** (see Chapter 6) may be set at planning materiality, but it is usually reduced to, say 75% or even 50% of planning materiality so as to take account of sampling risk. The tolerable error is used to determine sample size.

Audit evaluation

5.16 The level of materiality must be reviewed constantly as the audit progresses and changes may be required because:

(a) draft accounts are altered (due to material error and so on) and therefore overall materiality changes;

(b) external factors cause changes in the control or inherent risk estimates;

(c) such changes as are in (b) are caused by errors found during testing.

5.17 At the end of the testing process planning materiality will once again be used to determine whether adjustments should be made to the financial statements. All errors discovered during the audit which are not material on their own are added together. Projected errors are calculated by applying the error found in a sample to the population as a whole. (Note that a projected error greater than tolerable error in any one account will probably lead to further testing.)

6 EXPERTS, AUDIT STAFFING AND SERVICE ORGANISATIONS

> **KEY TERMS**
>
> **An expert** is a person or firm possessing special skill, knowledge and experience in a particular field other than auditing.

6.1 Professional audit staff are highly trained and educated, but their experience and training is limited to accountancy and audit matters. In certain situations it will therefore be necessary to employ someone else with different expert knowledge, in order to aid the auditors in reaching their opinion.

6.2 Auditors have **sole responsibility** for their opinion, but may use the work of an expert. An expert may be engaged:

(a) by a client to provide specialist advice on a particular matter which affects the financial statements; or

(b) by the auditors in order to obtain sufficient audit evidence regarding certain financial statement assertions.

Determining the need to use the work of an expert

> **SAS 520.1**
>
> When using the work performed by an expert, auditors should obtain sufficient appropriate audit evidence that such work is adequate for the purposes of an audit.

6.3 The following list of examples is given by the SAS of the audit evidence which might be obtained from the opinion, valuation etc of an expert.

(a) **Valuations of certain types of assets,** eg land and buildings, plant and machinery, works of art, precious stones, unquoted investments and intangible assets

(b) **Determination of quantities or physical condition of assets,** eg minerals stored in stockpiles, underground mineral and petroleum reserves and the remaining useful life of plant and machinery

(c) **Determination of amounts** using specialised techniques or methods, eg pensions accounting and actuarial valuations

(d) **The measurement of work completed** and **work in progress** on contracts in progress

(e) **Legal opinions** concerning interpretations of agreements, statutes and regulations, or on the outcome of litigation or disputes

6.4 When considering whether to use the work of an expert, the auditors should review:

(a) the **importance** of the matter being considered in the context of the financial statements;

(b) the **risk of misstatement** based on the nature and complexity of the matter being considered; and

(c) the **quantity** and **quality** of other available **relevant audit evidence.**

6.5 Once it is decided that an expert is required, the approach should be discussed with the management of the entity. Where the management is unwilling or unable to engage an expert, the auditors should consider engaging an expert themselves unless sufficient alternative audit evidence can be obtained. If unable to obtain sufficient appropriate audit evidence, the auditors should consider the implications for their audit report (see Chapter 12).

Competence and objectivity of the expert

SAS 520.2

When planning to use the work of an expert the auditors should assess the objectivity and professional qualifications, experience and resources of the expert.

6.6 This will involve considering:

(a) the expert's **professional certification,** or licensing by, or membership of, an appropriate professional body; and

(b) the expert's **experience and reputation** in the field in which the auditors are seeking audit evidence.

6.7 The risk that an expert's **objectivity** is **impaired** increases when the expert is:

(a) **employed** by the entity; or

(b) **related** in some other manner to the entity, for example, by being financially dependent upon, or having an investment in, the entity.

6.8 If the auditors have **reservations** about the competence or objectivity of the expert:

(a) they should **discuss** their **reservations** with management;

(b) they should **consider** whether **sufficient appropriate audit evidence** can be obtained;

(c) they *may* **undertake additional audit procedures** or seek evidence from another expert.

The auditors should then **consider** the **implications** for their report.

The expert's scope of work

SAS 520.3

The auditors should obtain sufficient appropriate audit evidence that the expert's scope of work is adequate for the purposes of their audit.

6.9 Written instructions usually cover the expert's terms of reference and such instructions may cover such matters as follows.

(a) The **objectives** and **scope** of the expert's work

(b) A **general outline** as to the specific matters the expert's report is to cover

(c) The **intended use** of the expert's work including the possible communication to third parties of the expert's identity and extent of involvement

(d) The **extent** of the **expert's access** to appropriate records and files

(e) Information regarding the **assumptions and methods intended** to be used by the expert and their consistency with those used in prior periods

6.10 If no such instructions exist, or are insufficient, then the auditors should communicate with the expert directly to obtain evidence of the scope of the expert's work.

Assessing the work of the expert

SAS 520.4

The auditors should assess the appropriateness of the expert's work as audit evidence regarding the financial statement assertions being considered.

6.11 Auditors should assess whether the substance of the expert's findings is properly reflected in the financial statements or supports the financial statement assertions. It will also require consideration of:

(a) the **source data used**;

(b) the **assumptions and methods used**;

(c) **when** the expert carried out the work;

(d) the reasons for any **changes in assumptions and methods** compared with those used in the prior period;

(e) the **results** of the expert's work in the light of the auditors' overall knowledge of the business and the results of other audit procedures.

6.12 When looking at source data, the auditors might carry out the following procedures.

(a) **Make enquiries** regarding any procedures undertaken by the expert to establish whether the source data is sufficient, relevant and reliable.

(b) **Review or test the data** used by the expert.

6.13   The auditors do *not* have the expertise to judge the assumptions and methods used; these are the responsibility of the expert. However, the auditors should seek to obtain an understanding of these assumptions etc, to consider their reasonableness based on other audit evidence, knowledge of the business and so on.

6.14   Where inconsistencies arise between the expert's work and other audit evidence, then the auditors should attempt to resolve them by discussion with both the entity and the expert. Additional procedures (including use of another expert) may be necessary.

6.15   Where the audit evidence from the expert is insufficient, and there is no satisfactory alternative source of evidence, then the auditors should consider the implications for their audit report.

6.16   The SAS makes the following very important point (our italics).

> 'When the auditors are satisfied that the work of an expert provides appropriate audit evidence, *reference is not made to the work of the expert in their report*. Such a reference may be misunderstood and interpreted as a qualification of the auditors' opinion or a division of responsibility, neither of which is appropriate.'

See Chapter 12 on audit reports.

Exam focus point

Expert opinions are generally obtained in 'difficult' audit areas, for example valuation of assets, and hence the topic has proved popular with examiners.

Staffing audits

6.17   When planning the audit the partner or manager must decide how many staff are to be allocated to the assignment, how experienced (which grade) and whether any of them will require special knowledge, skills or experience. For example, the client may undertake complicated leasing transactions, so an auditor with some experience of leasing would be required.

6.18   The partner will look at the staffing of the audit in previous years and he will need to decide whether that level of staffing was acceptable. He might judge this by looking at the amount of overtime worked last year and whether the budgeted cost was over or under run. This must be gauged with reference to any unexpected problems which arose in the previous year and whether they are likely to recur.

Using a service organisation

6.19   In April 1998 the Auditing Practices Board published draft SAS 480 *Audit evidence considerations when an entity uses a service organisation*. This SAS contains a number of points that are relevant if the client uses a service organisation.

SAS 480.1

User entity auditors should identify whether a reporting entity uses service organisations and assess the effect of any such use on the procedures necessary to obtain sufficient appropriate audit evidence to determine with reasonable confidence whether the user entity's financial statements are free of material misstatements.

KEY TERMS

- **Service organisation** is any entity that provides services to another.

- **User entity** is a reporting entity which uses the services of a service organisation.

- **User entity auditors** are the auditors appointed to report on the user entity's financial statements.

- **Relevant activities** are activities undertaken by a service organisation which are relevant to the conduct of the audit. Relevant activities:

  (a) relate directly to the preparation of the user entity's financial statements, including the maintenance of accounting records which form the basis for those financial statements; or

  (b) relate directly to the reporting of material assets, liabilities and transactions which are required to be included or disclosed in the financial statements (excluding the charge for provision of the service concerned).

Planning

SAS 480.2

In planning the audit, user entity auditors should determine whether activities undertaken by service organisations are relevant to the audit.

6.20 Examples of relevant activities include:

- maintenance of the user entity's accounting records
- other finance functions
- custody and management of assets
- undertaking or arranging transactions

SAS 480.3

User entity auditors should obtain and document an understanding of:

(a) the contractual terms which apply to relevant activities undertaken by service organisations; and

(b) the way that the user entity monitors the activities so as to ensure that it meets its fiduciary and other legal responsibilities.

6.21 User entity auditors may consider:

(a) whether the terms contain an **adequate specification** of the information to be provided to the user entity and responsibilities for initiating transactions;

(b) the way that **accounting records** relating to relevant activities are maintained;

(c) whether the user entity has **rights of access to accounting records** prepared by the service organisation concerning the activities undertaken, and relevant underlying information held by it, and the conditions in which such access may be sought;

(d) whether the terms take proper account of any **requirements of regulatory bodies** concerning the form of records to be maintained, or access to them;

(e) the process for establishing appropriate **performance standards**;

(f) whether the service organisation has agreed to **indemnify** the user entity in the event of a performance failure;

(g) whether the contractual terms permit the **user entity auditors access** to sources of audit evidence.

> **SAS 480.4**
>
> User entity auditors should determine the effect of relevant activities on their assessment of inherent risk.

6.22 Assessment of inherent risk may be affected by the following factors:

(a) the **nature** of the **services** provided

(b) the degree to which **authority** is **delegated** to the service organisations

(c) the **arrangements for ensuring** the **quality** of the service provided

(d) whether the activities involve **assets** which are susceptible to **loss or misappropriation**;

(e) the reputation for **integrity** of those responsible for direction and **management** of the service organisation.

> **SAS 480.5**
>
> The user entity auditors should assess whether the arrangements for maintaining all or part of the user entity's accounting records by a service organisation affects their reporting responsibilities in relation to accounting records arising from statute or other operation of law or regulation.

6.23 This area may cause auditors problems since it is not certain whether outsourcing the maintenance of accounting records fulfils the s 221 requirements of the Companies Act to keep proper accounting records. The terms of the outsourcing agreement and whether the user entity retains ownership of the accounting records may be relevant considerations.

6.24 Assessment of control risk may be influenced by the following factors:

(a) the **extent and nature of accounting records** maintained by the user entity's personnel;

(b) the **extent and nature of controls** operated by the user entity's personnel;

(c) **undertakings** by the service organisation about **provision of information** relating to the activity undertaken;

(d) arrangements for **access to underlying information**;

(e) **undertakings** by the service organisation for the **operation of internal controls**, and whether such controls are adequately specified, having regard to the size and complexity of the activities undertaken by the service organisation;

(f) the way in which the user determines whether the service organisation **complies** with its **contractual undertakings**, in particular the way in which it monitors compliance with applicable law and regulations;

(g) whether the service organisation provides information on the **design and operation** of **systems of control** (which may include the result of work undertaken by its internal audit function), possibly accompanied by reports from its external auditors.

Audit evidence

SAS 480.6

Based on their understanding of the aspects of the user entity's accounting system and control environment relating to relevant activities, user entity auditors should:

(a) assess whether sufficient appropriate audit evidence concerning the relevant financial statement assertions is available from records held at the user entity; and

(b) determine effective procedures to obtain evidence necessary for the audit either by direct access to records kept by service organisations or their auditors.

6.25 Sometimes the most efficient audit approach will be to obtain information from the user entity and confirmation from the service organisation. This approach may not always provide sufficient audit evidence, especially where the service organisation can initiate transactions or process cash receipts without user organisation approval.

6.26 In addition if the service organisation maintains accounting records for the user entity the auditors will require direct access to those records to obtain sufficient audit evidence.

6.27 Audit procedures that the user entity auditors might consider include:

(a) **inspecting records** or documents held by the user entity;

(b) **establishing** the **effectiveness of controls**;

(c) **obtaining representations** to confirm balances and transactions from the service organisation;

(d) performing **analytical review** procedures on the records maintained by the user entity or on the returns received from the service organisation;

(e) **inspecting records and documents** held by the service organisation;

(f) **requesting** the **service organisation auditors** or the user entity's internal audit function to perform specified procedures;

(g) **reviewing information** from the service organisation and its auditors concerning the **design and operation of its control systems**.

SAS 480.7

When using a report issued by the service organisation auditors or the user entity's internal audit function, the user entity's auditors should consider the scope of the work performed and assess whether the report is sufficient and appropriate for its intended use by the user auditor.

6.28 The user entity auditors should consider whether the report:

(a) **addresses financial statement assertions** that are relevant to the user entity auditor's examination;

(b) **provides an adequate level of assurance** concerning relevant aspects of the **systems' design, implementation and operation** over a specified period, and takes into account considerations of materiality determined by reference to the user entity's financial statements; and

(c) **covers the period** during which the user entity auditors intend to rely on an assessment of control risk at the service organisation.

Reporting

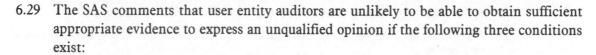

SAS 480.8

If user entity auditors conclude that evidence from records held by a service organisation is necessary in order to form an opinion on the user entity's financial statements and they are unable to obtain such evidence, they should

(a)   include a description of the factors leading to the lack of evidence in the basis of opinion section of their report; and

(b)   qualify their opinion or issue a disclaimer of opinion on the financial statements.

6.29   The SAS comments that user entity auditors are unlikely to be able to obtain sufficient appropriate evidence to express an unqualified opinion if the following three conditions exist:

(a)   the user entity does not maintain adequate records of, or controls over, the activities undertaken by the service organisation or cause such records to be maintained independently of the service organisation; and

(b)   the service organisation has not made available a report from its auditors concerning the operation of aspects of its systems of controls which the user entity auditors consider sufficient for the purposes of their audit; and

(c)   the user entity auditors are unable to carry out such tests as they consider appropriate at the service organisation itself, nor has it been possible for those tests to be undertaken by the service organisation's auditors.

Question 2

You are the manager in charge of the audit of Ruddington Furniture plc for the year ended 31 July 19X2, and you have been asked to describe the work which should be carried out in planning the audit and in monitoring its progress.

Ruddington Furniture plc buys domestic furniture from manufacturers and sells it to the general public. The company's head office and main warehouse are on the same site, and there are sales branches with associated warehouses in different parts of the country.

Your firm has been auditor of the company for a number of years. All the company's accounting records are maintained on the computer at head office. When a sale takes place at the branch, the salesman checks that the furniture the customer requires is in stock, and if it is, the customer pays for the items by cash, cheque or credit card (or charge card) and collects them from the warehouse. Where the items are not in stock, it is possible to find whether they are available at another local branch, or an order can be placed for the stock.

In previous years' audits there have been problems at branches of the actual stock being less than the computer book stock quantities. Also, problems have been experienced in identifying and valuing damaged stock and goods returned by customers. The company has a small internal audit department and their work includes periodic visits to branches.

The company was subject to a management buy-out in February 19X0 which resulted in high gearing. You understand that because of a recession in the furniture trade the company has liquidity problems and that currently it is negotiating with the bank to obtain additional finance.

Required

List and describe the matters you will consider and the work you will carry out in planning the audit.

Answer

In planning the audit the following matters should be taken into consideration.

(a) The audit files for the previous year should be examined in detail and any important matters should be considered which arise therefrom which might have a bearing on the current year's audit.

(b) Any recent changes in legislation or accounting standards which might affect the financial statements of Ruddington Furniture plc should be considered.

(c) If possible, the management accounts for the year should be obtained from the company. These should be examined to gain information about the trading performance of the company, perhaps in comparison with any budget which is available. Any significant changes in the management or key employees of the company, as well as in the accounting system and procedures, should be noted.

(d) The management of the company should be consulted in advance and the timing of the audit should be agreed. In particular:

   (i) the timing of the stocktake and the level of attendance by the auditors;

   (ii) the timing of significant phases of the preparation of the financial statements;

   (iii) the extent to which analyses and summaries can be prepared by the company's employees;

   (iv) the relevance of any work to be carried out by the enterprise's internal auditors.

(e) In terms of the stocktaking procedures, these should be reviewed in detail. In addition, it would be useful to obtain the results of any stock counts during the year, to consider whether problems still exist in the comparison between book and actual stock levels.

(f) In the light of the known liquidity problems of the company, it would be prudent to obtain any forecasts and budgets for the following year or years. This may be useful in performing any post balance sheet review, particularly if there is any considerable period between the end of the audit and the date the directors plan to sign the accounts (and the AGM).

(g) The internal auditors may be of use in the performance of the external audit. Their work should be examined to determine whether it is reliable and relevant, and some of the tests they have performed should be reperformed for this purpose. If it is decided that their work can be relied upon, this may reduce some of the testing the external auditors can perform. The internal audit work should highlight problem areas within the company and reduce the risks of the external auditor missing any fraud or errors.

(h) It should be possible at this stage to decide what the general audit approach is to be. It should be the case that a company of the size of Ruddington Furniture will have a strong system of internal control, as is indicated to some extent by the presence of the internal audit department. A risk-based audit approach is therefore most likely.

(i) It will be necessary to determine which audit staff are to be used. The staff chosen should be suitably qualified and experienced. The number of staff needs to be determined, particularly in relation to the number of stocktake visits the auditors will undertake. Larger branches should be visited and smaller branches in rotation over a few years.

(j) A timetable should be prepared for the audit, including the items for the principal phases of the audit, the date the audit report will be signed and an estimate of fees, costs and profit.

---

7   THE OVERALL AUDIT PLAN

SAS 200.2

Auditors should develop and document an overall audit plan describing the expected scope and conduct of the audit.

7.1 The SAS goes on to list matters which auditors should consider in developing the overall audit plan.

OVERALL AUDIT PLAN

Knowledge of the entity's business	General economic factors and industry conditions
	Important characteristics of the client, (a) business, (b) principal business strategies, (c) financial performance, (d) reporting requirements, including changes since the previous audit
	The operating style and control consciousness of directors and management
	The auditors' cumulative knowledge of the accounting and control systems and any expected changes in the period
Risk and materiality	The setting of materiality for audit planning purposes
	The expected assessments of risks or error and identification of significant audit areas
	Any indication that misstatements that could have a material effect on the financial statements might arise because of fraud or for any other reason
	The identification of complex accounting areas including those involving estimates
Nature, timing and extent of procedures	The relative importance of tests of control and substantive procedures
	The use of information technology by the client or the auditors
	The use made of work of any internal audit function
	Procedures which need to be carried out at or before the year end
	The timing of significant phases of the preparation of the financial statements
Co-ordination, direction, supervision and review	The involvement of other auditors
	The involvement of experts, other third parties and internal auditors
	The number of locations
	Staffing requirements

Other matters	Any regulatory requirements arising from the decision to retain the engagement
	The possibility that the going concern basis may be inappropriate
	The terms of the engagement and any statutory responsibilities
	The nature and timing of reports or other communication with the entity that are expected under the engagement

8   THE AUDIT PROGRAMME

SAS 200.3

Auditors should develop and document the nature, timing and extent of planned audit procedures required to implement the overall audit plan.

8.1   The auditors must, when developing the audit plan, consider the risks of error as well as the necessary audit evidence required to fulfil the procedures. Other considerations include:

(a)   **co-ordination** of **audit work** with any work on preparing the financial statements;
(b)   **timing** of **tests** of **controls** and substantive procedures;
(c)   **co-ordination** of any **assistance** expected from the entity;
(d)   the **composition** of the **audit team**; and
(e)   the **involvement** of **other auditors** or **experts**.

8.2   The audit programme may contain references to other matters such as the audit **objectives, timing, sample size** and **basis of selection** for each area. The audit programme's main use is highlighted by SAS 200.

'It serves as a set of instructions to the audit team and as a means to control and record the proper execution of the work.'

8.3   The level of detail and complexity depends not only on the complexity and size of the audit, but also the experience of the members of the audit team and the extent of other documentation.

Chapter roundup

- **Client screening** can be very important in avoiding embarrassing or damaging situations after an audit has been carried out.

- A variety of screening procedures may be carried out, depending on the relative size of audit firm and company.

- Whatever the size or importance of the engagement, some documentation should be retained on client screening, no matter how rudimentary.

- The main functions of the engagement letter are:
  - to **specify** the **respective responsibilities** of directors and auditors;
  - to lay down the **scope** of the **auditors'** work.

- The auditors will formulate an **overall audit plan** which will be translated into a **detailed audit programme** for audit staff to follow.

- In formulating the audit plan the auditors will consider:
  - knowledge of the entity's business;
  - risk and materiality;
  - nature, timing and extent of procedures;
  - co-ordination, direction, supervision and review.

- Any changes in the audit approach during the audit should be documented very carefully.

- When a new client is acquired the auditors must obtain **knowledge of the business** from various sources.

- Knowledge of the business can be used to:
  - **assess risks**;
  - **develop an** effective and efficient **audit plan**;
  - evaluate audit evidence.

- **Materiality** should be calculated at the planning stages of all audits. The calculation or estimation of materiality should be based on experience and judgement. The materiality chosen should be reviewed during the audit.

- The auditors may only rely on other **experts** once specific audit procedures have taken place.

Quick quiz

1   What are the main factors auditors will consider when deciding whether to accept a new client (see para 1.4)

2   When should an engagement letter be sent to audit clients? (2.4)

3   When might the necessity for a new engagement letter be indicated? (2.10)

4   What is the difference between an *audit plan* and an *audit programme* according to SAS 200 *Planning*? (3.3)

5   What are the objectives of planning work? (3.4)

6   Which sources of knowledge are mentioned by SAS 210 *Knowledge of the business*? (4.7)

7   Which audit areas might be most affected by knowledge of the business? (4.11)

8   How is materiality defined? (5.1)

9   How should the competence and objectives of an outside expert be assessed? (6.6)

10 What matters will the auditors' written instructions to an expert usually cover? (6.9)

11 What matters will the auditors consider when assessing the work of an expert? (6.11)

12 What factors will affect the content of an audit plan? (7.1)

The question below acts as revision on planning and control of audits

Question to try	Level	Marks	Time
3	Revision	n/a	45 mins

Chapter 4

AUDIT EVIDENCE AND DOCUMENTATION

Chapter topic list	Syllabus reference
1 Audit evidence	Revision
2 Documenting the audit process	Revision

Introduction

Before we can start the audit, we must determine what kind of evidence we are looking for; particularly what kinds of evidence would satisfy the auditors and what kinds would not.

We will then look at how audit evidence is documented and the kinds of working papers which should be kept on file.

Particularly important in this chapter are the financial statement assertions and factors affecting the reliability of audit evidence. You may be asked for the audit tests for certain areas of the financial statement. These should be centred on the financial statement assertions. Your Paper 6 material covers in detail the audit tests that affect the balance sheet, and you may wish to revise these now.

There have also been a number of questions in paper 10 on the strength of specific audit evidence.

1   AUDIT EVIDENCE   12/96

KEY TERM

Audit evidence is the information auditors obtain in arriving at the conclusions on which their report is based. Audit evidence comprises source documents and accounting records underlying the financial statement assertions and corroborative evidence from other sources.

1.1   In order to reach a position in which they can express a professional opinion, the auditors need to gather evidence from various sources. SAS 400 *Audit evidence* covers this area.

SAS 400.1

Auditors should obtain sufficient appropriate audit evidence to be able to draw reasonable conclusions on which to base the audit opinion.

1.2   Audit evidence can be obtained in many ways, often with a mix of tests of controls and substantive procedures, although sometimes only substantive procedures will be used;

along with enquiries as to the adequacy of the accounting system as a basis for the preparation of the financial statements.

Sufficient appropriate audit evidence

1.3 'Sufficiency' and 'appropriateness' are interrelated and apply to both tests of controls and substantive procedures.

   (a) **Sufficiency** is the measure of the **quantity** of audit evidence.
   (b) **Appropriateness** is the measure of the **quality** or **reliability** of the audit evidence.

1.4 Auditors are essentially looking for enough reliable audit evidence. Audit evidence usually indicates what is probable rather than what is definite (is usually persuasive rather than conclusive). However, auditors cannot give absolute but only reasonable assurance that the financial statements are free from misstatement, so not _all_ sources of evidence will be examined.

Sufficiency of audit evidence

1.5 The auditors' judgement as to what is sufficient appropriate audit evidence is influenced by factors such as the following.

   (a) The **assessment** of the **nature and degree** of **risk of misstatement** at **both the** financial statement level and the account balance or class of transactions level

   (b) The **nature** of the **accounting and internal control systems,** including the control environment

   (c) The **materiality** of the item being examined

   (d) The **experience gained during previous audits** and the auditors' **knowledge of the business** and **industry**

   (e) The **results of audit procedures,** and from any audit work carried out in the course of preparing the financial statements, including indications of fraud or error

   (f) The **source** and **reliability of information** available

1.6 If they are unable to obtain sufficient appropriate audit evidence, the auditors should consider the implications for their report.

Tests of control

SAS 400.2

In seeking to obtain audit evidence from tests of control, auditors should consider the sufficiency and appropriateness of the audit evidence to support the assessed level of control risk.

1.7 There are two aspects of the relevant parts of the accounting and internal control systems about which auditors should seek to obtain audit evidence.

   (a) **Design:** the accounting and internal control systems are capable of preventing or detecting material misstatements.

   (b) **Operation:** the systems exist and have operated effectively throughout the relevant period.

Substantive procedures

SAS 400.3

In seeking to obtain audit evidence from substantive procedures, auditors should consider the extent to which that evidence together with any evidence from tests of controls supports the relevant financial statement assertions.

1.8 Substantive procedures are designed to support the financial statement assertions.

KEY TERM

Financial statement assertions are the representations of the directors that are embodied in the financial statements. By approving the financial statements, the directors are making representations about the information therein. These representations or assertions may be described in general terms in a number of ways, one of which is as follows.

Existence An asset or liability exists at a given date

Rights and obligations An asset or liability pertains to the entity at a given date

Occurrence A transaction or event took place which pertains to the entity during the relevant period

Completeness There are no unrecorded assets, liabilities, transactions or events, or undisclosed items

Valuation An asset or liability is recorded at an appropriate carrying value

Measurement A transaction or event is recorded in the proper amount and revenue or expense is allocated to the proper period

Presentation and disclosure An item is disclosed, classified and described in accordance with the applicable reporting framework (eg relevant legislation and applicable accounting standards).

1.9 Audit evidence is usually obtained to support each financial statement assertion and evidence from one does not compensate for failure to obtain evidence for another. However, tests may provide audit evidence of more than one assertion.

1.10 Where tests of control provide satisfactory evidence as to the effectiveness of accounting and internal control systems, the extent of relevant **substantive procedures** may be **reduced**, but *not* entirely **eliminated**. Substantive procedures may also be incorporated within other procedures such as tests of control.

Reliability of evidence

1.11 The reliability of audit evidence is influenced by its source (internal or external) and by its nature (visual, documentary or oral). The following generalisations may help in assessing that reliability.

(a) Audit evidence from **external sources** (eg confirmation received from a third party) is **more reliable** than that obtained from the **entity's records**.

(b) Audit evidence obtained from the **entity's records** is more reliable when the related accounting and internal **control system operates effectively.**

(c) Evidence obtained **directly by auditors** is **more reliable** than that obtained by or **from the entity**.

(d) Evidence in the **form of documents and written representations** is **more reliable** than **oral representations**.

(e) **Original documents** are **more reliable** than **photocopies, telexes or facsimiles**.

1.12 Consistency of audit evidence from different sources will have a corroborating effect, making the evidence more persuasive. Where such evidence is **inconsistent**, the auditors must determine what additional procedures are necessary to resolve the inconsistency.

1.13 Auditors must consider the cost-benefit relationship of obtaining evidence _but_ any difficulty or expense is not in itself a valid basis for omitting a necessary procedure.

Exam focus point

You may be asked to consider how strong certain evidence is from the auditor's viewpoint, for example evidence obtained from the Internet (December 96 exam).

Procedures for obtaining audit evidence

1.14 Auditors obtain evidence by one or more of the following procedures.

(a) Inspection
(b) Observation
(c) Enquiry and confirmation
(d) Computation
(e) Analytical procedures

Inspection

1.15 The reliability of audit evidence obtained by _inspection_ of _records and documents_ varies according to the nature/source and effectiveness of internal controls over their processing. Three major categories of documentary evidence exist, given here in _descending_ degrees of reliability as audit evidence.

(a) Created and provided to auditors by third parties
(b) Created by third parties and held by the entity
(c) Created and held by the entity

1.16 Inspection of tangible assets provides reliable audit evidence about their _existence_ but not necessarily as to their ownership or value.

Observation

1.17 The standard examples of observation are attendance at the stocktake, or procedures which leave no audit trail.

Enquiries

1.18 Enquiries may range from formal written ones to third parties to oral ones to persons inside the entity. Responses may provide auditors with:

(a)   information not previously possessed; or

(b)   corroborative audit evidence.

Confirmations

1.19   Examples of confirmations include direct confirmation of debts by debtors of the entity or bank balances by the entity's bank.

Computations

1.20   Examples of computations include the adding up of bank reconciliations or ledger accounts.

Analytical procedures

1.21   Analytical procedures were discussed in the previous chapter. We will see in Chapter 15 how they can be used for substantive tests.

Question

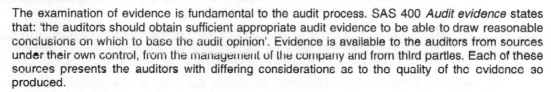

The examination of evidence is fundamental to the audit process. SAS 400 *Audit evidence* states that: 'the auditors should obtain sufficient appropriate audit evidence to be able to draw reasonable conclusions on which to base the audit opinion'. Evidence is available to the auditors from sources under their own control, from the management of the company and from third parties. Each of these sources presents the auditors with differing considerations as to the quality of the evidence so produced.

Required

(a)   Discuss the quality of the following types of audit evidence, giving two examples of each form of evidence.

(i)   Evidence originated by the auditors
(ii)   Evidence created by third parties
(iii)   Evidence created by the management of the client

(b)   Describe the general considerations which the auditors must bear in mind when evaluating audit evidence.

Answer

(a)   (i)   There is little risk that evidence originated by the auditors can be manipulated by management. It is therefore, in general, the most reliable type of audit evidence. Examples include the following.

(1)   Analytical procedures, such as the calculation of ratios and trends in order to examine unusual variations

(2)   Physical inspection or observation, such as attendance at physical stocktakes or inspection of a fixed asset

(3)   Re-performance of calculations making up figures in the accounts, such as the computation of total stock values

(ii)   Third party evidence is more reliable than client-produced evidence to the extent that it is obtained from sources independent of the client. Its reliability will be reduced if it is obtained from sources which are not independent, or if there is a risk that client personnel may be able to and have reason to suppress or manipulate it. This, for instance, is an argument against having replies to circularisations sent to the client instead of the auditors.

Examples of third party evidence include the following.

(1)   Circularisation of debtors or creditors and other requests from the auditors for confirming evidence, such as requests for confirmation of bank balances.

(2)   Reports produced by experts, such as property valuations, actuarial valuations, legal opinions. In evaluating such evidence, the auditors need to take into account the qualifications of the expert, his or her independence of the client and the terms of reference under which the work was carried out.

(3)   Documents held by the client which were issued by third parties, such as invoices, price lists and statements. These may sometimes be manipulated by the client, to the extent that items may be suppressed or altered, and to this extent they are less reliable than confirmations received direct.

(iii)   The auditors cannot place the same degree of reliance on evidence produced by client management as on that produced outside the client organisation. It will, however, often be necessary to place some reliance on the client's evidence. The auditors will need to apply judgement in doing so, taking into account previous experience of the client's reliability and the extent to which the client's representations appear compatible with other audit findings, as well as the materiality of the item under discussion. Examples of evidence originating from client management include the following.

(1)   The company's accounting records and supporting schedules. Although these are prepared by management, the auditors have a statutory right to examine such records in full: this right enhances the quality of this information.

(2)   The client's explanations of, for instance, apparently unusual fluctuations in results. Such evidence requires interpretation by the auditors and, being oral evidence, only limited reliance can be placed upon it.

(3)   Information provided to the auditors about the internal control system. The auditors need to check that this information is accurate and up-to-date, and that it does not simply describe an idealised system which is not adhered to in practice.

(b)   Audit evidence will often not be wholly conclusive. The auditors must obtain evidence which is sufficient and appropriate to form the basis for their audit conclusions. The evidence gathered should also be relevant to those conclusions, and sufficiently reliable ultimately to form the basis for the audit opinion. The auditors must exercise skill and judgement to ensure that evidence is correctly interpreted and that only valid inferences are drawn from it.

Certain general principles can be stated. Written evidence is preferable to oral evidence; independent evidence obtained from outside the organisation is more reliable than that obtained internally; and that evidence generated by the auditors is more reliable than that obtained from others.

2   DOCUMENTING THE AUDIT PROCESS

2.1   All audit work must be documented: the working papers are the tangible evidence of the work done in support of the audit opinion.

SAS 230.1

Auditors should document in their working papers matters which are important in supporting their report.

> **KEY TERM**
>
> **Working papers** are the material the auditors prepare or obtain, and retain in connection with the performance of the audit.
>
> Working papers may be in the form of data stored on paper, film, electronic media or other media.
>
> Working papers support, amongst other things, the statement in the auditors' report as to the auditors' compliance or otherwise with Auditing Standards to the extent that this is important in supporting their report.

2.2 Working papers are a record of:

(a) the **planning** and **performance** of the audit;

(b) the **supervision** and **review** of the audit work; and

(c) the **audit evidence** resulting from the audit work performed which the auditors consider necessary and on which they have relied to support their report.

Form and content of working papers

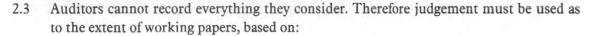

> **SAS 230.2**
>
> Working papers should record the auditors' planning, the nature, timing and extent of the audit procedures performed, and the conclusions drawn from the audit evidence obtained.
>
> **SAS 230.3**
>
> Auditors should record in their working papers their reasoning on all significant matters which require the exercise of judgement, and their conclusions thereon.

2.3 Auditors cannot record everything they consider. Therefore judgement must be used as to the extent of working papers, based on:

> 'What would be necessary to provide an experienced auditor, with no previous connection with the audit, with an understanding of the work performed and the basis of the decisions taken.'

2.4 Difficult areas of judgement or questions of principle may be questioned by a third party with the benefit of hindsight.

> 'In such circumstances it is important to be able to demonstrate the relevant facts that were known at the time the auditors reached their conclusion.'

2.5 The form and content of working papers are affected by matters such as:

(a) the **nature** of the **engagement**;

(b) the **form** of the **auditors' report**;

(c) the **nature** and **complexity** of the entity's **business**;

(d) the **nature** and **condition** of the **entity's accounting** and **internal control systems**;

(e) the **needs** in the particular circumstances for direction, supervision and review of the work of members of the audit team; and

(f) the **specific methodology** and technology the auditors use.

2.6   The SAS warns on the use of *standardised* working papers, eg checklists, specimen letters; they:

> 'may improve the efficiency with which such working papers are prepared and reviewed. While they facilitate the delegation of work and provide a means to control its quality, it is never appropriate to follow mechanically a standard approach to the conduct and documentation of the audit without regard to the need to exercise professional judgement.'

2.7   While auditors utilise schedules, analyses etc prepared by the entity, they require evidence that such information is properly prepared.

Examples of working papers

2.8   These include the following.

- Information concerning the legal and organisational structure of the client

- Extracts or copies of important legal documents, agreements and minutes

- Information concerning the client's industry, economic and legal environment

- Evidence of the planning process and any changes thereto

- Evidence of the auditors' understanding of the accounting and internal control systems

- Evidence of inherent and control risk assessments and any revisions

- Evidence of the auditors' consideration of the work of internal audit

- Analyses of transactions and balances

- Analyses of significant ratios and trends

- A record of the nature, timing, extent and results of auditing procedures

- Details of confirmation procedures on work carried out by other auditors

- Copies of communications with other auditors, experts and other third parties

- Copies of correspondence with the client, reports to directors or management and notes of discussions with the entity's directors or management concerning audit matters

- Letters of representation from the entity's directors or management

- A summary of the significant aspects of the audit including details of the information available, the amount involved, management's views, the conclusions reached and how these matters are resolved or treated

- Copies of the approved financial statements and auditors' reports

2.9   Working papers should show:

(a)   **when** and **by whom** the audit work was **performed**;

(b)   **when** and **by whom** it was **reviewed**. Detailed review points need not be retained as long as evidence of the extent of the review is shown on the working papers, including resolution of review points.

2.10   For recurring audits, working papers may be split between:

(a)   **permanent audit files**: updated with new information of continuing importance; and

(b) **current audit files**: contain information relating primarily to the audit of a single period.

Confidentiality, safe custody and ownership

> **SAS 230.4**
>
> Auditors should adopt appropriate procedures for maintaining the confidentiality and safe custody of their working papers.

2.11 Statute does not set down the period of retention of audit working papers; judgement must be used, and further consideration should be given to the matter before their destruction.

2.12 Working papers are the property of the auditors. They are not a substitute for, not part of, the entity's accounting records.

2.13 Auditors must follow ethical guidance on the confidentiality of audit working papers. They may, at their discretion, release parts of or whole working papers to the entity, as long as disclosure does not undermine 'the independence or validity of the audit process'. Information should not be made available to third parties without the permission of the entity.

Chapter roundup

- The auditors must be able to evaluate all types of audit evidence in terms of its sufficiency and appropriateness.

- Evidence can be in the form of **tests of controls** or **substantive procedures**.

- Tests of control concentrate on the **design** and **operation** of controls.

- Audit evidence should be found to support all of the **financial statement assertions**.
    - existence;
    - rights and obligations (ownership);
    - occurrence;
    - completeness;
    - valuation;
    - measurement;
    - presentation and disclosure.

- The **proper completion** of **working papers** is fundamental to the recording of the audit.

- You should be able to state what kind of **information** is usually found in working papers.

Quick quiz

1   Define 'sufficiency' and 'appropriateness' in relation to audit evidence. (see para 1.3)

2   What generalisation does SAS 400 make in relation to the sources and nature of audit evidence? (1.11)

3   What are the main procedures for obtaining audit evidence? (1.14)

4   What should the audit working papers record? (2.3)

5   What matters affect the form and content of working papers? (2.5)

6   How are working papers normally divided or classified on recurring audits? (2.10)

The revision question illustrates how the principles described in this chapter apply to certain balance sheet items

Question to try	Level	Marks	Time
4	Revision	20	36 mins

Part B
Advanced auditing practices and procedures

Chapter 5

PROFESSIONAL CODES OF ETHICS AND BEHAVIOUR

Chapter topic list	Syllabus reference
1 Due care, skill and competence	Revision
2 *Rules of Professional Conduct*	Revision
3 Statement 1: *Integrity, objectivity and independence*	Revision
4 Statement 2: *The professional duty of confidence*	Revision
5 Statement 3: *Advertising, publicity and obtaining professional work*	Revision
6 Areas of controversy	5(h)

Introduction

The ethical matters covered in this chapter are very important.

The first part of the chapter revises topics that were covered as part of Paper 6. Remember the key principle of Independence - that auditors should not only be independent but be seen to be independent. Auditors must consider whether they are independent of their clients when they accept appointment and subsequently be alert for threats to independence.

Section 6 takes the discussion on a number of currently controversial topics further than the Paper 6 material.

You should pay particular heed to the section on a practical approach to questions of ethics. Ethical matters have been examined in a number of different types of question in Paper 10, but most common is a situation where ethical issues have arisen on a high-risk client. However ethical issues are examined you must be able to apply ACCA's guidance on ethical matters to any given situation, but remember that common sense is a good guide.

1   DUE SKILL, CARE AND COMPETENCE

ACCA's *Rules of Professional Conduct*

'Members should carry out their professional work with due skill, care, diligence and expedition and with proper regard for the technical and professional standards expected of them as members.'

1.1   All accountants (not just auditors) in public practice are obliged by law to provide services of appropriate quality. Unless an accountant and client have agreed otherwise, there is an implied duty of care that an accountant owes to a client under s 13 Supply of Goods and Services Act 1982.

1.2   The professional guidance statement *Professional Liability* published in 1994 makes the following further points.

(a) The degree of skill and care will depend on the work: a higher degree will be required for work:

    (i)   of a specialised nature;

    (ii)   where negligence is likely to cause substantial loss.

(i) and (ii) particularly apply where the accountant represented himself as being experienced.

(b) The duty will not be absolute; opinions or advice will not give rise to claims just because they are proved wrong in the light of later events.

The auditors' duty of care

1.3 Thus auditors must employ **reasonable care** in all they do, in particular:

(a) Auditors must use **generally accepted auditing techniques** when seeking to satisfy themselves that the matters upon which they reports accurately reflect the true financial state of his client's business.

(b) If auditors come across any matter which puts them **upon inquiry** then they have a duty to investigate such a matter until they are able to resolve it to their own reasonable satisfaction. Auditors should not accept any explanation unless they have first carried out such investigations as will enable them properly to assess whether the explanation offered a reasonable one.

In Chapter 21 we will consider these points further when we see how the courts have interpreted the auditors' duty of care.

1.4 The guidance '*Managing the professional liability of accountants*' also shows how terms of engagement act in many circumstances to define the scope and responsibilities of the engagement, and to limit or exclude liability. In the case of most audits however statute, most importantly the Companies Act, lays down the responsibilities auditors have. The Companies Act also **forbids** auditors limiting or excluding liability to clients. However a letter of engagement is important for company audits as the letter should minimise the risk of misunderstanding between the auditor and client.

2   RULES OF PROFESSIONAL CONDUCT

2.1 There are a number of ethical issues which are of great importance in the client-auditor relationship. This onus is always on the auditor not only to be ethical but also to be *seen* to be ethical. To this end, the Association publishes *Rules of Professional Conduct. All* members *and* students of the ACCA must adhere to these rules. Guidance is in the form of:

(a) fundamental principles;

(b) specific guidance; and

(c) explanatory notes.

The fundamental principles

2.2 The fundamental principles state that members should:

(a) behave with **integrity** in all professional, business and personal financial relationships. Integrity implies not merely **honesty** but **fair dealing** and **truthfulness**;

(b)   strive for **objectivity** in all professional and business judgements. Objectivity is the state of mind which has regard to all considerations relevant to the task in hand but no other. It presupposes intellectual honesty;

(c)   not accept or perform work which they are not **competent** to undertake unless they obtain such advice and assistance as will enable them competently to carry out the work;

(d)   carry out their professional work with **due skill, care, diligence** and **expedition** and with proper regard for the technical and professional standards expected of them as members;

(e)   behave with **courtesy** and **consideration** towards all with whom they come into contact during the course of performing their work.

Specific guidance and explanatory material

2.3   The specific guidance and explanatory material in the *Rules of Professional Conduct* cover the following topics.

Statement	Title
1	Integrity, objectivity and independence
2	The professional duty of confidence
3	Advertising, publicity and obtaining professional work
4	Descriptions
5	Changes in professional appointments
6	Ownership of books and papers
7	Retention of books, files, working papers and other documents
8	Activities through corporate or non-corporate organisations
9	Fees
11	Professional liability of accountants and auditors
13	The incapacity or death of a sole practitioner
14	Clients' monies
17	Financial Services Act 1986
22	Corporate finance advice including takeovers
23	Confidentiality
24	The names of practising firms
25	Conflicts of interest
26	The ethical responsibilities of members in business

3   STATEMENT 1: INTEGRITY, OBJECTIVITY AND INDEPENDENCE

3.1   This is perhaps the most important ethical area for auditors.

3.2   Section A of this statement deals with *independence and the audit* (the other sections deal with areas outside the audit, which are not of interest in your syllabus).

ACCA Statement

'A member's objectivity must be beyond question if he (or she) is to report as an auditor. That objectivity can only be assured if the member is, and is seen to be, independent.'

'The threat to independence may be reduced by the nature and extent of the precautions taken by the practice to guard against loss of objectivity.'

3.3   The statement points out that, although the rules refer specifically to company audits under the Companies Acts, 'the spirit of the guidance applies equally to other audit situations'.

3.4   Most of the rest of this section of the statement is taken up with discussions and recommendations about **areas of risk,** and a summary is given below. The section concludes with some important definitions.

Undue dependence on an audit client   6/97

ACCA Statement

'Objectivity may be threatened or appear to be threatened by undue dependence on any audit client or group of connected clients.'

3.5   The statement recommends that, in general, the recurring work paid by one client or group of connected clients should not exceed **15%** of the gross practice income. In the case of **listed** and other **public interest** companies, the figure should be **10%** of the gross practice income.

3.6   New practices may not be able to satisfy such criteria and extra care will be necessary in such circumstances to safeguard independence.

3.7   A review of the risk to independence should be instituted for all large fees, certainly 10% (public interest 5%) and greater of gross practice income.

3.8   The statement also suggests that non-recurring fees might affect independence if they are large enough.

Overdue fees

ACCA Statement

'The existence of significant overdue fees from an audit client or group of associated clients can be a threat or appear to be a threat to objectivity akin to that of a loan.'

3.9   Firms must therefore ensure that overdue fees, along with fees from current work, could not be construed as a loan.

Actual or threatened litigation

ACCA Statement

'A firm's objectivity may be threatened or appear to be threatened when it is involved in, or even threatened with litigation in relation to a client.'

3.10 Litigation of certain sorts will represent a 'breakdown of the relationship of trust' between auditor and client. This would impair the independence of the auditor or cause the directors of the client to become unwilling to disclose information to the auditor. A dispute which is only in relation to audit fees may not cause such problems.

3.11 The point at which the firm should cease to act as auditors will vary from case to case. Auditors should be wary whenever it appears that litigation might occur.

Associated firms; influences outside the practice

ACCA Statement

'A firm's objectivity may be threatened or appear to be threatened as a result of pressures arising from associated practices or organisations, or from other external sources, such as bankers, solicitors, government or those introducing business.'

3.12 The problems of independence in relation to large and prestigious clients may arise in connection with the activities of an associated practice or organisation of the client. Factors to be considered by the firm include the closeness of the association and the strength of the associate's interest in the firm's retaining the client.

Family and other personal relationships

ACCA Statement

'A member's objectivity may be threatened or appear to be threatened as a consequence of a family or other close personal or business relationship.'

3.13 Problems arise if an officer or senior employee of an audit client is **closely connected** with the partner or senior staff member responsible for the conduct of the audit. In this context, closely connected people include (as well as the definition given below), adult children and their spouses, siblings and their spouses, any relative to whom regular financial assistance is given or who is indebted to the staff member or partner.

3.14 Proximity needs to be taken into account, including whether the partner or staff member is involved in the audit and the position of the person in the client's office (the more junior, the less risk).

3.15 S 27 CA 1989 prevents an officer or employee of a company (or their partner) from becoming an auditor of that company. The statement extends this prohibition for its members to two years after ceasing to be an officer or employee of the company.

Beneficial interests in shares and other investments

ACCA Statement

'A member's objectivity may be threatened or appear to be threatened where he (or she) holds a beneficial interest in the shares or other forms of investment in a company upon which the practice reports.'

3.16 Staff and partners should not have shareholdings in client businesses. (This includes beneficial shareholdings held by a spouse or minor child.)

(a) If shares are acquired involuntarily (by marriage or inheritance) then they should be disposed of at the earliest opportunity.

(b) Where an Act of Parliament or the articles of the client company require the auditor to be a shareholder, then the auditor should hold only the minimum number of shares and the holding should be disclosed in the accounts of the client company.

Beneficial holdings in unit trusts and so on are not precluded, nor are modest personal savings in a client building society or other similar institution.

Beneficial interests in trusts

ACCA Statement

'The objectivity of a practice may be threatened or appear to be threatened where a partner or a person closely connected with the partner has a beneficial interest in a trust having a shareholding in an audit client company.'

3.17 Where a trust, in which a partner or a person closely connected with a partner is a beneficiary, holds or acquires shares in a company audited by the practice:

(a) where the partner is and wishes to remain a trustee, the shareholding should be regarded as equivalent to a beneficial shareholding, and the practice should cease to report;

(b) where the partner is not a trustee, he should cease personally to report as soon as he becomes aware of the shareholding.

Where an employee has an interest in a trust having a shareholding in an audit client, that employee should not be employed on the audit of that client.

Trustee investments

ACCA Statement

'A member's objectivity may be threatened or appear to be threatened by trustee shareholdings and other trustee investments.'

3.18 The practice should not have a public company as an audit client if a partner (or the spouse of a partner) is a trustee of a trust holding shares in that company and the holding is in excess of **10%** of:

(a) the **issued share capital** of the company; or

(b)   the **total assets** comprised in the trust.

A trust holding of 10% or more (as described above) of *any* company will indicate problems with independence.

Voting on audit appointments

ACCA Statement

'Where a partner or staff member holds shares in any capacity in a company which is an audit client of the practice they should not be voted at any general meeting of the company in relation to the appointment, removal or remuneration of auditors.'

Loans

ACCA Statement

'Objectivity may be threatened or appear to be threatened by a loan to or from an audit client.'

3.19   No loans or guarantees should be undertaken unless they are with client financial institutions in the normal course of business (but the loan cannot be applied for partnership capital and the partner concerned must not be the engagement partner).

Goods and services; hospitality

ACCA Statement

'Objectivity may be threatened or appear to be threatened by acceptance of goods, services or hospitality from an audit client.'

Acceptance on normal commercial terms, or with only a modest benefit, is acceptable.

Provision of other services to audit clients

ACCA Statement

'There are occasions where objectivity may be threatened or appear to be threatened by the provision to an audit client of services other than the audit.'

3.20   Care must be taken to avoid performing executive functions or making executive decisions, particularly in the case of public interest or listed companies.

Review procedures

3.21   The statement recommends that:

ACCA Statement

'every audit firm should establish adequate review machinery, including an annual review, in order to satisfy itself that each engagement may properly be accepted or be continued having regard to the guidance given in this statement, and to identify situations where independence may be at risk and where the appropriate safeguards should be applied.'

3.22   Any additional safeguards required should be assessed by an independent partner, and might include rotation of the engagement partner or rotation of senior audit staff. In such circumstances, sole practitioners should consult another member externally.

KEY TERM

The following people will normally be regarded as **closely connected** with a person.

(a) His (or her) spouse or cohabitee other than a spouse from whom the person is separated, or, in the case of a shareholding, a spouse or cohabitee of whose financial affairs the person has been denied knowledge

(b) His (or her) minor children, including stepchildren

(c) A company in which he or she has a 20 per cent interest or more

The following persons will normally be regarded as being closely connected with a practice.

(a) A partner or, in the case of a corporate practice, a director or shareholder
(b) A person closely connected with (a)
(c) An employee of the practice

Note. The categories in these paragraphs are not exhaustive of the relationships which might threaten independence.

4   STATEMENT 2: THE PROFESSIONAL DUTY OF CONFIDENCE   6/96

Statement 23

4.1   Statement 23, which deals with confidentiality in general terms, makes it clear that information acquired in the course of professional work should not be disclosed except where consent has been obtained from the client, employer or other proper source, or where there is a public duty to disclose or where there is a legal or professional right or duty to disclose.

4.2   A member acquiring information in the course of professional work should neither use nor appear to use that information for his **personal advantage** or for the **advantage** of a **third party**.

4.3   In general, where there is a right (as opposed to a duty) to disclose information, a member should only make disclosure in pursuit of a public duty or professional obligation. Statement 2, discussed below, expands on the duty of confidence in relation to the defaults and unlawful acts of clients and others.

Statement 2

4.4   A member must make it clear to a client that he may only act for him if the client agrees to disclose in full to the member all information relevant to the engagement.

4.5   Where a member agrees to serve a client in a professional capacity both the member and the client should be aware that it is an implied term of that agreement that the member will not disclose the client's affairs to any other person save with the client's consent or within the terms of certain recognised exceptions.

4.6   The recognised exceptions are as follows.

   (a)   **Obligatory disclosure.**

      (i)   If a member knows or suspects his client to have committed the offence of treason he is obliged to disclose all the information at his disposal to a competent authority.

      (ii)   Under SAS 120 *Consideration of law and regulations* (see Chapter 11) auditors should consider whether non-compliance with laws and regulations affects the accounts. Auditors may have to include in their audit report a statement that non-compliance has led to significant uncertainties, or non-compliance means that they disagree with the way certain items have been treated in the accounts.

   (b)   **Voluntary disclosure.** In certain cases voluntary disclosure may be made by the member:

      (i)   where disclosure is reasonably necessary to protect the member's interests, for example to enable him to sue for fees or defend an action for, say, negligence;

      (ii)   where disclosure is compelled by process of law, for example where in an action a member is required to give evidence or discovery of documents;

      (iii)   where there is a public duty to disclose, say where an offence has been committed which is contrary to the public interest.

4.7   If an ACCA member is requested to assist the police, the Inland Revenue or other authority by providing information about a client's affairs in connection with enquiries being made, he should first enquire under what statutory authority the information is demanded. Unless he is satisfied that such statutory authority exists he should decline to give any information until he has obtained his client's authority. If the client's authority is not forthcoming and the demand for information is pressed the member should not accede unless so advised by his solicitor.

4.8   If an ACCA member knows or suspects that a client has committed a wrongful act he must give careful thought to his own position. He must ensure that he has not prejudiced himself by, for example, relying on information given by the client which subsequently proves to be incorrect.

4.9   However, it would be a criminal offence for a member to act positively, without lawful authority or reasonable excuse, in such a manner as to impede with intent the arrest or prosecution of a client whom he knows or believes to have committed an 'arrestable offence'.

5   STATEMENT 3: ADVERTISING, PUBLICITY AND OBTAINING PROFESSIONAL WORK   6/95

5.1   Guidance is given as follows.

(a)   Members should not obtain or seek work in an unprofessional manner.

(b)   Members can advertise but should have regard to relevant advertising codes and standards.

(c)   Members should not make disparaging references to or comparisons with the services of others.

(d)   Members should not quote fees without great care to not mislead as to the precise range of services and time commitment that fees are intended to cover, but they can offer free consultations to discuss level of fees.

(e)   No fees, commission or reward should be given to third parties in return for the introduction of clients.

6   AREAS OF CONTROVERSY

6.1   Auditing as a profession and as a concept has developed rapidly over the last 20 to 30 years. The demands on auditors have changed, as have the expectations of shareholders, creditors and managers about the audit role. Areas of controversy will be mentioned throughout this text, but here we will concentrate on some of the matters which are directly related to the auditors' independence, confidentiality and other qualities.

Independence   6/97

Multiple services

6.2   One of the more controversial independence arguments raging at the moment is the provision of other services to audit clients. One danger is the perception for example, that a company might give its auditors some lucrative consultancy work in exchange for a clean audit report. Another danger is that the auditors may end up making management decisions for the company and this would definitely harm their independence.

6.3   The problem exists for both large and small auditing firms, but in different ways. Small firms provide accountancy and taxation advice to their client, as well as general advice. Audit firms *cannot* perform accountancy work for public companies, but the auditors in these case provide consultancy services, corporate finance and taxation advice instead.

6.4   The problem with small or sole practitioners auditing very small companies is probably insurmountable. The DTI has now removed the requirement for some small companies to have an audit, and so for such companies this problem has been solved. Otherwise, the auditors must ensure that the **audit** work (as opposed to any accountancy or tax work) is planned and executed, and perhaps most importantly, properly **recorded**.

6.5   Some smaller firms which undertake both accountancy and audit work on clients have responded to the potential independence problem by requiring **different staff** to prepare and audit the accounts.

6.6   Larger audit firms have countered the problem by the use of separate departments for each service within the firm (consultancy, audit, taxation and so on). 'Chinese walls' supposedly operate between these departments, which means that no information is passed between them.

6.7 Another important safeguard is the **engagement letter**, which should make clear the extent of directors' responsibilities (ensuring accounts give a true and fair view, taxation matters are disclosed and so on).

6.8 Recent developments may have decreased the problems in this area. Some companies do now have a policy of using different audit firms for audit and non-audit work. Other companies make separate decisions as to who should provide audit and non-audit services. In some circumstances they may consider that one firm will provide the best audit service but another firm may be better at providing other services.

Opinion shopping

6.9 If a company is unhappy with the audit opinion which it receives (or may receive) from its current auditors, then it might approach other audit firms for a second opinion. The problem will be if the current auditors are pressurised into accepting the (more favourable) second opinion.

6.10 To avoid such a situation there should be constant communication between both sets of auditors. The second firm of auditors has a professional duty to seek permission for an approach to the current auditors from the client. Without such communication, the second opinion may be formed negligently.

Rotation of auditor appointments

6.11 It has been argued that the long-term nature of the company audit engagement tends to create a loss of auditor independence, due to an increasing familiarity with the company's management and staff, which works against the shareholders' and the public's interest. For this reason, it has been argued that there should be a rotation of the audit appointment every few years, preventing any unnecessary loss of independence which the present situation is thought to cause.

6.12 However, rotation of auditors may not be very popular in practice, owing to:

(a) the disadvantages of upsetting the client company with continual changes of audit staff;

(b) the high costs of recurring first audits;

(c) the possibility that set-up procedures will be less rigorous if the auditors know that the appointment is only for a short time;

(d) the ability of auditors to retain a fresh approach to the audit by rotating members of the audit staff internally so that no member is permanently assigned to it, including the reporting partner;

(e) the loss of trust and experience built up over time and the risk to audit effectiveness it would entail. The Cadbury Report on *The Financial Aspects of Corporate Governance* emphasises this point; it suggests that the accounting profession should draw up guidelines on the rotation of **audit partners**.

Audit committees

6.13 One American innovation which had an impact in this country is the audit committee. In the US already 80% of large companies have such committees and the Security and Exchange Commission have made it compulsory for all listed companies.

6.14 One of the main reasons for audit committees arises from the difficulty auditors have in combating instances where the executive directors of a company are determined to mislead them. As a result it is felt that an audit committee, preferably drawn from '**non-executive' directors** of a client company, would provide an invaluable independent liaison between the board and the auditors, thus strengthening the auditors' position and improving communication.

6.15 Other advantages that are claimed to arise from the existence of an audit committee include:

(a) it will lead to **increased confidence** in the credibility and objectivity of financial reports;

(b) by specialising in the problems of financial reporting and thus, to some extent, fulfilling the directors' responsibility in this area, it will allow the **executive** directors to **devote their attention to management**;

(c) in cases where the interests of the company, the executive directors and the employees conflict, the audit committee might provide an **impartial body** for the auditors to consult;

(d) the internal auditors will be able to report to the audit committee.

6.16 Opponents of audit committees argue that:

(a) there may be **difficulty selecting** sufficient non-executive directors with the necessary competence in auditing matters for the committee to be really effective;

(b) the establishment of such a **formalised reporting procedure** may **dissuade** the **auditors** from raising matters of judgement and limit them to reporting only on matters of fact;

(c) costs may be increased.

6.17 In the UK, the *Cadbury Report* recommended that audit committees should be compulsory under Stock Exchange rules in the UK and that the committee should consist entirely of non-executive directors, the majority of whom are independent of the company (this has been adopted by the Stock Exchange). The audit committee should have explicit authority and the resources to investigate any matters within their terms of reference.

6.18 In an appendix to the *Cadbury Report*, the Committee expands on the role and function of the audit committee.

'If they operate effectively, audit committees can bring significant benefits. In particular, they have the potential to:

(a) improve the quality of financial reporting, by reviewing the financial statements on behalf of the Board;

(b) create a climate of discipline and control which will reduce the opportunity for fraud;

(c) enable the non-executive directors to contribute an independent judgement and play a positive role;

(d) help the finance director, by providing a forum in which he can raise issues of concern, and which he can use to get things done which might otherwise be difficult;

(e) strengthen the position of the external auditor, by providing a channel of communication and forum for issues of concern;

(f) provide a framework within which the external auditor can assert his independence in the event of a dispute with management;

(g) strengthen the position of the internal audit function, by providing a greater degree of independence from management;

(h) increase public confidence in the credibility and objectivity of financial statements.'

6.19 The Committee warns, however, that the effectiveness of the audit committee may be compromised if it acts as a 'barrier' between the external auditors and the main (executive) board, or if it allows the main board to 'abdicate its responsibilities in the audit area' as this will weaken the board's responsibility for reviewing and approving the financial statements. The audit committee must also avoid falling under the influence of a dominant board member or getting in the way of exercise of the 'entrepreneurial skills' of the management. The audit committee will be ineffective if its members lack the 'understanding to deal adequately with the ... matters they are to face'.

6.20 In practice the main duties of the audit committee are likely to be as follows.

6.21 **Review of financial statements**. The committee should review both the half yearly and annual accounts. The committee should assess the overall appearance and presentation of the accounts, in particular the treatment of material changes from previous years, significant events and other exceptional items. The *Cadbury Report* lists the other main features the review should cover.

(a) Any changes in accounting policies and practices

(b) Major judgmental areas; these may include significant estimates and contingent liabilities

(c) Significant adjustments resulting from the audit

(d) The going concern assumption

(e) Compliance with accounting standards; in particular the committee should consider the effect of any changes in accounting standards

(f) Compliance with Stock Exchange and legal requirements

6.22 **Liaison with external auditors**. The audit committee's tasks here will include:

(a) being responsible for the appointment or removal of the external auditors as well as fixing their remuneration. The committee should also consider non-audit services provided by the external auditors, paying particular attention to whether there may be a conflict of interest;

(b) discussing the scope of the external audit prior to the start of the audit. This should include consideration of whether external audit's coverage of all areas and locations of the business is fair, and how much external audit will rely on the work of internal audit;

(c) acting as a forum for liaison between the external auditors, the internal auditors and the finance director;

(d) helping the external auditors to obtain the information they require and in resolving any problems they may encounter;

(e) making themselves available to the external auditors for consultation, with or without the presence of the company's management;

(f)   dealing with any serious reservations which the auditors may express either about the accounts, the records or the quality of the company's management.

6.23   **Review of internal audit**. The review should cover the following aspects of internal audit.

(a)   Standards including in particular objectivity, technical knowledge and professional standards

(b)   Scope, including how much emphasis is given to different types of review

(c)   Resources

(d)   Reporting arrangements

(e)   Work plan, especially whether internal audit's review of controls is reasonable and how much work is carried out on high risk areas

(f)   Liaison with external auditors

(g)   Results

6.24   **Review of internal control**. The audit committee can play a significant role in reviewing internal control.

(a)   Committee members can use their own experience to monitor continually the adequacy of internal control systems, focusing particularly on the control environment, management's attitude towards controls and overall management controls. The audit committee's review should cover legal compliance and ethics, for example listing rules, Financial Service Act requirements or environmental legislation.

(b)   Each year the committee should be responsible for reviewing the company's statement on internal controls prior to its approval by the board.

(c)   The committee should consider the recommendations of the auditors in the management letter and management's response. Because the committee's role is ongoing, it can also ensure that recommendations are publicised and see that actions are taken as appropriate.

6.25   **Investigations**. The committee will also be involved in implementing and reviewing the results of one-off investigations. The *Cadbury Report* recommends that audit committees should be given specific authority to investigate matters of concern, and in doing so have access to sufficient resources, appropriate information and outside professional help.

Peer reviews

6.26   Some people have suggested that a system of 'auditing the auditors' should be established and indeed there have already been examples of such reviews being carried out on a mandatory basis in the USA. It would involve either:

(a)   the profession as a whole establishing panels of experts to review and report on the practices and procedures of a firm of auditors; or simply,

(b)   another independent firm of auditors carrying out the review.

The main object of such an exercise is to improve the quality and performance of audit work generally, but undoubtedly an important part of the 'brief' of the reviewer would be to consider whether the firm under review was sufficiently independent of its clients.

Independence of auditors which are companies

6.27 The Companies Act 1989 provides for the possibility of incorporated firms being appointed as company auditors. Such firms are required to have rules preventing individuals who do not hold an appropriate qualification from exerting an influence over the conduct of an audit in such a way as to affect the independence or integrity of the auditor.

6.28 Discussion on this issue has focused mainly on the extent to which shares in an incorporated audit firm may be held by persons outside the firm. The 8th Directive allows up to 49% of the shares to be owned by outsiders, although many UK commentators have felt that the auditor's independence may be prejudiced if more than 25% of the shares are held externally.

Conflicts of interest

6.29 In some ways conflict of interest problems are similar to the difficulties firms have in maintaining independence. Conflicts of interest can arise in a variety of circumstances and each problem has to be dealt with on its own merits. There are no rules to deal with most of the situations, outside the Association's rules about independence and integrity, and the solution will usually be based on common sense as much as ethical behaviour.

6.30 We have already dealt with conflict of interest in terms of auditor independence, particularly in situations where there is a financial or personal interest in a client company.

6.31 Conflicts of interest can arise when a firm has two (or more) audit clients, both of whom have reason to be unhappy that their auditors are also auditors to the other company. This situation frequently arises when the companies are in direct competition with each other, and particularly when the auditors have access to particularly sensitive information. These situations are difficult for the auditors: it may involve the loss of a substantial client, even though the staff and engagement partners on each of the audits are different.

6.32 Most of these companies have this attitude because of the highly competitive nature of their industry. Others may be sensitive because of the work they do for governments in defence or other controversial areas.

Avoidance of conflicts of interest

6.33 In general, where conflicts of interest arise, there should be **full** and **frank explanation** to those involved by the audit firm, coupled with any action necessary to disengage from one or both positions.

6.34 Conflicts should, so far as possible, be avoided by not accepting any appointment or assignment in which conflict seems likely to occur.

6.35 This avoidance of clients causing a conflict of interest is more important for smaller audit firms. The larger firms can overcome a conflict by building a 'Chinese wall' within the firm. This would mean that the respective audits are undertaken by different audit 'groups', the engagement partners are different and all the other audit staff are allowed to work on one of the clients only.

6.36 An example of very competitive companies which appeared to agree with this type of arrangement was that of British Airways and British Caledonian (before they merged). Both companies were audited by the same large accountancy firm and yet the airline business is one of the most competitive in the world and confidential information is held at a premium.

6.37 It is possible, of course, that some clients might not agree to such an arrangement. The increasing number of mergers which have taken place within the accountancy profession recently have caused conflict of interest problems. For example, British Telecom was not happy when its auditors merged with the firm which audited Cable and Wireless. The new firm was forced to drop one of the audits.

6.38 A non-audit example of conflict of interest is a practice which advises a company upon the figures on which it bases a tender for a contract and which is then asked to become involved in advising a rival company tendering for the same contract. The conflict of interest is avoided by not taking up the work from the rival company.

6.39 Another situation which can arise is where two audit clients fall into dispute with each other. The auditors might be asked to arbitrate, but this would leave the auditors open to accusations of conflict of interest. It would be better to advise the companies to obtain arbitration from an independent accountant. The auditors should not investigate one client on behalf of another, nor pass on any knowledge of either client in such a situation. This is not always easy, particularly when the auditors can see the whole picture, but the companies cannot. The auditors must be extremely tactful and firm.

Exam focus point

Conflicts of interest is a topical area. One major objection to the proposed mergers between various of the Big Six firms was an increase in potential conflicts of interest.

Question

You are the auditor of Deanor Ltd and you prepare the accounts of Willoughby, an unincorporated business. Willoughby is a small business and its only accounting records are an analysed cash book and copies of sales and purchase invoices.

It appears from your preparation of the business's accounts that Deanor Ltd has not paid one of Willoughby's invoices for about £10,000, but the chairman of Deanor Ltd has told the proprietor of Willoughby that this invoice has been paid. The proprietor of Willoughby has asked you to carry out further investigations:

(a)   to confirm the invoice has not been paid, by producing a schedule of sales invoices to Deanor Ltd and cash received; and

(b)   to act on Willoughby's behalf over the dispute with Deanor Ltd.

The proprietor of Willoughby has said there are no staff in Willoughby's business who are capable of carrying out this work, and you are the only person who can help him.

Required

(a)   Consider the above situation and decide the action you should take in relation to the request by the proprietor of Willoughby, whether you should provide confirmation of whether the invoice has not been paid, by producing a schedule of sales invoices to Deanor and cash received, or act on Willoughby's behalf over the dispute with Deanor.

(b)   Assuming you decide to provide some help to Willoughby, you are required to consider whether you should look at Deanor's accounting records over this matter, and whether you should act on Deanor's behalf, if asked to do so by the company chairman.

Answer

Where a conflict of interest arises, the auditor/accountant should disclose the conflict in full to both parties. Ideally, I should act for neither party, but as I have discovered the problem in Willoughby's books and as no-one else is available to resolve the problem for them, then I will act for them in this matter. I should tell Deanor Ltd that I am acting for Willoughby in this matter.

In acting for Willoughby I may not examine the accounting records of Deanor Ltd, even if the directors of Deanor Ltd are willing I should do so.

This is a risky situation, because in a dispute of this nature I run the risk of alienating one or both of my clients and losing the fee income I receive from them.

Insider dealing

6.40 From the point of view of the auditors, insider dealing can be seen as an extension of the duty of confidentiality owed to clients. It does not just cover information passed to third parties, but also information used for personal gain.

Knowledge brought forward from Paper 2

Insider dealing can be described as dealing in securities whilst in possession of insider information as an insider, the securities being price-affected by the information.

These are various anti-avoidance measures in the legislation (including those relating to the disclosure of information to other parties. (Criminal Justice Act 1993)

6.41 You can see from this description of insider dealing that an auditor is likely to be in a position where he or she holds price-sensitive information about a client. Great care must be taken to ensure that the rules concerning insider dealing are not breached. Many firms insist that their staff sign forms annually which state that neither they nor any of their 'connected persons' have dealt in any client company shares (a list of client companies is often attached). Such forms are sometimes called '**independence declarations**'.

Fee negotiation and lowballing

6.42 The audit fee is a sensitive subject for most companies. It represents a cost for something the company often does not really want and the fees may be perceived as too high just for this reason. The directors of other companies may have a more positive attitude towards the benefit of an audit, but even they will often feel duty bound to obtain 'an audit' for as low a price as possible. The auditors, on the other hand, must ensure that they can provide a proper audit service for the fee negotiated.

6.43 There are various rules concerning the resignation or replacement of the auditors, but here we are merely concerned with how fee negotiations take place when obtaining the services of *new* auditors, whatever the reason for the change. There will, of course, be situations where newly formed companies will require auditors for the first time, but most appointments of auditors are through a change of auditors.

Tendering

6.44 Many large companies invite **tenders** for their audit work. The directors then have the opportunity to compare directly a range of offers. This is the type of situation usually faced by the larger auditing firms, although tenders can be invited for companies of any size. Generally, a tender will take the form of detailed written proposals and a presentation. Although the proposed level of **fees** charged will be a very important factor (and perhaps the deciding one), other aspects will be considered by the directors of the company concerned, including:

(a) the **level** of **expertise** each firm has in the industry;

(b) **similar companies** audited by each firm (good for expertise, worrying for confidentiality);

(c) **national** and **international presence** and so on.

6.45 Audit firms which tender for such audits will usually give at least an indication of the level of fees in the next few years, including likely overall rate rises.

6.46 In all situations, the auditors should quote a fee based on the estimated hours worked by each member of staff required on the audit, multiplied by the hourly rate commensurate with their grade, plus any expenses to be incurred during the audit (travel, subsistence and so on). Many audit firms will add a premium to the normal hourly charge out rate for specialist audits, such as banking or financial services.

Lowballing

6.47 Problems can arise when auditing firms appear to be charging less than this, or at least less than the 'market rate' for the audit. The practice of undercutting, usually at tender for the audit of large companies, has been called **lowballing**. In other cases, the audit fee has been reduced even though the auditors have remained the same. The problem here is that, if the audit is being performed for less than it is actually worth, then the auditors' independence is called into question.

6.48 This is always going to be a topical debate, but in terms of negotiating the audit fee the following factors need to be taken into account.

(a) The audit is perceived to have a fluctuating 'market price' as any other commodity or service. In a recession, prices would be expected to fall as companies aim to cut costs everywhere, and as auditors chase less work (supply falls). Audit firms are also reducing staffing levels and their own overhead costs should be lower.

(b) Companies can reduce external audit costs through various legitimate measures:

(i) extending the size and function of internal audit;
(ii) reducing the number of different audit firms used world-wide;
(iii) selling off subsidiary companies leaving a simplified group structure to audit;
(iv) the tender process itself simply makes auditors more competitive;
(v) exchange rate fluctuations in audit fees.

(c) Auditing firms have increased productivity, partly through the use of more sophisticated information technology techniques in auditing.

6.49 These factors will all be taken into account when the audit fee is negotiated. As far as undercutting or lowballing is concerned, the relevant professional bodies may issue new ethical rules to prevent it. In any case, an auditing firm lays itself open to accusations of loss of independence if it reduces its fees to below a certain level, particularly if it is difficult to see how such fees will cover direct labour costs. This is also true of firms which use the audit as a 'loss leader' to obtain profitable consultancy work from audit clients.

6.50   There is also a risk of a conflict of interest when non-audit services are offered to a client by the auditors. The possibility arises that the price of an 'acceptable' audit opinion is lucrative taxation or consulting work.

6.51   Where clients face difficulties paying an audit fee all at once, the auditors might offer to receive the fee over several months, or even the whole year, probably by direct debit.

A practical approach to questions of ethics

6.52   The following table summarises an approach to examination questions where ethical problems might arise.

DO	Note	DON'T
Identify the *key* facts as briefly as possible (one sentence?)	1	Merely paraphrase the question
Identify the major *principle(s)* at issue	2	Regurgitate the entire contents of the *Rules of Professional Conduct*
Consider alternative actions and their consequences	3	List every single possible action and then explain how all the unsuitable ones can be eliminated
Make a decision and recommend action as appropriate	4	Fail to make a decision or recommend action. Propose actions in breach of the *Rules of Professional Conduct*
Justify your decision	5	Be feeble. 'This should be done because it is ethical' is not terribly convincing

Notes

1   One sentence is an ideal to aim for.

2   (a)   Use the terminology of the *Rules of Professional Conduct*, but not *ad nauseam*. 'Integrity' is often more clearly described as 'honesty' (although the two words are not synonymous). Don't forget the words 'fairness', 'bias' and 'influence' when discussing 'objectivity'.

     (b)   Don't torture the situation to make it fit a principle: if, say, 'justice' is the most persuasive word for a situation don't be afraid of using it.

     (c)   If the law is involved, don't get carried away - this is not a law exam. 'The director has a statutory duty to ...' is sufficient: there is no need to go into legal detail.

3   A useful way of generating alternatives is to consider the problem from the other side of the fence: imagine you are the client/auditee company.

4   Making a decision is often very hard, but if you cannot do this you are simply not ready to take on the responsibilities of a qualified accountant. There are usually a number of decisions that could be justified, so don't be afraid of choosing the 'wrong' answer.

5   This is not actually as hard as you might think. By suggesting reporting, investigating and verifying facts and so on you are exhibiting **professional competence** and **due care**.

Chapter roundup

- The auditors' **duty of care** has been defined by case law over time.

- **Independence** is the most important characteristic of auditors. Guidance is given on the issue in the *Rules of Professional Conduct.*

- **Confidentiality** is also important. However auditors may be compelled by law or consider it desirable in the **public interest** to disclose details of clients' affairs to third parties.

- Current discussion is focused on the **other services** auditors sell to audit clients, **low-balling**, **conflicts of interest, opinion shopping** and the recommendations of the reports on **corporate governance**.

- Remember the approach to ethical questions.
  - Identify the key facts
  - Identify the major principle
  - Consider alternative actions and their consequences
  - Make a decision and recommend action
  - Justify your decision

Quick quiz

1   How does the Supply of Goods and Services Act 1982 affect the accountant? (see para 1.1)

2   List the fundamental principles of the *Rules of Professional Conduct.* (2.2)

3   How does Statement 1 describe the principle of independence? (3.2)

4   What is the maximum fee income which should be received from one client? (3.5)

5   What is the definition of a closely connected person? (3.22)

6   Under what circumstances is the auditor permitted to breach client confidentiality? (4.6 - 4.8)

7   What are the advantages and disadvantages of audit committees in terms of auditor independence? (6.14 - 6.16)

8   How can auditors avoid conflicts of interest? (6.33)

Question to try	Level	Marks	Time
5	Exam	20	36 mins

Chapter 6

INTERNAL CONTROLS, AUDIT RISK AND AUDIT SAMPLING

Chapter topic list	Syllabus reference
1 Internal controls and audit risk assessment	5(a), (g)
2 Audit sampling	5(a)
3 Sampling procedures	5(a)
4 Internal audit	5(a), (g)

Introduction

You should have studied these topics for previous papers, but they are fundamental to auditing and so we have covered them in some depth here.

The determination of **audit risk** is fundamental to audit planning and therefore Section 1 of this chapter is closely related to the audit planning matters covered in Chapter 3, particularly materiality and tolerable error.

In the Paper 10 exam questions on risk assessment often have an ethical dimension – a (usually) high risk client may put the auditor at risk of disobeying ethical guidance.

We have mentioned different types of audit tests in the previous chapters. Whatever type of test is chosen, the auditors need to decide how they will select the items to be tested from the whole population.

This is not as simple as it sounds. The auditors will want to select a sample which reflects, as closely as possible, the characteristics of the population from which the sample has been selected. If this is *not* the case, then the auditors cannot draw valid conclusions from the tests carried out on the sample.

The SAS on audit sampling has been produced by the APB and is discussed in Sections 2 and 3. Practical sampling methods range from the very simple to the very complex. The more sophisticated sampling techniques involve the use of probabilities and statistics. We will explain these practical aspects of sampling as simply as possible as you are not expected to understand the more complicated aspects of sampling theory. Sample theory is closely associated with audit risk.

Internal audit is included in this chapter as it functions as a type of internal control and because you should be aware of the SAS on the subject.

1   INTERNAL CONTROLS AND AUDIT RISK ASSESSMENT   6/95, 6/96

KEY TERMS

Audit risk is the risk that auditors may give an inappropriate opinion on the financial statements. Audit risk has three components; inherent risk, control risk and detection risk.

Inherent risk is the suspectibility of an account balance or class of transactions to material misstatement, either individually or when aggregated with misstatements in other balances or classes, irrespective of related internal controls.

Control risk is the risk that a misstatement:

(i) could occur in an account balance or class of transactions;

(ii) could be material, either individually or when aggregated with misstatements in other balances or classes; and

(iii) would not be prevented, or detected and corrected on a timely basis, by the accounting and internal control systems.

Detection risk is the risk that the auditors' substantive procedures do not detect a misstatement that exists in an account balance or class of transactions that could be material, either individually or when aggregated with misstatements in other balances or classes.

Exam focus point

Audit risk has been a popular topic in recent exams.

1.1 Audit risk is the risk that the auditors give an unqualified opinion on the accounts when they should have given a qualified opinion; *or* they give an opinion qualified for a particular reason where that reason was not justified. SAS 300 *Accounting and internal control and audit risk assessments* covers audit risk.

1.2 Audit risk can never be completely eliminated. The auditors are called upon to make subjective judgements in the course of forming an opinion and so fraud or error may possibly go undetected.

SAS 300.1

Auditors should:

(a) obtain an understanding of the accounting and internal control system sufficient to plan the audit and develop an effective audit approach; and

(b) use professional judgement to assess the components of audit risk and to design audit procedures to ensure it is reduced to an acceptably low level.

1.3 A **risk-centred methodology** gives the auditors an overall measure of risk, but at the same time it provides a quantification of each stage of the audit. The extent of detailed testing required is determined by a purely risk-based perspective. A diagrammatic view of the risk-based approach is given below.

1.4 Remember that materiality and audit risk are closely connected.

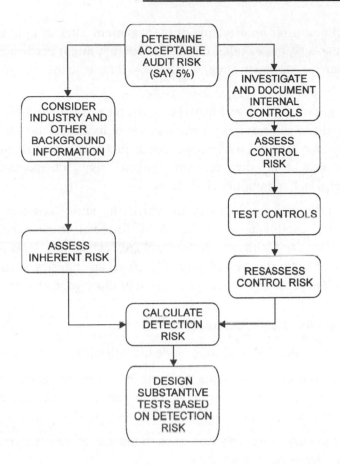

Inherent risk

SAS 300.2

In developing their audit approach and detailed procedures, auditors should assess inherent risk in relation to financial statement assertions about material account balances and classes of transactions, taking account of factors relevant both to the entity as a whole and to the specific assertions.

1.5   Inherent risk is the risk that items will be mis-stated due to the characteristics of those items, such as the fact that they are estimates or that they are important items in the accounts. The auditors must use their professional judgement and all available knowledge to assess inherent risk. If no such information or knowledge is available then the inherent risk is **high**.

1.6   The results of the assessment must be properly documented and, where inherent risk is assessed as not high, then audit work may be reduced. The SAS lists the relevant factors to be considered under two headings.

At the entity level

1.7   Consider:

(a)   The **integrity** and **attitude** to **risk** of **directors** and **management**. Dominance by a single person can cause problems.

(b)   **Management experience and knowledge** and changes in management during the period, eg inexperience may affect the preparation of the financial statements of the entity. Auditors will be particularly concerned with the quality of financial management.

(c) **Unusual pressures on directors or management,** such as tight reporting deadlines, market expectations or other circumstances that might predispose them to misstate the financial statements, eg a business that is close to breaching borrowing covenants.

(d) **The nature of the entity's business,** eg the potential for technological obsolescence of its products and services, or the number of locations and geographical spread of its production facilities. Over-dependence on a single product may cause problems; auditors should be alert for non-financial signs of stagnation eg out-of-date machinery, lack of computerisation, etc.

(e) **Factors affecting the industry** in which the entity operates, eg economic and competitive conditions as indicated by financial trends and ratios, regulatory requirements and changes in technology, consumer demand and accounting practices common to the industry. Clients in an industry with a high number of business failures may be under pressure to produce good results, or face bankruptcy.

At the account balance and class of transaction level

1.8   Relevant factors under this heading include the following.

(a) **Financial statement accounts** likely to be **prone** to **misstatement,** eg accounts which required adjustment in the previous period or which involve a high degree of estimation

(b) **The complexity of underlying transactions** and other events which might require the use of the work of an expert

(c) **The degree of judgement** involved in determining account balances

(d) **Susceptibility of assets to loss or misappropriation,** eg assets which are highly desirable and movable such as cash

(e) The **quality of the accounting systems**

(f) **The completion of unusual and complex transactions,** particularly at or near the period end

(g) **Transactions not subjected to ordinary processing**

(h) Areas which have experienced significant **staff changes** or which have other problems with staff eg low morale.

Control risk assessment

1.9   SAS 300 defines two elements in controls, the control environment and control procedures.

Control environment

KEY TERM

Control environment is the overall attitude, awareness and actions of directors and managers regarding internal controls and their importance in the entity. The control environment encompasses the management style, and corporate culture and values shared by all employees. It provides the background against which the various other controls are operated.

1.10 The SAS adds to the definition of the control environment that a strong control environment does not, by itself, ensure the effectiveness of the overall internal control system. This is a very important point, and the SAS lists the following factors which are reflected in the control environment.

(a) The **philosophy** and **operating style** of the directors and management

(b) The entity's **organisational structure** and methods of assigning authority and responsibility (including segregation of duties and supervisory controls)

(c) The directors' **methods of imposing control**, including the internal audit function, the functions of the board of directors and personnel policies and procedures

Control procedures

KEY TERM

Control procedures are those policies and procedures in addition to the control environment which are established to achieve the entity's specific objectives.

1.11 The definition of control procedures is extended in SAS 300. Control procedures include those designed to prevent or to detect and correct errors (the latter may be a focus of high level controls in small or owner-managed entities). The SAS lists some specific control procedures.

(a) Approval and control of documents

(b) Controls over computerised applications and the information technology environment

(c) Checking the arithmetical accuracy of the records

(d) Maintaining and reviewing control accounts and trial balances

(e) Reconciliations

(f) Comparing the results of cash, security and stock counts with accounting records

(g) Comparing internal data with external sources of information

(h) Limiting direct physical access to assets and records

Internal controls and their inherent limitations

1.12 SAS 300 states that the directors of an entity will set up internal controls in the accounting system to achieve objectives such as the following.

(a) Transactions are executed in accordance with proper general or specific **authorisation**.

(b) All transactions and other events are promptly recorded at the **correct amount**, in the **appropriate accounts** and in the **proper accounting period** so as to permit preparation of financial statements in accordance with the law and accounting standards.

(c) **Access to assets** is permitted only in accordance with proper authorisation.

(d) **Recorded assets** are **compared** with the **existing assets** at reasonable intervals and appropriate action is taken with regard to any differences.

1.13 However, any internal control system can only provide the directors with **reasonable assurance** that their objectives are reached, because of **inherent limitations**, such as the following.

(a) The usual requirement that the **cost** of an internal control is not **disproportionate** to the potential loss which may result from its absence.

(b) Most systematic internal controls tend to be directed at **routine transactions** rather than non-routine transactions.

(c) The potential for **human error** due to carelessness, distraction, mistakes of judgement and the misunderstanding of instructions.

(d) The possibility of **internal controls** being **bypassed** through collusion with parties outside or inside the organisation.

(e) The possibility that a person responsible for exercising an internal control could abuse that responsibility by **overriding** an internal control.

(f) The possibility that procedures may become **inadequate** due to changes in conditions or that compliance with procedures may deteriorate over time.

1.14 These factors show why auditors cannot obtain all their evidence from tests of the systems of internal control.

1.15 Auditors are only concerned with policies and procedures which are relevant to financial statement assertions. The understanding of relevant aspects of the accounting and internal control systems, together with inherent and control risk assessments, enables auditors:

(a) to **assess the adequacy** of the accounting system as a basis for preparing the financial statements;

(b) to **identify** the types of **potential misstatements** that could occur in the financial statements;

(c) to **consider factors** that affect the **risk of misstatements**; and

(d) **design appropriate audit procedures**.

1.16 When the auditors plan their work, they consider the likelihood of error in the light of **inherent risk** and the system of internal control (**control risk**) in order to determine the extent of work (and hence the level of **detection risk**) required to satisfy themselves that the risk of error in the financial statements is sufficiently low.

Accounting system and control environment

SAS 300.3

In planning the audit, auditors should obtain and document an understanding of the accounting system and control environment sufficient to determine their audit approach.

1.17 Auditors must obtain an **understanding** of the accounting system to enable them to identify and understand:

(a) **major classes of transactions** in the entity's operations;

(b) **how such transactions** are initiated;

(c) **significant accounting records**, supporting documents and accounts in the financial statements; and

(d) the **accounting and financial reporting process**, from the initiation of significant transactions and other events to their inclusion in the financial statements.

1.18 Having assessed the accounting system and control environment, the auditors can make a preliminary assessment of the adequacy of the system as a basis for the preparation of the financial statements, and of the likely mix of tests of control and substantive procedures.

1.19 During the above assessment, the auditors will obtain knowledge of the design and operation of the systems which will assist in the assessment of inherent risk. To obtain this knowledge, 'walk-through tests' are often performed. Walk-through tests involve tracing one or more transactions through the accounting system and observing the application of relevant aspects of the control system on these transactions.

1.20 The factors affecting the **nature, timing and extent** of the **procedures** performed in order to understand the systems include:

(a) **materiality** considerations;
(b) the **size and complexity** of the entity;
(c) their **assessment** of **inherent risk**;
(d) the **complexity** of the entity's computer systems;
(e) the **type of internal controls** involved; and
(f) the **nature of the entity's documentation** of specific internal controls.

1.21 The auditors will normally update previous knowledge of the systems in the following ways.

(a) **Enquiries** of appropriate supervisory and other personnel at various organisational levels within the entity, together with reference to documentation such as procedures manuals, job descriptions and systems descriptions

(b) **Inspection** of relevant documents and records produced by the systems

(c) **Observation** of the entity's activities and operations, include the information technology function's organisation, personnel performing control procedures and the nature of transaction processing

Control risk

SAS 300.4

If auditors, after obtaining an understanding of the accounting system and control environment, expect to be able to rely on their assessment of control risk to reduce the extent of their substantive procedures, they should make a preliminary assessment of control risk for material financial statement assertions, and should plan and perform tests of control to support that assessment.

1.22 No assessment is necessary when the auditors decide it is likely to be **inefficient** or **impossible** to rely on any assessment of control risk to reduce their substantive testing. In such cases control risk is assumed to be **high**. Under SAS 300, the key stages of assessing control risk are as follows.

Preliminary assessment of control risk

1.23 This evaluation of the accounting and control systems' effectiveness in correcting material misstatements will entail consideration of the design of the systems. Auditors should note:

(a) some control risk will always exist as internal controls have inherent limitations;

(b) where tests of controls provide audit evidence of effective control systems (ie control risk is low) then the extent of substantive testing may be reduced;

(c) where the control systems are not effective, or where an audit approach which relied on tests of controls would be inefficient, then audit evidence can be obtained entirely from substantive procedures and audit work from the preparation of financial statements.

Relationship between the assessments of inherent and control risks

1.24 Where inherent risk is high, management may institute a more rigorous accounting and control systems to prevent and detect material misstatements. This interrelationship means that inherent and control risks should often be assessed in combination.

Documentation of understanding and assessment of control risk

1.25 Where control risk is less than high, the auditors should document the basis for their conclusions. Common techniques are one or more of:

(a) narrative notes;
(b) questionnaires;
(c) checklists;
(d) flowcharts;

depending on the size and complexity of the entity.

Tests of control

KEY TERM

Tests of control are tests to obtain audit evidence about the effective operation of the accounting and internal control systems, that is, that properly designed controls identified in the preliminary assessment of control risk exist in fact and have operated effectively throughout the relevant period.

1.26 The SAS adds:

'They include tests of elements of the control environment where strengths in the control environment are used by auditors to reduce control risk assessments.'

1.27 Some procedures which were not designed or performed as tests of controls may qualify as such and may be used to support a control risk assessment as less than high.

1.28 Tests of control may include the following.

(a) **Corroborative enquires** about, and observation of, internal control functions

(b) **Inspection of documents** supporting controls or events to gain audit evidence that internal controls have operated properly, eg verifying that a transaction has been authorised or a reconciliation approved

(c) **Examination** of evidence of **management views**, eg minutes of management meetings at which financial results are reviewed and corrective action decided on

(d) **Reperformance** of control procedures, eg reconciliation of bank accounts, to ensure they were correctly performed by the entity

(e) **Testing** of the internal controls operating on **specific computerised applications** or over the overall information technology function, eg access or program change controls

1.29 Relevant factors for auditors to consider when obtaining evidence about the effective operation of internal controls are:

(a) **how they were applied**;
(b) the **consistency** with which they were applied during the period; and
(c) **by whom** they were applied.

1.30 Deviations in the operation of controls (caused by change of staff etc) may increase control risk and tests of control may need to be modified to confirm effective operation during and after any change.

1.31 Radical changes in controls, including a periodic breakdown in controls, should be considered as **separate periods** by the auditors.

1.32 The use of CAATs (Computer Assisted Audit Techniques) may be appropriate (see Chapter 8).

Quality and timeliness of audit evidence

1.33 Auditors' observations are usually more reliable audit evidence than merely making enquires. However, some test of controls, such as observation, only apply to one point in time, so additional procedures may be required to obtain evidence that controls are acting throughout the period.

1.34 In relation to tests before the period end, the SAS states:

> **SAS 300.5**
>
> If intending to rely on tests of control performed in advance of the period end, auditors should obtain sufficient appropriate audit evidence as to the nature and extent of any changes in design or operation of the entity's accounting and internal control systems within the accounting period since such procedures were performed.

1.35 Further evidence must be obtained to augment the results of tests carried out at an interim audit, ie before the period end. Factors to consider include:

(a) the **results** of the interim tests;

(b) the **length** of the remaining period;

(c) whether any **changes** have occurred in the accounting and internal control systems during the remaining period;

(d) the **nature and amount** of the **transactions** and other events and the balances involved;

(e) the **control environment**; and

(f) the **nature, timing** and **extent** of the **substantive procedures** which they plan to undertake.

1.36 Some consideration can be given to tests in previous years, while taking the above factors into account. However, the longer ago the tests took place, the less persuasive the resulting evidence that the control risk is less than high.

Final assessment of control risk

> ### SAS 300.6
>
> Having undertaken tests of control, auditors should evaluate whether the preliminary assessment of control risk is supported.

1.37 Deviations should be investigated, but in such cases the preliminary assessment may still be supported. Greater deviation may require the level of control risk to be revised; in such cases the nature, timing and extent of the auditors' planned substantive procedures should be modified.

Communication of weaknesses

1.38 The auditors may become aware of weaknesses in the system as a result of obtaining an understanding of those systems. Such weaknesses should be reported to management according to SAS 610 *Reports to directors or management* (see Chapter 9).

Question 1

An internal control system has been described as comprising 'the control environment and control procedures. It includes all the policies and procedures (internal controls) adopted by the directors and management of an entity to assist in achieving their objective of ensuring, as far as practicable, the orderly and efficient conduct of its business, including adherence to internal policies, the safeguarding of assets, the prevention and detection of fraud and error, the accuracy and completeness of the accounting records, and the timely preparation of reliable financial information'.

Explain the meaning and relevance to the auditors giving an opinion on financial statements of each of the management objectives above.

Answer

The auditors' objective in evaluating and testing internal controls is to determine the degree of reliance which they may place on the information contained in the accounting records. If they obtain reasonable assurance by means of tests of controls that the internal control system is effective in ensuring the completeness and accuracy of the accounting records and the validity of the entries therein, they may limit the extent of their substantive procedures.

(a) *'the orderly and efficient conduct of its business'*

An organisation which is efficient and conducts its affairs in an orderly manner is much more likely to be able to supply the auditors with sufficient appropriate audit evidence on which to base their audit opinion. More importantly, the level of inherent and control risk will be lower, giving extra assurance that the financial statements do not contain material errors.

(b) *'adherence to internal policies'*

Management is responsible for setting up an effective system of internal control and management policy provides the broad framework within which internal controls have to operate. Unless management does have a pre-determined set of policies, then it is very difficult to imagine how the company could be expected to operate efficiently. Management policy will cover all aspects of the company's activities and will range from broad corporate objectives to specific areas such as determining selling prices and wage rates.

Given that the auditors must have a sound understanding of the company's affairs generally, and of specific areas of control in particular, then the fact that management policies are followed will make the task of the auditors easier in that they will be able to rely more readily on the information produced by the systems established by management.

(c) *'safeguarding of assets'*

This objective may relate to the physical protection of assets (for example locking monies in a safe at night) or to less direct safeguarding (for example ensuring that there is adequate insurance cover for all assets). It can also be seen as relating to the maintenance of proper records in respect of all assets.

The auditors will be concerned to ensure that the company has properly safeguarded its assets so that they can form an opinion on the existence of specific assets and, more generally, on whether the company's records can be taken as a reliable basis for the preparation of financial statements. Reliance on the underlying records will be particularly significant where the figures in the financial statements are derived from such records rather than as the result of physical inspection.

(d) *'prevention and detection of fraud and error'*

The directors are responsible for taking reasonable steps to prevent and detect fraud. They are also responsible for preparing financial statements which give a true and fair view of the entity's affairs. However, the auditors must plan and perform their audit procedures and evaluate and report the results thereof, recognising that fraud or error may materially affect the financial statements. A strong system of internal control will give the auditors some assurance that frauds and errors are not occurring, unless management are colluding to overcome that system.

(e) *'accuracy and completeness of the accounting records'/'timely preparation of reliable financial information'*

This objective is most clearly related to statutory requirements relating to both management and auditors. The company has an obligation under the Companies Act 1985 to maintain proper accounting records. The auditors must form an opinion on whether the company has fulfilled this obligation and also conclude whether the financial statements are in agreement with the underlying records.

Detection risk

1.39 Detection risk is the risk that audit procedures will fail to detect material misstatements. Detection risk relates to substantive procedures and the inability of the auditors to examine all evidence. Audit evidence is usually persuasive rather than conclusive so some detection risk is usually present, allowing the auditors to seek 'reasonable confidence'.

1.40 The auditors' **inherent and control risk assessments** influence the **nature, timing and extent of substantive procedures** required to reduce detection risk and thereby audit risk. Misstatements discovered in substantive procedures may cause the auditors to modify their previous assessment of control risk.

> ### SAS 300.8
>
> Regardless of the assessed levels of inherent and control risks, auditors should perform some substantive procedures for financial statement assertions of material account balances and transaction classes.

1.41 **Substantive procedures can never be abandoned entirely** because control and inherent risk can never be assessed at a low enough level, although substantive procedures may be restricted to analytical procedures if appropriate.

1.42 Where the auditors' assessment of the components of audit risk changes during the audit, they should modify the planned substantive procedures based on the revised risk levels.

1.43   When both inherent and control risks are assessed as high, the auditors should consider whether substantive procedures can provide sufficient appropriate audit evidence to reduce detection risk, and therefore audit risk, to an acceptably low level.

1.44   When auditors determine that detection risk regarding a material financial statement assertion cannot be reduced to an acceptably low level, they should consider the implications for their report.

2   AUDIT SAMPLING

Purpose of SAS 430

The purpose is 'to set standards and provide guidance on the design and selection of an audit sample and the evaluation of the sample results. This SAS applies equally to both statistical and non-statistical sampling methods. It applies to any audit using sampling whether related to financial statements or not. Nothing contained in this statement is intended to preclude non-statistically based samples where there are reasonable grounds for believing that the results may be relied on for the purpose of the test.'

SAS 430.1

When using either statistical or non-statistical sampling methods, auditors should design and select an audit sample, perform audit procedures thereon and evaluate sample results so as to obtain appropriate audit evidence.

2.1   This SAS is based on the premise that auditors do not normally examine all the information available to them; it would be impractical to do so and using audit sampling will produce valid conclusions.

KEY TERMS

Audit sampling is the application of audit procedures to less than 100% of the items within an account balance or class of transactions to enable auditors to obtain and evaluate evidence about some characteristic of the items selected in order to form or assist in forming a conclusion concerning the population which makes up that account balance or class of transaction.

Sampling units are the individual items that make up the population.

Error is an unintentional mistake in the financial statements.

Tolerable error is the maximum error in the population that the auditors are willing to accept and still conclude that the audit objective has been achieved.

Sampling risk is the risk that the auditors' conclusion, based on a sample, may be different from the conclusion that would be reached if the entire population was subject to the same audit procedure.

Non-sampling risk is the risk that the auditors might use inappropriate procedures or might misinterpret evidence and thus fail to recognise an error.

2.2   The SAS points out that some testing procedures do *not* involve sampling, such as:

(a)   testing 100% of items in a population (this should be obvious);

(b)   testing all items with a certain characteristic (eg over a certain value) as selection is not representative.

2.3   The SAS distinguishes between **statistically based sampling**, which involves the use of techniques from which mathematically constructed conclusions about the population can be drawn, and **non-statistical methods**, from which auditors draw a judgmental opinion about the population.

Design of the sample

> ### SAS 430.2
>
> When designing the size and structure of an audit sample, auditors should consider the specific audit objectives, the nature of the population from which they wish to sample, and the sampling and selection methods.

Audit objectives

2.4   Auditors must consider the **specific audit objectives** to be achieved and the audit procedures which are most likely to achieve them. The auditors also need to consider the **nature and characteristics of the audit evidence** sought and **possible error conditions**. This will help them to define what constitutes an error and what population to use for sampling.

Population

2.5   The population from which the sample is drawn must be **appropriate** and **complete** for the specific audit objectives. The SAS distinguishes between situations where overstatement or understatement is being tested. The population may be divided into **sampling units** in a variety of ways, eg an individual debtors balance or, in monetary unit sampling, £1 of the total debtors balance. Auditors must define the sampling unit in order to obtain an efficient and effective sample to achieve the particular audit objectives.

2.6   To this end, stratification may be appropriate. Each sampling unit can only belong to one, specifically designed stratum, thus reducing the variability within each stratum. This enables the auditors to direct audit effort towards items which, for example, contain the greatest potential monetary error.

2.7   An example would be dividing a population by size of debtor so that all debtor balances under £1,000 were in one stratum, all balances from £1,000 to £5,000 in another and so on. Alternatively, auditors might split a population according to whether items were processed by different people; items processed by new staff might be particularly vulnerable to error.

Sample size

SAS 430.3

When determining sample sizes, auditors should consider sampling risk, the amount of error that would be acceptable and the extent to which they expect to find errors.

2.8 Examples of some factors affecting sample size are given in an appendix to the SAS, reproduced here.

Table 1: Some factors influencing sample size for tests of controls

Factor	Impact on sample size
Sampling risk	• The greater the reliance on the results of a test of control using audit sampling, the lower the sampling risk the auditors are willing to accept and, consequently, the larger the sample size. • The lower the assessment of control risk, the more likely the auditors are to place reliance on audit evidence from tests of control. • A high control risk assessment may result in a decision not to perform tests of control.
Tolerable error rate	The higher the tolerable error rate the lower the sample size and vice versa.
Expected error rate	• If errors are expected, a larger sample ordinarily needs to be examined to confirm that the actual error rate is less than the tolerable error rate. • High expected error rates may result in a decision not to perform tests of control.
Number of items in population	Virtually no effect on sample size unless population is small.

Table 2: Some factors influencing sample size for substantive tests

Factor	Impact on sample size
Inherent risk*	• The higher the assessment of inherent risk, the more audit evidence is required to support the auditors' conclusion.
Control risk*	• The higher the assessment of control risk, the greater the reliance on audit evidence obtained from substantive procedures. • A high control risk assessment may result in the decision not to perform tests of control and reliance entirely on substantive procedures.

Detection risk*	• Sampling risk for substantive tests is one form of detection risk. The lower the sampling risk the auditors are willing to accept, the larger the sample size.
	• Other substantive procedures may provide audit evidence regarding the same financial statement assertions and reduce detection risk. This may reduce the extent of the auditors' reliance on the results of a substantive procedure using audit sampling.
	• The lower the reliance on the results of a substantive procedure using audit sampling, the higher the sampling risk the auditors are willing to accept and, consequently, the smaller the sample size.
Tolerable error rate	The higher the monetary value of the tolerable error rate the smaller the sample size and vice versa.
Expected error rate	If errors are expected, a larger sample ordinarily needs to be examined to confirm that the actual error rate is less than the tolerable error rate.
Population value	The less material the monetary value of the population to the financial statements, the smaller the sample size that may be required.
Numbers of items in population	Virtually no effect on sample size unless population is small.
Stratification	If it is appropriate to stratify the population this may lead to a smaller sample size.

Note. The auditing standards and guidance included in SAS 220 *Audit materiality,* SAS 300 *Accounting and internal control systems and audit risk assessments* and SAS 400 *Audit evidence* are also relevant when using these tables.

Sampling risk

2.9   Sampling risk is encountered by the auditors in both tests of control and substantive procedures. It is the risk of drawing an incorrect conclusion from audit sampling and is part of detection risk. It affects different types of test as follows:

(a)   *Tests of control*:

(i)   the risk of placing a **higher than necessary assessment** on control risk, because the error in the sample is greater than the error in the total population; or

(ii)   the risk of placing a **lower than required assessment** on control risk, because the error in the sample is less than the error in the population as a whole.

(b)   *Substantive tests*:

(i)   the risk of concluding that a recorded account balance or class of transactions is **materially misstated when** it is **not**, because the error in the sample is greater than the error in the population as a whole; or

(ii)   the risk of concluding that a recorded account balance or class of transactions is **acceptable when** it is **materially misstated**, because the error in the sample is less than the error in the population as a whole.

2.10   The *greater* their reliance on the results of the procedure in question, the *lower* the sampling risk auditors will be willing to accept and the *larger* the sample size needs to be.

Sample size will therefore be considered in the context of overall risk assessment (see SAS 300 *Accounting and internal control systems and audit risk assessments* in Chapter 8).

2.11   The SAS also adds the following note regarding *non-sampling risk.*

> 'Sampling risk can be contrasted with non-sampling risk which arises when auditors use any audit procedures. Non-sampling risk arises because, for example, most audit evidence is persuasive rather than conclusive, or auditors might use inappropriate procedures or might misinterpret evidence and thus fail to recognise an error. Auditors attempt to reduce non-sampling risk to a negligible level by appropriate planning, direction, supervision and review.'

Tolerable error

2.12   This will still be considered during the planning stage.

(a)   In tests of control, the **tolerable error** is the **maximum rate of deviation from a prescribed control procedure** that auditors are willing to accept in the population and still conclude that the preliminary assessment of control risk is valid. Often this rate will be very low since auditors are likely to be concentrating on testing important controls.

(b)   In substantive procedures, the **tolerable error** is the **maximum monetary error** in an account balance or class of transactions that auditors are willing to accept so that, when the results of all audit procedures are considered, they are able to conclude, with reasonable assurance, that the financial statements are not materially misstated. Sometimes the tolerable error for substantive tests will be the materiality rate. Some accountancy firms set tolerable error as being a fixed percentage of materiality, say 50% or 70%, for reasons of safety.

Expected error

2.13   Larger samples will be required when errors are expected than would be required if none were expected, in order to conclude that the *actual* error is *less* than the *tolerable* error. The size and frequency of errors is important when assessing the sample size; for the same overall error, larger fewer errors will mean a bigger sample size than for smaller more frequent errors. If the expected error rate is high then sampling may not be appropriate. When considering expected error, the auditors should consider:

(a)   errors identified in previous audits;
(b)   changes in the entity's procedures;
(c)   evidence available from other procedures.

Selection of the sample

SAS 430.4

Auditors should select sample items in such a way that the sample can be expected to be representative of the population in respect of the characteristics being tested.

2.14   The SAS makes a very important point.

> 'For a sample to be representative of the population, all items in the population are required to have an equal or known probability of being selected.'

2.15   There are a number of selection methods available, but the SAS identifies three that are commonly used.

(a) **Random selection** ensures that all items in the population have an equal chance of selection, eg by use of random number tables.

(b) **Systematic selection** involves selecting items using a constant interval between selections, the first interval having a random start. When using systematic selection auditors must ensure that the population is not structured in such a manner that the sampling interval corresponds with a particular pattern in the population.

(c) **Haphazard selection** may be an acceptable alternative to random selection provided auditors are satisfied that the sample is representative of the entire population. This method requires care to guard against making a selection which is biased, for example towards items which are easily located, as they may not be representative.

2.16 In addition the auditors may also consider for certain tests:

(a) **Stratification:** This means dividing the population being sampled into sub-populations of items with similar characteristics. By stratifying, auditors can concentrate on particular sections of the population which they feel may be vulnerable to error (for example the transactions processed by a new purchase ledger clerk).

(b) **Sequence sampling:** Sequence sampling may be used to check whether certain items have particular characteristics. For example an auditor may use a sample of 50 consecutive cheques to check whether cheques are signed by authorised signatories rather than picking 50 single cheques throughout the year. Sequence sampling may however produce samples that are not representative of the population as a whole particularly if errors occurred only during a certain part of the period.

Evaluation of sample results

> ### SAS 430.5
>
> Having carried out, on each sample item, those audit procedures which are appropriate to the particular audit objective, auditors should:
>
> (a) analyse any errors detected in the sample; and
> (b) draw inferences for the population as a whole.

Analysis of errors in the sample

2.17 To begin with, the auditors must consider whether the items in question are **true errors**, as they defined them before the test, eg a misposting between customer accounts will not affect the total debtors. When the expected audit evidence regarding a specific sample item cannot be found, the auditors may be able to obtain sufficient appropriate audit evidence by performing alternative procedures. In such cases, the item is not treated as an error.

2.18 The **qualitative** aspects of errors should also be considered, including the nature and cause of the error and any possible effects the error might have on other parts of the audit.

2.19 Where common features are discovered in errors, the auditors may decide to identify all items in the population which possess the common feature (eg location), thereby producing a sub-population. Audit procedures could then be extended in this area and separate analysis could then be performed based on the items examined for each sub-population.

Inferences to be drawn from the population as a whole

2.20 The auditors should project the error results from the sample on to the relevant population. The projection method should be consistent with the method used to select the sampling unit. The auditors will:

(a) **estimate** the **probable error** in the population by extrapolating the errors found in the sample; and then

(b) **estimate** any **further error** that might not have been detected because of the imprecision of the technique (in addition to consideration of the qualitative aspects of the errors).

2.21 The auditors should then compare the projected population error (net of adjustments made by the entity in the case of substantive procedures) to the tolerable error, taking account of other audit procedures relevant to the specific control or financial statement assertion.

2.22 If the projected population error *exceeds* tolerable error, then the auditors should re-assess sampling risk. If it is unacceptable, they should consider extending auditing procedures or performing alternative procedures, either of which may result in a proposed adjustment to the financial statements.

2.23 **Section summary**

Key stages in the sampling process are:

- Determining **objectives** and **population**
- Determining **sample size**
- **Choosing method** of **sample selection**
- **Analysing** the **results** and **projecting errors**

3   SAMPLING PROCEDURES

Tests of controls: Attribute sampling

3.1 Attribute sampling is concerned with sampling units which can only take one of two possible values (say 0 or 1). It is generally used to provide information about either the rate of occurrence of an event or of certain characteristics in a population. It can thus be used to measure what proportion of items in a population have a particular property and what proportion of items do not have that property.

3.2 Attribute sampling deals only with rates of occurrence of events not monetary amounts and is therefore primarily used in tests of controls. Each occurrence of, or deviation from, a prescribed control procedure is given equal weight in the evaluation of the results, regardless of the monetary amount of the transaction. However, one statistical sampling approach, **monetary unit sampling**, uses attribute sampling theory to express a conclusion in monetary amounts.

3.3 In attribute sampling the sample size is calculated as:

$$\text{Sample size} = \frac{\text{Reliability factor}}{\text{Precision}}$$

where the *reliability factor*, taken from tables, is associated with the level of assurance the auditors want or need to obtain from the test. Such a table is given below and it shows the relationship between risk levels, and the reliability factor.

Risk level	Reliability factor	
	No errors expected	*One error expected*
1%	4.6	6.61
5%	3.0	4.75
10%	2.3	3.89
15%	1.9	3.38
20%	1.6	3.00
30%	1.2	2.44

3.4 The **precision level** is the number of errors the auditors are willing to accept in a population to be assured that the population is correct. For example, if the auditors decide that the population could be accepted as correct with no more than a 10% (say) risk that two or more out of every 100 items was incorrect, then the precision level would be 0.03 (in other words, less than three are incorrect).

Question 2

Calculate the sample sizes which should be used in tests of control in the following circumstances.

(a) No errors anticipated in the sample; accept 5% risk that four or more items in 100 are incorrect in the population.

(b) One error anticipated in the sample; accept 1% risk that three or more items in 100 are incorrect in the population.

Answer

(a) Sample size = $\dfrac{3.0}{0.05}$ = 60 items

(b) Sample size = $\dfrac{6.61}{0.04}$ = 165 items

3.5 Many auditing firms (particularly large firms) will standardise their approach to attribute sampling by giving set sample sizes for given planned levels of reliance. This standard approach is based on the assumption that the recommended sample sizes approximate to the sizes which would be obtained if the above reliability formula were applied.

3.6 Given below is a table which demonstrates this approach. The number of deviations allowed does not rise over two on the assumption that more than two deviations will automatically lead to the conclusion that testing of controls should not take place as the control(s) cannot be relied on.

Planned reliance (degree)	Deviations expected	Sample size
Low	0	15
	1	25
	2	40
Moderate	0	30
	1	50
	2	75
High	0	45
	1	80
	2	110

3.7   The test is then started. If it becomes apparent that the anticipated error rate of two or less has in fact been underestimated, the auditors may decide to abandon the half completed test and go straight away to substantive testing.

3.8   In order to interpret the results of the test and give an analysis of the degree of reliance warranted, a table such as the one shown below would be given.

	Degree of reliance warranted for number of errors found in sample						
Sample size	*0*	*1*	*2*	*3*	*4-5*	*6-7*	*8+*
15	L	N	N	N	N	N	N
25	L	L	N	N	N	N	N
30	M	L	N	N	N	N	N
40	M	L	L	N	N	N	N
45/50	H	M	L	L	N	N	N
75/80	H	H	M	M	L	L	N
110	H	H	H	M	M	L	L

Key   N = None   M = Moderate
         L = Low   H = High

3.9   Although the method of attribute sampling appears to be statistically acceptable, there is a perception problem which is at risk of being hidden by numbers. What does it really mean when the auditors state that they are 99% confident that a control will only fail once for every 100 times it is used?

Substantive procedures: Variables sampling

3.10   **Variables sampling** is concerned with sampling units which can take a value within a continuous range of possible values and is used to provide conclusions as to the monetary value of a population. The auditors can use it to:

   (a)   **estimate** the **value** of a **population** by extrapolating statistically the value of a representative sample of items drawn from the population;

   (b)   **determine** the **accuracy** of a **population** that has already been ascribed a value (generally described as 'hypothesis testing').

3.11   Thus auditors can use variables sampling both in an auditing context to test the amounts of populations such as debtors, payroll expense and fixed assets additions, and also in an accounting context to value populations such as stock by counting and pricing only a proportion of the items in the population.

3.12   The proper use of variables sampling involves the estimation of the number of units in a population *and* the calculation of the standard deviation of the population. This can be difficult and time consuming as test samples must be used to obtain the relevant information. To avoid these problems *Monetary Unit Sampling (MUS)* was developed.

Monetary unit sampling (MUS)

3.13   MUS has two main characteristics: items are selected for testing by weighting the items in proportion to their value and inferences are drawn based on 'attribute sampling' concepts.

3.14   MUS produces conclusions based on monetary amounts, *not* occurrence rates, by defining each £1 of a population as a separate sampling unit. Thus, a purchase ledger of

£3.6m is described as a population of 3.6m sampling units of £1; an individual balance of £4,000 merely represents 4,000 £1 sampling units.

3.15   We saw above that the sample size under attribute sampling was calculated as:

$$\text{Sample size} = \frac{\text{Reliability factor}}{\text{Precision}}$$

3.16   This formula is restated in monetary terms for MUS.

$$\text{Precision (as above)} = \frac{\text{Tolerable error}}{\text{Population value}}$$

Thus:

$$\text{Sample size} = \frac{\text{Reliability factor} \times \text{Population value}}{\text{Tolerable error}}$$

3.17   Having calculated the sample size, the auditors can then select the sample items. Firstly, the sampling interval must be calculated using either:

$$\text{Sampling interval} = \frac{\text{Population value}}{\text{Sample size}}$$

or

$$\text{Sampling interval} = \frac{\text{Tolerable error}}{\text{Reliability factor}}$$

3.18   Given a sample size of £X, the auditors will then select every X sampling unit in the population, starting from zero and added cumulatively (0, X, 2X etc), starting from a random point in the population.

Question 3

Using the information in (a) in Exercise 2 above, show the selection of sample items, given that:

(a)   tolerable error = £200,000;

(b)   population value = £5m;

(c)   random start at item 10,000;

(d)   the first ten ledger balances on the ledger in question are: £25,000; £27,250; £75,100; £8,450; £9,900; £1,720; £98,210; £227,190; £3,590; £48,620.

Answer

$$\text{Sample size} = \frac{\text{Reliability factor} \times \text{Population value}}{\text{Tolerable error}}$$

$$= \frac{3.0 \times 5,000,000}{200,000} = 75$$

$$\text{Sampling interval} = \frac{\text{Population value}}{\text{Sample size}}$$

$$= \frac{£5,000,000}{75} = £66,666$$

The sample will be selected as follows.

Ledger balance £	Value £	Cumulative value £	Select pound £
1	25,000	25,000	10,000
2	27,250	52,250	
3	75,100	127,350	76,666
4	8,450	135,800	
5	9,900	145,700	143,332
6	1,720	147,420	
7	98,210	245,630	209,998
8	227,190	472,820	276,664
			343,330
			409,996
9	3,590	476,410	
10	48,620	525,030	476,662
etc	etc	etc	etc

3.19 The sample in the above exercise will not be as great as 75 because of item 8 on the ledger (and other balances of a similar value will have the same effect). This demonstrates one of the advantages of MUS in that all items larger than the sampling interval will be selected. This selection of larger items gives a weighting which makes the reduction in the sample size acceptable.

Evaluation of MUS results

3.20 Where no errors are found in the sample, then the 'precision' achieved will be that predicted in terms of 'tolerable error' by the auditors before the test was carried out. The conclusion can then be drawn that the population from which the sample is drawn is not overstated by more than the monetary precision specified here (usually materiality).

3.21 This conclusion cannot be drawn when errors are found. It is then necessary to differentiate between two different types of error.

3.22 Where an error is in an item *larger* than the sampling interval, the auditors will be assured that the absolute amount of error in this top 'strata' of balances is known, because *all* such items have been examined in the test.

3.23 Where an error is found in an item which is *smaller* than the sampling interval, then it will be necessary to *project* the level of error on to the rest of the population.

3.24 This projection has two aspects.

(a) Estimating the probable error in the population.

(b) Adjusting the value of each error by a precision gap widening factor to arrive at the upper error limit. (The purpose of this is to estimate the error that may not have been found because of the imprecision of the estimation technique.)

3.25 Stage 1. *Calculate the most likely error*

The errors should be sorted into the two types mentioned above, over and under-statements. Let us use the data in Exercise 3 above and suppose that there are three errors of over-statements.

	Errors £	Item value £	% error	Sampling interval £	Expected value of error in sampling interval £
Higher value items	1,300	75,400	-	66,666	1,300
Lower value items	12,360	29,480	8%	66,666	5,333
	1,500	30,000	5%	66,666	3,333
Most likely error					9,966

3.26 Where an error is found in a lower-value item (value of item < sampling interval), the error is projected (or tainted) over the sampling interval (by multiplying sampling internal by % error). Where the error is in a higher-value item (value of item > sampling interval) the error is the exact amount of the error in the sample.

3.27 Stage 2. *Calculate upper error limit*

This involves precision gap widening. The errors are ranked in % terms and a precision gap factor applied to them, based on the risk accepted.

Error number	Precision gap widening factor	% error (tainting)	Sampling interval £	Precision gap widening £
1	0.75	8%	66,666	4,000
2	0.55	6%	66,666	2,200
				6,200

3.28 The upper error limit is calculated as follows.

	£
Sampling interval × reliability factor (66,666 × 3.0)	200,000
Most likely error	9,966
Precision gap widening	6,200
Upper error limit	216,166

The implications of this result is that there is a 5% risk that the error in the population will exceed £216,166.

3.29 If the upper error limit is greater than the tolerable error, the old audit brief recommended the following actions.

(a) Ask the client to adjust for any specific errors identified.

(b) Reconsider such aspects of the process as risk levels, tolerable error and sample size. Great care should be taken before original audit judgements are revised.

(c) Consider the need for further adjustments of the account balances concerned, for example additional debt provision.

(d) Consider the eventual form of the audit report - is a qualification or a disclaimer required?

These are consistent with the contents of SAS 430.

4   INTERNAL AUDIT

KEY TERM

Internal audit is an appraisal or monitoring activity established by management and directors, for the review of the accounting and internal control systems as a service to the entity. It functions by, amongst other things, examining, evaluating and reporting to management and the directors on the adequacy and effectiveness of components of the accounting and internal control systems.

4.1   SAS 500 *Considering the work of internal audit* examines the relationship between external and internal audit. It applies where the entity employs its own audit staff and when the internal audit function is undertaken by a third party or the external auditors. However, the SAS does *not* apply to situations where internal auditors assist external auditors in carrying out external audit tasks, but rather it applies only to internal audit activities which are relevant to the audit of the financial statements.

SAS 500.1

External auditors should consider the activities of internal audit and their effect, if any, on external audit procedures.

4.2   The SAS goes on to make a most important point.

> 'The external auditors have sole responsibility for the audit opinion expressed and for determining the nature, timing and extent of external audit procedures. All judgements relating to the audit of the financial statements are those of the external auditors. That responsibility is not reduced by any use made of internal audit work. However, internal audit work may serve to provide external auditors with audit evidence.'

Scope and objectives of internal audit

4.3   The scope and objectives of internal audit vary widely. Normally however, internal audit operates in one or more of the following broad areas.

- Review of the accounting and internal control systems

- Examination of financial and operating information

- Review of economy, efficiency and effectiveness

- Review of compliance with external regulations or internal policies

- Special investigations

Understanding and assessment of the role and scope of internal audit

SAS 500.2

The external auditors should obtain sufficient understanding of internal audit activities to assist in planning the audit and developing an effective audit approach

4.4   An effective IA function may reduce, modify or alter the timing of external audit procedures, but it can *never* eliminate them entirely. Where the IA function is deemed ineffective, it may still be useful to be aware of the IA conclusions. The effectiveness of IA will have a great impact on how the external auditors' assess the whole control system and the assessment of audit risk.

> ### SAS 500.3
>
> During the course of their planning the external auditors should perform an assessment of the internal audit function if they consider that it may be possible and desirable to rely on certain internal audit work in specific audit areas for the purpose of the external audit of the financial statements.

4.5   The following important criteria will be considered by the external auditors.

Organisational status

4.6   This involves assessing internal audit's specific status in the organisation and the effect this has on its ability to be objective.

4.7   In the ideal situation, the internal audit function reports to the highest level of management, but also has a direct line of communication to the entity's main board or audit committee, and is free of any other operating responsibility.

4.8   External auditors should consider any **constraints** or **restrictions** placed on internal audit. In particular, the internal auditors need to be free to communicate fully with the external auditors.

Scope of function

4.9   External auditors should assess the **nature** and **extent** of the **assignments** which internal audit performs. They should also consider whether management and the directors act on internal audit recommendations and how this is evidenced.

Technical competence

4.10   External auditors should ascertain whether internal audit work is performed by persons having **adequate technical training and proficiency** as internal auditors. External auditors may, for example, review the policies for hiring and training the internal audit staff and their experience and professional qualifications.

Due professional care

4.11   External auditors should assess whether internal audit work is **properly planned, supervised, reviewed and documented**. The existence of adequate audit manuals, work programmes and working papers may be considered.

Timing of liaison and co-ordination

4.12   All timing of IA work should be agreed as early as possible, and in particular how it co-ordinates with the external auditors' work. Liaison with the internal auditors should take place at regular intervals throughout the audit. Information on tests and conclusions should be passed both to and from IA.

Evaluating specific internal audit work

SAS 500.4

When the external auditors use specific internal audit work to reduce the extent of their audit procedures, they should evaluate that work to confirm its adequacy for their purposes.

4.13 The evaluation here will consider the scope of work and related audit programmes *and* whether the assessment of the IA function remains appropriate. This may include consideration of whether:

    (a) the work is performed by persons having **adequate technical training** and **proficiency** as internal auditors;

    (b) the work of assistants is **properly supervised, reviewed and documented**;

    (c) **sufficient appropriate audit evidence** is obtained to afford a reasonable basis for the conclusions reached;

    (d) the **conclusions** reached are **appropriate** in the circumstances;

    (e) any **reports** prepared by internal audit are **consistent** with the results of the work performed;

    (f) any **exceptions** or unusual matters disclosed by internal audit are **properly resolved**;

    (g) **amendments** to the external audit programme are **required** as a result of matters identified by internal audit work; and

    (h) there is a need to **test the work of internal audit** to confirm its adequacy.

4.14 If the external auditors decide that the IA work is not adequate, they should extend their procedures in order to obtain appropriate evidence.

Guidance for internal auditors

4.15 The auditing guideline *Guidance for internal auditors* is still examinable. We cover its main contents here.

KEY TERM

Internal audit is an independent appraisal function established by the management of an organisation for the review of the internal control system as a service to the organisation. It objectively examines, evaluates and reports on the adequacy of internal control as a contribution to the proper, economic, efficient and effective use of resources.

4.16 The essentials for effective internal auditing are as follows.

- Independence
- Staffing and training
- Constructive working relationships
- Due care

- Planning, controlling and recording

- Evaluation of the internal control system

- Evidence

- Reporting and follow-up

Exam focus point

You should remember the distinction between:

(a) assessing internal audit's effectiveness as part of the assessment of the accounting system (which external auditors should always do); and

(b) assessing the work of internal audit if its work is to be used as audit evidence (which will only happen if the external auditor is seeking to rely on the work of internal audit.)

Question 4

The growing recognition by management of the benefits of good internal control, and the complexities of an adequate system of internal control have led to the development of internal auditing as a form of control over all other internal controls. The emergence of the internal auditors as experts in internal control is the result of an evolutionary process similar in many ways to the evolution of independent auditing.

Required

(a) Explain why the internal and independent auditors' review of internal control procedures differ in purpose.

(b) Explain the reasons why internal auditors should or should not report their findings on internal control to the following selection of company officials:

(i)   the board of directors;
(ii) the chief accountant.

(c) Explain whether the independent auditors can place any reliance upon the internal auditors' work when the latter's main role is to be of service and assistance to management.

Answer

(a) The internal auditors review and test the system of internal control and report to management in order to improve the information received by managers and to help in their task of running the company. The internal auditors will recommend changes to the system to make sure that the management receives objective information which is efficiently produced. The internal auditors will also have a duty to search for and discover fraud.

The external auditors review the system of internal control in order to determine the extent of the substantive work required on the year end accounts. The external auditors report to the shareholders rather than the managers or directors.

External auditors usually however issue a letter of weakness to the managers, laying out any areas of weakness and recommendations for improvement in the system of internal control. The external auditors report on the truth and fairness of the financial statements, not directly on the system of internal control. The auditors do not have a specific duty to detect fraud, although they should plan their audit procedures so as to detect any material misstatement in the accounts on which they give an opinion.

(b) (i) *Board of directors*

A high level of independence is achieved by the internal auditors if they report directly to the Board. There may be problems with this approach.

(1) The members of the Board may not understand all the implications of the internal audit reports when accounting or technical information is required.

(2) The Board may not have enough time to spend considering the reports in sufficient depth. Important recommendations might therefore remain unimplemented.

A way around these problems might be to delegate the review of internal audit reports to an audit committee, which would act as a kind of sub-committee to the main board. The audit committee might be made up largely of non-executive directors who have more time and more independence from the day-to-day running of the company.

(ii)   *Chief accountant*

It would be inappropriate for internal audit to report to the chief accountant, who is largely in charge of running the system of internal control. It may be feasible for him or her to receive the report as well as the Board. Otherwise, the internal audit function cannot be effectively independent as the chief accountant could suppress unfavourable reports or could just not act on the recommendations of such reports.

(c)   The internal audit function is itself part of the system of internal control: it is an internal control over internal controls. As such, the external auditors should be able to test it and, if it is found to be reliable, they can rely on it.

To check the reliability of the work of the internal auditors, I would consider the following matters.

(i)   *The degree of independence of the internal auditors*

I would assess the organisational status and reporting responsibilities of the internal auditors and consider any restrictions placed upon them. Although internal auditors are employees of the enterprise and cannot therefore be independent of it, they should be able to plan and carry out their work as they wish and have access to senior management. They should be free of any responsibility which may create a conflict of interest, and of a situation where those staff on whom they are reporting are responsible for their or their staff's appointment, promotion or pay.

(ii)   *The scope and objectives of the internal audit function*

I would examine the internal auditors' formal terms of reference and ascertain the scope and objectives of internal audit assignments.

(iii)   *Quality of work*

I would consider whether the work of internal audit is properly planned, controlled, recorded and reviewed. Examples of good practice include the existence of an adequate audit manual, plans and procedures for supervision of individual assignments, and satisfactory arrangements for ensuring adequate quality control, reporting and follow-up.

(iv)   *Technical competence*

Internal audit should be performed by persons having adequate training and competence as auditors. Indications of technical competence may be membership of an appropriate professional body or attendance at regular training courses.

(v)   *Reports*

I would consider the quality of reports issued by internal audit and find out whether management considers and acts upon such reports.

If I find that where the internal auditors' work is reliable, I will be able to place reliance on that work when appropriate. This may mean that I will need to carry out less audit work.

However, it should be emphasised that I cannot rely totally on the internal auditors' work in relation to any particular audit objective. Internal audit work provides only one form of evidence, and the internal auditors are not independent of company management. I may be able to reduce the number of items which I test, but I will not be able to leave a particular type of test (for example, a debtors' circularisation) entirely to internal audit. I remain responsible for the opinion which I form on the accounts.

Chapter roundup

- **Audit risk** is the risk that the auditors may give an inappropriate opinion on the financial statements. A risk-based audit will make use of the risk model to determine the amount and extent of audit testing. Audit risk comprises **inherent**, **control** and **detection risk.**

- There are always inherent limitations to internal controls.

- The auditors must **understand** the **accounting system** and **control environment** in order to determine the audit approach.

- Auditors should assume **control risk** is high, unless it is assessed and the assessment confirmed by tests of controls.

- SAS 430 covers **audit sampling**. The main stages of sampling are:

  o   design of the sample
  o   selection of the sample
  o   evaluation of sample results

- **Sample sizes for tests of control** are influenced by:

  o   sampling risk
  o   tolerable error rate
  o   expected error rate

- **Sample sizes for substantive tests** are influenced by:

  o   inherent, control and detection risk
  o   tolerable error rate
  o   expected error rate
  o   population value
  o   stratification

- Sampling is not always possible or desirable and each set of circumstances must be judged for the appropriateness of testing procedures.

- **Attribute sampling** is suitable for **tests of controls** and it is based on calculation of a sample size in relation to a reliability factor and an acceptable precision level.

- **Variables sampling** is suitable for **substantive procedures** but in its true form it is time consuming and difficult.

- **Monetary unit sampling (MUS)** makes it much easier to test populations substantively, by adopting many of the techniques in attribute sampling.

- When evaluating results, auditors should:

  o   **analyse any errors**, considering the amounts and the reasons why they have occurred
  o   draw conclusions for the population as a whole

- The work of **internal audit** to some extent complements the work of external audit but there are several important differences.

- **External auditors** may rely on the work of internal audit provided it has been assessed as a reliable internal control. General criteria for assessment include:

  o   organisational status
  o   scope of function
  o   technical competence
  o   due professional care

Quick quiz

1   In relation to inherent risk, what factors should the auditors consider at the entity level? (see para 1.7) and at the account balance and class of transaction level? (1.8)

2   Define the control environment. (1.10)

3   What are the eight types of control procedure listed by SAS 300? (1.11)

4   What are the inherent limitations of an internal control system? (1.13)

5   Why must auditors obtain an understanding of the clients' accounting system? (1.15)

6   What types of procedure will be included in tests of control? (1.28)

7   Can substantive procedures ever be abandoned entirely? (1.41)

8   Define 'audit sampling'. (2.1)

9   How should the auditors proceed using audit sampling methods? (2.4)

10 What criteria must the population from which a sample is drawn fulfil? (2.5)

11 What is the effect of the expected error rate on sample sizes in tests of control and substantive tests? (2.8, *Tables*)

12 How does control risk affect tests of control? (2.9)

13 Which three methods of sample selection does SAS 430 identify? Define them. (2.15)

14 How should the auditors project the error results from the sample onto the relevant population? (2.20)

15 Define the 'precision level'. (3.4)

16 What is variables sampling? (3.10)

17 Can the internal auditors share the responsibility for the external auditors' opinion? (4.2)

18 What areas normally fall within the scope of internal audit? (4.3)

19 What criteria will be considered by the external auditors when deciding whether to rely on the work of internal audit? (4.6 - 4.11)

Question to try	Level	Marks	Time
6	Exam	25	45 mins

Chapter 7

SUBSTANTIVE TESTING AND ANALYTICAL REVIEW

Chapter topic list	Syllabus reference
1 Substantive procedures and directional testing	5(a)
2 Analytical procedures	5(a), (g)
3 Accounting estimates	5(a)

Introduction

The results of substantive analysis and testing has a direct impact on the financial accounts of a company.

Some aspects of substantive testing were covered in the last chapter, but the most important chapter relating to substantive testing is Chapter 4 which considers the nature of audit evidence. You should pay particular attention to what each type of test of detail can achieve. Scrutiny tests for example can be used to identify items that have not been included in the accounts, or unusual items which may indicate fraud or illegal acts.

You should be familiar with analytical procedures from your Paper 6 studies, but the new SAS on the subject is covered in full here. Analytical review was examined in June 1997, in a question where various financial indicators showed going concern problems.

1   SUBSTANTIVE PROCEDURES AND DIRECTIONAL TESTING   6/96

1.1   We saw earlier how the results of substantive procedures can affect the financial accounts. Most substantive tests will uncover absolute errors or errors which must be extrapolated across the rest of the population to produce an estimated expected error. Remember that adjustment will only be required for the total error if it is **material**. There are a few other points we can make about substantive testing.

Substantive analysis

1.2   Substantive analysis is the entire substantive section of the audit.

1.3   In this context, substantive testing is often referred to as 'tests of details'. The tests of details are of transactions and account balances. They will involve the following procedures.

(a)   Scrutiny of records for unusual items
(b)   Recomputation and test of clerical accuracy
(c)   Inspection of critical forms/documents
(d)   Confirmation
(e)   Observation and enquiry

(f)   Cut off tests

(g)   Analysis of accounts

(h)   Control account reconciliation

(i)   Physical inspection

(j)   Analytical procedures (see Section 2)

Directional testing

1.4   Broadly speaking, substantive procedures can be said to fall into two categories:

(a)   tests to discover errors (resulting in over- or under-statement); and

(b)   tests to discover omissions (resulting in under-statement).

Tests designed to discover errors

1.5   These tests will start with the **accounting records** in which the transactions are recorded and check from the entries to supporting documents or other evidence. Such tests should detect any over-statement and also any under-statement through causes other than omission.

Case example: test for errors

If the test is designed to ensure that sales are priced correctly, the test would begin with a sales invoice selected from the sales ledger. Prices would then be checked to the official price list.

Tests designed to discover omissions

1.6   These tests must start from **outside the accounting records** and then check back to those records. Understatements through omission will never be revealed by starting with the account itself as there is clearly no chance of selecting items that have been omitted from the account.

Case example: tests for omission

If the test is designed to discover whether all raw material purchases have been properly processed, the test would start, say, with goods received notes, to be checked to the stock records or purchase ledger.

Directional testing

1.7   For most systems auditors would include tests designed to discover both errors and omissions. The type of test, and direction of the test, should be recognised before selecting the test sample. If the sample which tested the accuracy and validity of the sales ledger were chosen from a file of sales invoices then it would not substantiate the fact that there were no errors in the sales ledger. The approach known as 'directional testing' applies this testing discipline.

1.8   Directional testing is particularly appropriate when testing the financial statement assertions of existence, completeness, rights and obligations, and valuation.

Directional testing and double entry

1.9 The concept of directional testing derives from the principle of double-entry bookkeeping, in that for every **debit** there is a **corresponding credit**, (assuming that the double entry is complete and that the accounting records balance). Therefore, any **misstatement** of a **debit entry** will result in either a corresponding **misstatement** of a **credit entry** or a **misstatement** in the opposite direction, of **another debit entry**. By designing audit tests carefully the auditors are able to use this principle in drawing audit conclusions, not only about the debit or credit entries that they have directly tested, but also about the corresponding credit or debit entries that are necessary to balance the books.

1.10 Tests are therefore designed in the following way.

Test item	Example
Test **debit items** (expenditure or assets) for overstatement by selecting debit entries recorded in the nominal ledger and checking value, existence and ownership	If a fixed asset entry in the nominal ledger of £1,000 is selected, it would be overstated if it should have been recorded at anything less than £1,000 or if the company did not own it, or indeed if it did not exist (eg it had been sold or the amount of £1,000 in fact represented a revenue expense)
Test **credit items** (income or liabilities) for understatement by selecting items from appropriate sources independent of the nominal ledger and ensuring that they result in the correct nominal ledger entry	Select a goods despatched note and check that the resultant sale has been recorded in the nominal ledger sales account. Sales would be understated if the nominal ledger did not reflect the transaction at all (completeness) or reflected it at less than full value (say if goods valued at £1,000 were recorded in the sales account at £900, there would be an understatement of £100).

1.11 The matrix set out below demonstrates how directional testing is applied to give assurance on all account areas in the financial statements.

Type of account	Purpose of primary test	Assets	Liabilities	Income	Expenses
			Primary test also gives comfort on		
Assets	Overstatement (O)	U	O	O	U
Liabilities	Understatement (U)	U	O	O	U
Income	Understatement (U)	U	O	O	U
Expense	Overstatement (O)	U	O	O	U

1.12 Thus, a test for the overstatement of an asset simultaneously gives comfort on understatement of other assets, overstatement of liabilities, overstatement of income and understatement of expenses.

Question 1

Fill in the blank spaces.

(a) Based on double-entry bookkeeping, it can be seen from the matrix that assets can only be *understated* by virtue of:

  (i)   other assets being _____; or
  (ii) liabilities being _____; or
  (iii) income being _____; or
  (iv) expenses being _____.

(b) Similarly, liabilities can only be *overstated* by virtue of:

  (i)   assets being _____; or
  (ii) other liabilities being _____; or
  (iii) income being _____; or
  (iv) expenses being _____.

Answer

(a) (i)   overstated   (b) (i)   overstated
    (ii) understated   (ii) understated
    (iii) understated   (iii) understated
    (iv) overstated   (iv) overstated

1.13 So, by performing the primary tests shown in the matrix, the auditors obtain audit assurance in other audit areas. Successful completion of the primary tests will therefore result in them having tested all account areas both for overstatement and understatement.

1.14 The major advantage of the directional audit approach is its cost-effectiveness.

(a) Assets and expenses are tested for overstatement only, and liabilities and income for understatement only, ie items are not tested for both overstatement and understatement.

(b) It audits directly the more likely types of transactional misstatement, ie unrecorded income and improper expense (arising intentionally or unintentionally).

2   ANALYTICAL PROCEDURES

> **KEY TERM**
>
> **Analytical procedures** are the analysis of relationships
>
> (a) between items of financial data, or between items of financial and non-financial data, deriving from the same period; or
>
> (b) between comparable financial information deriving from different periods to identify consistencies and predicted patterns or significant fluctuations and unexpected relationships, and the results of investigations thereof.

SAS 410.1

Auditors should apply analytical procedures at the planning and overall review stages of the audit.

2.1 In addition to the uses of analytical procedures above, they may also be used as substantive procedures, to obtain audit evidence directly.

Nature and purpose of analytical procedures

2.2 The SAS states that analytical procedures include:

(a) The **consideration** of **comparisons** with:

    (i) Comparable information for prior periods

    (ii) Anticipated results of the entity, from budgets or forecasts

    (iii) Predictive estimates prepared by the auditors, such as an estimation of the depreciation charge for the year

    (iv) Similar industry information, such as a comparison of the entity's ratio of sales to trade debtors with industry averages, or with the ratios relating to other entities of comparable size in the same industry.

(b) Those between elements of financial information that are expected to conform to a predicted pattern based on the entity's experience, such as the relationship of gross profit to sales.

(c) Those between financial information and relevant non-financial information, such as the relationship of payroll costs to number of employees.

2.3 A variety of methods can be used to perform the procedures discussed above, ranging from simple comparisons to complex analysis using statistics, on a company level, branch level or individual account level. The choice of procedures is a matter for the auditors' professional judgement.

Analytical procedures in planning the audit

SAS 410.2

Auditors should apply analytical procedures at the planning stage to assist in understanding the entity's business, in identifying areas of potential audit risk and in planning the nature, timing and extent of other audit procedures.

2.4 Possible sources of information about the client include:

- Interim financial information
- Budgets
- Management accounts
- Non-financial information
- Bank and cash records
- VAT returns
- Board minutes
- Discussions or correspondence with the client at the year-end.

Auditors may also use specific industry information or general knowledge of current industry conditions to assess the client's performance.

2.5 As well as helping to determine the nature, timing and extent of other audit procedures, such analytical procedures may also indicate aspects of the entity's business of which the auditors were previously unaware. Auditors are looking to see if developments in the client's business have had the expected effects. They will be particularly interested in changes in audit areas where problems have occurred in the past.

Analytical procedures as substantive procedures

2.6 SAS 410 *Analytical procedures* states that auditors must decide whether using available analytical procedures as substantive procedures will be effective and efficient in reducing **detection risk** for specific financial statement assertions. Auditors may efficiently use analytical data produced by the entity itself, provided they are satisfied that it has been properly prepared.

2.7 The SAS lists a number of factors which the auditors should consider when using analytical procedures as substantive procedures.

Factors to consider	Example
The **plausibility and predictability** of the relationships identified for comparison and evaluation	The strong relationship between certain selling expenses and turnover in businesses where the sales force is paid by commission
The **objectives** of the analytical procedures and the extent to which their results are reliable	
The degree to which information can be **disaggregated**	Analytical procedures may be more effective when applied to financial information on individual sections of an operation
The **availability of information**	Financial: budgets or forecasts
	Non-financial: eg the number of units produced or sold
The **relevance of the information** available	Whether budgets are established as results to be expected rather than as goals to be achieved
The **comparability of the information** available	Broad industry data may need to be supplemented to be comparable with that of an entity that produces and sells specialised products
The **knowledge gained during previous audits**	The effectiveness of the accounting and internal control systems
	The types of problems giving rise to accounting adjustments in prior periods

2.8 From our earlier coverage of audit evidence we can see that the information used in analytical procedures will be more reliable if it comes from sources independent from, rather than internal to, the entity. Internal information produced independently from the accounting function is more reliable than that originating from within it. The results of **other audit procedures** will help to determine the reliability of the information used in analytical procedures, as will the importance of the results of the procedure for the auditors' opinion.

2.9   The SAS identifies other factors which should be considered when determining the reliance that the auditors should place on the results of analytical procedures.

Reliability factors	Example
Other audit procedures directed towards the same financial statements assertions	Other procedures auditors undertake in reviewing the collectability of debtors, such as the review of subsequent cash receipts, may confirm or dispel questions arising from the application of analytical procedures to an aged profile of customers' accounts
The **accuracy** with which the expected results of analytical procedures can be predicted	Auditors normally expect greater consistency in comparing the relationship of gross profit to sales from one period to another than in comparing discretionary expenses, such as research or advertising
The **frequency** with which a relationship is observed	A pattern repeated monthly as opposed to annually

2.10   Reliance on the results of analytical procedures depends on the auditors' assessment of the **risk** that the procedures may identify relationships (between data) as expected, whereas a material misstatement exists (ie the relationships, in fact, do not exist).

Analytical procedures as part of the overall review

SAS 410.3

When completing the audit, auditors should apply analytical procedures in forming an overall conclusion as to whether the financial statements as a whole are consistent with their knowledge of the entity's business.

2.11   The conclusions from these analytical procedures should corroborate the conclusions formed from other audit procedures on parts of the financial statements. However, these analytical procedures may highlight areas which require further investigation and audit.

Investigating significant fluctuations or unexpected relationships

SAS 410.4

When significant fluctuations or unexpected relationships are identified that are inconsistent with other relevant information or that deviate from predicted patterns, auditors should investigate and obtain adequate explanations and appropriate corroborative evidence.

2.12 Investigations will start with enquires to management and then corroboration of management's responses:

(a) by comparing them with the auditors' knowledge of the entity's business and with other evidence obtained during the course of the audit; or

(b) if the analytical procedures are being carried out as substantive procedures, by undertaking additional audit procedures where appropriate to confirm the explanations received.

2.13 If explanations cannot be given by management, or if they are insufficient, the auditors must determine which further audit procedures to undertake to explain the fluctuation.

Practical techniques   6/97

2.14 When carrying out analytical procedures, auditors should remember that every industry is different and each company within an industry differs in certain respects.

2.15 Ratios mean very little when used in isolation. They should be calculated for previous periods and for comparable companies. This may involve a certain amount of initial research, but subsequently it is just a matter of adding new statistics to the existing information each year. The permanent file should contain a section with summarised accounts and the chosen ratios for prior years.

2.16 In addition to looking at the more usual ratios the auditors should consider examining other ratios that may be relevant to the particular clients' business, such as revenue per passenger mile for an airline operator client, or fees per partner for a professional office.

2.17 One further important technique is to examine important related accounts in conjunction with each other. It is often the case that revenue and expense accounts are related to balance sheet accounts and comparisons should be made to ensure that the relationships are reasonable.

Important accounting ratios	Gross profit margins, in total and by product, area and months/quarter (if possible).
	Debtors ratio (average collection period).
	Stock turnover ratio (stock divided into cost of sales).
	Current ratio (current assets to current liabilities).
	Quick or acid test ratio (liquid assets to current liabilities).
	Gearing ratio (debt capital to equity capital).
	Return on capital employed (profit before tax to total assets less current liabilities)

Related items	Creditors and purchases.
	Stocks and cost of sales.
	Fixed assets and depreciation, repairs and maintenance expense.
	Intangible assets and amortisation.
	Loans and interest expense.
	Investments and investment income.
	Debtors and bad debt expense.
	Debtors and sales.

2.18 Other areas that might be investigated as part of the analytical procedures include the following.

- **Examine changes** in **products, customers and levels** of **returns.**

- **Assess** the effect of **price and mix changes** on the cost of sales.

- **Consider** the effect of **inflation, industrial disputes, changes in production methods** and **changes in activity** on the charge for wages.

- **Obtain explanations** for all **major variances** analysed using a standard costing system. Particular attention should be paid to those relating to the over or under absorption of overheads since these may, inter alia, affect stock valuations.

- **Compare trends in production and sales** and assess the effect on any provisions for obsolete stocks.

- **Ensure** that **changes in the percentage labour or overhead content** of production costs are also reflected in the stock valuation.

- **Review other profit and loss expenditure,** comparing:
  - rent with annual rent per rental agreement;
  - rates with previous year and known rates increases;
  - interest payable on loans with outstanding balance and interest rate per loan agreement;
  - hire or leasing charges with annual rate per agreements;
  - vehicle running expenses to vehicles;
  - other items related to activity level with general price increase and change in relevant level of activity (for example telephone expenditure will increase disproportionately if export or import business increases);
  - other items not related to activity level with general price increases (or specific increases if known).

- **Review** profit and loss account for **items** which may have been **omitted** (eg scrap sales, training levy, special contributions to pension fund, provisions for dilapidation etc).

- **Ensure expected variations** arising from the following have occurred:
  - industry or local trends;
  - known disturbances of the trading pattern (for example strikes, depot closures, failure of suppliers).

2.19 Certain of the comparisons and ratios measuring liquidity and longer-term capital structure will assist in evaluating whether the company is a going concern, in addition to contributing to the overall view of the accounts. We shall see in Chapter 9 however, that there are factors other than declining ratios that may indicate going concern problems.

2.20 The working papers must contain the completed results of analytical procedures. They should include:

- the outline programme of the work;

- the summary of significant figures and relationships for the period;

- a summary of comparisons made with budgets and with previous years;

- details of all significant fluctuations or unexpected relationships considered;

- details of the results of investigations into such fluctuations/relationships;

- the audit conclusions reached;

- information considered necessary for assisting in the planning of subsequent audits.

Exam focus point

In the exam you may be given a set of figures (as in Question 2 below) and:

(a) asked to calculate changes, key ratios etc and hence identify significant areas of the accounts;

(b) asked what audit work will be required on these significant areas.

When analysing figures, make sure that the points which you make are consistent with each other.

Question 2

You are the manager responsible for the audit of Newstead Products Ltd for the year ended 30 September 19X9. The company is a wholesaler of do-it-yourself products. It operates from rented premises; its fixed assets comprises motor vehicles, a microcomputer and some minor fixtures and fittings. The accounting records (sales ledger, purchase ledger, nominal ledger and payroll) are maintained on a microcomputer by a bookkeeper, and a part-time accountant prepares the annual accounts and quarterly management accounts.

The summarised draft accounts for the year ended 30 September 19X9, and the previous year's audited accounts, are as follows.

PROFIT AND LOSS ACCOUNTS
FOR THE YEAR ENDED 30 SEPTEMBER

	19X9	19X8
	£	£
Sales	1,043,900	506,700
Cost of sales	680,600	355,200
Gross profit	363,300	151,500
Overheads	272,100	147,400
Profits before tax	91,200	4,100
Taxation	22,800	1,100
Retained profit	68,400	3,000

BALANCE SHEET AS AT 30 SEPTEMBER

	19X9	19X8
	£	£
Fixed assets	20,400	8,900
Current assets		
Stock	173,000	52,600

Trade debtors	239,200	95,500
Prepayments	5,500	1,500
	417,700	149,600
Current liabilities		
Trade creditors	178,800	71,300
Accruals	37,800	21,200
Taxation	22,800	1,100
Bank overdraft	86,100	20,700
	325,500	114,300
Net current assets	92,200	35,300
Net assets	112,600	44,200
Director's loan account	15,400	15,400
	97,200	28,800
Called up share capital	1,000	1,000
Profit and loss account	96,200	27,800
	97,200	28,800

The company sells low value items to a large number of customers. Most sales are on credit, with less than 5% of sales being in cash. It has over 700 'live' accounts on the sales ledger of which 70% are new customers in the past year. You have carried out audit checks on the accounting systems (ie compliance tests) and these tests have shown that the systems are generally reliable. However, there is no formal system for recording receipt of goods; the only record of receipt of goods is the supplier's delivery note, but as this is not dated by the goods received department, there is a greater risk of purchases cut-off errors. Your review of the accounts is to enable you to plan the audit of the year-end accounts, so that guidance is given to the audit staff and more time is spent in areas of highest audit risk.

Required

(a) Calculate appropriate ratios for both years, and comment on the financial performance of Newstead Products Ltd for the year ended 30 September 19X9, both in comparison with the previous year and in absolute terms.

(b) From your review of the financial statements and the other matters included in the question, suggest the amount of audit work you should perform and the particular procedures you should carry out to minimise the audit risk for the following items appearing in the final accounts:

    (i) stock and gross profit margin;
    (ii) trade debtors;
    (iii) trade creditors;
    (iv) bank overdraft and cash flow forecast.

Answer

(a) Key ratios derived from the accounts are as follows.

	19X9	19X8
Gross profit percentage	34.8%	29.9%
Net profit percentage	8.74%	0.81%
Expenses/sales (%)	26.1%	29.1%
Average age of stock (months)	3.1	1.8
Average age of debtors (months)	2.7	2.3
Average age of creditors (months)	3.2	2.4
Current ratio	1.28	1.31
Acid test ratio	0.75	0.85
Bank overdraft/shareholders' funds	0.89	0.72

Sales have increased in 19X9 by 106% over 19X8. This substantial increase in turnover has been accompanied by a significant improvement in the gross profit percentage from 29.9% to 34.8%. Over the same period, liquidity has declined, with the bank overdraft increasing from £20,700 to £86,100. The increase in stocks and creditors has been financed in part by this increase in the bank overdraft. The average age of stock held has increased significantly, raising the possibility that stocks have been overvalued. The average age of debtors has also increased, raising the possibility that debtors may be overstated. The average age of trade creditors has increased which suggests that, provided that cut off is correct and that there have not been significant misclassifications of amounts between account headings, the average settlement period has increased. This delay in settlement has been used as a source of finance for working capital requirements; presumably, creditors will not be prepared to allow much more lengthening of the settlement period.

As already mentioned, there is the possibility that stocks have been overvalued. Given also the absence of a proper system for recording purchases receipts, there could be errors in the accounts which go towards explaining the increase in gross profit margin.

Especially since sales have increased so much, it may be that sales vary significantly at different times of the year. The average age of stocks, debtors and creditors calculated above have been based on annual sales and cost of sales figures rather than on monthly figures. It should therefore be borne in mind that the increases in these ratios on a monthly basis may not be as high as those calculated above.

(b)   The particular points I would address are set out below.

    (i)   Stock values have increased by 229%, and the gross profit percentage has increased substantially. In considering whether stocks have been overvalued, I would consider the following.

        (1)   Has the counting of stocks been carried out completely and accurately? Have all stocks been counted once and once only, and has the summarisation of stocks been computed accurately?

        (2)   Is stock valued at the lower of cost and net realisable value (NRV)? In order to test for NRV, I would check a sample of stock lines of significant value to selling prices after the year end. If items are sold at less than cost, they should be valued at NRV.

        (3)   Is the recording of costs of stocks correct? I would check a sample of significant value items to the relevant purchase invoices, and check calculations.

        (4)   Are slow moving or obsolete stocks provided against, or otherwise correctly valued at the lower of cost and net realisable value? Records of stock movements are probably limited, but the techniques of enquiry and observation may help to identify any errors which may have been made.

        (5)   Has sales cut-off been performed correctly, with stock despatched before the year end being included as sales but not in year-end stocks, and stocks despatched after the year-end being recorded in year-end stocks but not in the year's sales? I would check a small sample of despatches each side of the year-end.

        (6)   In view of the lack of a proper system of recording the date goods were received, has the purchases cut-off been performed correctly? Goods received before the year-end should be recorded as purchases in the year, with the invoices either posted to the purchase ledger before the year end, or included in the year-end accruals. I would check a sample of goods received each side of the year-end to ensure correct treatment, and check the reconciliation of the statements of major suppliers.

        (7)   The increase in gross profit percentage should be discussed with management in order to establish if there is any known reason for the increase. Given the type of merchandise involved, it would be unusual for gross profit margins to fluctuate much, and so we can expect that management should be aware of any specific reason for the increase. A reasonableness check can be carried out on the gross profit percentage by checking sales prices from sales invoices with purchase prices from purchase invoices for sample of major stock lines and calculating a weighted gross profit margin to compare with that included in the accounts. the weighted gross profit margin is higher than that in the accounts, part of the difference may be due to wastage of stock or to some minor slow-moving items being sold with a lower gross profit margin.

    (ii)   Debtors have increased by 150%, and the average age of debtors has increased from 2.3 months to 2.7 months. The increase in the age of debtors suggests that the business may be allowing too much credit to customers, and that the level of the bad debt provision should be examined carefully.

         The reconciliation from the sales ledger control account to the listing of individual debtor balances should be checked, and any reconciling items should be explained.

         The ageing of debts in the sales ledger should be checked, and debts over three months old should be listed and reviewed. A positive debtors' circularisation should be carried out.

         Cash received from debtors after the balance sheet date should be reviewed. Any significant balances not cleared at the time of the audit should be discussed with management and investigated further where considered necessary.

A listing of doubtful debts should be obtained and discussed with management. The provisions made against doubtful debts should be reviewed by discussion with the credit controller and examination of correspondence files and supporting documentation.

Credit notes issued after the end of the year should be reviewed. If they provide credit in respect of goods despatched before the year end, a credit note provision should be made in the year-end accounts.

Sales cut-off will be checked, as already stated in (i) above.

(iii) The most important audit objective concerning creditors is normally that of completeness.

I would check the reconciliation from the purchase ledger control account to the list of individual purchase ledger balances, and investigate any reconciling items.

I would check from supplier statements to balances on the purchase ledger. Invoices included on suppliers' statements but not on the purchase ledger should be included in accruals provided that the goods are included in stocks.

Purchases cut-off should be checked, as already described in (i) above.

The average age of creditors has increased from 2.4 months to 3.2 months during 19X9. This raises the question of whether this increase in the average settlement period can be sustained, a point which is considered further below.

(iv) A standard letter confirming the overdraft balance will be obtained from the bank, and the bank reconciliation will be reviewed and reperformed. The overdraft has increased substantially during the year. This raises the question of whether the bank will be prepared to continue to finance the company to the level required. I shall therefore seek documentary evidence of the extent of the bank overdraft facility and check the date it is due for review. The facility available should be compared with anticipated overdraft requirements as shown in the company's cash flow forecast. The reliability of the forecast may be judged in part by considering the record of the accuracy of forecasts in periods to date. The figures included in the forecasts for sales, gross profit, and the average ages of stock, debtors and creditors, should be reviewed for reasonableness. I would enquire whether the company is experiencing any problems with suppliers, whose settlement periods are being stretched increasingly. I would check whether the cash flow forecast anticipates a similar average settlement period being maintained. I would assess whether, in the light of other information, this assumption is reasonable.

3 ACCOUNTING ESTIMATES

3.1 SAS 420 *Audit of accounting estimates* provides guidance on the audit of accounting estimates contained in financial statements.

SAS 420.1

Auditors should obtain sufficient appropriate audit evidence regarding accounting estimates.

KEY TERM

An **accounting estimate** is an approximation of the amount of an item in the absence of a precise means of measurement.   *(APB Glossary of terms)*

3.2 SAS 420 gives these examples.

- Allowances to reduce stocks and debtors to their estimated realisable value
- Depreciation provisions
- Accrued revenue
- Provision for a loss from a lawsuit

- Profits or losses on construction contracts in progress
- Provision to meet warranty claims

3.3 **Directors and management** are responsible for making accounting estimates included in the financial statements. These estimates are often made in conditions of uncertainty regarding the outcome of events and involve the use of judgement. The risk of a material misstatement therefore increases when accounting estimates are involved. Audit evidence supporting accounting estimates is generally less than conclusive and so auditors need to exercise greater judgement than in other areas of an audit.

The nature of accounting estimates

3.4 A great deal of skill and knowledge may be required to determine a very complex accounting estimate.

3.5 Accounting estimates may be produced as part of the routine operations of the accounting system, or may be a non-routine procedure at the period end. Where, as is frequently the case, a **formula** based on past experience is used to calculate the estimate, it should be reviewed regularly by management (eg actual vs estimate in prior periods).

Case examples: nature of accounting estimates

From a routine operation: a warranty provision calculated automatically as a percentage of sales revenue.

From a non-routine operation: a provision for legal costs and damages payable in an impending legal dispute.

Using a standard formula: the use of standard rates for depreciating each category of fixed assets.

3.6 If there is no objective data to assess the item, or if it is surrounded by uncertainty, the auditors should consider the implications for their report.

Audit procedures

SAS 420.2

Auditors should obtain sufficient appropriate evidence as to whether an accounting estimate is reasonable in the circumstances and, when required, is appropriately disclosed.

3.7 The auditors should gain an understanding of the procedures and methods used by management to make accounting estimates. This will aid the auditors' planning of their own procedures.

SAS 420.3

Auditors should adopt one or a combination of the following approaches in the audit of an accounting estimate:

(a) review and test the process used by management or the directors to develop the estimate;

(b) use an independent estimate for comparison with that prepared by management or the directors; or

(c) review subsequent events.

Review and testing the process

3.8 The auditors will carry out these steps.

- **Evaluate the data** and **consider the assumptions** on which the estimate is based
- **Test the calculations** involved in the estimate
- **Compare estimates** made for **prior periods** with **actual results** of those periods
- **Consider management's**/directors' **review and approval procedures**

Use of an independent estimate

3.9 Such an estimate (made or obtained by the auditors) may be compared with the accounting estimate. The auditors should evaluate the data, consider the assumptions and test the calculation procedures used to develop the independent estimate. Prior period independent assessments and actual results could also be compared.

Review of subsequent events

3.10 The auditors should review transactions or events after the period end which may reduce or even remove the need to test accounting estimates (as described above).

Evaluation of results of audit procedures

SAS 420.4

Auditors should make a final assessment of the reasonableness of the accounting estimate based on their knowledge of the business and whether the estimate is consistent with other audit evidence obtained during the audit.

3.11 Auditors must assess the differences between the amount of an estimate supported by evidence and the estimate calculated by management. If the difference is reasonable then no adjustment may be required; *but* the **cumulative differences** relating to accounting estimates should not be all in one direction, so that the cumulative effect on the financial statements is material.

3.12 If the auditors believe that the difference is unreasonable then an adjustment should be made. If the directors or management refuse to revise the estimate, then the difference is considered a misstatement and will be treated as such.

Chapter roundup

- **Analytical procedures** cover comparisons of financial data with other financial or non-financial data of the same or previous periods, also comparisons of financial data with expected data.

- Analytical procedures aim to **identify inconsistencies** or **significant fluctuations**.

- Analytical procedures must be undertaken at the **planning** stage of audits.

- Analytical procedures can be used as substantive procedures, depending on the **available information** and the plausibility and predictability of the relationships.

- Analytical review should be undertaken at the **final stage** of an audit on the final accounts.

- **Significant fluctuations** and **unexpected variations** should be investigated by enquiries of management, comparisons with other evidence and further audit procedures as required.

- Accounts may contain **accounting estimates** in a number of areas.

- Auditors can test accounting estimates by:

    o **Reviewing** and **testing** the management process
    o **Using an independent estimate**
    o **Reviewing subsequent events**

Quick quiz

1   What are the main methods used in 'substantive procedures'? (see para 1.3)

2   In directional testing, what are debit items and credit items tested for respectively? (1.10)

3   What factors should auditors consider when using analytical procedures as substantive procedures? (2.7 – 2.9)

4   What investigations will the auditors undertake when they find significant fluctuations or unexpected relationships during analytical procedures? (2.12)

5   List four sets of related accounts. (2.17)

6   Give four examples of accounting estimates. (3.2)

7   Who is responsible for making accounting estimates? (3.3)

8   How should the auditors assess accounting estimates? (3.7)

Question to try	Level	Marks	Time
7	Exam	15	27 mins

Chapter 8

COMPUTER AUDITING

Chapter topic list	Syllabus reference
1 Computers in audit administration	5 (a), (b), 6 (b)
2 Auditing in a computer environment	5 (a), (b), 6 (b)
3 Types of Computer Assisted Audit Techniques (CAATs)	5 (a), (b), 6 (b)
4 Controls in on-line and real-time systems	5 (a), 6 (b)
5 Control problems in small computer systems	5 (a), 6 (b)
6 Bureaux and software houses	5 (a), 6 (b)
7 Systems development	5 (a), 6 (b)
8 Computer fraud	5 (a), 6 (b)
9 Developments in the computerised environment	5 (a), 6 (b)
10 Year 2000	5 (a), 6 (b)

Introduction

Much of this material should be familiar to you from your Paper 6 studies. The first section covers some of the main audit tools the computer auditor is likely to meet in practice.

Auditing in a computer environment requires special knowledge and skills. It is true to say, however, that the principles of auditing and internal controls, discussed in earlier chapters, still apply. You should bear this in mind as you work through this chapter. Computers have simplified many audit tasks. An important decision when deciding how to test computerised systems is to decide whether Computer Assisted Audit Techniques should be used.

Key controls are **authorisation** and **access** controls. You should also appreciate the potential problems auditors face when auditing a computer system, in particular the **loss of audit trail**.

This chapter also covers current areas of particular concern to auditors, including **on-line systems**, **computer fraud**, use of the **Internet** and other developments in the computerised environment.

1   COMPUTERS IN AUDIT ADMINISTRATION   6/94, 6/95

1.1 These days it is unusual to find a business, whatever its size, without a computer of some sort. We will consider how the computerisation of client records affects the auditors in the rest of this chapter. To begin with, however, we will consider how auditors use computers themselves, as an audit tool to aid audit automation.

1.2 Until recently, auditing firms used computers for very basic administrative functions. Programs have now been developed which allow more sophisticated use of computers in the audit.

Working papers

1.3 **Automated** working paper packages have been developed which can make the documenting of audit work much easier. Such programs will aid preparation of working papers, lead schedules, trial balance and the financial statements themselves. These are automatically cross referenced and balanced by the computer. Whenever an adjustment is made, the computer will automatically update all the necessary schedules, including the trial balance, rather than the auditor having to do so manually (a laborious task!).

1.4 The **advantages** of automated working papers are as follows.

(a) The risk of errors is reduced.

(b) The working papers will be neater and easier to review.

(c) The time saved will be substantial as adjustments can be made easily to all working papers, including working papers summarising the key analytical information.

(d) Standard forms do not have to be carried to audit locations.

(e) Audit working papers can be transmitted for review via a modem, or fax facilities (if both the sending and receiving computers have fax boards and fax software).

1.5 Standard word processing software is all that is needed to develop and use a reasonably satisfactory system of electronic audit working papers. It can be used for other purposes such as drafting the audit report, preferably towards the end of the audit field work. A system combining office packages such as Word, Excel or Access may have special advantages as it can be designed to allow logical steps to be automated, as follows.

(a) *Automated checking of electronic working papers for completeness*

(i) Is there evidence of supervision and review on each schedule?
(ii) Is there an audit conclusion on each lead schedule?
(iii) Have all points raised by the auditors on 'audit point sheets' been answered?

(b) *Automated checking of electronic working papers for accuracy*

(i) Are all the totals of numeric data consistent?
(ii) Do numeric totals carry forward accurately to lead schedule?

(c) *Automated processing*

(i) Footing and crossfooting (standard word processing software can also do this).
(ii) Carry forward of numeric data to lead schedules.
(iii) Highlight proposed audit recommendations for audit management review.
(iv) Consolidate and reformat material contained within the audit working papers in order to prepare the draft audit report.

1.6 More generally, the audit can be assisted or facilitated by software dealing with graphics production image processing and desk-top publishing. Auditors may also benefit from on-line accessing and real-time file updating.

Statistical sampling and analytical procedures

1.7 Auditors can now use software packages to perform analytical procedures. These packages are most useful when information can be input directly from the client's computer system. This information can be added to year after year, building up cumulative data.

1.8 Such information can also be used for statistical sampling. The package can then perform such tasks as determining sample sizes, computing standard ratios, generating random numbers from a given sequence and evaluating results from tests based on samples.

Decision support systems

1.9 These systems involve judgmental processes which would normally only be carried out by a 'human' auditor. The main developments in this area include the automation of checklists, such as those used for internal control evaluation, statutory requirements and materiality estimations. These checklists are formulated so as to follow different logic paths in response to answers given at various stages of the checklist, including omitting questions.

Controls over audit computers

1.10 As with all computers (as we will see below), controls must be exercised over the input, processing and output of computers used on an audit. The main areas where controls should operate are:

(a)   security;
(b)   completeness (of input); and
(c)   accuracy (of input, processing and output).

Question 1

(a)   List two types of software which the auditors could use with a PC as an aid to audit work.

(b)   List five ways in which the auditors could use a PC as an audit aid.

(c)   What controls must be in place over a PC used in an audit?

Answer

(a)   Examples of software which the auditors might use on a PC in order to aid his audit work are as follows.

   (i)   Standard software for word processing and spreadsheets which can be used to carry out the tasks listed in (b) below.

   (ii)   'Expert' systems (often developed in house by the large audit firms) which will determine sample sizes based on specified risk criteria.

(b)   A PC may be used by the auditors in order to assist their audit work as follows.

   (i)   The production of time budgets and budgetary control. The time budget by area for the audit can be produced on the PC and actual hours worked can be input to obtain a variance. The variance which arises on the interim audit can be used as a basis for updating the final audit time budget.

   (ii)   The production of working papers, in particular lead schedules, trial balances and schedules of errors.

   (iii)   Analytical procedures can be more efficiently carried out on a PC as the necessary calculations can be carried out at much greater speed and year-on-year information built up.

   (iv)   The production and retention of audit programmes. These can then be reviewed and updated from year to year.

   (v)   The maintenance of permanent file information (for example systems) which can be updated from one year to the next.

(c)   Controls which must be exercised when PCs are used by the auditors in their work are as follows.

   (i)   Access controls for users by means of passwords.

(ii)   Back-up of data contained on files, regular production of hard copy; back-up disks held off the premises.

(iii)   Viral protection for programmes.

(iv)   Training for users.

(v)   Evaluation and testing of programs before use.

(vi)   Proper recording of input data, to ensure reasonableness of output.

2 AUDITING IN A COMPUTER ENVIRONMENT 6/94, 6/95

2.1   The expansion in the use of computers for accounting purposes will certainly continue. Auditors must therefore be able to cope with the special problems that arise when auditing in a computer environment and keep abreast of technical innovation.

2.2   First we look in a rather general way at the nature of controls in a computer environment. Broad guidance is provided for the auditor in the form of the old APC operational guideline *Auditing in a computer environment*. This guideline has not been replaced by a new APB auditing standard, so it is followed here as it still demonstrates best practice for the most part. The introduction to this guideline sets the scene.

> 'Computer systems record and process transactions in a manner which is significantly different from manual systems, giving rise to such possibilities as a lack of visible evidence and systematic errors. As a result, when auditing in a computer environment, the auditor will need to take into account additional considerations relating to the techniques available to him, the timing of his work, the form in which the accounting records are maintained, the internal controls which exist, the availability of the data and the length of time it is retained in readily usable form.'

2.3   Internal controls over computer-based accounting systems may be considered under the following two main headings.

KEY TERMS

Application controls relate to the transactions and standing data appertaining to each computer-based accounting system and are therefore specific to each such application.

The objectives of application controls, which may be manual or programmed, are to ensure the completeness and accuracy of the accounting records and the validity of the entries made in these records resulting from both manual and programmed processing.

General controls are controls, other than application controls, which relate to the environment within which computer based accounting systems are developed, maintained and operated, and which are therefore applicable to all the applications. The objectives of general controls are to ensure the proper development and implementation of applications and the integrity of program and data files and of computer operations. Like application controls, general controls may be either manual or programmed.

2.4   Application controls and general controls are inter-related. Strong general controls contribute to the assurance which may be obtained by an auditor in relation to application controls. On the other hand, unsatisfactory general controls may undermine strong application controls or exacerbate unsatisfactory application controls.

2.5   You have already studied application and general controls in your earlier studies. These exercises will help you revise typical or desirable application and general controls.

Question 2

To achieve the overall objectives of application controls, the specific requirements are:

(a)   controls over the completeness, accuracy and authorisation of input;
(b)   controls over the completeness and accuracy of processing;
(c)   controls over the maintenance of master files and the standing data contained therein.

Required

List the typical controls which would fulfil those requirements.

Answer

(a)   *Controls over input*

Control techniques for ensuring the completeness of input in a timely fashion include:

(i)   manual or programmed agreement of control totals;

(ii)   one for one checking of processed output to source documents;

(iii)   manual or programmed sequence checking;

(iv)   programmed matching of input to a control file, containing details of expected input;

(v)   procedures over resubmission of rejected controls.

Controls over the accuracy of Input are concerned with the data fields on input transactions. Control should be exercised not only over value fields, such as invoice amounts, but also important reference fields, such as account number or date of payment. Some of the completeness control techniques, such as a batch total, will also control accuracy but others, such as sequence checks, will not. Additional techniques to ensure accuracy include:

(i)   programmed check digit verification (a check digit included in a reference number is arithmetically checked to ensure that it bears the required relationship to the rest of the number);

(ii)   programmed reasonableness checks, including checking the logical relationship between two or more files;

(iii)   programmed existence checks against valid codes;

(iv)   manual scrutiny of output.

Controls over authorisation involve checking that all transactions are authorised and that the Individual who authorised each transaction was so empowered. This will generally involve a clerical review of input transactions, although a programmed check to detect transactions that exceed authorisation limits may be possible. The clerical review should be done either after a control total has been established or after processing, to ensure that unauthorised transactions cannot be introduced after the review.

(b)   *Controls over processing*

Controls are required to ensure that:

(i)   all input data is processed;

(ii)   the correct master files and standing data files are used;

(iii)   the processing of each transaction is accurate;

(iv)   the updating of data, and any new data generated during processing, is accurate and authorised;

(v)   output reports are complete and accurate.

The control techniques used to ensure the completeness and accuracy of input may also be used to ensure the completeness and accuracy of processing provided the techniques are applied to the results of processing, such as a batch reconciliation produced after the update and not the one produced after the initial edit. Another technique for ensuring the completeness and accuracy of processing is summary processing.

(c)   *Controls over master files and the standing data contained therein*

Techniques for ensuring the completeness, accuracy and authorisation of amendments to master files and standing data files and for ensuring the completeness and accuracy of the processing of these amendments are similar to the techniques for transaction input. However, in view of the greater importance of master files and standing data, there is often sufficient justification for using the more costly control techniques such as one for one checking. It may also be appropriate to users to check all master files and standing data, perhaps on a cyclical basis.

Controls are also required to ensure the continuing correctness of master files and the standing data contained therein. Frequently control techniques such as record counts or hash totals for the file, are established and checked by the user each time the file is used.

Question 3

To achieve the overall objectives of general controls identified in Paragraph 2.3 (b) above, controls are required:

(a)   over application development;
(b)   to prevent or detect unauthorised changes to programs;
(c)   to ensure that all program changes are adequately tested and documented;
(d)   to prevent or detect errors during program execution;
(e)   to prevent unauthorised amendments to data files;
(f)   to ensure that systems software is properly installed and maintained;
(g)   to ensure that proper documentation is kept; and
(h)   to ensure continuity of operations.

Required

Comment on the type of controls which should be found under each of these headings.

Answer

(a)   *Controls over application development*

The auditors might consider the adequacy of such matters as: system design standards, programming standards, documentation controls and standards, testing procedures, approval of development stages by users and computer management, internal audit involvement, segregation of duties for system design, programming and operations, training and supervision.

(b)   *Controls to prevent or detect unauthorised changes to programs*

This covers both accidental and fraudulent corruption of program logic during program maintenance or program execution. In addition to such matters as the segregation of duties and the training and supervision of staff for program maintenance, the auditors would consider such matters as: authorisation of jobs prior to processing, the record of program changes and its review to detect unauthorised changes, password protection of programs, emergency modification procedures, integrity of back up copies of programs, physical protection of production programs and programs stored off-line, and comparison of production programs to controlled copies. For program execution, the auditors would consider: the operations manual procedures to prevent access to programs during execution, controls over use of utility programs, restricted access to the computer and remote terminals, review of job accounting reports and investigation of unusual delays, and rotation of duties.

(c)   *Controls to ensure that all program changes are adequately tested and documented*

As program changes may range from a small alteration of an output report to a major redesign, most installations will have more than one set of standards for testing and documenting changes. The auditors would consider the adequacy of such matters as: testing procedures, documentation controls and standards, approval of changes by users and computer management, internal audit involvement, and segregation of duties, training and supervision of the staff involved.

(d)   *Controls to prevent or detect errors during program execution*

The auditors might consider the adequacy of operations controls included in the systems software, use of job control procedure libraries, an operations manual detailing set up and execution procedures, job scheduling, emergency back up procedures and training and supervision. These procedures should provide protection against errors such as incorrect data files, wrong versions of production programs, running programs in the wrong sequence, incorrect response to a program request and job control errors.

(e) *Controls to prevent unauthorised amendment to data files*

Controls to prevent unauthorised amendments to data files are dependent upon the application controls over the file, the manner in which the file is maintained and the file management software used. The auditors might consider the adequacy of such general control procedures as: authorisation of jobs prior to processing, procedures to detect unauthorised amendments, password protection and procedures for recording and investigating unauthorised access attempts, emergency modification procedures, integrity of back up files, physical protection of data files, restricted use of utility programs and the segregation of duties.

(f) *Controls to ensure that systems software is properly installed and maintained*

Systems software includes the operating system, teleprocessing monitors, data base management systems, spooling systems and other software used to increase the efficiency of processing and to control processing. The auditors should consider not only the controls exercised by the software but also the controls over the software, such as: frequency of amendments, amendment procedures, access controls and the segregation of duties.

(g) *Controls to ensure that proper documentation is kept*

Proper documentation aids efficient and accurate operations by users and computer personnel, setting up and amendments to applications, and recovery from disaster. The auditors would consider such matters as: quality of documentation, quality of standards used, enforcement of standards, internal audit involvement and updating procedures.

(h) *Controls to ensure continuity of operation*

As part of their overall assessment of the enterprise the auditors might consider the back up procedures, testing of back up facilities and procedures, protection of equipment against fire and other hazards, emergency and disaster recovery procedures, maintenance agreements and insurance.

The auditors' approach

2.6 Audits are performed in a computer environment wherever computer-based accounting systems, large or small, are operated by an enterprise, or by a third party on behalf of the enterprise, for the purpose of processing information supporting the amounts included in the financial statements.

2.7 The nature of computer-based accounting systems is such that the auditors are afforded opportunities to use either the enterprise's or another computer to assist them in the performance of their audit work. Techniques performed with computers in this way are known as Computer Assisted Audit Techniques (CAATs) of which the following are the major categories according to the old APC guideline:

(a) **Use of audit software**: computer programs used for audit purposes to examine the contents of the enterprise's computer files.

(b) **Use of test data**: data used by the auditors for computer processing to test the operation of the enterprise's computer programs.

2.8 Audit software and test data are considered in detail in the next section.

Knowledge and skills

2.9 When auditing in a computer environment, the auditors should obtain a basic understanding of the fundamentals of data processing and a level of technical computer knowledge and skills which, depending on the circumstances, may need to be extensive.

Planning, controlling and recording

Planning an audit in a computer environment

2.10 As part of their planning considerations, auditors should decide at an early stage what effect the system itself and the way it is operated will have on the timing of and the manner in which they will need to perform and record their work. In this respect they may have had the opportunity to consider these matters during the development and implementation of the system.

2.11 The auditors should also consider the use of CAATs, as this may have a significant effect on the nature, extent and timing of audit tests. In certain circumstances the auditors will need to use CAATs in order to obtain the evidence they require, whereas in other circumstances they may use CAATs to improve the efficiency or effectiveness of the audit.

2.12 In choosing the appropriate combination of CAATs and manual procedures, the auditors will need to take the following points into account.

(a) Computer programs often perform functions of which **no visible evidence** is available. In these circumstances it will frequently not be practicable for the auditors to perform tests manually.

(b) In many audit situations the auditors will have the choice of performing a test either **manually** or with the **assistance of a CAAT**. In making this choice, they will be influenced by the respective efficiency of the alternatives, taking into account:

   (i) the extent of tests of controls or substantive procedures achieved by both alternatives;

   (ii) the pattern of cost associated with the CAAT;

   (iii) the ability to incorporate within the use of the CAAT a number of different audit tests.

(c) In some cases, the auditors will need to report within a comparatively **short time-scale**. In such cases it may be more efficient to use CAATs because they are quicker to apply, even though manual methods are practicable and may cost less.

(d) If using a CAAT, auditors should ensure that the **required computer facilities, computer files** and **programs are available**. Furthermore, given that enterprises do not retain copies of computer files and programs for an indefinite period, the auditors should plan the use of any CAAT in good time so that these copies are retained for their use.

(e) The operation of some CAATs requires **frequent attendance** or access by the auditors. The auditors may be able to reduce the level of their tests by taking account of CAATs performed by the internal auditors, but the extent to which they can do this in any given situation will depend, amongst other things, on their assessment of the effectiveness and relevance of the internal audit function.

(f) Where the enterprise's accounting records include computer data, the auditors will need to have **access** to that **data**. Further, where the auditors wish to perform a CAAT, it is often necessary for the enterprise to make computer facilities available to the auditors to enable them to discharge their responsibilities.

Controlling of CAATs

2.13 Where CAATs are used, however, particular attention should be paid to:

(a) the need to **co-ordinate the work of staff** with specialist computer skills with the work of others engaged on the audit;

(b) the **approval and review** of the **technical work** by someone with the necessary computer expertise.

Auditors may use a CAAT on copies of computer records or programs, provided they have taken steps to gain reasonable assurance that the copies are identical to the originals.

Internal control evaluation

2.14 The principles relating to internal controls are the same in a computer environment as in any other environment, but there are additional considerations which are discussed in the following paragraphs.

2.15 For application controls, an integrated set of internal control questions may be used covering controls over both the manual part and the programmed part of the application, and the impact of relevant general controls.

2.16 Where preliminary evaluation of the application controls and general controls discloses the absence of, or uncompensated weaknesses in, controls, and therefore the auditors cannot rely on the controls, they should move directly to substantive procedures which may be assisted by the use of CAATs.

2.17 However, where preliminary evaluation reveals application controls or general controls which may meet the auditors' objectives, they carry out tests of controls if they wish to rely on those controls. In determining whether they wish to place reliance on application controls or general controls, the auditors will be influenced by the cost effectiveness and ease of testing and by the following matters.

(a) Before auditors place reliance on application controls which involve computer programs, they need to obtain reasonable assurance that the programs have operated properly, by evaluating and testing the effect of relevant general controls or by other tests on specific parts of the programs.

(b) Sometimes a programmed accounting procedure may not be subject to effective application controls. In such circumstances, in order to put themselves in a position to limit the extent of substantive procedures, the auditors may choose to perform tests of controls by testing the relevant general controls either manually or by using CAATs, to gain assurance of the continued and proper operation of the programmed accounting procedure.

(c) In a computer environment there is the possibility of systematic errors. This may take place because of program faults or hardware malfunction in computer operations. However, many such potential recurrent errors should be prevented or detected by general controls over the development and implementation of applications, the integrity of the program and data files, and of computer operations.

(d) The extent to which the auditors can rely on general controls may be limited because many of these controls might not be evidenced, or because they could have been performed inconsistently. In such circumstances, which are particularly common where small computers are involved, the auditors may obtain assurance from tests on manual application controls or by tests on specific parts of the programs.

2.18 Procedures the auditors may consider include observing the control in operation, examining documentary evidence of its operation, or performing it again themselves. In the case of programmed application controls, the auditors may test specific parts of the programs, or re-perform them, by taking advantage of CAATs. They may also obtain evidence by testing relevant general controls.

Review of financial statements

2.19 CAATs (particularly audit software) may be of assistance to auditors in carrying out certain aspects of this work (for example analytical review).

Working papers

2.20 Where a CAAT is used, the working papers should indicate the work performed by the CAAT, the results of the CAAT, the auditors' conclusions, the manner in which any technical problems were resolved and may include any recommendations about the modification of the CAAT for future audits.

Audit trails

2.21 The original purpose of an **audit trail** was to preserve details of all stages of processing on *paper*. This meant that transactions could be followed stage-by-stage through a system to ensure that they had been processed correctly: thus a sales system transaction record could be traced right through the system because the audit trail would show a reference to the customer order, delivery note, invoice and cheque receipt.

Around the computer?

2.22 Traditionally, therefore, it was widely considered that auditors could fulfil their function without having any detailed knowledge of what was going on inside the computer.

2.23 The auditors would commonly audit **'round the computer'**, ignoring the procedures which take place within the computer programs and concentrating solely on the input and corresponding output. Audit procedures would include checking authorisation, coding and control totals of input and checking the output with source documents and clerical control totals.

2.24 However, besides consuming vast amounts of paper and computer and printer time, the traditional approach does not reflect the modern reality of computerised accounting, where computers are used to manipulate and interpret data to assist in the management of the business, as much as to satisfy the record-keeping and reporting requirements of company law. As the complexity of computer systems has increased there has been a corresponding *loss* of audit trail.

Through the computer

2.25 The 'round the computer approach' is now frowned upon. Typical audit problems that arise as audit trails move further away from the hard copy trail include:

(a) testing computer generated totals when no detailed analysis is available;
(b) testing the completeness of output in the absence of control totals.

It is recognised that one of the principal problems facing the auditors is that of acquiring an understanding of the workings of electronic data processing and of the computer itself.

2.26   Auditors now customarily audit '**through the computer**'. This involves an examination of the detailed processing routines of the computer to determine whether the controls in the system are adequate to ensure complete and correct processing of all data. In these situations it will often be necessary to employ computer assisted audit techniques.

3   TYPES OF COMPUTER ASSISTED AUDIT TECHNIQUES (CAATS)

3.1   There is no mystique about using a computer to help with auditing. You probably use common computer assisted audit techniques all the time in your daily work without realising it.

(a)   Most modern accounting systems allow data to be manipulated in various ways and extracted into an **ad hoc report**. Even the popular (but relatively tiny) Sage Sterling system allows its database to be quizzed in quite sophisticated ways.

(b)   Even if reporting capabilities are limited, the data can often be exported directly into a **spreadsheet** package (sometimes using simple Windows-type cut and paste facilities in very modern systems) and then analysed, say, by sorting in order of highest balances, or recalculating totals using the SUM function.

(c)   Most systems have **searching** facilities that are much quicker to use than searching through print-outs by hand. This offsets the so-called 'loss of audit trail' to a significant extent. The trail is still there, even though it may have to be followed through in electronic form.

3.2   There are a variety of packages specially designed either to ease the auditing task itself (for example selecting records to investigate, based on various **statistical sampling** techniques or calculating **audit risk**), or to carry out audit **interrogations** of computerised data automatically. There are also a variety of ways of testing the processing that is carried out.

3.3   Much of this work can now be done using PCs such as laptops that are independent of the organisation's systems. (In the past this has been problematic because the storage capacity and speed of PCs rendered them unable to cope with large volumes of data, but with advances in PC technology this is not much of a problem today.)

Using the right files

3.4   Before any audit software is run, the auditors should check the identity and version of the data files and programs used, whether they are taken from the company's records and systems or supplied by themselves. This will normally involve checking with external evidence, such as control totals, and looking at file lengths, dates, times or other file properties.

Audit interrogation software

3.5   Interrogation software performs the sort of checks on data that auditors might otherwise have to perform by hand.

3.6   The case example below will give you a clear idea of what interrogation software can achieve.

Case example: ACL for Windows

Here are some extracts (from some marketing blurb) about one of the leading CAAT products, ACL for Windows.

'ACL for Windows is PC software that allows users to independently and interactively read, analyse, interrogate and report on data from virtually any mainframe, mini or microcomputer. ACL for Windows is the industry standard and is specifically designed for the non-technical user.

Ease of use: an intuitive interface with pull down menus and point and click features

Built-in audit and data analysis functionality: our powerful commands are specifically designed for audit and data analysis, requiring no additional programming or technical expertise

Interactive interrogation capability: interrogate your data interactively, following your train of thought and investigating exceptions as they arise

Unlimited file size capability: analyse 100% of your data file with complete confidence in your results

High quality reporting features: once you've completed your analysis, create high quality, multi-line reports to support your findings

Here are just a few of the many uses of ACL.

Identify trends, pinpoint exceptions and potential areas of concern

Locate errors and potential fraud by comparing and analysing files according to end user criteria

Recalculate and verify balances

Identify control issues and ensure compliance with standards

Age and analyse accounts receivable, payables or any other time-sensitive transactions

Recover expenses or lost revenues by testing for duplicate payments, gaps in invoice numbers or unbilled services

Test for unauthorised employee/supplier relationships

Automate repetitive tasks by creating custom ACL applications or batches

---

3.7 Although audit interrogation software may be used during many tests of controls and substantive procedures, its use is particularly appropriate during substantive testing of transactions and especially balances. By using audit software, the auditors may scrutinise large volumes of data and concentrate skilled manual resources on the investigation of results, rather than on the extraction of information.

3.8 Major considerations when deciding whether to use file interrogation software are as follows.

(a) As a minimum auditors will require a **basic understanding** of data processing and the enterprise's computer application, together with a detailed knowledge of the audit software and the computer files to be used.

(b) Depending on the complexity of the application, the auditors may need to have a sound appreciation of systems analysis, operating systems and, where program code is used, experience of the programming language to be utilised.

(c) Auditors will need to consider how easy it is to transfer the client's data onto the auditors' PC.

(d) The client may lack full knowledge of the computer system, and hence may not be able to explain fully all the information it produces.

Test data

3.9 An obvious way of seeing whether a system is **processing** data in the way that it should be is to input some test data and see what happens. The expected results can be calculated in advance and then compared with the results that actually arise.

3.10 The problem with test data is that any resulting corruption of the data files has to be corrected. This is difficult with modern real-time systems, which often have built in (and highly desirable) controls to ensure that data entered *cannot* easily be removed without leaving a mark. Consequently test data is used less and less as a CAAT.

Embedded audit facilities

3.11 The results of using test data would, in any case, be completely distorted if the programs used to process it were not the ones *normally* used for processing. For example a fraudulent member of the IT department might substitute a version of the program that gave the correct results, purely for the duration of the test, and then replace it with a version that syphoned off the company's funds into his own bank account.

3.12 To allow a **continuous** review of the data recorded and the manner in which it is treated by the system, it may be possible to use CAATs referred to as 'embedded audit facilities'.

3.13 An embedded facility consists of audit modules that are incorporated into the computer element of the enterprise's accounting system. Two frequently encountered examples are Integrated Test Facility (ITF) and Systems Control and Review File (SCARF).

Integrated test facility

3.14 Integrated Test Facility involves the creation of a fictitious entity (for example a department or a customer) within the framework of the regular application. Transactions are then posted to the fictitious entity along with the regular transactions. The results produced by the normal processing cycle are compared with what should have been produced, which is predetermined by other means.

3.15 It is important to ensure that the fictitious entities do not become part of the financial reporting of the organisation. Several methods can be adopted to prevent this. The simplest and most secure method is to make reversing journal entries at appropriate cut-off dates. ITF enables management and auditors to keep a constant check on the internal processing functions applied to all types of valid and invalid transactions.

SCARF

3.16 SCARF is a relatively simple technique to build into an application. It is best described by illustrating an example, in this case, a general (nominal) ledger application.

3.17 Each general ledger account would have two 'auditors' fields: a Yes/No field indicating whether or not SCARF applies to this account; and a monetary value which is a threshold amount set by the auditors. The system would be set up so that only the auditors could specify whether an account was a SCARF account or not and what the monetary value would be.

3.18 Subsequently all transactions posted to a SCARF account which had a value in excess of the threshold amount would also be written to a separate SCARF file. This technique thus enables the auditors to monitor material transactions or sensitive accounts with ease and provides an assurance that all such transactions are under scrutiny.

Simulation

3.19   Simulation (or 'parallel simulation)' entails the preparation of a separate program that simulates the processing of the organisation's real system. Real data can then be passed not only through the system proper but also through the simulated program. For example the simulation program may be used to re-perform controls such as those used to identify any missing items from a sequence.

Program logic and coding

3.20   Two further types of CAATs worth mentioning are:

(a)   **logical path analysis,** which will draw flowcharts of the program logic; and

(b)   **code comparison programs**, which compare the original specified program to the current program to detect unauthorised amendments.

Knowledge-based systems

3.21   Decision support systems' and expert systems can be used to assist with the auditors' own judgement and decisions. This is likely to save time and money as such methods increase the efficiency of the audit procedures used, and the maintenance of audit records. Other cost savings include the reduction in the number of staff required, and the fact that routine tasks can be assigned to technicians, who are helped by the expert system.

Question 4

When auditing a computer based accounting system, it is possible for most of the audit to be completed using conventional audit techniques. In some computer based systems, however, it is necessary for the auditors to employ computer assisted audit techniques (CAATs).

Required

(a)   Outline the major types of CAATs and describe the potential benefits that might be derived from using them.

(b)   Briefly explain the use that the auditors could make of such a test pack when examining a sales ledger system maintained on a computer system.

Answer

(a)   Audit techniques that involve, directly or indirectly, the use of a client's computer are referred to as Computer Assisted Audit Techniques (CAATs), of which the following are two principal categories.

    (i)   *Audit software*: computer programs used for audit purposes to examine the contents of the client's computer files.

    (ii)   *Test data*: data used by the auditors for computer processing to test the operation of the enterprise's computer programs.

The benefits of using CAATs are as follows.

    (i)   By using computer audit programs, the auditors can scrutinise large volumes of data and concentrate skilled manual resources on the investigation of results, rather than on the extraction of information.

    (ii)   Once the programs have been written and tested, the costs of operation are relatively low, indeed the auditors do not necessarily have to be present during its use (though there are frequently practical advantages in the auditors attending).

(b)   The auditors could use a test pack to test the sales ledger system by including data in the pack which would normally be processed through the system, such as:

    (i)   sales;
    (ii)   credits allowed;
    (iii)   cash receipts;
    (iv)   discounts allowed.

The processing of the input would involve:

(i)   production of sales invoices (with correct discounts);

(ii)   production of credit notes;

(iii) posting of cash received, invoices and credit notes to individual debtor's accounts to appear on statements;

(iv)   posting all transactions to the sales ledger control account and producing balances.

The result produced would be compared with those predicted in the test pack. Errors should appear on exception reports produced by the computer, for example, a customer credit limit being breached.

4   CONTROLS IN ON-LINE AND REAL-TIME SYSTEMS

Nature of on-line and real-time systems

4.1   Whilst traditional batch processing is still a common method of using a computer to process accounting data there is a rapid increase in the use of an on-line system, including those in real-time.

4.2   **On-line** systems provide the facilities for data to be passed to and from the central computer via remote terminals. **Real-time** systems are a further development of on-line systems and permit immediate updating of computer held files. The data input and file update phases are therefore merged and the system accepts individual transactions rather than batches of data.

4.3   Real-time systems, which are often referred to as one-write systems, are the computerised equivalent of bookkeeping systems like Kalamazoo or Twinlock. In those systems, several accounting records are prepared simultaneously by the use of carbon paper between specially aligned sheets of paper, the bottom sheet being, say, a sales day book, followed by the customer's account, then the customer's statement.

4.4   Most computers can operate in real time. The following paragraphs are concerned primarily with larger, multi-terminal, on-line systems.

Controls in real-time systems

4.5   There are certain control problems associated with most real-time systems. The main points to remember are as follows. We are concerned primarily with larger, multi-user systems. By **terminals** we mean either dumb terminals or networked PCs.

Segregation of duties

4.6   The same person is often responsible for producing *and* processing the same information. To compensate for the reduction in internal check, supervisory controls should be strengthened. The role of the systems administrators is particularly important; they should be responsible for backing up files, authorising users, controlling the file server and investigating problems.

Data file security

4.7   The ability of a person using a remote terminal to gain access to databases at will results in the need for special controls to ensure that files are neither read nor written to (nor destroyed), either accidentally or deliberately, without proper authority.

(a)   The controls may be partly **physical**. For example:

(i)   **access to terminals** is **restricted** to authorised personnel;

(ii) the **terminals** and the **rooms** in which they are kept are **locked** when not in use.

(b) They may be partly controlled by the **operating system**, including the following.

(i) The use of **passwords** (or lockwords), or **special badges** or keys, sometimes linked to a user's personal identification code which must be used before the terminal operator can gain access to the computer/particular files.

In some systems one password or other identification is required before it is possible to read a file, a second before it is possible to write new data and yet a third if both operations are permitted. Obviously, the code given to a particular individual will depend on his job function and status within the organisation.

(ii) **Restriction** by the operating system of **certain users** to **certain files**. For example, the PC in the wages department may only be given access to the wages files.

(iii) **Logging** of all **attempted violations** of the above controls possibly accompanied by the automatic shut down of the PC or terminal used. Obviously all violations should be speedily and thoroughly investigated.

(c) Application controls may include **validity checks** on input and **reporting of unusual transactions**.

4.8 Passwords are particularly important. There are various procedures that can be implemented to prevent unauthorised use of passwords.

(a) Passwords should be **changed regularly**, eg every month, and if possible changed by the user.

(b) Passwords should be of a **reasonable length**; and possibly mix numbers and words to prevent their being guessed.

(c) Passwords should **not be displayed** when being input.

(d) **Re-use** of old passwords should **not be permitted**.

(e) The system should automatically "**log-off**" if a terminal is not used for a certain time.

(f) If someone tries to log on with the **wrong password**, the terminal should be **disabled** after two or three wrong attempts.

Program security

4.9 The points discussed above apply equally to the use of programs.

Server security

4.10 Access controls on the file server are particularly important, since interference here can damage the whole system. The server should not also be used as a normal terminal, and it should be in secure accommodation.

Back-ups

4.11 Back-ups must be taken at least daily, and separately on a weekly basis. In a real time system it may be necessary to have a cut off time after which no further transactions are ever posted. Attempts to open a file when a back-up is in progress can sometimes corrupt the process. Stray transactions posted after the back-up has been done could be lost if there is some sort of accident and the back-up data has to be restored in full the next day.

4.12 On the other hand, immediate access to files allows more sophisticated checks to be performed. For example it allows more extensive use of computer matching, where the information input may be checked for accuracy against that held on file. Moreover, in spite of the potential for abuse, there is a distinct advantage to enabling users to correct certain types of error immediately.

Database management systems (DBMS)

4.13 DBMS are normally designed for use in real-time environments. They enable elements of data to be accessed by different programs. This avoids the duplication of data which inevitably occurs in a traditional system.

4.14 As data is normally only stored once, and may be accessible to all users that require it, the principal control problems raised concern the authorisation of data amendments and restriction of access to data. Any data amendments must take into account the requirements of all the users. An **administration function** should be set up to run and control the day to day operation of the database, thereby enhancing segregation of duties (this function will be independent of the systems development personnel and programmers and data processing manager). The following controls, some of which are common to all real-time systems, might also be incorporated into DBMS.

Controls to prevent or detect unauthorised changes to programs

4.15 These include:

- **no access** to **live program** files by any personnel except for the operations personnel at the central computer;

- **password protection** of programs;

- **restricted access** to the central computer and terminal;

- **maintenance of a console** log and scrutiny by the data processing manager and by an independent party such as the internal auditors.

- **periodic comparison** of live production programs to control copies and supporting documentation.

Controls to prevent or detect errors during operation

4.16 These include:

- **restriction of access** to terminals by use of passwords and restrictions of programs themselves to certain fields;

- **satisfactory application controls** over input, processing and master files and their contents, including retrospective batching (see Paragraph 5.5);

- use of **operations manuals** and training of all users;

- **maintenance of logs** showing unauthorised attempts to access and regular scrutiny by the data processing manager and internal auditors;

- **physical protection** of data files;
- **training** in emergency procedures.

Controls to ensure integrity of the database system

4.17 These include:

- **restriction of access** to the data dictionary (this contains standard descriptions, including definitions, characteristics and inter-relationship of data;

- **segregation of duties** between the data processing manager, the database administration function and systems development personnel;

- **liaison** between the database administration function and systems development personnel to ensure integrity of systems specifications;

- **preparation and update** as necessary of user manuals in conjunction with the data dictionary.

4.18 The audit of DBMS creates particular problems as the two principal CAATs, test data and audit software, tend to work unsatisfactorily on the programs and files contained within such systems. The auditors may, however, be able to use **embedded audit facilities**. Close liaison with the internal auditors may also provide audit comfort. The auditors should if possible be involved at the evaluation, design and development stages so that they are able to determine their audit requirements and identify control problems *before* implementation.

5   CONTROL PROBLEMS IN SMALL COMPUTER SYSTEMS

5.1 In this section we look at the control and audit problems peculiar to PCs.

Summary of the control problems

5.2 The majority of the potential problems arise due to the departure from the formal structure of the traditional data processing department, where a controlled environment was provided over the acquisition, maintenance and distribution of computer information. In the world of the PC this controlled structure does not exist and the environment is more informal.

5.3 The problems surrounding PCs can be grouped under three headings:

- **lack** of **planning** over the **acquisition** and **use of PCs**;
- **lack** of **documentary evidence**; and
- **lack** of **security** and **confidentiality**.

5.4 All these areas could produce problems for the auditors, giving them difficulties when attempting to assess the documentation, the adequacy of design processes and testing, the completeness, accuracy and authority of data and, of course, audit trails. Each of the three problem areas is now considered in more detail.

Lack of planning over the acquisition and use of PCs

5.5 When an organisation sets out to acquire a computer system, a series of steps should be undertaken before making the decision to purchase.

Choosing a supplier

5.6   A feasibility study should be carried out, examining the requirements, the costs and the benefits, to ensure that the expense is justified. Suppliers should be invited to tender, and responses from the suppliers should be evaluated and compared. All interested parties within the organisation should be identified and involved throughout the whole procedure.

5.7   When assessing tenders, the organisation should consider what software and hardware it wants to buy, and also who should supply it. Selecting the right accounting software is obviously vital. Important considerations include the following.

   (a)   The **uses** of the accounts software package. The package should be able to accommodate existing accounting records and be capable of expansion in the future. The package must also be capable of generating year-end and other necessary reports. The company may wish to buy separate software for stock control or payroll applications.

   (b)   The **security** of the software package.

   (c)   The **audit trail** given by the package.

   (d)   Whether the software will be regularly **upgraded** for technical changes such as changes in tax rates.

   (e)   Whether the accounting software forms part of a package designed for the use of businesses in the industry in which the company operates.

5.8   The company should also consider the following general factors.

   (a)   Whether to purchase all equipment and software from the **same supplier**.

   (b)   The **reputation** of the supplier. Well-known suppliers may have the better **reputation**, but may be significantly more expensive.

   (c)   The **support facilities** offered by the supplier (see below).

   (d)   Whether the hardware and software purchased will be able to cope with **normal workloads** and **busy periods**.

   (e)   The **expected useful life** of the software and equipment purchased.

Suitability

5.9   There is a risk that the client will not have the expertise to evaluate the relative merits of systems. This could give rise to compatibility and/or capacity problems thereby restricting future developments, unless in the last resort, the entire system is replaced. Many first time users tend to purchase standard software packages which creates an even greater risk as regards suitability, for such systems may not fit precisely the company's trading methods. Moreover, the first time user is unlikely to have the expertise required to tailor such packages.

Support facilities

5.10 The support facilities offered by the supplier and/or software house should be ascertained to ensure that:

   (a)   in the event of machine breakdown, **prompt service** and, if necessary, backup facilities are available;

   (b)   any **bugs** in the programme can be **sorted out**;

   (c)   **minor modifications** to the program can be carried out;

    (d) **adequate** systems **documentation** and operator manuals have been provided, such documentation falling into three generally accepted categories:

        (i) **program documentation**: which states in detail how each program within each part of the system operates, what files are being opened and accessed, and what functions are being performed;

        (ii) **operator instructions**: which are designed to be 'desk-top' instructions enabling the PC user to access and use the system as required;

        (iii) **user manual**: which is the 'layman's guide' to the operation of the whole system and would usually include the operator instructions; and

    (e) operators have received **adequate instruction**.

Standards

5.11 In a formal data processing environment there will normally be standards covering controls and accounting principles to which all procedures regarding hardware and software should conform. With PCs, where the time taken from ordering, through installation to operation, may be a matter of weeks only, there is great danger that standards are not set.

5.12 Strict disciplines must be imposed to ensure that recognised systems development controls are applied and sufficient administration procedures are implemented.

Lack of documentary evidence

5.13 We have identified that many PCs operate in real time via VDUs, which allows users to have direct access to the computer thus enabling them to input data, update files and make one-off enquiries on data held on files. The necessity for edit programs and hard copy is avoided.

5.14 Control can be enhanced by ensuring that edit programs are in-built at the design stage and by incorporating into the system a user-usage file which logs details of the user's identification, the application involved, the records accessed or updated and so on. Such a file can be reviewed periodically by a responsible official and the auditor. It may be prudent to implement manual controls to ensure that transactions can only be processed when supported by an appropriate initiating document. Similarly, manual batching can be imposed.

Lack of security and confidentiality

Lack of segregation of duties

5.15 Poor segregation of duties all too easily occurs since frequently the same person prepares the data, feeds it into the computer, supervises the processing and acts as end user. This lack of division of duties leads to enhanced opportunities for fraud, the user having access to assets and the recording and disposal of assets. The auditors may well have to perform extensive substantive verification work to compensate for this serious lack of control.

Lack of control over users

5.16   Because PCs do not require a protected environment the terminals are readily available to any user. In order to safeguard the records, controls to prevent unauthorised users from using the computer are necessary (use of locks, passwords and so on).

Lack of control over alterations to programs

5.17   We have emphasised that a lack of expertise, particularly in the case of first time users, may lead to imprudent purchase in terms of capacity and compatibility. Conversely, there are dangers arising because of the relative ease with which expertise may be acquired once a machine is installed and operational. PCs employ high level languages and a working knowledge can be grasped within a short time. In the wrong hands there is a danger that programs might be altered without detection or that programs are written at the time data is being processed without adequate testing.

5.18   Stringent supervisory arrangements are required to prevent unauthorised personnel from having access to the programs together with programmed controls preventing unauthorised running. A degree of security will be guaranteed to the extent that the programs are permanently etched onto silicon chips and are hence an integral part of the hardware ('ROMs'). Such programs can only be altered by specialist electronics engineers.

6   BUREAUX AND SOFTWARE HOUSES

6.1   Computer service bureaux are third party service organisations who provide EDP facilities to their clients. Most bureaux are members of COSBA (Computer Services and Bureaux Association) which provides a code of practice for its members.

6.2   The main types of bureaux are:

   (a)   independent companies formed to provide specialist computing services;

   (b)   computer manufacturers with bureaux;

   (c)   computer users (for example universities) with spare capacity who hire out computer time when it is not required for their own purposes. This type of bureau is now much less common than it was some years ago.

Planning and control exercised by the user

6.3   When a system using a bureau is set up it is essential that a full feasibility study and system design should be carried out. In practice the bureau may provide assistance in performing these tasks.

6.4   A *small* DP department should be set up to liaise with the bureau and to ensure that adequate systems controls are maintained. The controls kept by the client should cover:

   •   physical movement of data to and from the bureau;
   •   accuracy and completeness of processing;
   •   resubmission of rejected data;
   •   correct distribution of output;
   •   system testing involving all clerical procedures at the user company;
   •   control over the maintenance of data on master files;
   •   adequate back-up facilities both for processing and for file reconstruction;
   •   security of data.

The audit approach where controls are in the hands of third parties

6.5   The guideline *Auditing in a computer environment* implies that, wherever possible, the auditors would opt to obtain assurance by testing their client's controls, provided they are adequate, rather than by seeking to rely on controls operated by the bureau. This may be feasible, and cost effective, where, for instance, batch processing is involved. Visible data is generally abundant and loss of audit trail is normally not encountered. Reliance will be sought from the user controls at the input and output stages which should provide evidence of the proper functioning of programmed procedures performed by the bureau. However, the auditors will also be concerned with the operation of general controls at the bureau:

(a)   **security** over the **client's data** (sensitive information such as names of customers and employees should be coded if necessary);

(b)   **adequate facilities** for **reconstruction**; and

(c)   **control over master file data** (all master file amendments should be printed out and checked to ensure that they have all been authorised by the user).

6.6   Where the auditors wish to evaluate and test the controls at the bureau (whether general and/or application), and permission is obtained, they have two options:

(a)   a **separate examination of controls** by the **auditors** of each of the bureau's clients (unlikely to be feasible);

(b)   an **examination of controls** by a **third party reviewer** (probably another firm of auditors, perhaps even the bureau's own auditors) and issue of a report which can be made available to auditors of each of the bureau's clients.

6.7   The second option also has some problems.

(a)   Auditors may be unwilling to place reliance on an examination of controls commissioned by the computer bureau.

(b)   The interaction between the general controls exercised by the bureau and the application controls exercised by the client may be unclear.

(c)   It is often the case that different users place varying degrees of reliance on certain controls and auditors need to gain different levels of knowledge about these controls.

6.8   The auditors may conclude that they can rely on an examination by a third party review if they are satisfied that all the procedures which they themselves would have wished to perform have indeed been carried out and with the same level of expertise as they would have applied. This is likely to involve consultations with the third party reviewers. Remember that the bureau is the client of the third party reviewers and as such must give permission before a consultation can take place.

6.9   Where the auditors are unable to rely on an examination by a third party reviewer and are not granted permission to perform their own examination of the controls at the bureau, they may have to resort to extensive substantive testing (unless they can obtain sufficient assurance from the user controls). There is no reason why the auditors should not employ CAATs such as test data and audit software to assist them where their client uses a bureau. In the case of audit software, permission of the client *and* bureau would normally be necessary.

7   SYSTEMS DEVELOPMENT

7.1   When an audit client computerises the business, the implications for the auditors are great. The whole nature of the audit will change and the auditors must obtain the requisite knowledge to audit the system. The auditors may also be involved in the process of installing a computer system by giving advice and help. In any case, the auditors will want to audit the implementation of a new system as well as its continued use and maintenance.

Knowledge brought forward from Paper 5

Systems development is covered in your Paper 5 studies.

SYSTEMS DEVELOPMENT LIFE CYCLE	
Feasibility study	Briefly review the existing system
	Identify possible alternative solutions
Systems investigation	Obtain details of current requirements and user needs such as data volumes, processing cycles and timescales
	Identify current problems and restrictions
Systems analysis	Consider why current methods are used and identify better alternatives
Systems design	Determine what inputs, processing and storage facilities are necessary to produce the outputs required
	Consider matters such as program design, file design and security
	Prepare a detailed specification of the new system.
Systems implementation	Write or acquire software, test it, convert files, install hardware and start running the new system
Review and maintenance	Ensure that the new system meets current objectives, and that it continues to do so

---

7.2   The auditors reviewing the development process will want to satisfy themselves that each of these stages is being completed in a controlled manner with thorough coverage of the issues involved and reasonable solutions. The influence of the user on the development should be pervasive and the auditors must ensure that this has been the case. In particular the system must not be implemented until the users are happy with it.

7.3   The auditors will be involved at the systems design stage to check that various rules are clearly established. Factors auditors should consider include:

- whether risks have been considered
- access to the system
- controls over data and operations
- adequacy of testing procedures
- arrangements for data conversion
- continuity of processing
- audit arrangements including the use of CAATs
- compliance with the Data Protection Act and other relevant regulations

7.4   The auditors should review the **program specifications** and ensure that they are formally accepted by the programmer and are in accordance with the organisation's development standards. The auditors should also review the issuing of amendments to program specifications and satisfy themselves that they are being processed in a formal manner.

7.5 The auditors will review the programming work to satisfy themselves that standards laid down have been complied with. It is unlikely that they will review the program code itself for this purpose, but they will confirm that all programming work has been test-checked by other programmers.

7.6 The programmer will **test the programs** against test data. The auditors will review the **program file** which contains information on how each program works. The system should also be tested in detail using the test data, not only by the programmer, but also (separately) by the user.

7.7 The auditors should check that **test plans** are **adequate,** and include **anticipated results** for comparison with actual results. The auditors should **confirm** that the **testing** is **satisfactory** and that all data requirements and key controls have been tested. The auditors should also check the **security** of the testing process.

7.8 Audit can be invaluable in ensuring that no system goes live with **inadequately trained staff** or without a **full procedures manual** in the computer *and* user departments. Training can only be completed with hands on experience once the system is up and running. Good **file conversion procedures** are crucial and the auditors must satisfy themselves that the size and nature of the task has been allowed for. The auditors should enquire about the file conversion procedures very early in the system development.

7.9 Where the auditors are required to formally sign-off the system they would only do so if they were satisfied that:

(a) the system meets user requirements; and the programs, which function satisfactorily and have been tested thoroughly, have been developed with adequate controls incorporated and are auditable;

(b) the master files are complete and accurate;

(c) a satisfactory implementation program has been devised and that data will be converted satisfactorily.

7.10 **Implementation** is often done in phases, possibly linked to a phased construction of the master files. Parallel running of the old and new systems should occur, at least for the first sections to be implemented until confidence is built up.

7.11 After implementation, a **post-installation audit** should take place. The user department should be involved in this and approve the findings. The objective of this audit is to check that design objectives have been met.

7.12 The ongoing **maintenance** task of a computer system is facilitated if the initial development of the system was well controlled. **Good documentation, proper authorisation of all program** modifications and the **continued analysis** of performance data of the system are the hallmarks of sound maintenance which the auditors will look for. In some cases the auditors will feature in the program change control process, even though in theory this is unsound.

Small companies

7.13   In the case of a small business, the system will probably be bought in as a package. A summary of the control procedures in this situation is as follows.

- Define the objectives of the system and ensure those needs are met.
- Purchase from a reputable supplier.
- Review the available documentation.
- Assess the viability of the supplier to ensure future support will be available.
- Enter a maintenance contract.
- Identify other users of that system and ask for their opinion of that system.
- Control the conversion of files from the old to the new system.

Section summary

7.14   The main procedures over the in-house development of a system is as follows.

- Adopt a **recognised** and **documented system** analysis and design method.
- Full **documentation** must be completed throughout the development stage.
- **Review** and **approval** should be carried out throughout the development stages.
- **Test data** with pre-determined results must be used on all system areas.
- **Full testing** should be carried out prior to implementation.
- **Approval** of **system documentation** by external auditors.
- **Full training schemes** should be set up.
- **User documentation** should be reviewed prior to implementation.
- **Controlled file conversion** from old to new system.
- **Review** of **ability** of **development staff**.

8   COMPUTER FRAUD

Major categories of computer fraud

8.1   Computer fraud usually involves the theft of funds by dishonest use of a computer system. The type of computer fraud depends on the point in the system at which the fraud is perpetrated.

(a)   **Input fraud.** Data input is falsified; good examples are putting a non-existent employee on the salary file or a non-existent supplier to the purchases file.

(b)   **Processing fraud.** A programmer or someone who has broken into this part of the system may alter a program. For example, in a large organisation, a 'patch' might be used to change a program so that 10 pence was deduced from every employee's pay cheque and sent to a fictitious account to which the perpetrator had access. A 'patch' is a change to a program which is characterised by its speed and ease of implementation.

(c)   **Output fraud.** Output documents may be stolen or tampered with and control totals may be altered. Cheques are the most likely document to be stolen, but other documents may be stolen to hide a fraud.

(d)   **Fraudulent use of the computer system.** Employees may feel that they can use the computer system for their own purposes and this may take up valuable processing time. This is probably quite rare, but there was a case of a newspaper publisher's computer system being used by an employee to produce another publication!

Recent developments increasing the risk of fraud

8.2 Over the last few years there have been rapid developments in all aspects of computer technology and these have increased the opportunities that are available to commit a fraud. The most important of the recent developments are as follows.

(a) **Computer literacy**. The proportion of the population which is computer literate is growing all the time. Once people know how to use a computer, the dishonest ones among them may attempt computer fraud. It is much easier to 'hide' an electronic transaction: it is not 'visible', or not in the same sense as a paper-based one, in any case.

(b) **Communications**. The use of telephone links and other public communication systems has increased the ability of people outside the company breaking into the computer system. These 'hackers' could not have operated when access was only possible on site.

(c) **Reduction in internal checks**. The more computers are used, the fewer the tasks left to personnel to carry out. A consequence of this is often a reduction in the number of internal checks carried out for any transaction.

(d) Improvements in the **quality of software** and the increase in **implementation of good software** has not kept pace with the improvements in hardware. Distributed systems and networked PCs have become very common but this has caused the control over central databases and programs to be relaxed.

Planned approach to counteract computer fraud

8.3 Management must have a clear policy to counteract the threat of computer fraud. Employees are the most likely perpetrators of fraud (and directors). A dishonest employee will be rare, but temptation should be avoided by giving no opportunity or motive to staff. The company should attempt to prevent dishonesty, opportunity and motive in a comprehensive approach.

(a) All **staff** should be **properly trained** and should fully appreciate their role in the computer function. They should also be aware of the consequences of any fraud they might perpetrate.

(b) **Management policy on fraud** should be **clear and firm**. Management should have a positive approach to both the possibility and prevention of computer fraud.

(c) A **study** should be carried out to examine where the company is **exposed to possible fraud**. In the computer area itself controls in the system and training will both be important. Other areas should also be examined, such as recruitment and personnel policies.

(d) As a result of the study undertaken in (iii) above, the company should map out an approach or **plan** in each area of the business **to tackle and prevent fraud**.

(e) The **plan** produced must be **implemented properly** across the company. Regular reports of progress should be made to the board. Particular attention should be paid to changes in programs and the purchase and implementation of new software and hardware.

Controls to prevent computer fraud

8.4 As with all controls in a system, the three areas to examine are prevention, detection and correction. Key controls are likely to include the following.

(a) Access to computer terminals and to other parts of the computer should be restricted.

(b) Access to sensitive areas of the system should be logged and monitored.

(c) Error logs and reports should be monitored and investigated on a regular basis.

(d) Staff recruitment should include careful vetting, including taking up all references.

(e) Expert system software may be used to monitor unusual transactions.

9   DEVELOPMENTS IN THE COMPUTERISED ENVIRONMENT

9.1   In this section we identify one or two modern developments in technology that could have audit implications.

The Internet   12/96

9.2   Many auditors are now finding their clients conducting business through the Internet. As always, the principal audit concerns will be controls over the use of the Internet, and the strength of audit evidence obtained through the Internet.

Controls over the Internet

9.3   Possible control problems include:

(a) Unauthorised use of the Internet. Staff may for example use the Internet for unauthorised purchases. Even just accessing data can have costs. Although access to the Internet is priced at the cost of a local call, finding and downloading data can often be a very slow process. A simple enquiry might turn out to cost the price of an hour long local call.

(b) People may be able to access businesses' internal systems via the Internet, and obtain confidential information, or launch a virus which disrupts internal systems.

9.4   Controls to combat these risks include:

(a) **Passwords, user-identification procedures** and **access control logs**. These controls can all be used to limit access.

(b) **Disabling certain terminals**. This means that the terminals affected cannot receive or copy certain data.

(c) **Firewalls**. These disable part of the communication technology that normally allows two-way communication, so external contacts are denied access to part of the system.

(d) **Authorisation**. This technique makes sure that a message has come from an authorised sender.

(e) **Virus control software**. This should be constantly in use and should be regularly updated.

(f) **Physical controls**. Measures should be taken to protect data from physical threats such as a fire that destroys communications equipment, or damage to cables resulting in the loss of data being transmitted.

Audit evidence

9.5 Certain general observations can be made about audit evidence obtained through the Internet.

(a) Internet evidence generated by the auditor will be stronger than evidence generated by the client. Comfort may be obtained if the auditor can access the Internet and test what the client has posted.

(b) Internet evidence can be obtained in written form and is thus stronger than oral evidence.

(c) If the internal controls mentioned above are strong, the auditors will have more confidence in the quality of the evidence.

E-mail

9.6 E-mail may have numerous advantages in reducing office paperwork and speeding up communication, but it also has dangers from an audit point of view. For example, an unscrupulous employee in a large organisation might find it quite easy to send an e-mail from his or her boss's computer authorising a substantial bonus or pay-rise.

Question 5

What controls could be put in place to prevent this from happening?

Networks

9.7 Control of network systems is of the utmost importance. The auditors must be able to analyse the risks of unauthorised access such as line tapping or interception and to evaluate preventative measures.

9.8 **Authentication** programmes and *encryption* are used for security. The auditor must understand such matters and should be able to make recommendations on implementation. Password security is also extremely important, and the auditors may be called upon to recommend complex password procedures for sophisticated systems.

Electronic data interchange (EDI)

9.9 Electronic data interchange is now used very widely because it cuts out the task of re-inputting data that has already been input into a system in electronic form, saving time and improving accuracy.

9.10 However this raises a number of audit issues. How can the receiving organisation be sure that data transmitted by EDI is authentic? What authorisation measures are in place to ensure that transactions above a certain value are properly authorised before being transmitted or accepted? What is the legal position of the two parties if a transaction is disputed? Can an organisation rely on its EDI partner to operate adequate controls?

9.11 Again encryption and authentication offer some help, as do transaction logs that identify the originator of any transactions generated and transmitted.

Exam focus point

Recent exams have asked about practical computer problems such as use of the Internet and purchase of a system by a small company. Another topical issue is coping with Year 2000 problems (see below).

10 YEAR 2000

10.1 One current computer issue of significant concern is the effect of Year 2000 on systems and business operations. Year 2000 problems have arisen because a number of computer systems identify years using 2 digits only. The digits 00 (or maybe 99) may therefore be identified as 1900 or as a special code or error condition, resulting possibly in errors or failure of the computer systems.

10.2 The Audit Faculty of the Institute of Chartered Accounts in England and Wales produced guidance on this area in Autumn 1997 and this guidance has subsequently been incorporated into an APB Practice Note. The guidance is based on the following principles:

(a) the directors are responsible for ensuring the business adequately addresses the issue;

(b) the auditors' responsibilities outlined in statute and Auditing Standards have not changed;

(c) the auditors need to make appropriate enquiries to obtain a sufficient understanding of any material impact on the accounts. The guidance points out that in many cases the year 2000 may not impact upon the accounts directly; its main impact may be to do with the efficiency of the business.

10.3 The guidance recommends auditors communicate with the directors formally that the issue of the Year 2000 will be considered only insofar as it affects auditors' responsibilities under statute and SASs. If auditors are asked to help the client with preparations for the year 2000, this would be a separate engagement requiring a separate engagement letter.

10.4 When analysing the effect of the Year 2000 management may consider:

(a) the **computer environment** including hardware, system software, network and communications software;

(b) **application software** developed in-house by an IT function;

(c) user developed application software;

(d) **packaged software,** considering not just the base package but the way in which it has been implemented;

(e) software provided and operated by **third parties** under outsourcing arrangements or on a computer bureau basis;

(f) **embedded systems** in computer controlled equipment used in the business, for example in manufacturing processes and environment/process control, or in the products sold.

10.5 Management should also consider effects of the Year 2000 on suppliers or customers.

10.6 In addition management ought to plan appropriately, considering the following:

(a) creating an appropriate overall project structure;

(b) defining the individual projects (for replacement or fixing of systems);

(c) planning to resource these projects including estimates for:

   (i) costs;
   (ii) time;
   (iii) hardware capacity;
   (iv) securing external resources;

(d) developing a testing and implementation strategy;

(e) identifying constraints such as:

   (i) resource availability and retention;
   (ii) realistic ability to secure further resources;

(f) developing a high level plan for the overall programme of projects;

(g) reviewing and updating the plan in-line with actual progress;

(h) identifying alternative actions for systems issues which will not be addressed in time (contingency or damage limitations plans).

10.7 Management should ensure that any impact that has a material financial effect is reflected in the accounts. Matters to consider include:

(a) the **write down of assets** such as software or computer controlled equipment that may be rendered inoperable;

(b) **disclosure and treatment of costs** that can be foreseen or disclosure of commitments;

(c) **capitalisation of costs**. However, depending on the entity's accounting policies, capitalisation would only be on new equipment or software or where the life was enhanced or extended. Auditors should also consider the accuracy of any allocation of costs between expense and capitalisation;

(d) **disclosure of contingent liabilities** such as for rectifications under warranties, litigation or compensation;

(e) **consequential taxation adjustments.**

10.8 Management should also consider how the effect of year 2000 might cause errors prior to 31 December 1999. For example if the system carries out calculations involving future dates, errors may occur as soon as dates beyond 31 December 1999 are included.

10.9 Other matters for directors to consider include a possibly increased risk of fraud and whether to make a statement in the accounts about the impact of the year 2000.

Audit considerations

10.10 Auditors need to consider at the planning stage:

(a) the **significance** of **computers** and date sensitive aspects of business operations generally;

(b) the **nature** of the **key computer systems** which generate specific accounting information;

(c)   the **dependence** of the entities' systems and activities on third parties (eg outsourcers, customers, suppliers) where failure of the third party systems would have a direct impact on amounts or disclosures in the financial statements;

(d)   any **increased risk of error** in accounting information or other information supporting items in the financial statements;

(e)   the potential impact, if any, on the **going concern** basis;

(f)   the possible impact on **specific financial statement amounts or disclosures**.

10.11 When considering the directors' review of the systems and plans, auditors should consider:

(a)   whether the **impact analysis** was carried out **systematically** and the quality of records documenting that process;

(b)   whether all **significant business units** were **involved** in the process;

(c)   information (or test results) obtained from **IT suppliers** on packaged systems and outsourced systems;

(d)   the **skills, knowledge and experience of the staff** involved in the impact analysis;

(e)   whether **systems replacement or modification projects** are being led by staff with experience of such projects (either internal or provided by external suppliers or advisers);

(f)   **resources** committed to the systems projects identified;

(g)   **timescales** allocated for the systems projects identified;

(h)   **monitoring of progress** against plans;

(i)   whether any **slippage** against the plan has resulted in action.

Reporting to management and shareholders

10.12 Auditors will report material weaknesses in internal control related to the year 2000; they may report if they feel management has not considered the impact of the year 2000 sufficiently. Auditors must however stress the limitations of the work on which the comments are based, and that failure to report on something does not mean it will be functioning properly.

10.13 The following matters may have an impact on the audit report.

(a)   **lack of information** from the business;

(b)   **going concern** considerations; if systems or machinery become inoperable, or major suppliers or customers are likely to have year 2000 problems. If the auditors believe that there may be going concern problems, they should consider:

    (i)   disclosure in the accounts;
    (ii)   alternative plans of directors;
    (iii)   how quickly the business might fail;

(c)   any other statements made by the directors in the accounts.

Chapter roundup

- You must recognise the practical impact of computerisation in recent years and the fact that all auditors will encounter computer-based systems in their professional work.

- Remember, for this paper, that exam questions will **assume that a client's system is computerised.**

- Computers have several uses in **audit administration** and **management** including:

  - linked computerised working papers
  - statistical sampling
  - analytical procedures.

- Auditors may use a number of **computer assisted audit techniques** including:

  - audit interrogation software
  - test data
  - embedded audit facilities
  - simulation
  - logical path analysis
  - code comparison programs.

- The majority of modern systems are **real-time systems**, where users have instant and direct access to data. Important real-time controls are:

  - segregation of duties
  - data file security
  - program security
  - back-ups.

- Many small companies use **personal computers** (PCs). The major problems with the use of PCs are:

  - lack of planning over acquisition and use
  - lack of documentary evidence
  - lack of security and confidentiality

- **Bureaux** and **software houses** can offer help in certain areas but auditors may have problems assessing controls over their use.

- **Systems development controls** and **contingency planning** should be in place for all systems.

- **Computer fraud** can occur at the input, processing or output stages, or could involve fraudulent use of the computer system.

- Modern developments that improve access to data may undermine controls.

Quick quiz

1   What are the main advantages in using an automated working papers package?   (see para 1.4)

2   What are the definitions of application controls and general controls? (2.3)

3   What are the two principal categories of CAAT? (2.7)

4   What factors will determine whether the auditors perform a test manually or by using a CAAT? (2.12)

5   In what circumstances may the reliance that the auditors wish to place on general controls be limited? (2.17(d))

6   What is meant by 'audit trail'? (2.21)

7   What factors will determine the uses auditors make of file interrogation software? (3.8)

8   What is the advantage of an embedded audit facility? (3.12)

9   What is an 'integrated test facility'? (3.14)

10   What control problems and strengths can be identified in on-line computer systems?   (4.6 - 4.12)

11   Suggest three categories of controls which might be incorporated into database management systems. (4.15 - 4.17)

12   What are the major control problems surrounding the use of PC's? (5.3)

13   What controls should be exercised by a user of a computer bureau over the data transmitted to the bureau? (6.4)

14   What are the main stages of the systems development life cycle? (7.1)

15   What are the major categories of computer fraud? (8.1)

16   What controls can a business implement over employees' use of the Internet? (9.4)

17   Why is the Year 2000 potentially a problem for many computer systems? (10.1)

Question 8 is designed as revision on controls over a computer system in a small company, and the audit approach to those controls

Question to try	Level	Marks	Time
8	Revision	n/a	36 mins

Chapter 9

FORMING AN AUDIT JUDGEMENT

Chapter topic list		Syllabus reference
1	Overall review of financial statements	5(c)
2	Opening balances and comparatives	5(e)
3	Unaudited published information	5(f)
4	Subsequent events	5(d)
5	Contingencies	5(d)
6	Going concern	5(d)
7	Management representations	5(g)
8	Reporting to management	5(g)
9	Completion of the audit	5(c),(d),(e)

Introduction

At the end of an audit, after the bulk of the audit work has been completed but before the auditors can give an opinion, there are various procedures which they must undertake.

Although each of these procedures are separated here for studying purposes, they are linked by their common aim of giving assurance as to the company's stability and the validity of the financial statements.

These procedures are extremely important; failure to carry them out can lead to the gravest consequences for the auditors. Given this fact, they tend to be fairly standard in most audit approaches. A useful summary of these procedures is given in the checklist at the end of this chapter and you should refer to the checklist throughout this chapter. Note that quality control matters should be raised at this stage of the audit (see Chapter 12), and analytical procedures will be used (see Chapter 7).

This chapter contains a number of topics that are very examinable. These include **post balance sheet events** and **contingencies** which may be examined as part of a question involving accounting issues, and **going concern** (which remains a problem for auditors and was examined in June 1997).

1 OVERALL REVIEW OF FINANCIAL STATEMENTS

1.1 Once the bulk of the substantive procedures have been carried out, the auditors will have a draft set of financial statements which should be supported by appropriate and sufficient audit evidence. SAS 470 *Overall review of financial statements* covers the beginning of the end of the audit process.

SAS 470.1

Auditors should carry out such a review of the financial statements as is sufficient, in conjunction with the conclusions drawn from the other audit evidence obtained, to give them a reasonable basis for their opinion on the financial statements.

1.2   This review requires appropriate skill and experience on the part of the auditors.

Compliance with accounting regulations

SAS 470.2

Auditors should consider whether the information presented in the financial statements is in accordance with statutory requirements and that the accounting policies employed are in accordance with accounting standards, properly disclosed, consistently applied and appropriate to the entity.

1.3   The SAS goes on to list the factors which the auditors should consider when examining the **accounting policies**.

(a)   Policies **commonly adopted** in **particular industries**.

(b)   Policies for which there is substantial **authoritative support**.

(c)   Whether any **departures from applicable accounting standards are necessary** for the financial statements to give a true and fair view.

(d)   Whether the **financial statements reflect** the **substance** of the underlying transactions and not merely their form.

1.4   The SAS suggests that, when compliance with statutory requirements and accounting standards is considered, the auditors may find it useful to use a **checklist**. In fact, it is quite common, particularly in large firms which audit plcs and other complex businesses, to have a variety of pre-printed checklists for different types of client.

Review for consistency and reasonableness

SAS 470.3

Auditors should consider whether the financial statements as a whole and the assertions contained therein are consistent with their knowledge of the entity's business and with the results of other audit procedures, and the manner of disclosure is fair.

1.5   The SAS lists the principal considerations:

(a)   Whether the financial statements adequately reflect the **information** and **explanations** previously obtained and conclusions previously reached during the course of the audit.

(b)   Whether it reveals any **new factors** which may affect the presentation of, or disclosure in, the financial statements.

(c) Whether **analytical procedures** applied when completing the audit, such as comparing the information in the financial statements with other pertinent data, **produce results** which assist in arriving at the overall conclusion as to whether the financial statements as a whole are consistent with their knowledge of the entity's business.

(d) Whether the **presentation** adopted in the financial statements may have been **unduly influenced by the directors' desire** to present matters in a favourable or unfavourable light.

(e) The potential impact on the financial statements of the **aggregate of uncorrected misstatements** (including those arising from bias in making accounting estimates) identified during the course of the audit and the preceding period's audit, if any.

2   OPENING BALANCES AND COMPARATIVES

> ### KEY TERMS
>
> **Opening balances** are those account balances that exist at the beginning of the period. Opening balances are based upon the closing balances of the preceding period and reflect the effect of transactions of preceding periods and accounting policies applied in the preceding period.
>
> **Comparatives** are the corresponding amounts and other related disclosures from the preceding period which are part of the current period's financial statements as required by relevant legislation and applicable accounting standards. Such comparatives are intended to be read in relation to the amounts and other disclosures related to the current period.

2.1   SAS 450 *Opening balances and comparatives* covers this area. It is appropriate to consider such matters at the planning stage as well as the final stages of the audit as the outcome of the relevant audit procedures could have a substantial impact on the audit of current year transactions and balances.

> ### SAS 450.1
>
> Auditors should obtain sufficient appropriate audit evidence that amounts derived from the preceding period's financial statements are free from material misstatements and are appropriately incorporated in the financial statements for the current period.

2.2   Note that the preceding period accounts, when new auditors are appointed, may have been reported on by the predecessor auditors or they may have been *unaudited*.

Opening balances

SAS 450.2

Auditors should obtain sufficient appropriate audit evidence that:

(a)   opening balances have been appropriately brought forward;

(b)   opening balances do not contain errors or misstatements which materially affect the current period's financial statements; and

(c)   appropriate accounting policies are consistently applied or changes in accounting policies have been properly accounted for and adequately disclosed.

2.3   If the auditors are unable to obtain sufficient appropriate audit evidence, then they should consider the implications for their audit report.

2.4   The SAS goes on to look at opening balances from the point of view of both **continuing auditors** and **incoming auditors**.

KEY TERMS

Continuing auditors are the auditors who audited and reported on the preceding period's financial statements and continue as the auditors for the current period.

Predecessor auditors are the auditors who previously audited and reported on the financial statements of an entity, and who have been replaced by the incoming auditors.

Incoming auditors are the auditors who are auditing and reporting on the current period's financial statements, not having audited and reported on those for the preceding period.

Continuing auditors

2.5   Audit procedures need not extend beyond ensuring that opening balances have been appropriately brought forward and the current accounting policies have been consistently applied, *if*:

(a)   the continuing auditors issued an unqualified report on the preceding periods' financial statements; *and*

(b)   the audit of the current period does not reveal any matters which cast doubt on those financial statements.

2.6   If a **qualified audit report** was issued on the preceding period's financial statements then the auditors should consider whether the matter which gave rise to the qualification has been **adequately resolved** and properly dealt with in the **current period's financial statements**. This is in addition to the procedures above.

Incoming auditors

2.7   This situation is obviously more difficult. Appropriate and sufficient audit evidence is required on the opening balances and this depends on matters such as the following.

(a)   The **accounting policies** followed by the entity.

(b) Whether the **preceding period's financial statements were audited** and, if so, whether the auditors' report was **qualified**.

(c) The **nature of the opening balances**, including the risk of their misstatement.

(d) The **materiality of the opening balances** relative to the current period's financial statements.

2.8 The **procedures given** for continuing auditors should be carried out. Other procedures suggested by the SAS are as follows.

(a) **Consultations with management** and review of records, working papers and accounting and control procedures for the preceding period.

(b) **Substantive testing of any opening balances** in respect of which the results of other procedures are considered unsatisfactory.

2.9 In relation to (b) above, the SAS mentions the specific situation where the entity has taken advantage in the previous year of the exemptions from audit for smaller companies (ss 249A to 249E CA 1985). If insufficient evidence is available on opening balances then the auditors should consider the implications for their audit report.

2.10 Consultations with predecessor auditors will not normally be necessary as the above procedures will be sufficient. Predecessor auditors have no legal or ethical duty to provide information and would not normally be expected to release relevant working papers. However:

> 'they are expected to cooperate with incoming auditors to provide clarification of, or information on, specific accounting matters where this is necessary to resolve any particular difficulties.'

Comparatives

12/97

2.11 Opening balances will, in the current year's financial statements, become comparative figures which must be disclosed.

SAS 450.3

Auditors should obtain sufficient appropriate audit evidence that:

(a) the accounting policies used for the comparatives are consistent with those of the current period and appropriate adjustments and disclosures have been made where this is not the case;

(b) the comparatives agree with the amounts and other disclosures presented in the preceding period and are free from errors in the context of the financial statements of the current period; and

(c) where comparatives have been adjusted as required by relevant legislation and accounting standards, appropriate disclosures have been made.

2.12 The SAS then goes on to discuss the status of comparatives from an audit perspective.

> 'The comparatives form part of the financial statements on which the auditors express an opinion, although they are not required to express an opinion on the comparatives as such. Their responsibility is to establish whether the comparatives are the amounts which appeared in the preceding period's financial statements or, where appropriate, have been restated either to achieve consistency and comparability with the current period's amounts or to reflect a change of accounting policy or the correction of a fundamental error.'

2.13 Where the auditors are unable to obtain sufficient appropriate audit evidence to support the comparatives they must consider the implications for their report.

2.14 The SAS then discusses these implications in various situations.

Continuing auditors

2.15 The extent of audit procedures for comparatives will be significantly less then those for current year balances; normally they will be limited to a **check that balances have been brought forward correctly**. Materiality of any misstatements should be considered in relationship to *current* period figures.

2.16 The auditors' report on the previous period financial statements may have been qualified. Where the qualification matter is still **unresolved**, two situations may apply.

(a) If the matter is material in the context of the current period's opening balances as well as comparatives, the report on the current period's financial statements should be **qualified regarding opening balances and comparatives**.

(b) If the matter does not affect opening balances but is material in the context of the current period's financial statements, the report on the current period's financial statements should **refer to the comparatives**.

   (i) If comparatives are **required by law or regulation**, the reference will be in the form of a **qualification on the grounds of non-compliance** with that requirement.

   (ii) If comparatives are presented solely as **good practice**, the reference should be in the form of an **explanatory paragraph**.

2.17 Where a previous qualification has been resolved and dealt with properly in the financial statements then no mention of the qualification needs to be made in the current audit report. If, however, the matter was material to the current period, then it should be mentioned in the current report, including an explanation of how it has been resolved. It is also possible that a qualification will still be necessary, eg if a provision has been made in the current year which should have been made in the previous period.

2.18 There are circumstances (which should be unusual) where the auditors became aware of a material misstatement which affects the preceding period's financial statements on which the auditors' report was *not* qualified. The following will apply.

(a) If the preceding period's financial statements have been revised and reissued with a new auditors' report, the auditors should ensure that the comparatives agree with the revised financial statements.

(b) If the preceding period's financial statements have *not* been revised and reissued but the comparatives have been properly restated, the auditors should not qualify their report providing adequate disclosure has been given.

(c) If the preceding period's financial statements have *not* been revised and reissued, and the comparatives have *not* been properly restated, the auditors should consider the implications for their report.

Incoming auditors: audited comparatives

2.19 In this situation, the preceding period's financial statements have been audited by other auditors. The incoming auditors only bear audit responsibility for the comparatives in the context of the financial statements as a whole. The incoming auditors will use the knowledge gained in the current audit to decide whether the previous period's financial statements have been properly reflected as comparatives in the current period's financial statements.

2.20 The procedures above should be considered should such a situation arise.

Incoming auditors: unaudited comparatives

2.21 In this situation (eg where the company took advantage of the small company audit exemption in the previous period) the auditors should check that there is clear **disclosure** in the current financial statements that the comparatives are unaudited. They must still undertake the duties mentioned above as far as is appropriate. If there is not sufficient appropriate evidence, or if disclosure is inadequate, the auditors should consider the implications for their reports.

FRS 3

2.22 It is worth noting here that prior period adjustments will affect the figures for the previous year. The auditors should ensure that any prior period adjustment is correctly stated and disclosed according to FRS 3 *Reporting financial performance.*

Question 1

An auditing standard has been issued on *Opening balances and comparatives*, and one of the matters it considers is where one firm of auditors takes over from another firm. You have recently been appointed auditor of Lowdham Castings Ltd, a company which has been trading for about thirty years, and are carrying out the audit for the year ended 30 September 19X6. The company's turnover is about £500,000 and its normal profit before tax is about £30,000.

Required

Discuss your responsibilities in relation to the comparatives included in the accounts for the year ended 30 September 19X6. You should also consider the information you would require from the retiring auditors.

Answer

Consideration of the financial statements of the preceding period is necessary in the audit of the current period's financial statements in relation to three main aspects.

(a) *Opening position:* obtaining satisfaction that those amounts which have a direct effect on the current period's results or closing position have been properly brought forward.

(b) *Accounting policies:* determining whether the accounting policies adopted for the current period are consistent with those of the previous period.

(c) *Comparatives:* determining that the comparatives are properly shown in the current period's financial statements.

The auditors' main concern will therefore be to satisfy themselves that there were no material misstatements in the previous year's financial statements which may have a bearing upon their work in the current year.

The new auditors do not have to 're-audit' the previous year's financial statements, but they will have to pay more attention to them than would normally be the case where they had themselves been the auditors in the earlier period. A useful source of audit evidence will clearly be the previous auditors, and, with the client's permission, they should be contacted to see if they are prepared to co-operate. Certainly, any known areas of weakness should be discussed with the previous auditors and it is also possible that they might be prepared to provide copies of their working papers (although there is no legal or ethical provision which requires the previous auditors to co-operate in this way).

3   UNAUDITED PUBLISHED INFORMATION

3.1   The APB's SAS 160 *Other information in documents containing audited financial statements* provides guidance for auditors in this area. However, the SAS states clearly that:

> 'Nothing in this SAS refers to other information which is released in conjunction with financial statements without the auditors' knowledge or consent.'

3.2   The SAS uses the term 'other information' by which it means financial and non-financial information *other than* the audited financial statements and the auditors' report, which an entity may include in its annual report, either by custom or statute. Examples are:

(a)   a directors' report (required by statute);

(b)   a chairman's statement;

(c)   an operating and financial review;

(d)   financial summaries;

(e)   employment data;

(f)   planned capital expenditures;

(g)   financial ratios; and

(h)   selected quarterly data.

3.3   Auditors have no responsibility to report that other information is properly stated because an audit is only an expression of opinion on the truth and fairness of the financial statements. However, they may be engaged separately, or required by statute, to report on elements of other information, eg review the directors' statement of compliance with the Cadbury Code.

3.4   The SAS then moves on to the auditors' general responsibilities towards 'other information'.

SAS 160.1

Auditors should read the other information. If as a result they become aware of any apparent misstatements therein, or identify any material inconsistencies with the audited financial statements, they should seek to resolve them.

3.5   This SAS covers all types of entity, because the credibility of the financial statements and the related auditors' report will always be undermined by any inconsistencies between the financial statements and the other information, or by misstatements within the other information. For some entities there will be specific legal requirements to follow, eg relating to the directors' report of a limited company.

Auditors' consideration of other information

SAS 160.2

If auditors identify an inconsistency between the financial statements and the other information, or a misstatement within the other information, they should consider whether an amendment is required to the financial statements or to the other information and should seek to resolve the matter through discussion with the directors.

3.6   A **misstatement** within other information exists when it is stated incorrectly or presented in a misleading manner.

3.7   An **inconsistency** exists when the other information contradicts, or appears to contradict information contained in the financial statements. This could lead to doubts about audit evidence or even the auditors' opinion.

Unresolved misstatements and inconsistencies

> ### SAS 160.3
>
> If, after discussion with the directors, the auditors conclude that the financial statements require amendment and no such amendment is made, they should consider the implications for their report. If, after discussion with the directors, the auditors conclude that the other information requires amendment and no such amendment is made, they should consider appropriate actions.

3.8   In some circumstances, the auditors have a statutory duty to consider the directors' report. S 235 Companies Act 1985 states that:

> 'the auditors shall consider whether the information given in the directors' report for the financial year for which the accounts are prepared is consistent with those accounts; and if they are of opinion that it is not they shall state that fact in their report.'

3.9   The Act does not provide any assistance as to what is meant by an 'inconsistency' or indeed what matters may give rise to an inconsistency in this context. What is in no doubt, however, is that this requirement is not equivalent to forming an opinion on the directors' report itself. Where there are no inconsistencies, the directors' report need not be mentioned.

3.10   Matters which may require resolution or reference in an explanatory paragraph within the auditors' report include:

(a)   an **inconsistency between amounts or narrative** appearing in the financial statements and the directors' report;

(b)   an **inconsistency between the basis of preparation** of related items appearing in the financial statements and the directors' report, where the figures themselves are not directly comparable and the different bases are not disclosed;

(c)   an **inconsistency between figures** contained in the financial statements **and a narrative interpretation** of the effect of those figures in the directors' report.

The effect on the auditors' report will be shown in the next chapter where we discuss all aspects of the auditors' report.

3.11   Apart from the situation described above, where other information contains misstatements or inconsistencies with the financial statements and the auditors are unable to resolve them by discussion with the directors, then it may be appropriate:

(a)   to seek legal advice; and/or
(b)   to speak at the general meeting (s 390 CA 1985); and/or
(c)   to resign (but note s 394 CA 1985 regarding a statement on reasons for resigning).

The flow chart below is provided by the SAS to help in determining the correct course of action.

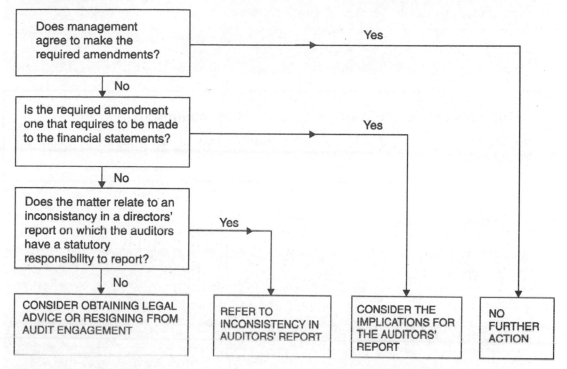

DETERMINING A COURSE OF ACTION REGARDING MATERIAL
MISSTATEMENTS AND INCONSISTENCIES

The process described below is to be followed in respect of each individual material inconsistency between the financial statements and the other information, and each material misstatement within the other information.

Timing considerations

3.12 SAS 600 *Auditors' reports on financial statements* (see Chapter 12) requires all other information to be approved by the entity, and the auditors to consider all necessary evidence, before the audit opinion is expressed.

4   SUBSEQUENT EVENTS

4.1 Before describing the steps taken by the auditors to obtain reasonable assurance in respect of subsequent events (also called post balance sheet events - the terms are interchangeable) it is prudent to revise the accounting requirements of the relevant accounting standard SSAP 17 *Accounting for post balance sheet events*. The review of subsequent events is closely connected to the audit of contingencies (Section 5) and the going concern review (Section 6).

SSAP 17

KEY TERMS

Post balance sheet events are those events, both favourable and unfavourable, which occur between the balance sheet date and the date on which the financial statements are approved by the board of directors.

Adjusting events are post balance sheet events which provide additional evidence of conditions existing at the balance sheet date. They include events which because of statutory conventional requirements are reflected in financial statements.

Non-adjusting events are post balance sheet events which concern conditions which did not exist at the balance sheet date.

> The date on which the financial statements are approved by the board of directors is the date the board of directors formally approves a set of documents as the financial statements. In respect of unincorporated enterprises the date of approval is the corresponding date. In respect of group accounts, the date of approval is the date when the group accounts are formally approved by the board of directors of the holding company.'

Knowledge brought forward from Paper 10 (Accounting)

You should refer to the Paper 10 Accounting Text for details of accounting for post balance sheet events.

SAS 150 *Subsequent events*

KEY TERMS

Subsequent events are those relevant events (favourable or unfavourable) which occur and those facts which are discovered between the period end and the laying of the financial statements before the members or equivalent.

Relevant events are those which:

- provide additional evidence relating to conditions existing at the balance sheet date; or

- concern conditions which did not exist at the balance sheet date, but which may be of such materiality that their disclosure is required to ensure the financial statements are not misleading.

SAS 150.1

Auditors should consider the effect of subsequent events on the financial statements and on their report.

4.2 The SAS does *not* provide guidance on:

> 'facts discovered after the laying of the financial statements before the members. Such facts may result in the directors issuing revised accounts as defined by relevant legislation.'

SAS 150.2

Auditors should perform procedures designed to obtain sufficient appropriate audit evidence that all material subsequent events up to the date of their report which require adjustment of, or disclosure in, the financial statements have been identified and properly reflected therein.

Audit procedures

4.3 Audit procedures should be applied to any matters examined during the audit which may be susceptible to change after the year end. They are in addition to tests on specific transactions after the period end, eg cut-off tests.

4.4   The following procedures will generally be important.

- **Enquire into,** and **consider** the **effectiveness** of, the **procedures** management has established to ensure that subsequent events are identified.

- **Read minutes of the meetings** of members, the board of directors and audit and executive committees held after the period end.

- **Enquire** about **matters discussed** at meetings for which minutes are not yet available.

- **Review relevant accounting records** and reading the entity's latest available financial information, such as interim financial statements, budgets, cash flow forecasts and other related management reports.

- **Make enquires of management** as to whether any subsequent events have occurred which might affect the financial statements.

4.5   The SAS lists specific enquires which should be made of management.

- The current status of items involving subjective judgement or which were accounted for on the basis of preliminary data, for example litigation in progress.

- Whether new commitments, borrowings or guarantees have been entered into.

- Whether sales of assets have occurred or are planned.

- Whether the issue of new shares or debentures, or an agreement to merge or to liquidate, has been made or is planned.

- Whether any assets have been destroyed, for example by fire or flood.

- Whether there have been any developments regarding risk areas and contingencies (warranties, guarantees etc).

- Whether any unusual accounting adjustments have been made or are contemplated.

- Whether any events have occurred or are likely to occur which might bring into question the appropriateness of accounting polices or estimates used in the financial statements as would be the case, for example, if such events might call into question the validity of the going concern basis.

4.6   These procedures should be performed as near as possible to the date of the auditors' report. Reviews and updates of these procedures may be required, depending on the length of the time between the procedures and the signing of the auditors' report and the susceptibility of the items to change over time.

Subsequent events discovered after the date of the auditors' report but before the financial statements are issued

4.7   The financial statements are the directors' responsibility. The directors should therefore inform the auditors of any material subsequent events between the date of the auditors' report and the date the financial statements are issued. The auditors do *not* have any obligation to perform procedures, or make enquiries regarding the financial statements *after* the date of their report.

SAS 150.3

When, after the date of their report but before the financial statements are issued, auditors become aware of subsequent events which may materially affect the financial statements, they should establish whether the financial statements need amendment, should discuss the matter with the directors and should consider the implications for their report, taking additional action as appropriate.

4.8 When the financial statements are amended, the auditors should extend the procedures discussed above to the date of their new report, carry out any other appropriate procedures and issue a new audit report dated the day it is signed.

4.9 The situation where the statements are not amended but the auditors feel that they should be is discussed below.

Subsequent events discovered after the financial statements have been issued but before their laying before the members, or equivalent

4.10 Auditors have no obligations to perform procedures or make enquiries regarding the financial statements *after* they have been issued.

SAS 150.4

When, after the financial statements have been issued, but before they have been laid before the members or equivalent, auditors become aware of subsequent events which, had they occurred and been known of at the date of their report, might have caused them to issue a different report, they should consider whether the financial statements need amendment, should discuss the matter with the directors, and should consider the implications for their report, taking additional action as appropriate.

4.11 The SAS distinguishes between two cases:

(a) an event which occurred before the date of the auditors' report, but which the auditors became aware of thereafter; and

(b) an event which occurred after the date of the auditors' report.

4.12 Under (a), the auditors and directors should consider whether the financial statements should be revised (eg under ss 245 to 245(c) CA 1985). In situation (b) there is no statutory provision for revising financial statements. The auditors might take legal advice on withdrawing their report. In *both* cases, a statement by the directors or auditors at the AGM may be feasible, but in any event legal advice may be helpful.

4.13 The SAS gives the appropriate procedures which the auditors should undertake when the directors revise the financial statements.

(a) **Carry out the audit procedures** necessary in the circumstances.

(b) **Consider**, where appropriate, whether Stock Exchange regulations require the **revision to be publicised.**

(c) **Consider** whether there is any requirement, in the case of businesses authorised under the Financial Services Act 1986 or other regulated businesses, to **communicate with the appropriate regulator.**

(d) **Review the steps taken by the directors** to ensure that anyone in receipt of the previously issued financial statements together with the auditors' report thereon is informed of the situation.

(e) **Issue a new report** on the revised financial statements.

4.14 When the auditors issue a **new report** they:

(a) **refer in their report to the note to the financial statements** which more extensively discusses the reason for the revision of the previously issued financial statements, or set out such reason in their report;

(b) **refer to the earlier report** issued by them on the financial statements;

(c) **date** their new report **not earlier** than the date the revised financial statements are approved; and

(d) **have regard** to the **guidance** relating to reports on revised annual financial statements and directors' reports as set out in APB's Practice Note 8 *Reports by auditors under company legislation in the United Kingdom.*

4.15 Where the directors do *not* revise the financial statements but the auditors feel they should be revised, and where the statements have been issued but not yet laid before the members; or if the directors do not intend to make an appropriate statement at the AGM, then the auditors should consider steps to take, on a timely basis, to prevent reliance on their report eg a statement at the AGM. Remember that the auditors have no right to communicate to the members directly in writing.

5   CONTINGENCIES

5.1 Again, we will look at the accounting requirements here first.

SSAP 18

> **KEY TERM**
>
> **Contingency** is a condition which exists at the balance sheet date, where the outcome will be confirmed only on the occurrence or non-occurrence of one or more uncertain future events. A contingent gain or loss is a gain or loss dependent on a contingency.'

> **Knowledge brought forward from Paper 10 (Accounting)**
>
> You should refer to the Paper 10 Accounting Text for details of accounting for contingencies.

Contingencies: obtaining audit evidence

5.2 The audit of contingencies is the subject of an early guidance statement (U16) published by the ICAEW in 1970. Although this statement predates the accounting standard, SSAP 18, its recommendations are still broadly relevant to contingencies such as legal claims. The statement suggests the following audit procedures:

- **Review the client's system of recording claims** and the procedure for bringing these to the attention of the management or board.

- **Discuss the arrangements for instructing solicitors** with the official responsible for legal matters.

- **Examine the minutes of the Board of Directors** and or executive or other relevant committee for references to, or indications of, possible claims.

- **Examine bills rendered by solicitors** and correspondence with them, in which connection the solicitors should be requested to furnish bills or estimates of charges to date, or to confirm that they have no unbilled charges.

- **Obtain a list of matters referred to solicitors** from the appropriate director or official with estimates of the possible ultimate liabilities.

- **Obtain written assurances** from the appropriate directors or officials that they are not aware of any matters referred to solicitors other than those disclosed.

- **Consider whether contingencies from last year** may still be applicable.

- Consider whether **the nature of the client's business** makes certain contingencies likely (eg warranty claims).

Note. These procedures may not provide the auditors with adequate information of the likely amounts for which the company is responsible.

Representations from solicitors

5.3 In appropriate circumstances, the auditors may decide to obtain written representations in respect of legal actions from the company's legal advisers. Requests for such confirmation should be kept within the solicitor-client relationship and should thus be issued by the client with a request that a copy of the reply be sent direct to the auditors. As with a debtors' circularisation it should be appreciated that the auditors do not have a right to communicate with third parties directly.

5.4 In order to ascertain whether the information provided by the directors is complete auditors may request solicitors to advise whether they have matters in hand which are not listed in the letter of request, and to provide information as to the likely amounts involved. However the Council of the Law Society has advised solicitors that it is unable to recommend them to comply with requests for information which are more widely drawn than the specimen form of wording set out below.

In connection with the preparation and audit of our accounts for the year ended .... the directors have made estimates of the amounts of the ultimate liabilities (including costs) which might be incurred and are regarded as material in relation to the following matters on which you have been consulted. We should be obliged if you would confirm that in your opinion these estimates are reasonable.

Matter   *Estimated liability, including costs*

....

5.5 Despite the above views of the Council of the Law Society regarding non-specific enquiries, there may be circumstances in which it is necessary as an audit procedure for an enquiry of a general nature to be addressed to the solicitors in order to confirm that the information provided by the directors is complete in all material particulars.

5.6 If the outcome of their enquiries appears satisfactory, the auditors would not normally regard the absence of a corroboration of the completeness of a list of legal matters as a reason in itself for qualifying their report.

5.7   If the enquiries lead to the discovery of significant matters not previously identified, the auditors will wish to extend their enquiries and to request their client to address further enquiries to, and arrange a meeting with, the solicitors, at which the auditors will wish to be present.

5.8   If, having regard to all the circumstances, the auditors are unable to satisfy themselves that they have received all the information they require for the purpose of their audit, they must qualify their report.

Exam focus point

You should appreciate that the problems of accounting for contingencies makes their audit difficult.

Question 2

You are currently engaged in the audit of Riah Ltd for the year ended 30 April 19X1. It has been brought to your attention that after the year end, one of the company's three factories was closed following a strike by the employees over their claim for a 25% pay increase; the employees were dismissed and management do not intend to re-open the factory.

Required

(a)   Describe the audit work that should be carried out in order to determine whether the closure has been correctly treated in the accounts of Riah Ltd for the year to 30 April 19X1.

(b)   Identify the items that should be included in any provision for closure costs to be made in the accounts.

Answer

(a)   The closure of the factory should be investigated according to SSAP 17 *Accounting for post balance sheet events.*

The following audit work should be carried out to determine whether the closure was an adjusting or non-adjusting event as described by SSAP 17. This would depend on whether the decision to close was made before or after the year end.

(i)   Check the board minutes to determine when the decision was taken by the board to close the factory.

(ii)   Find out how long the strike had been going on before the year end and what the effect had been on the results of the company.

(iii)   Consider other sources of information, such as press reports and correspondence with the trade union to determine when it was decided to close the factory.

The effect of the closure would certainly be material to the results of the company. Thus, if the decision to close was taken before the year end then full provision for closure costs should be taken in the accounts under consideration. If the decision was taken after the year end, then the costs and circumstances surrounding the closure should be disclosed by way of a note in the 30 April 19X1 accounts.

(b)   The following costs should be considered for inclusion in the provision.

(i)   *Property*. Any land and buildings should be valued at current market value, with provisions made for any diminution in value (which will cause a loss on sale).

(ii)   *Fixed assets*. Any assets which will not be used elsewhere in the organisation should be valued at scrap or sale value. Any potential loss must be provided for.

(iii)   *Stocks and work in progress*. Any stocks which cannot be used elsewhere in the organisation should be valued at resale value (which may be insignificant) and any possible losses on sale should be provided in full.

(iv)   *Debtors*. Any uncollectable debts should be provided for in the costs of closure.

(v)   *Damages*. Damages may be payable for breach of contract. This will normally arise when a contract cannot be completed. The costs of such damages, and any legal fees, should be provided in the closure costs.

(vi)   *Redundancy payments.* The company will almost certainly be liable for a statutory minimum in redundancy payments and these will be included in the provision.

(vii)   *Additional or run-down costs.* The factory will probably take some time to close down and any extra costs, such as wages, gas, electricity or rent should be included in the closure cost.

6   GOING CONCERN

6.1   SAS 130 *Going concern basis in financial statements* was developed separately from the bulk of the other auditing standards because of its importance. This arises from the exposure of the auditors should they miss the going concern problems of a client and the difficulties surrounding the determination of going concern status in any given situation.

Going concern as an accounting concept

> **KEY TERM**
>
> The **going concern** concept: the enterprise will continue in operational existence for the foreseeable future. This means in particular that the profit and loss account and balance sheet assume no intention or necessity to liquidate or curtail significantly the scale of operation. (SSAP 2)

6.2   The SSAP definition is supported by legal requirements (Para 10 Sch 4 CA 1985 etc). Under these requirements, the financial statements of an entity are assumed to be prepared on a going concern basis. Thus, in financial statements:

(a)   assets are recognised and measured on the basis that the entity expects to recover (through use or realisation) the recorded amounts in the normal course of business; and

(b)   liabilities are recognised and measured on the basis that they will be discharged in the normal course of business.

6.3   Where the going concern basis is *not* appropriate:

(a)   the entity may not be able to recover the amounts recorded in respect of assets; and
(b)   there may be changes in the amounts and dates of maturities of liabilities.

Therefore, if material, the amounts and classification of assets and liabilities would need to be adjusted.

6.4   Consequently, the *directors* must satisfy themselves that the going concern basis is appropriate. Even where it is, further disclosure may be required to give a true and fair view. Under the SAS, the auditors should carry out procedures to provide them with assurance that:

(a)   the **going concern basis** used in the preparation of the financial statements as a whole is **appropriate**; and

(b)   there are **adequate disclosures** regarding that basis in the financial statements in order that they give a true and fair view.

6.5   The auditors must consider whether the entity will continue as a going concern for the foreseeable future, so both the current and future circumstances of the business must be considered.

The applicability and scope of this SAS

> **SAS 130.1**
>
> When forming an opinion as to whether financial statements give a true a fair view, the auditors should consider the entity's ability to continue as a going concern, and any relevant disclosures in the financial statements.

6.6   The SAS gives guidance to auditors in the context of the going concern basis in financial statements which are required to be properly prepared under CA 1985 and to show a true and fair view. The SAS does *not* give guidance relating to the going concern in any other context, eg *Cadbury Report* matters.

Foreseeable future

6.7   SSAP 2 uses the term 'foreseeable future' but does not define it. The SAS recognises that any consideration of foreseeable future involves 'making a judgement, at a particular point in time, about future events which are inherently uncertain'. The SAS suggests that the following factors are relevant.

(a)   In general terms, the degree of **uncertainty increases significantly** the **further into the future** the consideration is taken. The manner in which the uncertainty increases with time depends on the circumstances of each particular entity.

(b)   Any judgement about the future is based on **information available at the time** at which it is made. Subsequent events can overturn a judgement which was reasonable at the time it was made.

6.8   In other words, the 'foreseeable future' depends on the specific circumstances at a point in time, including the nature of the business, its associated risks and external influences. As a consequence there can never be any certainty in relation to going concern. The auditors' judgement is only valid at that time and can be 'overturned by subsequent events'.

Consideration of going concern by the directors

6.9   The directors must assess going concern by looking at a period into the future and considering all available and relevant information. The SAS states that a minimum length for this period cannot be specified; it would be 'artificial and arbitrary' as there is no 'cut off point' after which the directors would change their approach. The length of the period is likely to depend upon:

(a)   the entity's reporting and budgeting systems; and
(b)   the nature of the entity, including its size and complexity.

6.10   Any limit to this period (eg to less than one year) will cause the directors to consider whether any further disclosures should be made to explain the use of the going concern basis.

Audit procedures

6.11   The audit procedures will be based on the directors' deliberations and the information they used. The auditors must assess whether the audit evidence is sufficient and appropriate and whether they agree with the directors' judgement. They should consider:

(a) the nature of the entity (its size and the complexity of its circumstances, for instance);

(b) whether the information relates to future events, and if so how far into the future those events lie.

A lengthy appendix to the SAS gives examples of how auditors might apply the SAS in different circumstances.

Audit evidence   6/97

SAS 130.2

The auditors should assess the adequacy of the means by which the directors have satisfied themselves that:

(a) it is appropriate for them to adopt the going concern basis in preparing the financial statements; and

(b) the financial statements include such disclosures, if any, relating to going concern as are necessary for them to give a true and fair view.

For this purpose:

(i) the auditors should make enquiries of the directors and examine appropriate available financial information; and

(ii) having regard to the future period to which the directors have paid particular attention in assessing going concern, the auditors should plan and perform procedures specifically designed to identify any material matters which could indicate concern about the entity's ability to continue as a going concern.

Preliminary assessment

6.12 The auditors' approach includes a preliminary assessment, when the overall audit plan is being developed, of the risk that the entity may be unable to continue as a going concern. The auditors should consider.

(a) **Whether the period** to which the directors have paid particular attention in assessing going concern is **reasonable**.

(b) The **systems,** or other means (formal or informal), **for timely identification of warnings of future risks** and uncertainties the entity might face.

(c) **Budget and/or forecast information** (cash flow information in particular) produced by the entity, and the quality of the systems (or other means, formal or informal) in place for producing this information and keeping it up to date.

(d) Whether the **key assumptions** underlying the budgets and/or forecasts appear appropriate in the circumstances, including:

(i) projected profit;
(ii) forecast levels of working capital;
(iii) the completeness of forecast expenditure;
(iv) whether the client will have sufficient cash at periods of maximum need;
(v) the financing of capital expenditure and long-term plans.

(e) The **sensitivity of budgets and/or forecasts** to variable factors both within the control of the directors and outside their control.

(f)   Any **obligations, undertakings or guarantees** arranged with other entities (in particular, lenders, suppliers and group companies) for the giving or receiving of support.

(g)   The **existence, adequacy and terms of borrowing facilities**, and supplier credit.

(h)   The **directors' plans** for resolving any matters giving rise to the concern (if any) about the appropriateness of the going concern basis. In particular, the auditors may need to consider:

(i)   whether the plans are realistic;

(ii)   whether there is a reasonable expectation that the plans are likely to resolve any problems foreseen; and

(iii)   whether the directors are likely to put the plans into practice effectively.

6.13   The nature and scope of the auditors' procedures will depend on the circumstances; the extent will depend mainly on the excess of the financial resources available over the financial resources required.

6.14   The auditors' and directors' procedures can be very simple in some cases, particularly in the case of smaller companies, where budgets and forecasts are not normally prepared and no specific systems are in place to monitor going concern matters.

The auditors' examination of borrowing facilities

6.15   The auditors will usually:

(a)   obtain confirmations of the existence and terms of bank facilities; and
(b)   make their own assessment of the intentions of the bankers relating thereto.

6.16   These procedures will become more vital in any of the following circumstances (for example).

(a)   There is a **low margin** of **financial resources** available to the entity.

(b)   The entity is **dependent on borrowing facilities** shortly due for renewal.

(c)   Correspondence between the bankers and the entity reveals that the **last renewal** of facilities was **agreed with difficulty,** or that, since the last review of facilities, the bankers have imposed additional conditions as a prerequisite for continued lending.

(d)   A **significant deterioration in cash flow** is projected.

(e)   The **value of assets granted** as security for the borrowings is **declining.**

(f)   The entity has **breached the terms of borrowing covenants,** or there are indications of potential breaches.

6.17   If the auditors cannot satisfy themselves then, in accordance with the audit reporting standard (SAS 600), they should consider whether the relevant matters need to be:

(a)   **disclosed in the financial statements** in order that they give a true and fair view, and/or

(b)   **referred to in the auditors' report** (by an explanatory paragraph or a qualified opinion).

6.18   The SAS also contains guidance regarding the auditors' examination of the entity's banking facilities the drafting of which has been assisted by the British Bankers Association, to improve communication between directors, auditors and bankers.

SAS 130.3

The auditors should determine and document the extent of their concern (if any) about the entity's ability to continue as a going concern. In determining the extent of their concern, the auditors should take account of all relevant information of which they have become aware during their audit.

6.19   The following are given as examples of indicators of an entity's inability to continue as a going concern.

Going concern	
Financial	An excess of liabilities over assets
	Net current liabilities
	Necessary borrowing facilities have not been agreed
	Default on terms of loan agreements, and potential breaches of covenant
	Significant liquidity or cash flow problems
	Major losses or cash flow problems which have arisen since the balance sheet date and which threaten the entity's continued existence
	Substantial sales of fixed assets not intended to be replaced
	Major restructuring of debts
	Denial of (or reduction in) normal terms of trade credit by suppliers
	Major debt repayment falling due where refinancing is necessary to the entity's continued existence
	Inability to pay debts as they fall due
Operational	Fundamental changes to the market or technology to which the entity is unable to adapt adequately
	Externally forced reductions in operations (for example, as a result of legislation or regulatory action)
	Loss of key management or staff, labour difficulties or excessive dependence on a few product lines where the market is depressed
	Loss of key suppliers or customers or technical developments which render a key product obsolete
Other	Major litigation in which an adverse judgement would imperil the entity's continued existence
	Issues which involve a range of possible outcomes so wide that an unfavourable result could affect the appropriateness of the going concern basis

Exam focus point

Any question on going concern is likely to ask you to identify signs that a particular client may not be a going concern.

6.20 Auditors may still obtain sufficient appropriate audit evidence in such situations to conclude that the going concern basis is still appropriate. However if these signs are present, and cause auditors concern, further procedures such as discussions with the directors and further work on forecasts may be required.

6.21 Where auditors consider that there is a significant level of concern about the going concern basis, or where they disagree with the preparation of the accounts on a going concern basis, they might write to the directors suggesting the need to take suitable advice. Legal advice might be required about the implications of trading while insolvent.

Written confirmations of representations from the directors

SAS 130.4

The auditors should consider the need to obtain written confirmations of representations from the directors regarding:

(a) the directors' assessment that the company is a going concern; and

(b) any relevant disclosures in the financial statements.

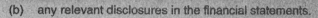

6.22 Representations may be critical in terms of audit evidence. If they do *not* receive such representations the auditors should consider whether:

(a) there is a limitation of scope in their work and a qualified opinion is required in 'except for' or 'disclaimer' terms; or

(b) the failure of the directors to provide written confirmation could indicate concern.

Assessing disclosures in the financial statements

SAS 130.5

The auditors should consider whether the financial statements are required to include disclosures relating to going concern in order to give a true and fair view.

6.23 The main concern here is **sufficiency** of disclosure:

(a) where there are going concern worries; and
(b) where the future period the directors have considered is less than one year.

6.24 The auditors must assess whether the statements show a true and fair view and hence whether their opinion should be qualified, as well as whether all matters have been satisfactorily disclosed.

Reporting on the financial statements

6.25   The SAS summarises, in flowchart form, how auditors formulate their opinion as to whether the financial statements give a true and fair view and this is shown overleaf.

SAS 130.6

Where the auditors consider that there is a significant level of concern about the entity's ability to continue as a going concern, but do not disagree with the preparation of the financial statements on the going concern basis, they should include an explanatory paragraph when setting out the basis of their opinion. They should not quality their opinion on these grounds alone, provided the disclosures in the financial statements of the matters giving rise to the concern are adequate for the financial statements to give a true and fair view.

6.26   **Clarity of communication** is of primary importance here. Where the auditors have concluded that there is a significant level of concern about the entity's ability to continue as a going concern, the following matters must be included in the financial statements for disclosure to be regarded as adequate.

- A statement that the financial statements have been prepared on the **going concern basis**

- A statement of the **pertinent factors**

- The **nature** of the concern

- A statement of the **assumptions** adopted by the directors, which should be clearly distinguishable from the pertinent facts

- (Where appropriate and practicable) a statement regarding the directors' **plans for resolving the matters** giving rise to the concern

- Details of any **relevant actions** by the directors

SAS 130.7

If the period to which the directors have paid particular attention in assessing going concern is less than one year from the date of approval of the financial statements, and the directors have not disclosed that fact, the auditors should do so within the section of their report setting out the basis of their opinion, unless the fact is clear from any other references in their report. They should not qualify their opinion on the financial statements on these grounds alone.

6.27   Disclosure of the period reviewed may have been given elsewhere, eg in the *Operating and Financial Review*. The auditors must assess whether the directors have considered a period of at least one year from the date of approval of the financial statements, and that there is sufficient evidence of this.

6.28   The auditors will qualify their opinion if they consider that the directors have not taken adequate steps to satisfy themselves that it is appropriate for them to adopt the going concern basis. This will be a limitation in the scope of the auditors' work.

SAS 130.8

Where the auditors disagree with the preparation of the financial statements on the going concern basis, they should issue an adverse audit opinion.

Going concern presumption is inappropriate

6.29 Where the going concern presumption is **inappropriate**:

(a) even disclosure in the financial statements of the matters giving rise to this conclusion is *not* sufficient for them to give a true and fair view; and

(b) the effect on financial statements prepared on that basis is so material or pervasive that the financial statements are seriously misleading.

Accordingly, an **adverse opinion** is appropriate in such cases.

Financial statements not prepared on the going concern basis

SAS 130.9

In rare circumstances, in order to give a true and fair view, the directors may have prepared financial statements on a basis other than that of a going concern. If the auditors consider this other basis to be appropriate in the specific circumstances, and if the financial statements contain the necessary disclosures, the auditors should not qualify their opinion in this respect.

6.30 Under such circumstances, the accounts may be prepared on a basis that reflects the fact that assets may need to be realised other than in the ordinary course of operations. The auditors may wish to refer to the basis on which the financial statements are prepared.

6.31 **Section summary**

- Director and auditor assessment of the going concern basis should take place over the **foreseeable future.**

- Auditors should make a **preliminary assessment** of going concern and be alert during the audit for **signs** of **going concern problems.**

- Specific audit procedures include **assessment** of **client forecasts,** examination of **borrowing facilities** and obtaining **representations** from the directors.

- Auditors may **qualify** the audit report because they disagree with the use of the **going concern basis** or **extent of disclosure.**

- Alternatively auditors may consider it appropriate to give an unqualified opinion with a **fundamental uncertainty** paragraph.

*Going concern and reporting
on the financial statements*

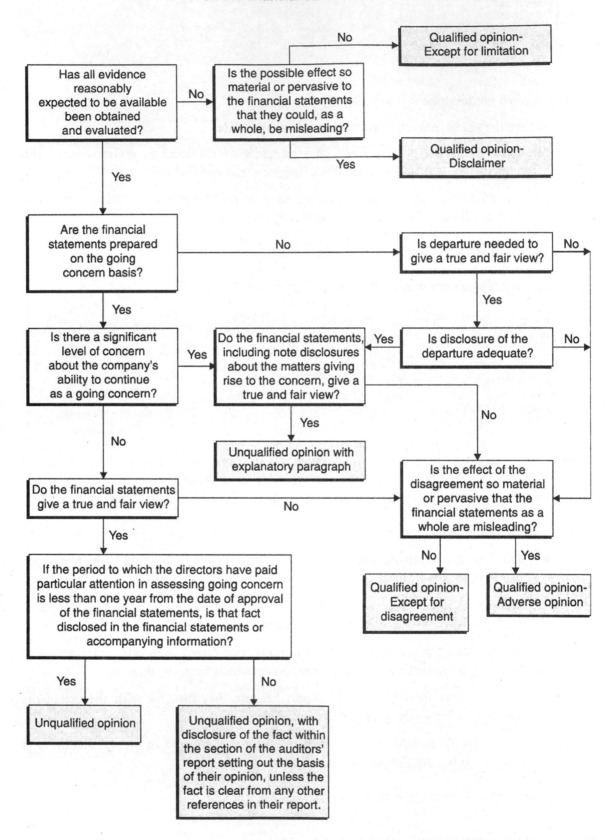

7   MANANGEMENT REPRESENTATIONS   6/95

Purpose of SAS 440
The purpose is to establish standards and provide guidance on the use of management representations as audit evidence, the procedures to be applied in evaluating and documenting management representations and the action to be taken if management refuses to provide confirmation of appropriate representations.

7.1   The auditors receive many representations during the audit, both unsolicited and in response to specific questions. Some of these representations may be critical to obtaining sufficient appropriate audit evidence. Representations may also be required for general matters, eg full availability of accounting records.

7.2   Written confirmation of oral representations avoids confusion and disagreement. The written confirmation may take the form of:

(a)   a **representation letter** from **management** (see example below);

(b)   a **letter from the auditors** outlining their understanding of management's representations, duly acknowledged and confirmed in writing by management; or

(c)   **minutes of meetings of the board** or directors, or similar body, at which such representations are approved.

SAS 440.1

Auditors should obtain written confirmation of appropriate representations from management before their report is issued.

Acknowledgement by directors of their responsibility for the financial statements

SAS 440.2

The auditors should obtain evidence that the directors acknowledge their collective responsibility for the preparation of the financial statements and have approved the financial statements.

7.3   Auditors normally do this when they receive a signed copy of the financial statements which incorporate a relevant statement of the directors' responsibilities. Alternatively, the auditors may obtain such evidence from:

(a)   relevant minutes of meetings of the board of directors or similar body, or by attending such a meeting; or

(b)   a written representation from the directors.

Representations by management as audit evidence

7.4   In addition to representations relating to responsibility for the financial statements, the auditors may wish to rely on management representations as audit evidence.

SAS 440.3

Auditors should obtain written confirmation of representations from management on matters material to the financial statements when those representations are critical to obtaining sufficient appropriate audit evidence.

7.5 Such matters should be discussed with those responsible for giving the written confirmation, to ensure that they understand what they are confirming. Written confirmations are normally required of appropriately senior management. Only matters which are material to the financial statements should be included in a letter of representation.

7.6 When the auditors receive such representations they should:

(a) **seek corroborative audit evidence**;

(b) **evaluate** whether the **representations** made by management appear **reasonable** and are **consistent** with other audit evidence obtained, including other representations; and

(c) **consider** whether the **individuals** making the representations can be expected to be **well-informed** on the particular matters.

7.7 The SAS then makes a very important point.

'Representations by management cannot be a substitute for other audit evidence that auditors expect to be available. If auditors are unable to obtain sufficient appropriate audit evidence regarding a matter which has, or may have, a material effect on the financial statements and such audit evidence is expected to be available, this constitutes a limitation in the scope of the audit, even if a representation from management has been received on the matter. In these circumstances it may be necessary for them to consider the implications for their report.'

7.8 There are two instances given in the SAS where management representations *may* be the only audit evidence available.

(a) **Knowledge of the facts is confined to management,** eg the facts are a matter of management intention.

(b) **The matter is principally one of judgement or opinion,** eg the trading position of a particular customer.

7.9 In exceptional circumstances, the matter may be so significant that the auditors should refer to the representations in their report as being relevant to a proper understanding of the basis of their opinion.

7.10 There may be occasions when the representations received do not agree with other audit evidence obtained.

SAS 440.4

If a representation appears to be contradicted by other audit evidence, the auditors should investigate the circumstances to resolve the matter and consider whether it casts doubt on the reliability of other representations.

7.11 Investigations of such situations will normally begin with further enquiries of management; the representations may have been misunderstood or, alternatively, the other evidence misinterpreted. If explanations are insufficient or unforthcoming, then further audit procedures may be required.

Basic elements of a management representation letter

7.12   A management representation letter should:

- be addressed to the auditors;
- contain specified information;
- be appropriately dated; and
- be approved by those with specific knowledge of the relevant matters.

7.13   The auditors will normally request that the letter is:

(a)   discussed and agreed by the board of directors (or equivalent);

(b)   signed on its behalf by the chairman and secretary before the auditors approve the financial statements. The whole board is then aware of the representation on which the auditors are relying; s 389A CA 1985 may be mentioned, under which it is an offence to mislead the auditors.

7.14   The letter will usually be **dated on** the day the financial statements are **approved**, but if there is any significant delay between the representation letter and the date of the auditors' report, then the auditors should consider the need to obtain further representations.

Action if management refuses to provide written confirmation of representations

SAS 440.5

If management refuses to provide written confirmation of a representation that the auditors consider necessary, the auditors should consider the implications of this scope limitation for their report.

7.15   In these circumstances, the auditors should consider whether it is appropriate to rely on other representations made by management during the audit.

Example of a management representation letter

7.16   An *example* of a management representation letter is provided in an appendix to the SAS. It is *not* a standard letter, and representations do not have to be confirmed in letter form.

(Company letterhead)

(To the auditors) (Date)

We confirm to the best of our knowledge and belief, and having made appropriate enquiries of other directors and officials of the company, the following representations given to you in connection with your audit of the financial statements for the period ended 31 December 19...

(1) We acknowledge as directors our responsibilities under the Companies Act 1985 for preparing financial statements which give a true and fair view and for making accurate representations to you. All the accounting records have been made available to you for the purpose of your audit and all the transactions undertaken by the company have been properly reflected and recorded in the accounting records. All other records and related information, including minutes of all management and shareholders' meetings, have been made available to you.

(2) The legal claim by ABC Limited has been settled out of court by a payment of £258,000. No further amounts are expected to be paid, and no similar claims have been received.

(3) In connection with deferred tax not provided, the following assumptions reflect the intentions and expectations of the company:

(a) capital investment of £450,000 is planned over the next three years;

(b) there are no plans to sell revalued properties; and

(c) we are not aware of any indications that the situation is likely to change so as to necessitate the inclusion of a provision for tax payable in the financial statements.

(4) The company has not had, or entered into, at any time during the period any arrangement, transaction or agreement to provide credit facilities (including loans, quasi-loans or credit transactions) for directors or to guarantee or provide security for such matters.

(5) There have been no events since the balance sheet date which necessitate revision of the figures included in the financial statements or inclusion of a note thereto.

As minuted by the board of directors at its meeting on .... (date)

....

Chairman   Secretary

Exam focus point

The most important points to remember about a letter of representation are:

(a) the circumstances in which it can be used;
(b) the auditors' response if the client fails to agree to it.

You should also be able to draft appropriate representations if asked.

Question 3

Procedures regarding written representations should be agreed at an early stage in order to reduce the possibility of the auditors being faced with a refusal by management to co-operate in providing such representations. In the case of a new engagement it is good practice to draw the directors' attention to the fact that the auditors will seek representations as part of their normal audit procedures in a paragraph in the letter of engagement.

Required

(a) State why directors sometimes refuse to co-operate with representations.

(b) What actions should the auditors take if the directors refuse to sign the letter of representation?

Answer

(a) In the past one of the reasons why management refused to co-operate was that they considered the representation letter to be an attempt by the auditors to shift responsibility for the audit opinion: an attitude with some justification, as the auditors frequently sought representations in respect of virtually all the material figures in the balance sheet involving *any* degree of judgement and opinion. Now that representations are to be confined to material matters that are *principally* areas of judgement and opinion and matters where knowledge of the facts is confined to management, there should be relatively few representations to be sought and this approach should hence lessen the reluctance of management to co-operate.

(b) However, management may at the outset indicate that they are not willing to sign letters of representation or to pass minutes requested by the auditors. If they do so indicate, the auditors should inform management that they will themselves prepare a statement in writing setting out their understanding of the principal representations that have been made to them during the course of the audit, and they should send this statement to management with a request for confirmation that their understanding of the representations is correct.

If management disagrees with the auditors' statement of representations, discussions should be held to clarify the matters in doubt and, if necessary, a revised statement prepared and agreed. Should management fail to reply, the auditors should follow the matter up to try to ensure that their understanding of the position, as set out in his statement, is correct.

In rare circumstances the auditors may be unable to obtain the written representations which they require. This may be, for instance, because of a refusal by management to co-operate, or because management properly declines to give the representations required on the grounds of its own uncertainty regarding the particular matter. In either case, if the auditors are unable to satisfy themselves, they may have to conclude that they have not received all the information and explanations that they require, and consequently may need to consider qualifying their audit report.

8   REPORTING TO MANAGEMENT

8.1   We mentioned in previous chapters that the auditors would report any weaknesses discovered in the system of internal control to the management of the company. This report usually takes the form of a **management letter,** but other types of report are acceptable.

8.2   SAS 610 *Reports to directors or management* covers this topic.

Purpose of SAS 610

The purpose is to establish standards and provide guidance on auditors' reports to directors, including any audit committee, or to management, at an appropriate level, of weaknesses in the accounting and internal control systems and other matters, including errors, identified during the audit.

SAS 610.1

Auditors should consider the matters which have come to their attention during the audit and whether they should be included in a report to directors or management.

8.3   The main purposes of reports to directors or management are for auditors to communicate points that have come to their attention during the audit:

(a) on the **design** and **operation** of the **accounting and internal control systems** and to make suggestions for their improvement;

(b) of **other constructive advice,** eg comments on potential economies or improvements in efficiency; and

(c) on other matters, eg comments on adjusted and unadjusted errors in the financial statements or on particular accounting policies and practices.

8.4 Note that such a report to management is *not* a substitute for a qualified audit report (see Chapter 12), when such a qualification is required. Inconsistencies between reports to management and the auditors' report should be avoided.

Material weaknesses in the accounting and internal control systems

SAS 610.2

When material weaknesses in the accounting and internal control systems are identified during the audit, auditors should report them in writing to the directors, the audit committee or an appropriate level of management on a timely basis.

8.5 A **material weakness** is one which may result in a **material misstatement** in the financial statements. If it is corrected by management, it need not be reported, but the discovery and correction should be documented.

8.6 To be effective, the report should be made as soon as possible after completion of the audit procedures . A written report is usual, but some matters may be raised orally with a file note to record the auditors' observation and the directors' response. As soon as an accounting breakdown is identified or serious weaknesses are apparent senior management should be informed without delay.

8.7 Where no report is felt to be necessary, the auditors should inform the directors that no material weaknesses have been found.

Interim letters

8.8 Where the audit work is performed on more than one visit, the auditors will normally report to management after the interim audit work has been completed as well as after the final visit, particularly if there are procedures that need to be improved before the financial year end.

Final letters

8.9 The final management letter can cover:

(a) **additional matters** under the same headings as the interim letter, if sent;

(b) details of **inefficiencies or delays** in the agreed timetable for preparation of the accounts or of workings schedules which delayed the completion of the audit and may have resulted in increased costs;

(c) any **significant differences** between the accounts and any management accounts or budgets which not only caused audit problems but also detract from the value of management information;

(d) any results of the auditors' **analytical procedures** of which management may not be aware and may be of benefit to them.

Other matters regarding reports to directors or management

8.10   If the auditors choose not to send a formal letter or report but consider it preferable to discuss any weaknesses with management, the discussion should be **minuted** or otherwise recorded in writing. Management should be provided with a copy of the note to ensure the discussion has been fairly reflected. The written record of any such discussions should be filed with the audit working papers.

8.11   The auditors should explain in their report to management that it **only** includes those matters which came to their attention as a result of the audit procedures, and that it should not be regarded as a comprehensive statement of all weaknesses that exist or all improvements that might be made.

8.12   The auditors should request a **reply** to all the points raised, indicating what action management intends to take as a result of the comments made in the report. It should be made clear in the report that the auditors expect at least an acknowledgement of the report or, where they consider it appropriate, the directors' discussion of the report to be recorded in the board minutes.

8.13   If previous points have not been dealt with effectively and they are still considered significant, the auditors should enquire why action has not been taken.

8.14   The report may contain matters of varying levels of significance and thus make it difficult for senior management to identify points of significance. The auditors can deal with this by giving the report a **'tiered' structure** so that major points are dealt with by the directors or the audit committee and minor points are considered by less senior personnel.

8.15   Other points to note about the management letter are as follows.

(a)   The recommendations should take the form of **suggestions** backed up by **reason and logic.**

(b)   The letter should be in **formal terms** unless the client requests otherwise.

(c)   **Weaknesses** that **management** are aware of but **choose not to do anything about** should be mentioned to protect the auditors.

(d)   If management or staff have **agreed to changes**, this should be mentioned in a letter.

Third parties interested in reports to directors or management

8.16   Any report made to directors or management should be regarded as a confidential communication. The auditors should therefore not normally reveal the contents of the report to any third party without the prior written consent of the directors or management of the company.

8.17   In practice, the auditors have little control over what happens to the report once it has been despatched. Occasionally management may provide third parties with copies of the report, for example their bankers or certain regulatory authorities.

8.18   Thus care should be taken to protect the auditors' position from exposure to liability in negligence to any third parties who may seek to rely on the report. Accordingly, the auditors should state clearly in their report that it has been prepared for the private use of the client. Auditors will normally state in their report to directors or management that:

(a) the report has been prepared for the **sole use** of the entity;

(b) it must **not be disclosed to a third party**, or quoted or referred to, without the written consent of the auditors; and

(c) **no responsibility** is assumed by the auditors to any other person.

8.19 As a general rule liability in negligence to a third party may only arise in circumstances where auditors carry out work for an entity knowing:

(a) that their work is to be relied upon by a third party;

(b) the purpose for which that third party intends to rely on it; and

(c) that the third party may suffer financial loss if the report is relied on having been negligently prepared.

An express disclaimer of liability normally provides protections against an unforeseen liability to a third party. See Chapter 12 for further discussion of these matters.

Specimen management letter

8.20 A specimen letter is provided below which demonstrates how the principles described in the previous paragraphs are put into practice.

Exam focus point

You may be asked to draft paragraphs for a management letter in the exam. You should follow the format we have used .

SPECIMEN MANAGEMENT LETTER

AB & Co
Certified Accountants
29 High Street
London, N10 4KB

The Board of Directors,
Manufacturing Co Limited,
15 South Street
London, S20 1CX

Members of the board,   1 April 198X

Financial statements for the year ended 31 May 198X

In accordance with our normal practice we set out in this letter certain matters which arose as a result of our review of the accounting systems and procedures operated by your company during our recent interim audit.

We would point out that the matters dealt with in this letter came to our notice during the conduct of our normal audit procedures which are designed primarily for the purpose of expressing our opinion on the financial statements of your company. In consequence our work did not encompass a detailed review of all aspects of the system and cannot be relied on necessarily to disclose defalcations or other irregularities or to include all possible improvements in internal control.

1   *Purchases: ordering procedures*

Present system
During the course of our work we discovered that it was the practice of the stores to order certain goods from X Ltd orally without preparing either a purchase requisition or purchase order.

Implications
There is therefore the possibility of liabilities being set up for unauthorised items and at a non-competitive price.

Recommendations

We recommend that the buying department should be responsible for such orders and, if they are placed orally, an official order should be raised as confirmation.

2   *Purchase ledger reconciliation*

Present system

Although your procedures require that the purchase ledger is reconciled against the control account on the nominal ledger at the end of every month, this was not done in December or January.

Implications

The balance on the purchase ledger was short by some £2,120 of the nominal ledger control account at 31 January 198X for which no explanation could be offered. This implies a serious breakdown in the purchase invoice and/or cash payment batching and posting procedures.

Recommendations

It is important in future that this reconciliation is performed regularly by a responsible official independent of the day to day purchase ledger, cashier and nominal ledger functions.

3   *Sales ledger: credit control*

Present system

As at 28 February 198X debtors account for approximately 12 weeks' sales, although your standard credit terms are cash within 30 days of statement, equivalent to an average of about 40 days (6 weeks) of sales.

Implications

This has resulted in increased overdraft usage and difficulty in settling some key suppliers accounts on time.

Recommendations

We recommend that a more structured system of debt collection be considered using standard letters and that statements should be sent out a week earlier if possible.

4   *Preparation of payroll and maintenance of personnel records*

Present system

Under your present system, just two members of staff are entirely and equally responsible for the maintenance of personnel records and preparation of the payroll. Furthermore, the only independent check of any nature on the payroll is that the chief accountant confirms that the amount of the wages cheque presented to him for signature agrees with the total of the net wages column in the payroll. This latter check does not involve any consideration of the reasonableness of the amount of the total net wages cheque or the monies being shown as due to individual employees.

Implications

It is a serious weakness of your present system, that so much responsibility is vested in the hands of just two people. This situation is made worse by the fact that there is no clearly defined division of duties as between the two of them. In our opinion, it would be far too easy for fraud to take place in this area (eg by inserting the names of 'dummy workmen' into the personnel records and hence on to the payroll) and/or for clerical errors to go undetected.

Recommendations

(i)   Some person other than the two wages clerks be made responsible for maintaining the personnel records and for periodically (but on a surprise basis) checking them against the details on the payroll;

(ii)   The two wages clerks be allocated specific duties in relation to the preparation of the payroll, with each clerk independently reviewing the work of the other;

(iii)   When the payroll is presented in support of the cheque for signature to the chief accountant, that he should be responsible for assessing the reasonableness of the overall charge for wages that week.

Our comments have been discussed with your finance director and the chief accountant and these matters will be considered by us again during future audits. We look forward to receiving your comments on the points made. Should you require any further information or explanations do not hesitate to contact us.

This letter has been produced for the sole use of your company. It must not be disclosed to a third party, or quoted or referred to, without our written consent. No responsibility is assumed by us to any other person.

We should like to take this opportunity of thanking your staff for their co-operation and assistance during the course of our audit.

Yours faithfully

ABC & Co

Question 4

List the most important reasons for the auditors to give a management letter to a client.

Answer

The principal purposes of a management letter are as follows.

(a) To enable the auditors to highlight weaknesses in the accounting records, systems and controls which they have identified during the course of their audit, and which may lead to material errors.

(b) To provide management with constructive advice on various aspects of the business which the auditors may have identified during the course of the audit.

(c) To highlight matters that may have an effect on future audits.

(d) To comply with specific requirements as laid down by, for example, local authorities, housing associations.

Reporting externally on internal control

8.21 One aspect of the recent debate on corporate governance has been whether directors and auditors should report in the accounts on the effectiveness of internal controls. In 1992 the Cadbury report recommended that directors should make a statement in the accounts on the effectiveness of internal control and the accountancy profession should develop guidance on how auditors should report.

8.22 In 1994 a Working Group on Internal Control published guidance for directors, suggesting that directors should evaluate the effectiveness of internal controls, considering the following criteria:

(a) control environment;
(b) identification and evaluation of risks and control objectives;
(c) information and communication;
(d) control procedures;
(e) monitoring and corrective action.

8.23 The discussion paper recommended that the statement by the directors should include the following elements:

(a) an **acknowledgement** by directors that they are responsible for the company's system of internal financial control;

(b) an **explanation** that such a system can only provide **reasonable** and not absolute **assurance against** material misstatement or **loss**;

(c) a description of the **key procedures** that the directors have established and which are designed to provide effective financial control;

(d) confirmation that the **directors** (or a board committee) have **reviewed the effectiveness** of the system of internal financial control; and

(e) **information** about those **weaknesses** in internal financial control that have resulted in material losses, contingencies or uncertainties which require disclosure in the financial statements or the auditors' report on the financial statements.

8.24 Subsequently the Auditing Practices Board published a bulletin *Disclosures relating to corporate governance,* covering a number of corporate governance issues. This paper recommended that there should be a wider debate about auditors reporting on the effectiveness of internal controls. Pending the outcome of this debate, the bulletin noted the problems facing auditors reporting on director statements about internal financial control because:

(a) a form of wording for directors' statements was not set out in the discussion paper;

(b) the discussion paper required directors to confirm they had reviewed internal financial control, not whether they had concluded on effectiveness;

(c) however some directors might wish to give an opinion on the effectiveness of internal financial control or extend their report to cover other aspects of internal control.

8.25 The bulletin suggested that auditors should state the following as part of their report on corporate governance:

' with respect to the directors' statements on internal financial control on page ..., in our opinion the directors have provided the disclosures required by the Code (as supplemented by the related guidance for directors) and the directors' statement on internal financial control only is not inconsistent with the information of which we are aware from our audit work on the financial statements.'

8.26 Subsequently in 1995 the Auditing Practices Board published a discussion paper on *Internal financial control effectiveness.* This paper attempted to discuss the wider issues involved including whether auditors should report on the **quality of the directors' review** or on **internal financial control effectiveness**, and if so, what form the report should take. The paper observed that auditors would need to do significantly more work if they were to report on effectiveness; on the other hand, the assurance given on the accounts would be enhanced.

8.27 Other issues discussed in the paper included:

(a) the **definition** of a **material weakness**;

(b) whether directors and auditors should report on **financial information used within the business** and the **safeguarding of assets** against unauthorised use of disposition;

(c) whether auditors should review controls **up to the date the directors approve the financial statements,** and whether if they did significant extra audit work would be involved;

(d) whether the value of auditor reporting on internal control financial effectiveness would be reduced if **auditor liability** on such reporting was **limited**.

8.28 Experience suggested that directors of many companies were unwilling to report on effectiveness. In January 1998 the Hampel report on corporate governance suggested that directors should report on all aspects of internal control (not just financial control) but that they need not report on effectiveness. Auditors should report **privately** to directors on internal control, but need not report **publicly**.

8.29 In March 1998 the Auditing Practices Board published a further consultation draft *Providing assurance on internal control*. The paper highlighted various ways in which auditors could give assurance on internal controls:

(a) a **limited scope controls opinion engagement** where the auditors would make a statement that an accompanying report by the directors of the entity described fairly the control activities in place at a specified date, and a statement that specified control activities operated at a date or for a period.

(b) a **controls opinion engagement** which might cover:

(i) the process undertaken by management in making an assertion on the adequacy of internal control;

(ii) the design of the internal control system;

(iii) internal control adequacy.

8.30 An appendix to the paper set out the difficulties auditors faced when publicly reporting on internal control.

(a) **public reports** may be **susceptible to misinterpretation** if the readers do not know about the terms of engagement;

(b) there is **no set of control objectives or criteria** that are applicable for all organisations that provide an objective benchmark against which accountants can assess controls;

(c) it is **difficult to communicate the weaknesses** of internal controls;

(d) **readers do not see** what is being reported on.

8.31 The paper argues that private reporting has the following advantages:

(a) it **minimises** the risk of the **expectation gap**;

(b) **public reporting** of deficiencies is **problematic**, particularly discussing the implications of deficiencies;

(c) the **risk of litigation** and the fact that internal control evaluation is subjective may mean that accountants are more cautious about reporting deficiencies publicly than they would be privately;

(d) private reporting means that there can be **timely reporting** on contemplated systems changes.

8.32 Critics of recent developments have argued that listed company directors ought to be able to report on the effectiveness of internal controls, and that this is part of the responsibility and accountability expected of listed company directors. The debate is likely to continue over the next few years.

9 COMPLETION OF THE AUDIT

9.1 Most of the audit evidence contributing to the auditors' judgement of sufficiency has been obtained from substantive procedures, analytical procedures, reliance on internal controls (where applicable) and review of financial statements, but there are, nevertheless, some small but significant pieces still to be fitted into the audit evidence jigsaw.

Summarising errors

SAS 220.3

In evaluating whether the financial statements give a true a fair view, auditors should assess the materiality of the aggregate of uncorrected misstatements.

9.2 The aggregate of uncorrected misstatements comprises:

(a) **specific misstatements** identified by the auditors, including uncorrected misstatements identified during the audit of the previous period if they affect the current period's financial statements; and

(b) their **best estimate** of **other misstatements** which cannot be quantified specifically.

9.3 If the auditors consider that the aggregate of misstatements may be material, they must consider reducing audit risk by extending audit procedures or requesting the directors to adjust the financial statements (which the directors may wish to do anyway).

9.4 The auditors should consider the implications for their audit report if:

(a) the directors refuse to adjust; *and*

(b) the extended audit procedures do not enable the auditors to conclude that the aggregate of uncorrected misstatements is not material.

9.5 The summary of errors will not only list errors from the current year, but also those in the previous year(s). This will allow errors to be highlighted which are reversals of errors in the previous year, such as in the valuation of closing/opening stock. Cumulative errors may also be shown, which have increased from year to year. It is normal to show both the balance sheet and the profit and loss effect, as in the example given here.

SCHEDULE OF UNADJUSTED ERRORS

		19X2				19X1			
		P & L account		Balance sheet		P & L account		Balance sheet	
		Dr	Cr	Dr	Cr	Dr	Cr	Dr	Cr
		£	£	£	£	£	£	£	£
(a)	ABC Ltd debt unprovided	10,470			10,470	4,523			4,523
(b)	Opening/ closing stock under-valued*	21,540			21,540		21,540	21,540	
(c)	Closing stock undervalued		34,105	34,105					
(d)	Opening unaccrued expense								
	Telephone*		453	453		453			453
	Electricity*		905	905		905			905
(e)	Closing unaccrued expenses								
	Telephone	427			427				
	Electricity	1,128			1,128				
(f)	Obsolete stock write off	2,528			2,528	3,211			3,211
Total		36,093	35,463	35,463	36,093	9,092	21,540	21,540	9,092
	*Cancelling items	21,540			21,540				
			453	453					
			905	905					
		14,553	34,105	34,105	14,553				

9.6 The schedule will be used by the audit manager and partner to decide whether the client should be requested to make adjustments to the financial statements to correct the errors.

9.7 In practice the client will normally adjust the financial statements to take account of such errors during the course of the audit. This will frequently apply to both material and immaterial items, for the sake of accuracy.

Completion checklists

9.8 Audit firms frequently use checklists which must be signed off to ensure that all final procedures have been carried out, all material amounts are supported by sufficient appropriate evidence, etc. An example is shown below.

Chapter roundup

- The auditors must perform and document an **overall review** of the financial statements before they can reach an opinion, covering:

  o compliance with statute and accounting standards
  o consistency with audit evidence
  o overall reasonableness

- Specific procedures must be applied to **opening balances** at a new audit client.

- The auditors' responsibilities for **comparatives** relate mainly to **consistency**, although comparatives and opening balances can have an impact on current results.

- **Unaudited published information** includes the **directors' report,** and other statements such as the **chairman's statement** and an **operating and financial review.** Auditors have a statutory responsibility to report inconsistencies between the directors' report and accounts.

- Auditors should consider the effect of **subsequent events** (after the balance sheet date) on the accounts.

- Auditors have a responsibility to **review subsequent events** before they sign their audit report, and may have to take action if they become aware of subsequent events between the date they sign their audit report and the date the financial statements are laid before members.

- The audit of **contingencies** involves reviewing the company's dealing with solicitors, and is generally connected to the subsequent events review.

- Evaluation of going concern is most important. Auditors should consider the **future plans** of directors and any signs of **going concern problems** which may be noted throughout the audit. **Bank facilities** may have to be confirmed.

- When reporting on the accounts, auditors should consider whether the going concern basis is **appropriate,** and whether **disclosure** of going concern problems is **sufficient**.

- **Representations from management** should generally be restricted to matters that cannot be verified by other audit procedures.

- Any representations should be **compared** with other evidence and their **sufficiency** assessed.

- As part of their completion procedures, auditors should consider whether the **aggregate of uncorrected misstatements** is material.

Quick quiz

1   What matters should the auditors consider when examining accounting policies? (see para 1.3)

2   What are the principal considerations in a review of the financial statements for consistency and reasonableness? (1.5)

3   What are the auditors' duties in relation to opening balances? (2.3) and comparatives? (2.11)

4   What two situations might exist in the current period where a previous qualification matter is still unresolved? (2.16)

5   What are the auditors' general responsibilities in relation to 'other information'? (3.4)

6   What types of inconsistencies might arise between the financial statements and 'other information'? (3.10)

7   What procedures should the auditors undertake to identify subsequent events and when should they be carried out? (4.4)

8   What procedures should the auditors carry out to verify the existence of contingencies? (5.2)

9   Give the SSAP 2 definition of 'going concern'. (6.2)

10   What factors affect 'foreseeable future' and what does the term signify? (6.7, 6.8)

11   When will it be vital for the auditors to examine borrowing facilities? (6.16)

12   What should the auditors do when they receive management representations? (7.6)

13   Can representations take the place of audit evidence? (7.7)

14   What are the main purposes of reports to directors? (8.3)

Questions to try	Level	Marks	Time
9	Exam	25	45 mins

Audit completion checklist

Client:
Period ended:
Instructions:
1   All questions must be answered by ticking one of the columns as appropriate.
2   Any 'No' answer must be referenced to the 'points for partner' schedule.

Section 1 - To be completed by the manager

	Yes	No	N/A	Reference to points for partner schedule
Permanent audit file				
1 Have the following been updated in the course of the audit:				
(a) Flowcharts and related documentation for:				
(i) computer systems?				
(ii) non-computer systems?				
(b) Internal /key control evaluation questionnaire conclusions?				
(c) Details of the client organisation?				
(d) Financial history?				
2 Is a current letter of engagement in force?				
Transaction (interim) audit file				
3 Were walk-through tests performed to confirm our record of the accounting systems?				
4 Was the audit programme tailored?				
5 Was adequate audit attention given to internal control weaknesses?				
6 Were levels of audit testing (compliance and substantive) appropriate?				
7 Have audit programmes been signed off as complete?				
8 Are there adequate explanations of work done and are conclusions drawn?				
9 Is there evidence of the review of work?				
10 Have weaknesses arising on the interim audit been reported to management in a formal letter				
11 Has the client replied to the weaknesses already notified in respect of matters arising from the previous year's audit?				
12 Have major internal control weaknesses previously notified been rectified?				
Final (balance sheet) audit file				
13 Have lead schedules been prepared for each audit area and cross-referenced and agreed with the financial statements?				
14 Have all the working papers been initialled and dated by the members of staff who prepared them?				

	Yes	No	N/A	Reference to points for partner schedule
15 Have all the working papers been cross-referenced?				
16 Do the working papers show comparative figures where appropriate?				
17 Have audit conclusions been drawn for each balance sheet audit area as appropriate?				
18 Has the balance sheet audit programme been completed, initialled and cross-referenced to the working papers?				
19 Have the necessary profit and loss account schedules been prepared and do they agree with the detailed accounts?				
20 Current assets:				
(a) Were debtors circularised and were the results satisfactory?				
(b) Was the client's stocktaking attended and were the results satisfactory?				
(c) Is the basis of stock and work in progress valuation satisfactory and correctly disclosed in the accounts?				
21 Liabilities:				
(a) Were creditors circularised and were the results satisfactory?				
(b) Have all liabilities, contingent liabilities, and capital commitments been fully accounted for or noted in the accounts?				
Audit completion				
22 Have formal representations been obtained or has a draft letter been set up (including representations in respect of each director regarding transactions involving himself and his connected persons required to be disclosed by the Companies Act 1985)?				
23 Have all audit queries been satisfactorily answered?				
24 Post balance sheet event review:				
(a) Has a comprehensive review been performed and evidenced?				
(b) Has the review been carried out at the most recent date possible with regard to the anticipated date of the audit report?				
25 Have all audit queries been satisfactorily answered?				
26 Have all closing adjustments been agreed with the client?				
27 Are you satisfied that all material instances where we have not received the information and explanations we require have been referred to in the points for partner schedule?				

	Yes	No	N/A	Reference to points for partner schedule
28	**Review of working papers**			
(a)	Have you reviewed all the working papers? (If not, briefly describe review procedure adopted)			
(b)	Have arrangements been made for the financial statements to be reviews by:			
(i)	a second partner (a brief review or special review)? and/or			
(ii)	the audit review panel?			
(c)	Has the planning memorandum and, where applicable, client risk evaluation questionnaire been completed?			
	Subsidiary and associated companies			
29	Where secondary auditors have been involved in the audit of subsidiary and associated companies, have we:			
(a)	Sent our group accounts audit questionnaire?			
(b)	Received satisfactory answers? or			
(c)	Reviewed and approved the working papers of secondary auditors?			
30	Have all accounts of subsidiary and associated companies been approved by the directors and audited?			
31	If any of the audit reports have been qualified has the fact and nature of the qualification been referred to in the points for partner schedule?			
	Financial statements and directors report			
32	Is the financial statements layout in accordance with the firm's standard accounts pack?			
33	Has the analytical review memorandum been properly completed and are the review conclusions consistent with the conclusions drawn in respect of our other audit work?			
34	Is the reliance placed on analytical review reasonable in the circumstances?			
35	Is any proposed dividend covered by the distributable profits as disclosed in the financial statements?			
36	Has the firm's accounting disclosure checklist been completed to ensure that the financial statements and directors' report comply with:			
(a)	the Companies Act 1985?			
(b)	Statements of Standard Accounting Practice and Financial Reporting Standards?			
(c)	Stock Exchange requirements?			
(d)	Other reporting requirements?			

	Yes	No	N/A	Reference to points for partner schedule
37	Has the directors' report been reviewed for consistency with the financial statements?			
38	Has other financial information to be issued with the audited financial statements (eg contained in the Chairman's Statement or Employee Accounts) been reviewed for consistency with the financial statements?			

.... Audit Manager   Date ....

Section II - To be completed by the reporting partner

	Yes	No	Comments
1	Has Section I of the checklist been satisfactorily completed?		
2	Have all the points on the 'points for partner' schedule been satisfactorily resolved or are there any material matters outstanding which should be referred to the audit panel?		
3	Has your review of the current and permanent file indicated that the working paper evidence is sufficient to enable you to form an opinion on the financial statements, having regard to the firm's audit manual procedures?		
4	Are the conclusions you have drawn from your overall review of the financial statements based on your knowledge of the client, consideration of the analytical review memorandum, review of post balance sheet events and where appropriate, client risk evaluation questionnaire, consistent with those contained in the detailed working papers?		
5	Have all improvements which you consider could be made in the conduct of future audits been noted on 'points forward' (for consideration at the audit debriefing)?		
6 (a)	Are there any specialist areas in which the client could benefit from our expertise, for example tax planning?		
(b)	Has the provision of such services been drawn to his attention?		

I confirm that the report of the auditors will be unqualified*/unqualified with an explanatory paragraph*/qualified* as set out in the attached draft financial statements.

.... Date

Reporting Partner

*Delete as appropriate

Chapter 10

GROUP AUDITS

Chapter topic list	Syllabus reference
1 Group accounting and the holding company auditors	5(b)
2 Principal auditors and other auditors	5(b)
3 The consolidation	5(b)
4 Reporting on group accounts	5(b)
5 Joint audits	5(b)
6 Auditing foreign subsidiaries	5(b)

Introduction

This is a new auditing topic for you, one which is concerned with practical difficulties of communication between auditors and the problems of geography.

In auditing group accounts, as in so many other areas, the auditors require detailed accounting knowledge in order to fulfil their responsibilities. Your studies in financial accounting should have made you familiar with the extensive statutory and professional requirements governing the preparation of group accounts.

You should also refer to the audit report required for group companies in Chapter 12.

The integrated accounting and auditing question in the exam has often been about groups and group auditing. Recent questions have often focused on situations where the various parts of a group are audited by a number of different auditors (thus testing your ability to apply SAS 510).

1   GROUP ACCOUNTING AND THE HOLDING COMPANY AUDITORS

6/94

Knowledge brought forward from Paper 10 (Accounting)

FRS 2 *Accounting for subsidiaries.*

SSAP 1 *Accounting for associated companies*

FRS 6 *Acquisitions and mergers*

FRS 7 *Fair values in acquisition accounting*

Companies Act 1989 provisions relating to groups

KEY TERMS

Principal auditors are the auditors with responsibility for reporting on the financial statements of an entity when those financial statements include financial information of one or more components audited by other auditors.

Other auditors are auditors, other than the principal auditors, with responsibility for reporting on the financial information of a component which is included in the financial statements audited by the principal auditors. Other auditors include affiliated firms, whether using the same name or not, and correspondent firms, as well as unrelated auditors.

Component is a division, branch, subsidiary, joint venture, associated undertaking or other entity whose financial information is included in financial statements audited by the principal auditors.

Responsibility of principal auditors

1.1   The duty of the principal auditors is:

> 'To report on whether in their opinion the group accounts give a true and fair view of the state of affairs as at the end of the year, and the profit and loss for the year, of the undertakings included in the consolidation as a whole, so far as concerns members of the company' (s 235 Companies Act 1985).

1.2   The principal auditors have **sole responsibility** for this opinion even where the group financial statements include amounts derived from accounts which have not been audited by them. As a result, they cannot discharge their responsibility to report on the group financial statements by an unquestioning acceptance of component companies' financial statements, whether audited or not.

Rights of principal auditors

1.3   The principal auditors have all the statutory rights and powers in respect of their audit of the holding company that we identified in the context of the audit of non-group companies in earlier chapters (for example right of access at all times to the holding company's books, accounts and vouchers).

1.4   The principal auditors also have the following rights:

(a)   the **right to require from the other auditors** of a UK-incorporated company such **information and explanations** as they may reasonably require (s 389A(3) CA 1985); and

(b)   the right to **require the parent company** to take all reasonable steps to **obtain reasonable information** and explanations from the subsidiary and this will include foreign subsidiaries (s 389A(4) CA 1985).

1.5   Even where their responsibilities in this regard are not set down by statute (for example where the component company is an associated company not a subsidiary), the other auditors should appreciate that the component company's financial statements will ultimately form a part of the group financial statements. In principle, the other auditors should therefore be prepared to co-operate with the principal auditors and make available such information as the principal auditors may require.

1.6   It should be made clear however, that the relationship between principal and other auditors is *not* that between a principal and an agent.

2   PRINCIPAL AUDITORS AND OTHER AUDITORS   6/94, 12/97

2.1   The principal auditors must decide how to take account of the work carried out by the other auditors. The extent of the procedures adopted by the principal auditors will be determined by the **materiality** of the amounts derived from the financial statements of components of the group, and the **level of risk** that the auditors are willing to accept that such statements contain material errors.

2.2   The APB has produced an auditing standard on this subject. SAS 510 *The relationship between principal auditors and other auditors.*

SAS 510.1
When using the work of other auditors, principal auditors should determine how that work will affect their audit

Acceptance as principal auditors   12/96

SAS 510.2
Auditors should consider whether their own participation is sufficient to enable them to act as principal auditors

2.3   The principal auditors should not be so far removed from large parts of the group audit that they are unable to form an opinion. The SAS suggests that, in this context, the principal auditors should consider the following.

* The **materiality** of the portion of the financial statement which they do not audit

* The **degree of their knowledge** regarding the business of the components

* The **nature of their relationship** with the firms acting as other auditors

* Their **ability** where necessary to **perform additional procedures** to enable them to act as principal auditors

* The **risk of material misstatements** in the financial statements of the components audited by other auditors

Exam focus point
In addition to these points, the prospective auditor should also consider the general points relating to acceptance of appointment discussed in Chapter 3.

Principal auditors' procedures   12/96, 12/97

SAS 510.3
When planning to use the work of other auditors, principal auditors should consider the professional qualifications, experience and resources of the other auditors in the context of the specific assignment.

2.4   The initial enquires of this nature will be concerned with:

(a)   the other auditors' **membership of a professional body**;

(b)   the **reputation** of any firm to which the other auditors are affiliated. If necessary, further enquires can be made of third parties, the other auditors' professional body, or discussion with the other auditors. A review of previous audit work by the other auditors may have a bearing.

> **SAS 510.4**
> Principal auditors should obtain sufficient appropriate audit evidence that the work of the other auditors is adequate for the principal auditors' purposes.

2.5   In order to obtain such evidence at the planning stage, the principal auditors should advise the other auditors of the use they intend to make of their work and make arrangement for the co-ordination of their audit efforts. The principal auditors will inform the other auditors about the following matters.

- **Areas** requiring **special consideration** (key risks, control environment)
- Procedures for the **identification** of **discloseable inter-entity transactions**
- Procedures for notifying principal auditors of **unusual circumstances**
- The **timetable** for completion of the audit
- The **independence requirements**
- The **relevant accounting, auditing** and **reporting requirements**

The other auditors should give representations on independence and accounting, auditing and reporting requirements.

2.6   The nature, timing and extent of the principal auditors' procedures will depend on the individual circumstances of the engagement, and their assessment of the other auditors. Factors that may be taken into account include the following.

- **Assessment** of other auditors
- **Risks**
- **Materiality** of components
- **Relationships** with the client.

2.7   Procedures that the principal auditors may use include the following.

- **Discussions** with the other auditors about their audit procedures
- **Review** of a **written summary** of those procedures (perhaps using a questionnaire or checklist
- **Review** of the other auditors' **working papers**

2.8   These procedures may be undertaken during a visit to the other auditors. They may be considered unnecessary if evidence has already been obtained of adequate quality control over the other auditors' work, for example, through inter-firm reviews within affiliated firms.

2.9   Having received the agreed work, documentation etc from the other auditors:

SAS 510.5

The principal auditors should consider the significant findings of the other auditors. (SAS 510.5)

2.10 This consideration may involve:

(a) **Discussions** with the other auditors and with the directors or management of the component

(b) **Review** of copies of **reports to directors** or **management** issued by the other auditors

(c) **Supplementary tests**, performed by the principal auditors or by the other auditors, on the financial statements of the component

Co-operation between auditors

SAS 510.6

Other auditors, knowing the context in which the principal auditors intend to use their work, should co-operate with and assist the principal auditors.

Information supplied by other auditors

2.11 Where the component is a subsidiary the other auditors will have a **statutory** duty to co-operate as mentioned in Section 1 above.

2.12 If there is no such statutory obligation, but the principal auditors state their intention to use the other auditors' work, then the other auditors may need to obtain permission from the component to communicate with the principal auditors on the auditing matters. Where this permission is refused, the other auditors should inform the principal auditors of the refusal, so that the principal auditors can agree with the directors of the entity they audit what action to take.

2.13 The other auditors should draw to the attention of the principal auditors any matters they discover in their audit which they feel is likely to be relevant to the principal auditors' work. They may do so:

(a) by **direct communication** (with permission from the component or where there is a statutory obligation);

(b) by **reference** in their **audit report**.

2.14 If the other auditors are unable to perform any aspect of their work as requested, they should inform the principal auditors.

Information supplied by principal auditors

2.15 The other auditors have sole responsibility for their audit opinion on the financial statments of the component they audit. They should **not** rely on the principal auditors informing them of matters which might have an impact on the financial statements of the component. If they wish to do so, they should seek representations directly from the directors or management of the entity audited by the principal auditors.

2.16   The principal auditors have no obligation, statutory or otherwise, to provide information to other auditors. Where during the course of their audit, they discover matters which they consider may be relevant to the other auditors' work, they should discuss and agree an appropriate course of action with the directors of the entity which they audit. This may involve the principal auditors communicating directly with the other auditors, or the directors informing the component or the other auditors.

2.17   If the circumstances are such that the information cannot be passed to the other auditors, for example due to sensitive commercial considerations, the principal auditors should take **no further action**. To divulge such information in these situations would be a breach of client confidentiality.

Reporting considerations

2.18   The SAS makes the following important points about the principal auditors' report.

> 'When the principal auditors are satisfied that the work of the other auditors is adequate for the purposes of their audit, no reference to the other auditors is made in the principal auditors' report.
>
> The principal auditors have sole responsibility for their audit opinion and a reference to the other auditors in the principal auditors' report may be misunderstood and interpreted as a qualification of their opinion or a division of responsibility, neither of which is appropriate.'

2.19   The principal auditors must consider the implications for their report when they *cannot* obtain sufficient evidence about the work of the other auditors, and it has not been possible to perform additional procedures in respect of the component's financial statements.

2.20   The reports of other auditors on the component's financial statements may contain a qualified opinion or an explanatory paragraph referring to an uncertainty. In such cases the principal auditors should consider whether the subject of the qualification or fundamental uncertainty is of **such nature and significance**, in relation to the financial statements of the entity on which they are reporting, that it should be reflected in their audit report.

Other aspects of the audit requiring consideration in a group context

2.21   The following points must be considered at the planning stages of a group audit.

Engagement letters

2.22   SAS 140 *Engagement letters* states that when the auditors of a parent entity are also auditors of the component, a separate engagement letter may, in many cases, be unnecessary. The factors which influence the decision whether or not to agree a separate engagement letter with the component include the following.

- Who appoints the auditors of the component
- Whether a separate report is to be issued on the component
- Whether the terms for each component are the same
- Legal and regulatory requirements
- The extent of any work performed by other auditors
- The degree of ownership by the parent

2.23   If the auditors send one letter relating to the group as a whole, it should identify the components for which they are appointed as auditors. The directors of the parent entity should be requested to forward the letter to the boards of directors of the components concerned. Each board should be requested to confirm that the terms of the engagement letter are accepted.

Control environment and systems

2.24 Assessment of the control environment and systems in accordance with SAS 300 *Accounting and internal control systems and audit risk assessments* will include assessment of the overall group control environment. Factors to consider include:

- Organisational structure of the group
- Level of involvement of the parent company in components
- Degree of autonomy of management of components
- Supervision of components' management by parent company
- Information systems, and information received centrally on a regular basis
- Role of internal audit in review of components

Subsequent events

2.25 SAS 150 *Subsequent events* states that, when planning reliance on other auditors, principal auditors should satisfy themselves that the other auditors have performed appropriate procedures relating to the subsequent events in the period up to the date of the principal auditors' report.

Management representations

2.26 SAS 440 *Management representations* makes the following comments about obtaining representations in a group situation.

(a) When the auditors have responsibility for reporting on group financial statements, where appropriate they should obtain **written confirmation** of representations relating to specific matters regarding both the group financial statements and the financial statements of the parent undertaking.

(b) How they obtain these representations depends on the group's methods of delegation of management control and authority.

    (i) They may be able to obtain the required representations regarding the group financial statements from the management of the parent undertaking because of the level of their involvement in the management of the group.

    (ii) They may obtain certain representations regarding matters material to the group financial statements directly from the management of the subsidiary undertakings, or by seeing relevant representations by management to the auditors of those subsidiary undertakings, in addition to those obtained from the management of the parent undertaking.

Reports to directors or management

2.27 When reporting to management in a group situation, SAS 610 *Reports to directors or management* states that the directors or management of the parent undertaking of a group of companies may wish to be informed of significant points arising in the reports to the directors or management to its subsidiary undertakings.

2.28 In these circumstances, permission is required from the directors or management of the subsidiary undertakings to disclose the contents of any reports to directors or management to the parent undertaking or the principal auditors. Normally, such arrangements for groups are established at the planning stage and are recorded in the instructions to the auditors of subsidiary undertakings and relevant engagement letters.

Exam focus point
Most recent questions on group audits have partly been about relations with other auditors and assessment of their work.

Question 1

You are the main auditor of Mouldings Holdings plc, which has subsidiaries in the UK and overseas, many of which are audited by other firms. All subsidiaries are involved in the manufacture or distribution of plastic goods and have accounting periods coterminous with that of the holding company.

You are required to state why you would wish to review the work of the auditors of the subsidiaries not audited by you and to detail the work you would wish to carry out in performing such a review.

Answer

(a) Reasons for reviewing the work of other auditors

The main consideration which concerns the audit of all group accounts is that the holding company's auditors (the 'principal' auditors) are responsible to the members of that company for the audit opinion on the whole of the group accounts.

It may be stated (in the notes to the financial statements) that the financial statements of certain subsidiaries have been audited by other firms, but this does not absolve the principal auditors from any of their responsibilities.

These responsibilities are imposed by statute. S 235 (2) Companies Act 1985 requires the auditors of a holding company to report to its members on the truth and fairness of the view given by the financial statements of the company and its subsidiaries dealt with in the group accounts. Furthermore, the Act provides the principal auditors with powers (389A) to obtain such information and explanations as they reasonably require from the subsidiary companies and their auditors, or from the parent company in the case of overseas subsidiaries, in order that they can discharge their responsibilities as holding company auditors.

The auditing standard SAS 510 The relationship between principal auditors and other auditors clarifies how the principal auditors can carry out a review of the audits of subsidiaries in order to satisfy themselves that, with the inclusion of figures not audited by themselves, the group accounts give a true and fair view.

The scope, standard and independence of the work carried out by the auditors of subsidiary companies (the 'other' auditors) are the most important matters which need to be examined by the principal auditors before relying on financial statements not audited by them. The principal auditors need to be satisfied that all material areas of the financial statements of subsidiaries have been audited satisfactorily and in a manner compatible with that of the principal auditors themselves.

(b) Work to be carried out by principal auditors in reviewing the other auditors' work

(i) Send a questionnaire to all other auditors requesting detailed information on their work, including:

(1) an explanation of their general approach (in order to make an assessment of the standards of their work);

(2) details of the accounting policies of major subsidiaries (to ensure that these are compatible within the group);

(3) the other auditors' opinion of the subsidiaries' overall level of internal control, and the reliability of their accounting records;

(4) any limitations placed on the scope of the auditors' work;

(5) any qualifications, and the reasons for them, made or likely to be made to their audit reports.

(ii) Carry out a detailed review of the other auditors' working papers on each subsidiary whose results materially affect the view given by the group financial statements. This review will enable the principal auditors to ascertain whether (*inter alia*):

(1) an up to date permanent file exists with details of the nature of the subsidiary's business, its staff organisation, its accounting records, previous year's financial statements and copies of important legal documents;

(2) the systems examination has been properly completed, documented and reported on to management after discussion;

(3) tests of controls and substantive procedures have been properly and appropriately carried out, and audit programmes properly completed and signed;

(4) all other working papers are comprehensive and explicit;

(5) the overall review of the financial statements has been adequately carried out, and adequate use of analytical procedures has been undertaken throughout the audit;

(6) the financial statements agree in all respects with the accounting records and comply with all relevant legal requirements and accounting standards;

(7) minutes of board and general meetings have been scrutinised and important matters noted;

(8) the audit work has been carried out in accordance with approved auditing standards;

(9) the financial statements agree in all respects with the accounting records and comply with all relevant legal and professional requirements;

(10) the audit work has been properly reviewed within the firm of auditors and any laid-down quality control procedures adhered to;

(11) any points requiring discussion with the holding company's management have been noted and brought to the principal auditors' attention (including any matters which might warrant a qualification in the audit report on the subsidiary company's financial statements);

(12) adequate audit evidence has been obtained to form a basis for the audit opinion on both the subsidiaries' financial statements and those of the group.

If the principal auditors are not satisfied as a result of the above review, they should arrange for further audit work to be carried out either by the other auditors on their behalf, or jointly with them. The other auditors are fully responsible for their own work; any additional tests are those required for the purpose of the audit of the group financial statements.

3   THE CONSOLIDATION   6/94, 6/95

3.1   After receiving and reviewing all the subsidiaries' (and associates') accounts, the principal auditors will be in a position to audit the consolidated accounts (the principal auditors may well have been responsible for the audit of some or indeed all of the subsidiary and associated companies, in which case the techniques described earlier will only apply where there are other auditors.)

3.2   An important part of the work on the consolidation will be checking the consolidation adjustments. Consolidation adjustments generally fall into two categories:

° permanent consolidation adjustments; and

° consolidation adjustments for the current year.

Permanent consolidation adjustments should be recorded on the permanent file, for reference in future years. Current year consolidation adjustments such as intra-group sales, charges, unrealised profits, or adjustments to ensure consistent accounting policies are followed, should be recorded on the consolidation working papers.

3.3 The audit steps involved in the consolidation process may be summarised as follows.

- Check the **transposition** from the audited accounts of each subsidiary/associate to the consolidation schedules.

- Check that adjustments made on consolidation are appropriate and consistent with the previous year. This will involve:

  ° **recording** the **dates** and **costs** of **acquisitions** of subsidiaries and the assets acquired;

  ° **calculating goodwill** and **pre-acquisition reserves** arising on consolidation;

  ° **preparing** an overall **reconciliation** of movements on reserves and minority interests.

- Check for acquisitions:

  ° whether **acquisition** or **merger accounting** has been **appropriately used;**

  ° the **appropriateness** of the **date** used as the date for acquisition;

  ° the **treatment** of the **results** of **investments** acquired during the year;

  ° if acquisition accounting has been used, that the **fair value** of **acquired assets** and **liabilities** is reasonable;

  ° **goodwill** has been **calculated correctly** and if amortised, period of amortisation is reasonable.

- Check for disposals:

  ° the **appropriateness** of the **date** used as the date for disposal;

  ° whether the **results** of the **investment** have been **included** up to the date of disposal, and whether figures used are reasonable.

  (Audited figures may not be available, and management accounts may have to be used. The auditor should consider whether these are reliable and prepared on a basis consistent with previous years.)

- **Consider** whether **previous treatment** of **existing subsidiaries** or **associates** is still **correct** (consider level of influence, degree of support).

- Verify the **arithmetical accuracy** of the consolidation workings.

- **Review** the **consolidated accounts** for **compliance** with the Companies Act 1985, SSAPs, FRSs and other relevant regulations. Care will need to be taken where:

  ° group companies do not have coterminous accounting periods;

  ° subsidiaries are not consolidated;

  ° accounting policies of group members differ because foreign subsidiaries operate under different rules;

  Other important areas include:

  ° treatment of participating interests and associates;

  ° treatment of goodwill and intangible assets;

  ° foreign currency translation;

  ° treatment of loss-making subsidiaries

  ° treatment of restrictions on distribution of profits of a subsidiary

- **Review** the **consolidated accounts** to confirm that they give a true and fair view in the circumstances.

3.4 The principal auditors are often requested to carry out the consolidation work even where the accounts of the subsidiaries have been prepared by the client. In these circumstances the auditors are of course acting as accountants *and* auditors and care must be taken to ensure that the *audit* function is carried out and evidenced.

Question 2

Your firm is the auditor of Beeston Industries plc, which has a number of UK subsidiaries (and no overseas subsidiaries), some of which are audited by other firms of professional accountants. You have been asked to consider the work which should be carried out to ensure that inter-company transactions and balances are correctly treated in the group accounts.

Required

(a) List and briefly describe the audit work you would perform to check that inter-company balances agree, and to state why inter-company balances should agree, and the consequences of them not agreeing.

(b) List and briefly describe the audit work you would perform to verify that inter-company profit in stock has been correctly accounted for in the group accounts.

Answer

(a) Inter-company balances should agree because, in the preparation of consolidated accounts, it is necessary to cancel them out. If they do not cancel out then the group accounts will be displaying an item which has no value outside of the group and profits may be correspondingly under or over-stated. The audit work required to check that inter-company balances agree would be as follows.

    (i) Obtain and review a copy of the holding company's instructions to all group members relating to the procedures for reconciliation and agreement of year end inter-company balances. Particular attention should be paid to the treatment of 'in transit' items to ensure that there is a proper cut-off.

    (ii) Obtain a schedule of inter-company balances from all group companies and check the details therein to the summary prepared by the holding company. The details on these schedules should also be independently confirmed in writing by the other auditors involved.

    (iii) Confirmation of nil balances should also be confirmed by both the group companies concerned and their respective auditors.

    (iv) The details on the schedules in (iii) above should also be agreed to the details in the financial statements of the individual group companies which are submitted to the holding company for consolidation purposes.

(b) Where one company in a group supplies goods to another company at cost plus a percentage, and such goods remain in stock at the year end, then the group stocks will contain an element of unrealised profit. In the preparation of the group accounts, best accounting practice requires that a provision should be made for this unrealised profit.

In order to verify that inter-company profit in stock has been correctly accounted for in the group accounts, the audit work required would be as follows.

    (i) Confirm the group's procedures for identification of such stocks and their notification to the parent company who will be responsible for making the required provision.

    (ii) Obtain and review schedules of inter-group stock from group companies and confirm that the same categories of stock have been included as in previous years.

    (iii) Select a sample of invoices for goods purchased from group companies and check to see that as necessary these have been included in year end inter-group stock and obtain confirmation from other auditors that they have satisfactorily completed a similar exercise.

(iv) Check the calculation of the provision for unrealised profit and confirm that this has been arrived at on a consistent basis with that used in earlier years, after making due allowance for any known changes in the profit margins operated by various group companies.

(v) Check the schedules of inter-group stock against the various stock sheets and consider whether the level of inter-group stock appears to be reasonable in comparison with previous years, ensuring that satisfactory explanations are obtained for any material differences.

4   REPORTING ON GROUP ACCOUNTS

4.1   The principal auditors should *not* ordinarily refer in their report to the name of any other auditors, or to the fact that other companies have been audited by other auditors. The principal auditors cannot delegate the responsibility for their opinion; any such reference might mislead the reader into believing otherwise.

4.2   If the principal auditors form an unqualified opinion on the group accounts, the report wording and presentation would be as shown in Chapter 12 but would vary in referring to a group rather than a company. Such a report would be appropriate irrespective of whether the principal auditors are also auditors of all or any of the subsidiary and associated companies within the group.

4.3   In the event of any restriction in the scope of their audit of the group financial statements the principal auditors should consider qualifying their report. This example of an uncertainty would give rise to a limitation of scope qualification or disclaimer dependent on the auditors' assessment of the materiality of the problem (see Chapter 12 on the audit report).

5   JOINT AUDITS

5.1   The relationship between principal and other auditors discussed in the previous sections is **not** the same as that between the auditors involved in a joint audit.

5.2   A joint audit can be defined as one 'where two or more auditors are responsible for an audit engagement and jointly produce an audit report to the client'.

Reasons for joint audits

5.3   Two or more firms of accountants could act as joint auditors for a number of reasons.

(a) **Takeover.** The holding company may insist that their auditors act jointly with those of the new subsidiary.

(b) **Locational problems.** A company operating from widely dispersed locations may find it convenient to have joint auditors.

(c) **Political problems.** Overseas subsidiaries may need to employ local auditors to satisfy the laws of the country in which they operate. It is sometimes found that these local auditors act jointly with those of the holding company.

(d) Companies preferring to use **local accountants**, while at the same time enjoying the wider range of services provided by a large national firm.

5.4   There are several practical points that must be borne in mind before accepting a joint audit. In particular it will be necessary to assess the **experience** and **standards** of the other firm by looking at the audit techniques used, by scrutinising their working papers and establishing whether they have had experience in similar jobs.

5.5   Joint audits are not mentioned by the new SAS on engagement letters, but the old operational guideline *Engagement letters* advised that, where there are joint auditors, the audit engagement should be explained in similar terms by each set of auditors. The auditors should agree whether joint or separate letters should be sent to the client. Separate letters would normally need to be sent where other services are provided.

5.6   Once a joint position has been accepted the **programme** to be adopted and the **split** of the **detailed work** will have to be discussed. Sometimes, the division of work will be dictated by the circumstances, perhaps because of **locational problems** or because of **varying expertise** (one firm may have a stronger computer auditing section). Where such considerations do not apply, often the work is done on a rotational basis, as this ensures that each firm gets a complete view of the whole enterprise.

5.7   One of the major criticisms of joint audits is that they may be expensive. This is probably true, but if the two firms have organised the work between them properly the difference should be minimal. Furthermore, an increase in the fees may be justified by improved services not least because the two firms of accountants are likely to work as efficiently as possible from a sense of professional pride.

5.8   Both firms must sign the audit report and both are responsible for the whole audit whether or not they carried out a particular area of the audit programme. It follows that both firms will be **jointly liable** in the event of litigation.

6   AUDITING FOREIGN SUBSIDIARIES   12/95

6.1   When a UK auditing firm has a UK client which owns overseas subsidiaries, the UK client may:

(a)   choose to have the foreign subsidiaries audited by local firms (as has been assumed in Sections 1 to 4 above); or

(b)   request that the UK auditors undertake the audit of the foreign subsidiaries.

6.2   The very large auditing firms have no difficulty with this second approach. They have offices located worldwide and can therefore pass on the audit of foreign subsidiaries to these offices with assurances of the standard of the audit which will be performed. For smaller auditing firms, such a request to audit foreign subsidiaries would be quite unusual (although by no means out of the question) because of the extra costs likely to be incurred by such an approach.

6.3   Even when the UK auditors are a large firm however, and local offices audit the foreign subsidiaries, it is often the case that the 'principal' auditors at the client's UK head office will undertake an audit visit to a major foreign subsidiary each year. This is particularly the case with world-wide clients, such as major airlines.

6.4   There are some obvious immediate difficulties in UK auditors working overseas, namely the differences in language and culture. These problems can usually be overcome, through the use of translators, good preparation and the fortunate use of English as a second language in many countries.

6.5 A summary of the difficulties and possible solutions involved would include the following.

(a) **Language difficulties** might be overcome by finding a member of the UK office who speaks the relevant language, or a translator.

(b) **Cultural differences** should be tackled by the UK auditors learning as much as possible about the country before leaving the UK.

(c) **Differences in local accounting and auditing conventions,** as well as legislation, can again be tackled by study before the audit begins.

(d) Some countries may have very **specific problems**, including civil unrest, high inflation or hyper inflation, currency restrictions and so on. The auditors will need to consider how such issues should be tackled in the audit (as well as the eventual consolidation).

(e) The auditors may face difficulties obtaining the necessary **permit to work** or even enter the country in question. The client company should help the auditors as much as possible in this respect.

(f) The auditors must ensure that they have **sufficient support** in their base office in the UK to help them if any difficulty arises.

Exam focus point

A number of recent questions on group audits have had an international dimension, since the problems of obtaining sufficient audit evidence and assurance on the work of other auditors can be acute.

Chapter roundup

- Principal company auditors have a duty to report on the truth and fairness of group accounts. They have the right to require from auditors of subsidiaries the **information** and **explanations** they require, and to require the principal company to obtain the necessary **information** and **explanations** from subsidiaries.

- Principal auditors should consider whether their **involvement** in the group audit is **sufficient** for them to act as principal auditors.

- The reliance placed on other auditors will depend on a variety of factors.

  ° **Assessment** of the other firms' **independence** and **competence**
  ° **Reviews** of other firms' work

- You should revise the regulations for group accounting in FRS 2, FRS 6 and FRS 7 and CA 1985 in your financial accounting study material.

- Consolidation procedures include:

  ° checking **consolidation adjustments** have been correctly made;
  ° checking **treatment of additions and disposals** has been correct;
  ° arithmetical checks.

- Auditing a **foreign subsidiary** can pose practical problems for auditors. An appreciation of the features of doing business and auditing in the country concerned is vital.

Quick quiz

1   What special rights are granted to the principal auditors by the Companies Act 1985 in relation to other auditors? (see paras 1.3 - 1.4)

2   What factors should the principal auditors consider before accepting a group engagement? (2.3)

3   What enquiries should the principal auditors make about the other auditors? (2.4)

4   What matters should the principal auditors communicate to the other auditors? (2.5)

5   What duties does SAS 510 impose on other auditors to co-operate with principal auditors? (2.11 - 2.14)

6   Should the principal auditors mention the reports of other auditors in their report on the holding company? (2.18)

7   What factors should be considered when determining the necessity for separate engagement letters for group companies? (2.22)

8   List the audit steps involved in the consolidation process. (3.2)

9   In what circumstances might joint auditors be appointed by a company or group? (5.3)

Question to try	Level	Marks	Time
10	Exam	20	36 mins

Chapter 11

DIRECTORS, LAW AND REGULATIONS AND FRAUD

Chapter topic list	Syllabus reference
1 Directors' emoluments	5(d)
2 Transactions with directors	5(d)
3 Related party transactions	5(d)
4 Law and regulations	5(d)
5 Fraud and error	5(d)

Introduction

The transactions of directors are a sensitive issue, particularly (in the current economic climate) in relation to pay. Although disclosure of directors' transactions is governed by statute, the Cadbury Report has suggested fuller disclosure and other measures such as the restriction of the length of directors' service contracts.

The audit of transactions with directors is important because of the impact it can have on the audit report; if the accounts do not disclose the relevant information, then the auditors are obliged to do so in their report.

The last part of the chapter deals with SAS 460 *Related party transactions*, SAS 120 *Consideration of law and regulations*, and SAS 110 *Fraud and error*.

These SASs can be difficult to apply, but the consequences for the auditor of failing to identify problems or take appropriate action can be very serious.

Exam focus point

Topics in this chapter are important because of the implications for the audit report (emoluments etc) and because they are topical (because FRS 8 has come out recently). A question might link a number of topics in this chapter.

1   DIRECTORS' EMOLUMENTS

1.1   The legal requirements which relate to disclosure of directors' emoluments are complex and are now contained in Schedule 6 of the CA 1985.

1.2   Auditors have a duty to include in their report the required disclosure particulars of **directors' emoluments** and **transactions** with directors, if they have not been fully disclosed in the accounts.

Audit approach

1.3 Auditors will have carried out an evaluation of salaries payroll procedures, including the system in operation for directors' salaries, earlier in the audit.

1.4 At the year end, they can probably concentrate on limited substantive work designed to ensure that:

(a) the final figures in the accounting records are complete. Certain figures such as directors' bonuses and commissions may not be computed until the last moment);

(b) the disclosure requirements in respect of directors have been complied with.

1.5 Auditors may have particular problems here in relation to non-recurring payments and benefits in kind, as, if they have no previous knowledge of the existence of such items, they are often difficult to detect. Consideration should always be given as to whether some of the more common types of benefit exist (for example a company car or cheap loans).

1.6 Auditors should carry out the following general procedures.

- **Ascertain** whether **monies payable** or **benefits in kind** provided have been properly approved in accordance with the company's memorandum and articles of association and that they are **not prohibited** by the Act.

- **Confirm** that all **monies payable** and **benefits receivable** in relation to the current accounting period have been **properly accounted for**, unless the right to any of these has been waived by inspecting:

  o salary records,

  o service contracts,

  o P11Ds,

  o pension records

- **Review directors' service contracts, salary records, board minutes** and other records for evidence of **emoluments** that have **not been disclosed**.

- **Review** the **company's procedures** to ensure that all directors are made aware of and properly discharge their statutory responsibility (s 232(3)) to advise the board of all disclosable emoluments.

- **Review** the **procedures** for ensuring that any **payments** made to **former directors** of the company are **identified** and properly **disclosed**.

- **Consider** the need for any amounts included in directors' remuneration to be **further disclosed** in accordance with the provisions of the Companies Act 1985 (for example property rented by directors from a company at below market rental).

Further disclosures

1.7 The following disclosures may require special attention.

(a) **Compensation for loss of office***:* generally speaking these payments are disclosable but doubt often arises over whether the approval of the company in general meeting is required.

(b) **Emoluments** paid **other than by the company itself***:* disclosure is required regardless of who actually makes the payment but it may be difficult to obtain the necessary information.

(c) **Benefits in kind** are disclosable as well as fees and salaries and these are frequently difficult to quantify.

(d) The Companies Act 1989 amends the 1985 Act to require disclosure of:

    (i) **'Golden hellos'** (amounts paid to obtain the services of a director); and

    (ii) **Payments** made to **'connected persons'** or to a body corporate controlled by a director.

(e) **Share options** granted to directors.

(f) Amounts payable under **long-term incentive schemes**.

(g) **Retirement benefits** that are in **excess** of what directors are **entitled** to under the pension scheme.

Compensation for loss of office

1.8 In the normal course of events, statute requires that any payments made to a director in compensation for loss of office (or in connection with his retirement) should have received the **prior** approval of the company in general meeting.

1.9 The following difficulties in interpretation may, however, arise and legal advice may be required.

(a) The prior approval of the members is *not* required in respect of payments which are made *bona fide* by way of **damages** for breach of contract or by way of pension in respect of past services.

Auditors must **ascertain** the **terms** and **length** of the **unexpired portion** of the director's service contract and consider the reasonableness of the payments made against this background.

(b) Where a payment made is described as **ex gratia** it could be considered to be unrelated to the office and therefore not requiring the prior approval of the members.

Auditors should consider carefully all the circumstances surrounding the payment and not automatically assume that approval was not required.

(c) Where a payment is made to a director after he or she has resigned, it has been argued that the prior approval of the members is not required, as the Act does not require the prior approval of payments made to past directors.

Payments made by persons other than the company

1.10 As noted earlier, directors' emoluments must be disclosed even if they have not been paid by the company itself. This would most commonly arise in the following situations:

(a) where payment is made either by a holding company or fellow subsidiary;

(b) where payment is made by a management company which is not part of the group or a company owned by the director, a charge being made to the company (where financial statements are being reported on) for the services of the director.

In addition to being remuneration, any such arrangement may also require disclosure under the provisions of the Companies Act 1985 in relation to transactions in which directors have a material interest.

1.11 In either of the above cases a blanket charge may be made to the company by the other company involved, covering not merely the director's emoluments but also other costs (such as general administration costs). In this situation the amount requiring disclosure may not be separately identifiable (in the case of payments made by another group company there may be no recharge at all).

1.12 Auditors would therefore be justified in accepting an apportionment, especially where no recharge is made and the director is a director of several group companies.

1.13 Auditors should also bear in mind that the information is only disclosable 'so far as ..... the company has the right to obtain it from the persons concerned'. Where the necessary information cannot be obtained, then the facts should be disclosed by way of note.

1.14 Auditors may be faced with a further complication if a company claims that emoluments paid by its parent company were purely in respect of the director's services to the parent company. If this is the case, then such emoluments are only disclosable in the accounts of the parent company if the director is also a director of the parent company (unless the parent company is a foreign company). The auditors must consider the acceptability of such a claim in the light of what they know about the company.

Valuation of benefits in kind

1.15 In accordance with the Companies Act 1985 the amount to be disclosed for a benefit in kind is its **estimated money value**. The Act gives no guidance as to how this phrase should be interpreted. Taxable amounts are often used but it is difficult to reconcile these with 'money values' for certain types of benefit. Perhaps more useful information for members would be to consider a value based upon the **personal benefit** derived by the director.

1.16 Where the value used is based upon estimates the auditors must **ensure** that such **estimates** are made **at an appropriate level** (for example by the board of directors). On occasions it may be almost impossible to place a meaningful value on the benefit. In such cases it might be advisable for the directors to provide an explanatory note at the foot of the directors' emoluments note.

Golden hellos

1.17 Under the Companies Act 1985 rules emoluments in respect of a person's accepting office as director shall be treated as emoluments in respect of his services as director.

Payments to connected persons and controlled bodies corporate

1.18 The Companies Act 1985 requires disclosure of payments to **connected persons** and **controlled bodies** corporate within the aggregate figures for directors' emoluments. The definition of 'connected person' and 'controlled' bodies corporate in the Companies Act 1985 provisions requiring disclosure of payments to such persons is as defined for the directors' loans legislation. It will include:

    (a) spouses;

    (b) children;

    (c) partners;

    (d) some trusts;

    (e) bodies corporate in which a director has a significant holding (generally, over 20%).

1.19 From the audit point of view, identifying connected persons and controlled bodies corporate is likely to present the biggest problem in checking that these disclosures have been properly made. If the company fails to make the required disclosures, then auditors have a statutory responsibility to include the necessary details in their audit report, insofar as they are reasonably able to do so.

Share options

1.20 UITF Abstract 12 *Disclosure of directors' share options* requires the disclosure of share options granted to individual directors, together with details of the exercise price, market price at date of exercise etc. However, this abstract is *not* legally enforceable. The form shown below assumes that the company would disclose options granted to directors in full.

Directors' notification

1.21 The form below is an example of a form to be submitted annually by each director to the company secretary containing information about emoluments. Auditors should obtain copies of these forms and will often, in addition, obtain a confirmation statement of aggregate emoluments from the company secretary.

1.22 Note that the following form enquires about related party transactions: see Section 3 below.

CERTIFICATE OF DIRECTORS' REMUNERATION, INTERESTS IN SHARES ETC, AND INTEREST IN CONTRACTS FOR THE YEAR ENDED ....

I, ..., hereby give notice in accordance with the provisions of section 232(3) of the Companies Act 1985 that the emoluments received and receivable by me, including amounts paid to persons connected with me and bodies corporate controlled by me, in respect of my services to the company or its subsidiary undertakings as referred to in Part I of Schedule 6 to the Companies Act 1985 are as follows.

	From the company £	From its subsidiary undertakings £	From other persons £
A Remuneration for current financial year			
1 Emoluments			
(i) Services as a director:			
Fees as a director			
(ii) Management or executive services:			
Remuneration including bonuses and commissions			
Expense allowance assessed to UK tax			
The estimated money value of benefits received otherwise than in cash			
Pension scheme contributions			
(iii) Remuneration in respect of accepting office as director			
Total emoluments			
2 Pensions paid, otherwise than under a duly constituted scheme:			
Monetary amount of pensions paid/payable in cash including amounts payable to dependants and nominees			
Estimated money value of pensions payable otherwise than in cash			
Total pensions			
3 Compensation for loss of office:			
Monetary amount of compensation for loss of office paid/payable otherwise than in cash			
Estimated money value of compensation for loss of office paid/payable otherwise than in cash			
Total compensation for loss of office			
4 Consideration paid by the company to third parties in respect of my services as a director:			
Monetary amount of payments to third parties for making available my services as director			
Estimated money value of consideration to third parties paid/payable otherwise than in cash			
Total payments to third parties			
TOTAL for current year			
Emoluments in respect of the current year which I have waived			

	From the company £	From its subsidiary undertakings £	From other persons £
B Adjustment in respect of previous years Expense allowances and benefits not previous included, now charged to UK income tax Other adjustments (specify):			

C   Disclosure of nature of benefits in kind

I hereby confirm

1   The amount for pensions includes an estimated money value of £........ in respect of .... [*nature of pension in kind*] which was given to me.

2   The amount for compensation for loss of office includes an estimated money value of £........ in respect of .... [*nature of compensation in kind*] which was given to me.

3   The amount of consideration paid to third parties in respect of my service includes an estimated money value of £........ in respect of .... [*nature of consideration in kind*].

II   I hereby confirm that my interests, including those of my spouse and infant children, in the shares and debentures of the company or other body corporate in the same group required to be disclosed in the directors' report, were as follows.

Description of shares	At beginning of year (or date of appointment)	At end of year

III   I hereby confirm that the following rights to subscribe for shares in or debentures of the company or any other body corporate in the same group were granted to or exercised by me (including those of my spouse and infant children) during the year to which this certificate relates.

Description of option/right	At beginning of year (or date of appointment)	Granted	Exercised	At end of year

IV   I confirm that during the year to which this certificate relates, neither I nor any person connected with me had an interest in any contract, transaction, arrangement or agreement with the company or any of its subsidiaries (other than my contract of service) required to be disclosed in the accounts, except:

Date of contract arrangement or agreement	Principal terms	Value of contract, arrangement or agreement	Parties to contract arrangement or agreement	Nature of director's interest

> **V** I further confirm that neither I, nor any person connected with me, was indebted at any time during the financial year ended .... in respect of any loan, quasi-loan or credit transaction granted by:
>
> (i)   the company;
> (ii) any subsidiary; or
> (iii) any person under a guarantee or on security provided by the company or any of its subsidiary companies.
>
> Signed ....   Date ....

Question 1

List the general audit procedures required to ensure that directors' emoluments have been correctly accounted for and disclosed.

Answer

See Paragraph 1.6

2   TRANSACTIONS WITH DIRECTORS

Accounting requirements

2.1   Under s 330 Companies Act 1985 no company may:

(a)   **make a loan to a director**, or to a director of its holding company;

(b)   **guarantee or provide security** in connection with a loan made to such a director by another party;

(c)   **arrange** to have **assigned** to it, or to assume, rights or liabilities under a transaction which would have been prohibited if it had initially been entered into by the company (this clause is designed to prevent the basic rule in (a) and (b) being circumvented by involving third parties);

(d)   **take part** in any sort of **arrangement** whereby a third party receives some benefit from the company, its holding company, subsidiary or fellow subsidiary and, in return, enters into a transaction with a director which would have been prohibited if it had been entered into by the company.

2.2   No **relevant** company may enter into, guarantee or provide security in connection with:

(a)   a **loan agreement** with a **person 'connected' with a director** or a director of its holding company;

(b)   a **quasi-loan** with such a **director or connected person**;

(c)   a **credit transaction** with such a **director or connected person**.

2.3   S 330 introduces some important terms which are defined in s 331.

> **KEY TERMS**
>
> - **Relevant company** means any public company and any private company which is a member of a group containing one or more public companies.
>
> - **Persons connected with a director** include:
>
>   (a) the spouse and infant children of the director;
>
>   (b) companies with which the director is associated, (a director is associated with a company if, together with any persons connected with him, he holds more than 20% of the equity capital or voting rights of the company);
>
>   (c) the trustee of a trust of which the director or a person connected with him is a beneficiary;
>
>   (d) any partners of the director or of a person connected with him.
>
> - **Quasi-loan** is made to a person when a company pays or agrees to pay money for or on behalf of that person on the understanding that the money will be reimbursed by that person. A typical example is where a director uses a company credit card to buy goods for his personal use on the understanding that he will reimburse the company at a later time.
>
> - **Credit transaction** includes any transaction involving the acquisition of land, goods or services for which payment is deferred. It includes leasing transactions.

Exceptions to general prohibitions

2.4   There are certain exceptions to the general prohibitions above. These are summarised in the table below.

Type of transaction	Conditions	Limits	
		Private companies (directors)	**Relevant companies Directors and (connected persons)**
Funds for business expenditure	Approved by members	None	£10,000 in total outstanding per director
Loans etc between holding company and subsidiary		None	None
Quasi-loans	Repayable within two months	None	None
Credit transactions	In ordinary course of business/arm's length	None	None
	Not in ordinary course of business	None	£5,000 in total outstanding per director
Loans etc to subsidiary associated with director		None	None
Loans etc by money-lending companies	For purchase/ improvement of principal residence	£100,000 in total	£100,000 in total
	Others, in ordinary course of business /arm's length	None	£100,000 in total (except banks)

(a) **De minimis exemption** (small loans). A company is not prohibited from making loans to any of its directors or to any director of its holding company, provided the aggregate of the relevant amounts does not exceed **£5,000.**

(b) **Quasi-loans** to directors of **relevant** companies are permitted provided they are paid within **two months**, and the total outstanding to the company and its subsidiaries does not exceed **£5,000.**

(c) A company is not prohibited from doing anything to provide any of its directors with funds to meet expenditure **incurred by** him for the **purposes of the company** or to enable him **properly to perform his duties** as officer of the company or to enable any of its directors to avoid incurring such expenditure. Such expenditure must however be approved either by:

(i) **prior approval** of the company in general meeting; or

(ii) **retroactive approval** at or before the **next annual general meeting** after the loan is made. Failing this, the loan must be repaid within six months of the conclusion of that meeting.

The **purpose and amount** must be **disclosed** at the general meeting during which approval of the loan is sought. In the case of a **relevant company** this exception is restricted in that such a company may not enter into any transaction if the aggregate of the **relevant amounts** exceeds £10,000.

(d)   A company is not prohibited from:

   (i)   making a **loan** or **quasi-loan** to its **holding company;**

   (ii)   entering into a **guarantee** or **providing any security** in connection with such a loan or quasi-loan;

   (iii)   entering into a **credit transaction** as creditor for its holding company;

   (iv)   entering into a **guarantee** or **providing any security** in connection with such a credit transaction.

(e)   **Intra-group transactions.** Where a director of a relevant company or of its holding company is associated with a subsidiary of either of those companies, the relevant company is not prohibited by reason of that association alone from making a loan or quasi-loan to the *subsidiary*, nor is it prohibited from entering into a guarantee or providing any security in connection with such a loan or quasi-loan.

(f)   All **credit transactions** made in the **ordinary course** of the company's business can be for unlimited amounts; if not in the ordinary course of business, the **relevant amount** is limited to £5,000, for **relevant** companies.

(g)   **Transactions** entered into by **money-lending companies** in the ordinary course of their business and on terms that are no more favourable than those that would be available to an unconnected person of similar standing. In the case of a **relevant** company the 'relevant amount' must not exceed **£100,000** (but see (h) below).

(h)   For transactions entered into by recognised banks the provisions are the same as in (g) but without any financial limit (but see (i) below).

(i)   **Loans** made to **directors of money-lending companies or recognised banks for the purchase or improvement of their sole or main residence** provided that they are granted on terms that are no more favourable than those given to other employees and the **relevant amount** does not exceed £100,000.

Note. The **relevant amount** is the value of all existing transactions between, on the one hand, the party in relation to whom a new transaction is being contemplated and any persons connected with him and, on the other hand, the company and any of its subsidiaries or fellow subsidiaries, plus the value of the transaction being contemplated.

2.5   In general a loan or other transaction which is entered into in contravention of the Act is **voidable** at the instance of the company. If a relevant company makes an arrangement which breaches s 330, the director(s) responsible and other persons aware of the illegality of the transaction may be criminally liable. The director (or connected person) is also liable to account to the company for any gain he has made.

Directors' contracts of employment

2.6   Under s 319 CA 1985, a company may not incorporate into any agreement a term that a director's employment with the company (or within the group if he is a director of the holding company) is to continue or may be **continued otherwise than at the company's option** for a period that exceeds **five** years unless:

   (a)   the company has the **absolute right** to terminate the employment by notice; or

   (b)   the term has been **approved** by the company in **general meeting.**

2.7   The Act goes further than the Stock Exchange Listing Agreement which requires that no service contract shall be longer than ten years unless approved by the company in general meeting. The *Cadbury Report* has now suggested that directors' contracts should be no longer than **three** years although this requirement is not mandatory.

Substantial property transactions

2.8 The 1985 Act contains restrictions in respect of substantial property transactions between companies and their directors. The basic rule under s 320 is that any **acquisition or disposal** by the company of a **non-cash** asset **from or to** a **director**, a **director of its holding company** or a **connected person** is **prohibited**. The major exceptions are:

(a) **arrangements approved** by the company in **general meeting**;

(b) arrangements when the value of the assets is **less than £1,000** or, **if greater**, is **less than the lower of £50,000 and 10%** of the company's **net assets** (as reported in the last accounts);

(c) if the **asset** is to be **acquired by** a **holding company from** any of its **wholly owned subsidiaries** or **from** a **holding company by any** of its **wholly owned subsidiaries**, or **by one wholly owned subsidiary** to **another wholly owned subsidiary** of the same holding company;

(d) the arrangement is entered into by a company which is being **wound up** (unless the winding-up is a members' voluntary winding-up.)

Disclosure requirements

2.9 The disclosure requirements relate to:

(a) any **loans**, **quasi-loans** or **other arrangements** specified in s 330 that the company or one of its subsidiaries has entered into or agreed to enter into;

(b) any other **transaction** or **arrangement** with the company or one of its subsidiaries in which a director of the company, its holding company or a person connected with such **director** had, either directly or indirectly a **material interest**.

2.10 The term 'material' is not defined by the Act. It is left to the opinion of the majority of the other directors or, failing their agreement, to the court.

2.11 The main information which should be disclosed is:

(a) the **principal terms** of the transaction or arrangement;

(b) a **statement** that it **took place** or existed during the year;

(c) the **name of the director involved** and, where relevant, the name of the connected person;

(d) as regards **loans**:

    (i) the **amount of the liability** (including interest) at both the beginning and the end of the financial year and the maximum amount during the year;

    (ii) the **amount of any unpaid interest**;

    (iii) the **amount of any provision** the company has made against the debt;

(e) **similar requirement**s existing for **guarantees, loans, quasi loans** and so forth;

(f) the **'value'** of any other **transactions** which would mean, for example, the disclosure of the arm's length value of any goods, land or services;

(g) for officers other than directors, the Act requires the disclosure of the **aggregate amount outstanding** at the end of the year and the **number of officers** involved for each of the following types of transaction:

    (i) **loans** and **related guarantees**;

(ii)   **quasi-loans** and **related guarantees**;

(iii)   **credit transactions** and **related guarantees**.

2.12   There are exemptions from disclosure. These are the principal ones:

(a)   **transactions** etc between **two companies** where the interest of a director of one solely arises because he is also a director of the other;

(b)   **service contracts** (these must however be available for inspection by members under s 318);

(c)   **credit transactions** (and **related agreements**) when the aggregate amount outstanding on all such transactions for the director involved does not **exceed £5,000**;

(d)   **any transaction** or **arrangement** where the aggregate value of all such transactions is **less than £1,000** or, if it exceeds £1,000, is less than the **lower of £5,000** or **1%** of the **company's net assets**;

(e)   any **transaction** etc which was **not entered** into during the financial year and which did not subsist at any time during that year.

Audit approach

2.13   How can the auditors ensure, so far as they are reasonably able to, that all statutory disclosure requirements have been complied with? The approach below reflects the guidance provided in an APC audit brief entitled *Directors' loans, other transactions and remuneration*. The APB has not replaced this guidance.

Identification of transactions

2.14   Auditors may find it difficult to obtain sufficient assurance that they have identified all disclosable transactions because of:

(a)   the **low value of certain transactions**, making them difficult to detect when using normal audit procedures;

(b)   the **requirements of the Act** for **disclosure of transactions** between the company and the connected persons of a director, given that it may not always be easy for the auditors to identify such connected persons;

(c)   the fact that there may be little or no **documentary evidence** of **transactions** requiring disclosure, given that the Act covers not just formal agreements and arrangements, but also informal ones.

In the light of the above, the auditors' approach must often be largely dependent on their own vigilance and on management representations.

Complexity of legislation

2.15   The complexity of the legislation may give rise to difficulties of interpretation. For example, the Act does not actually include a definition of a loan; the auditors must be aware that not every form of indebtedness amounts to a loan. Advances of expenses or remuneration on account may constitute a loan if the monies are outstanding for a long time.

Company procedures

2.16 Auditors should enquire as to the company's procedures for ensuring that all disclosable transactions are properly identified and recorded. Such procedures are likely to include the following.

- **Advise** all **directors** and **officers** that they have a **responsibility** to disclose transactions in which they have an interest, either directly or through connected persons. (Such disclosure should take place at a meeting of the directors of the company.)

- **Record** all **transactions** notified in the minutes of directors' meetings.

- **Maintain** a **register** in which details of all transactions requiring disclosure are recorded.

- **Establish** some **method** of:

  ° **identifying proposed transactions** which will require the approval of the members in general meeting; and

  ° **ensuring** that the **company does not enter** into any **illegal transaction**.

- **Monitor the system** by checking on a regular basis (as a minimum, once a year) that each director is in agreement with the company's record of his disclosable transactions and is satisfied that such records are both complete and accurate.

- **Obtain** from **each director** at the end of each financial year a **formal statement** indicating the disclosures necessary for the purposes of the statutory accounts. This statement might conveniently be combined with the directors' emoluments letter.

2.17 The company secretary is likely to establish the necessary procedures in a larger company. With smaller organisations, auditors may well find that there may be no formalised procedures or that they are inadequate. Auditors should **advise each director** of his statutory responsibilities together with a **written request** for **confirmation** of any disclosable transaction in which he has an interest (and consider advising the company about instituting formalised procedures).

2.18 An example of a form requiring such information is given at the end of this section.

Audit procedures

2.19 Further audit procedures to be adopted should include the following.

- **Inspect** the **board minutes** and other records of transactions with directors and connected persons to consider their adequacy and whether or not they appear to have been kept up to date.

- **Examine** any **agreements** and **contracts** involving **directors and connected persons**, including tracing the details of such transactions to any source documentation available.

- **Consider** whether **transactions** disclosed are on **commercial** terms.

- **Assess** the **recoverability** of amounts due from directors or connected persons.

- **Review** the **legality** of the disclosable transactions recorded by the company. Where auditors are of the opinion that a transaction is illegal, they should:

     °   immediately advise the directors of their view;

     °   give careful consideration as to whether any reference to the matter will be required in the audit report.

- **Advise** the **client** to **seek legal advice** in those cases where there are doubts as to the legality and/or disclosable nature of a transaction;

    (°   should the client decline to do so; or if

     °   the auditors are still not satisfied with the advice received by the client

then they should consider taking independent legal advice on the matter).

- **Consider** the **possibility** that the **company's details** of **disclosable transactions** may be incomplete as regards those directors (and connected persons) who have not been in office throughout the year.

- **Review subsequent events** in order to consider whether they might have any impact on the matters requiring disclosure.

Formal disclosure statement

2.20   Finally, auditors should consider obtaining written representations from each director giving confirmation of any disclosable transaction which relates to himself and any persons connected with him. An appropriate form of letter might be as follows.

Dear Sirs,

Transactions involving directors and connected persons

(Companies Act 1985 s 232, Sch 6 Part II)

I hereby confirm that I have examined the financial statements of Standard plc as at 31 December 19XX and that these financial statements contain all the information required by section 232 and Sch 6 Part II of the Companies Act 1985 in respect of myself and all persons connected with me.

Yours faithfully,

An alternative form of letter might make reference to an **attached list of transactions** (where financial statements incorporating the information are not available). In these circumstances the auditors would need to check that the information on the list was correctly transferred to the financial statements.

2.21   In the case of those companies where more formal procedures have been established, copies of the formal disclosure statement mentioned above might have been prepared by each director and addressed to the company secretary. In addition to these, auditors may wish to obtain a statement from the company secretary on behalf of the board covering directors' transactions in aggregate.

2.22   As in the case of directors' emoluments, if a company does not comply with the disclosures of the Act, it is the responsibility of the auditors to include the details in their report as far as they are reasonably able to do so. The report would be qualified on the grounds of disagreement: failure to comply with legislation, and a paragraph such as the following might be included.

'The following details of a loan required by s 232 of the Companies Act 1985 to be disclosed in the financial statements, have not been so disclosed. During the year, the company made a loan of £8,000 to Mr A X, a minor son of Mr B X, a director of the company. The maximum amount of the liability (including interest) during the year amounted to £8,300. The amount of the liability at the end of the year was £7,300 of which £3,000 was interest due but not paid at that date.'

To: The Secretary .... Limited/plc

CERTIFICATE OF DIRECTOR'S INDEBTEDNESS TO THE COMPANY FOR THE YEAR ENDED
....

I confirm that the details set out below provide all the information required to be disclosed in the company's accounts by Schedule 6 to the Companies Act 1985 in respect of my indebtedness to the company or any of its subsidiary companies.

1 Indebtedness to the company or any subsidiaries	Loans		Quasi-loans		Credit transactions	
	Com-pany £	Subsid-iaries £	Com-pany £	Subsid-iaries £	Com-pany £	Subsid-iaries £
(a) Amount outstanding: at beginning of period						
at end of period						
(b) Maximum amount out-standing during period						
(c) Amount of any interest due but unpaid						

2   Details of principal terms of loans, quasi-loans or credit transactions:

3   In respect of loans, quasi-loans or credit transactions guaranteed or secured by the company or any of its subsidiary companies:

	Company £	Subsidiaries £
(a) Amount of company's, or subsidiaries', liability: at beginning of period		
at end of period		
(b) Maximum potential liability of company or subsidiary		
(c) Any amount paid or incurred by company or subsidiary in fulfilling guarantee or discharging security		

Signed ....   Date ....

Question 2

Sketch the table shown in Paragraph 2.8 listing the CA 1985 limits for the transactions of directors.

---

3   RELATED PARTY TRANSACTIONS

3.1   Central to a number of DTI investigations have been companies trading with organisations or individuals **other than at arm's length**. Such transactions were made possible by a degree of control or influence exercised by directors over both parties to the transactions, and in some cases resulted in financial loss to shareholders, creditors or both.

3.2   Some types of related party transactions are covered by existing statutory or Stock Exchange requirements, such as the provisions of the Companies Act 1985 covering transactions by directors and connected persons discussed above and 'Class IV' circulars which listed companies are required to send to shareholders when an acquisition or disposal of assets is made from or to a director, substantial shareholder or associate.

3.3   The accounting for related party transactions is dealt with in FRS 8 *Related party disclosures*. This FRS is covered in full in the accounting text for Paper 10.

Knowledge brought forward from Paper 10 Accounting

Related parties are defined as two or more parties, (where) at any time during the financial period:

(a)   one party has either direct or indirect control of the other party; or

(b)   the parties are subject to common control from the same source; or

(c)   one party has influence over the financial and operating policies of the other party to an extent that that other party might be inhibited from pursuing at all times its own separate interests; or

(d)   the parties, in entering a transactions, are subject to influence from the same source to such an extent that one of the parties to the transaction has subordinated its own separate interests.'

Related party transactions are the transfer of assets or liabilities or the performance of services by, to or for a related party irrespective of whether a price is charged.'

FRS 8 can be summarised as follows.

(a)   FRS 8 requires the disclosure of:

     (i)   **information** on **related party transactions**; and

     (ii)   the **name of** the party **controlling** the **reporting entity** and, if different, that of the **ultimate controlling party** whether or not any transactions between the reporting entity and those parties have taken place.

   Aggregated disclosures are allowed subject to certain restrictions.

   Related parties are defined below.

(b)   No disclosure is required in consolidated financial statements of intragroup transactions and balances eliminated on consolidation. A parent undertaking is not required to provide related party disclosures in its own financial statements when those statements are presented with consolidated financial statements of its group.

(c)   Disclosure is not required in the financial statements of subsidiary undertakings, 90% or more of whose voting rights are controlled within the group, of transactions with entities that are part of the group or investees of the group qualifying as related parties provided that the consolidated financial statements in which that subsidiary is included are publicly available.

The auditors should consider the implications for their report if:

SAS 460 *Related parties*

3.4   The purpose of the SAS is:

> 'to establish standards and provide guidance on auditing related party transactions, establishing the ultimate controlling party of the reporting entity and their respective disclosure in financial statements. Disclosure requirements with respect to related party transactions and control of an entity are found, for example, in companies legislation, accounting standards and stock exchange listing rules.'

SAS 460.1

The auditors should plan and perform the audit with the objective of obtaining sufficient audit evidence regarding the adequacy of the disclosure of related party transactions and control of the entity in the financial statements.

Inherent difficulties of detection

3.5   It may not be self-evident to management whether a party is related. Furthermore, many accounting systems are not designed to either distinguish or summarise related party transactions, so management will have to carry out additional analysis of accounting information.

3.6   An audit cannot be expected to detect all material related party transactions. The risk that undisclosed related party transactions will not be detected by the auditors is especially high when:

(a)   related party transactions have taken place without charge;

(b)   related party transactions are not self-evident to the auditors;

(c)   transactions are with a party that the auditors could not reasonably be expected to know is a related party; or

(d)   active steps have been taken by directors or management to conceal either the full terms of a transaction, or that a transaction is, in substance, with a related party.

Responsibilities of the directors

3.7   The directors are responsible for the identification of related party transactions. Such transactions should be properly approved as they are frequently not at arm's length. The directors are also responsible for the *disclosure* of related party transactions.

Quality of audit evidence

3.8   Such evidence may:

(a)   be limited; or
(b)   although not limited, be created by the related party.

Evidence is most reliable when obtained from or created by third parties. The auditors can, if other audit work does not indicate contrary evidence, accept representations from the directors. The auditors should, however, have a degree of scepticism.

Identification of related parties and transactions

SAS 460.2

When planning the audit the auditors should assess the risk that material undisclosed related party transactions may exist.

3.9   Control systems should be instituted by the directors to identify related party transactions. In general, the higher the auditors' assessment of control risk, with respect to related parties, the more emphasis is placed on substantive procedures when developing the audit programme.

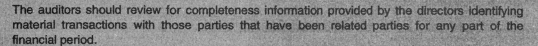

SAS 460.3

The auditors should review for completeness information provided by the directors identifying material transactions with those parties that have been related parties for any part of the financial period.

3.10 The following examples are given of audit procedures.

- **Review minutes** of meetings of shareholders and directors and other relevant statutory records such as the register of directors' interests.

- **Review accounting records** for large or unusual transactions or balances, in particular transactions recognised at or near the end of the financial period.

- **Review confirmations of loans receivable** and payable and confirmations from banks. Such a review may indicate the relationship, if any, of guarantors to the entity.

- **Review investment transactions**, for example purchase or sale of an interest in a joint venture or other entity.

3.11 The following substantive procedures are suggested, the extent of which should be determined as a result of tests of controls and the procedures listed above.

- **Enquire of management** and the directors as to whether transactions have taken place with related parties that are required to be disclosed by the disclosure requirements, such as FRS 8, that are applicable to the entity.

- **Review prior year working papers** for names of known related parties.

- **Enquire** as to the **names** of all pension and other trusts established for the benefit of employees and the names of their management and trustees.

- **Enquire** as to the **affiliation** of directors and officers with other entities.

- **Review the register of interests in shares** to determine the names of principal shareholders.

- **Enquire of other auditors** currently involved in the audit, or predecessor auditors, as to their knowledge of additional related parties.

- **Review the entity's tax returns**, listing documents supplied to Stock Exchanges, returns made under companies legislation and other information supplied to regulatory agencies for evidence of the existence of related parties.

- **Review invoices and correspondence** from lawyers for indications of the existence of related parties or related party transactions.

SAS 460.4

The auditors should be alert for evidence of material related party transactions that are not included in the information provided by the directors

3.12 The following evidence is suggested of the type mentioned in SAS 460.4.

- Transactions which have **abnormal terms of trade**, such as unusual prices, interest rates, guarantees and repayment terms.

- Transactions which appear to **lack a logical business reason** for their occurrence.

- Transactions in which **substance differs from form**.

- Transactions **processed or approved in a non-routine manner** or by personnel who do not ordinarily deal with such transactions.

- **Unusual transactions** which are entered into shortly before or after the end of the financial period.

Examining identified related party transactions and disclosures

SAS 460.5

The auditors should obtain sufficient appropriate audit evidence that material identified related party transactions are properly recorded and disclosed in the financial statements.

3.13 The following procedures are suggested when the audit evidence about a related party transaction is limited.

(a) **Discuss** the **purpose** of **the transaction** with management or the directors.

(b) **Confirm** the **terms** and **amount** of the **transaction** with the related party.

(c) **Corroborate** with the **related party** the **explanation** of the purpose of the transaction and, if necessary, confirm that the transaction is *bona-fide*.

Disclosure relating to control of the entity

SAS 460.6

The auditors should obtain sufficient appropriate audit evidence that disclosures in the financial statements relating to control of the entity are properly stated.

Directors' representations

SAS 460.7

The auditors should obtain written representations from the directors concerning the completeness of information provided regarding the related party and control disclosures in the financial statements.

Audit conclusions and reporting

SAS 460.8

The auditors should consider the implications for their report if:

(a) they are unable to obtain sufficient appropriate audit evidence concerning related parties and transactions with such parties; or

(b) the disclosure of related party transactions or the controlling party of the entity in the financial statements is not adequate.

Problems with applying SAS 460

3.14   Problems auditors have had when applying SAS 460 include the following.

Identification of controlling party

3.15   Auditors may find it very difficult to identify the controlling party if the entity is part of a multi-national group. If the controlling party is a trust, auditors may have problems determining who if anyone controls the trust.

3.16   Alternatively the directors may state that they do not know the identity of the controlling party or that there is no controlling party. These statements may be difficult to disprove.

Materiality

3.17   This problem has two aspects:

(a)   Auditors may not be able to determine whether transactions are material to related parties who are individuals (directors, key management and their families).

(b)   Auditors may have particular problems applying the definition of materiality (an item is material if it affects the decisions of the users of the accounts). As materiality depends on circumstances as well as amounts, auditors have to decide whether the fact that certain transactions are on normal commercial terms influences whether they are disclosed.

4   LAW AND REGULATIONS

4.1   The standard which has been brought out on this subject is very long. The SASs in SAS 120 *Consideration of law and regulations* are as follows and these summarise the APB's approach to the subject.

SAS 120

Auditors should plan and perform their audit procedures, and evaluate and report on the results thereof, recognising that non-compliance by the entity with law or regulations may materially affect the financial statements. (SAS 120.1)

The auditors' consideration of compliance with law and regulations

The auditors should obtain sufficient appropriate audit evidence about compliance with those laws and regulations which relate directly to the preparation of, or the inclusion or disclosure of specific items in, the financial statements. (SAS 120.2)

The auditors should perform procedures to help identify possible or actual instances of non-compliance with those laws and regulations which provide a legal framework within which the entity conducts its business and which are central to the entity's ability to conduct its business and hence to its financial statements, by:

(a)   obtaining a general understanding of the legal and regulatory framework applicable to the entity and the industry, and of the procedures followed to ensure compliance with that framework;

(b)   inspecting correspondence with relevant licensing or regulatory authorities;

(c)   enquiring of the directors as to whether they are on notice of any such possible instances of non-compliance with law or regulations; and

(d)   obtaining written confirmation from the directors that they have disclosed to the auditors all those events of which they are aware which involve possible non-compliance, together with the actual or contingent consequences which may arise therefrom. (SAS 120.3)

When carrying out their procedures for the purpose of forming an opinion on the financial statements, the auditors should in addition be alert for instances of possible or actual non-compliance with law or regulations which might affect the financial statements. (SAS 120.4)

When the auditors become aware of information which indicates that non-compliance with law or regulations may exist, they should obtain an understanding of the nature of the act and the circumstances in which it has occurred and sufficient other information to evaluate the possible effect on the financial statements. (SAS 120.5)

When the auditors become aware of or suspect that there may be non-compliance with law or regulations, they should document their findings and, subject to any requirement to report them direct to a third party, discuss them with the appropriate level of management. (SAS 120.6)

The auditors should consider the implications of suspected or actual non-compliance with law or regulations in relation to other aspects of the audit, particularly the reliability or management representations. (SAS 120.7)

Reporting to management

The auditors should, as soon as practicable (save where SAS 120.15 applies) either:

(a)   communicate with management, the board of directors or the audit committee, or

(b)   obtain evidence that they are appropriately informed,

regarding any suspected or actual non-compliance with law or regulations that comes to the auditors' attention. (SAS 120.8)

If, in the auditors' judgement, the suspected or actual non-compliance with law or regulations is material or is believed to be intentional, the auditors should communicate the finding without delay. (SAS 120.9)

Reporting to addressees of the auditors' report on the financial statements

Where the auditors conclude that the view given by the financial statements could be affected by a level of uncertainty concerning the consequences of a suspected or actual non-compliance which, in their opinion, is fundamental, they should include an explanatory paragraph referring to the matter in their report. (SAS 120.10)

Where the auditors conclude that a suspected or actual instance of non-compliance with law or regulation has a material effect on the financial statements and they disagree with the accounting treatment or with the extent, or the lack, of any disclosure in the financial statements of the instance of its consequences they should issue an adverse or qualified opinion. If the auditors are unable to determine whether non-compliance with law or regulations has occurred because of limitation in the scope of their work, they should issue a disclaimer or a qualified opinion. (SAS 120.11)

Reporting to third parties

When the auditors become aware of a suspected or actual non-compliance with law and regulations which gives rise to a statutory duty to report, they should make a report to the appropriate authority without undue delay. (SAS 120.12)

Where the auditors become aware of a suspected or actual instance of non-compliance with law or regulations which does not give rise to a statutory duty to report to an appropriate authority they should:

(a)   consider whether the matter may be one that ought to be reported to a proper authority in the public interest; and where this is the case

(b)   except in the circumstances covered in SAS 120.15, discuss the matter with the board of directors including any audit committee. (SAS 120.13)

   Where, having considered any views expressed on behalf of the entity and in the light of any legal advice obtained, the auditors conclude that the matter ought to be reported to an appropriate authority in the public interest, they should notify the directors in writing of their view and, if the entity does not voluntarily do so itself or is unable to provide evidence that the matter has been reported, they should report it themselves. (SAS 120.14)

   Auditors should report a matter direct to a proper authority in the public interest and without discussing the matter with the entity if they conclude that the suspected or actual instance of non-compliance has caused them no longer to have confidence in the integrity of the directors. (SAS 120.15)

> **Overseas activities**
>
> Where any of the activities of a company or group are carried on outside the United Kingdom or the Republic of Ireland, the auditors should take steps to ensure that the audit work in relation to the detection and reporting of any non-compliance with local law and regulations is planned and carried out in accordance with the requirements of this SAS. (SAS 120.16)

4.2 The SAS draws a distinction between the responsibilities of the directors and the responsibilities of the auditors.

4.3 The **directors** should take the appropriate steps and establish arrangements to ensure compliance with law and regulations and to prevent and detect any non-compliance. In addition, they are responsible for the financial statements showing a true and fair view.

4.4 The **auditors** have no duty to prevent non-compliance with laws and regulations but they should 'plan, perform and evaluate their audit work in order to have a reasonable expectation of detecting material misstatement in the financial statements', including those arising from non-compliance with laws and regulations.

4.5 In an appendix to the SAS there is a list of examples of the type of information that may come to the auditors' attention and may indicate that non-compliance with law or regulations has occurred.

  (a) Investigation by government departments or payment of fines or penalties

  (b) Payments for unspecified services or loans to consultants, related parties, employees or government employees

  (c) Sales commissions or agents' fees that appear excessive in relation to those normally paid by the entity or in its industry or to the services actually received

  (d) Purchasing at pricing significantly above or below market price

  (e) Unusual payments in cash, purchases in the form of cashiers' cheques payable to bearer or transfers to numbered bank accounts

  (f) Unusual transactions with companies registered in tax havens

  (g) Payments for goods or services made other than to the country from which the goods or services originated

  (h) Existence of an accounting system that fails, whether by design or by accident, to provide adequate audit trail or sufficient evidence

  (i) Unauthorised transactions or improperly recorded transactions

  (j) Media comment

Assessment of law and regulations in practice

4.6 SAS 120 has proved difficult for auditors to apply in practice. The Institute of Chartered Accountants in England and Wales recently issued a Technical Release on this area *'Consideration of law and regulations: Guidance and Questionnaire for Auditors.'* Significant aspects of applying SAS 120 in practice highlighted by the Technical Release were as follows.

Distinction between types of law

4.7   The most difficult distinction in practice is between:

(a)   laws which are **central** to the ability of the client to conduct its business;

(b)   other laws and regulations.

4.8   The Technical Release points out that:

(a)   For some businesses, certain laws and regulations will be central, for other businesses the *same* laws and regulations will not be central.

(b)   For some businesses, laws and regulations which were not central last year may be central this year, (for example where the maximum penalty for a first offence is a warning, but subsequent infringements may lead to closure of the business).

Procedures that should be performed

4.9   The Technical Release echoes the distinction that the SAS makes between checking systems of compliance and checking actual compliance. One example given is emissions from a chemical factory; auditors would review the company's systems for keeping these under control, and would also review correspondence with the environmental authority. However, the auditors would not be expected to check the actual emissions. The Technical Release poses the question how far checking compliance procedures might go.

Interaction with SAS 110

4.10   One example given in the Technical Release is of possible illegal payments (maybe bribes) to secure contracts abroad. The laws breached may not be central to the entity's ability to carry on business but breaches could result in adverse publicity and have possible financial consequences. There is therefore an audit risk which auditors have to address under SAS 110 *Fraud and error* by performing audit tests on payments sent abroad with the aim of having a reasonable expectation of being able to detect material fraud or irregularities.

Reporting

4.11   The Technical Release highlights various issues which procedures under SAS 120 may identify that may impact upon the audit report.

(a)   The need for **possible provisions**:

(i)   for fines, legal expenses, rectification costs;
(ii)   for indirect costs, for example loss in value of stock.

(b)   **Going concern doubts** (because of uncertain future sales).

(c)   **Scope limitation**, perhaps caused by unhelpful management responses to queries.

4.12   Auditors should also consider whether they have a statutory duty to report breaches to third parties.

Money laundering

4.13   One area of laws and regulations which has caused auditors particular difficulty is money laundering. The APB issued Practice Notice 12 *Money Laundering* in May 1997 on the subject. Although this Practice Note is not listed as an examinable document, you do need to know what money laundering is and have a general awareness of how it impacts upon the audit.

> **KEY TERM**
>
> **Money laundering** covers any activity by which the apparent source and ownership of money representing the proceeds of income are changed so that the money appears to have been obtained legitimately.

4.14 There are five criminal offences which relate to money laundering.

- **Assisting** another to retain the proceeds of criminal conduct

- **Acquisition, possession or use** of the proceeds of criminal conduct

- **Concealing** the proceeds of criminal activity

- **Failure to disclose** knowledge or suspicion of money laundering (only money laundering related to drug trafficking or terrorism)

- **Tipping off** (disclosing information to any person if disclosure may prejudice an investigation into:

  o   drug trafficking;

  o   drug money laundering;

  o   terrorist related activities;

  o   laundering the proceeds of criminal conduct).

4.15 The Practice Note suggests that the auditors are likely to be affected by money laundering legislation in the following ways.

Appointment

4.16 At minimum, auditors will seek to gain knowledge of the potential client's directors and management so as to fulfil the SAS 210 requirements of obtaining knowledge that is sufficient to enable them to understand the business.

4.17 In addition the money laundering regulations require auditors to carry out identity checks on the client if they are providing certain non-audit services (for example investment business advice) that constitute 'relevant financial business'. In practice many firms now extend these identification procedures to all new clients.

Planning and substantive testing

4.18 Auditor responsibilities under SAS 110 and 120 will influence the audit work that is planned and carried out.

4.19 The Practice Note lists a number of factors which may indicate both fraud and money laundering.

    (a)   *Factors arising from action by the entity or its directors*

         These include:

- Complex corporate structure where complexity does not seem to be warranted

- Complex or unusual transactions, possibly with related parties

- Transactions with little commercial logic taking place in the normal course of business

- Transactions not in the normal course of business

- Transactions where there is a lack of information or explanations, or where explanations are unsatisfactory

- Transactions at an undervalue

- Transactions with companies whose identity is difficult to establish as they are registered in countries known for their commercial secrecy

- Extensive or unusual related party transactions

- Many large cash transactions when not expected

- Payments for unspecified services, or payments for services that appear excessive in relation to the services provided

- The forming of companies or trusts with no apparent commercial or other purpose

- Long delays in the production of company or trust accounts

- Foreign travel which is apparently unnecessary and extensive

(b) *Factors arising from action by a third party*

Circumstances which may indicate that third parties are using transactions with an entity to launder criminal proceeds include:

- A customer establishing a pattern of small transactions and then having one or two substantially larger ones

- Unusual transactions or a pattern of trading with one customer that is different from the norm

- A customer setting up a transaction that appears to be of no commercial advantage or logic

- A customer requesting special arrangements for vague purposes

- Unusual transactions with companies registered overseas

- Requests for settlement in bank accounts or jurisdictions which would be unusual for a normal commercial transaction

4.20 The Practice Note points out that these signs may not be apparent when assessing risk at the planning stage. Nevertheless auditors should be alert, particularly for a significant unusual pattern of activity.

4.21 As regards laws and regulations, the Practice Note draws a distinction between various types of entity.

(a) Entities where the money laundering laws and regulations are central to the business. These include:

(i) financial sector entities offering services that are governed by Money Laundering Regulations;

(ii) public sector entities which are required to comply with specific regulations on money laundering.

(b) Entities where the money laundering laws and regulations are not central, but which may be more likely to be run for money laundering purposes or to be used to launder criminal proceeds. Examples given by the Practice Note include:

    (i)   import/export companies;

    (ii)   business which are cash-based (for example, antique businesses, art dealers, auction houses, casinos or garages).

(c)   Other entities.

Reporting

4.22 Reporting money laundering can cause problems for auditors because of the possibility of breaching the laws relating to **tipping off**. Auditors will not only avoid reporting to management if they suspect management of being involved with money laundering, but they will also have to take care when carrying out audit procedures to avoid problems with tipping off.

4.23 The Practice Note suggests that **preliminary enquiries** to ascertain the precise nature of a transaction will not give rise to a tipping-off offence unless the auditors know or suspect an investigation is being mounted or is proposed, and that auditor enquiries may prejudice the investigation. 'It is important that auditors only go so far as to establish their own satisfaction whether there is a suspected case of money laundering involving the directors and to consider the consequences for the report on the financial statements.'

4.24 As regards the audit report on the financial statements, auditors potentially face a dilemma. An unqualified report may effectively legitimise an illegal business which may constitute assisting another to retain the proceeds of criminal conduct'. On the other hand a qualified audit report or fundamental uncertainty paragraph may constitute tipping off. Legal advice, or advice from the Economic Unit of the National Criminal Intelligence Service (NCIS) may be necessary before the audit report is issued.

4.25 Auditors may also be required or wish to report suspicions of money laundering to appropriate authorities. Reports must be made in the following circumstances.

(a)   For any client, if the auditor has knowledge or suspicions of **drug money laundering** or arrangements facilitating the retention or control of **terrorist funds** or the proceeds of terrorist related activities, or the provision of financial assistance for terrorism. Reports should be made to NCIS.

(b)   For financial services, reports to the appropriate regulators under SAS 620 (see Chapter 12).

(c)   For public sector clients, to the appropriate authority.

4.26 In other circumstances auditors may feel that suspicions should be reported in the public interest. The Practice Note points out that statutory immunity is granted, from any legal action for breach of confidence, for having notified the Economic Crime Unit of NCIS of suspicions of money laundering, provided the report is made in good faith.

5   FRAUD AND ERROR   12/95, 6/97

5.1   The incidence of financial fraud, particularly in a computer environment, is increasing and has been a central feature in a number of financial scandals in recent years. This fact, together with the increasing sophistication of fraudsters, creates difficult problems for management and auditors. A few years ago the then Minister for Corporate and Consumer Affairs called on the profession to be 'the front line of the public's defences against fraud'.

5.2   There are some who would argue that the detection of fraud should be the auditors' principal function. This prevailing attitude clearly gives rise to a public expectation which is neither shared nor fulfilled by the profession.

5.3   SAS 110 *Fraud and error,* which is quite long and complicated, is covered briefly here.

Introduction

Auditors should plan and perform their audit procedures and evaluate and report the results thereof, recognising that fraud or error may materially affect the financial statements. (SAS 110.1)

The approach to be adopted by the auditors

When planning the audit the auditors should assess the risk that fraud or error may cause the financial statements to contain material misstatements. (SAS 110.2)
Based on their risk assessment, the auditors should design audit procedures so as to have a reasonable expectation of detecting misstatements arising from fraud or error which are material to the financial statements. (SAS 110.3)

Procedures when there is an indication that fraud or error may exist

When auditors become aware of information which indicates that fraud or error may exist, they should obtain an understanding of the nature of the event and the circumstances in which it has occurred, and sufficient other information to evaluate the possible effect on the financial statements. If the auditors believe that the indicated fraud or error could have a material effect on the financial statements, they should perform appropriate modified or additional procedures. (SAS 110.4)

When the auditors become aware of, or suspect that there may be, instances of error or fraudulent conduct, they should document their findings and, subject to any requirement to report them direct to a third party, discuss them with the appropriate level of management. (SAS 110.5)

The auditors should consider the implications of suspected or actual error or fraudulent conduct in relation to other aspects of the audit, particularly the reliability of management representations. (SAS 110.6)

Reporting to management

The auditors should as soon as practicable communicate their findings to the appropriate level of management, the board of directors or the audit committee if:

(a)   they suspect or discover fraud, even if the potential effect on the financial statements is immaterial (save where SAS 110.12 applies); or

(b)   material error is actually found to exist. (SAS 110.7)

Reporting to addressees of the auditors' report on the financial statements

Where the auditors conclude that the view given by the financial statements could be affected by a level of uncertainty concerning the consequences of a suspected or actual error or fraud which, in their opinion, is fundamental, they should include an explanatory paragraph referring to the matter in their report. (SAS 110.8)

Where the auditors conclude that a suspected or actual instance of fraud or error has a material effect on the financial statements and they disagree with the accounting treatment or with the extent, or the lack, of disclosure in the financial statements of the instance or of its consequences they should issue an adverse or qualified opinion. If the auditors are unable to determine whether fraud or error has occurred because of limitation in the scope of their work, they should issue a disclaimer or a qualified opinion. (SAS 110.9)

Reporting to third parties

Where the auditors become aware of a suspected or actual instance of fraud they should:

(a) consider whether the matter may be one that ought to be reported to a proper authority in the public interest; and where this is the case

(b) except in the circumstances covered in SAS 110.12, discuss the matter with the board of directors, including any audit committee. (SAS 110.10)

Where having considered any views expressed on behalf of the entity and in the light of any legal advice obtained, the auditors conclude that the matter ought to be reported to an appropriate authority in the public interest, they should notify the directors in writing of their view and, if the entity does not voluntarily do so itself or is unable to provide evidence that the matter has been reported, they should report it themselves. (SAS 110.11)

When a suspected or actual instance of fraud casts doubt on the integrity of the directors auditors should make a report direct to a proper authority in the public interest without delay and without informing the directors in advance. SAS 110.12)

Overseas activities

Where any of the activities of a company or group are carried on outside the United Kingdom or the Republic of Ireland, the auditors should take steps to ensure that the audit work in relation to the detection and reporting of any fraud and error is planned and carried out in accordance with the requirements of this SAS. (SAS 110.13)

KEY TERM

Fraud comprises both the use of deception to obtain an unjust or illegal financial advantage, and intentional misrepresentation by management, employees or third parties.

Error is an unintentional mistake.

5.4 The SAS emphasises that it is the responsibility of the directors to take reasonable steps to prevent and detect fraud. It is also their responsibility to prepare financial statements which give a true and fair view of the entity's affairs. The Cadbury Code has made a variety of suggestions to help directors fulfil their responsibilities.

5.5 In an appendix to the SAS there is a list of examples of conditions or events which may increase the risk of either fraud or error or both.

Fraud and error	
Previous experience or incidents which call into question the integrity or competence of management	Management dominated by one person (or a small group) and no effective oversight board or committee
	Complex corporate structure where complexity does not seem to be warranted
	High turnover rate of key accounting and financial personnel
	Personnel (key or otherwise) not taking holidays
	Significant and prolonged under-staffing of the accounting department
	Frequent changes of legal advisors or auditors

Particular financial reporting pressures within an entity	Industry volatility
	Inadequate working capital due to declining profits or too rapid expansion
	Deteriorating quality of earnings, for example increased risk taking with respect to credit sales, changes in business practice or selection of accounting policy alternatives that improve income
	The entity needs a rising profit trend to support the market price of its shares due to a contemplated public offering, a takeover or other reason
	Significant investment in an industry or product line noted for rapid change
	Pressure on accounting personnel to complete financial statements in an unreasonably short period of time
	Dominant owner-management
	Performance-based remuneration
Weaknesses in the design and operation of the accounting and internal controls system	A weak control environment within the entity
	Systems that, in their design, are inadequate to give reasonable assurance of preventing or detecting error or fraud
	Inadequate segregation of responsibilities in relation to functions involving the handling, recording or controlling of the entity's assets
	Indications that internal financial information is unreliable
	Evidence that internal controls have been overridden by management
	Ineffective monitoring of the operation of system which allows control overrides, breakdown or weakness to continue without proper corrective action
	Continuing failure to correct major weakness in internal control where such corrections are practicable and cost effective
Unusual transactions	Unusual transactions, especially near the year end, that have a significant effect on earnings
	Complex transactions or accounting treatments
	Unusual transactions with related parties
	Payments for services (for example to lawyers, consultants or agents) that appear excessive in relation to the services provided
Problems in obtaining sufficient appropriate audit evidence	Inadequate records, for example incomplete files, excessive adjustments to accounting records, transactions not recorded in accordance with normal procedures and out-of-balance control accounts

Inadequate documentation of transactions, such as lack of proper authorisation, supporting documents not available and alternation to documents (any of these documentation problems assume greater significance when they relate to large or unusual transactions)

An excessive number of differences between accounting records and third party confirmations, conflicting audit evidence and unexplainable changes in operating ratios

Evasive, delayed or unreasonable responses by management to audit inquires

Inappropriate attitude of management to the conduct of the audit, eg time pressure, scope limitation and other constraints

Some factors unique to an information systems environment which relate to the conditions and events described above

Inability to extract information from computer files due to lack of, or non-current, documentation of record contents or programs

Large numbers of program changes that are not documented, approved and tested

Inadequate overall balancing of computer transactions and data bases to the financial accounts

5.6 The Cadbury Committee said in its report that it would be pointless to place a duty on the auditors to detect material fraud because they will never be in a position to guarantee that no such fraud has taken place. The Committee does suggest, however, that legislation should be considered which would extend the statutory protection, already available to auditors in the financial sector, to the auditors of all companies, so that they can report any suspicions of fraud or other misdemeanour to the appropriate authorities, without breaching the confidence of the client.

Exam focus point

Questions in the exam may focus on the auditors' responsibility for detection of fraud, and the likelihood that certain procedures will detect fraud.

Chapter roundup

- The rules concerning directors' **emoluments** and directors' **transactions** are complicated but you should not lose sight of the basic thrust of the legislation.

- The auditors must ensure **proper disclosure** of directors' emoluments in the accounts, because any failure in disclosure must be remedied in the audit report.

- Transactions between **related parties** should be properly disclosed and accounted for in substance rather than form.

- The **responsibility** for ensuring compliance with **law and regulations** rest with the **management**. Where **breaches** are discovered by the auditors they need only be **disclosed** if **required by law** or where there is a **material effect** on the financial statements.

- Auditors may have difficulty **identifying related party transactions**, or **deciding** whether they are **material**.

- Auditors are thus particularly concerned with laws and regulations:

  - that **directly affect** the **financial statements**
  - that are **central** to the client's ability to conduct its business

- Auditors may have problems in deciding which laws and regulations are central to the client's business and whether and how breaches should be reported.

- Auditors who suspect **money laundering** may be taking place must be very careful.

- **Directors** (not auditors) are responsible for preventing fraud. Auditors should design procedures so as to have a **reasonable expectation** of detecting **material misstatements**, whether intentional or unintentional, in the accounts.

Quick quiz

1 What general procedures might the auditors perform to satisfy themselves that the accounts contain the correct disclosures in respect of directors' emoluments? (see para 1.6)

2 What types of disclosure of emoluments might require special attention? (1.7)

3 What information is required to be disclosed in respect of a loan to a director or connected person? (2.11)

4 What procedures might be instituted by a company to ensure that all disclosable transactions by directors are identified and recorded? (2.16)

5 In what circumstances might parties be considered to be 'related'? (3.3)

6 Why are related party transactions often difficult to detect? (3.6)

7 What substantive procedures might the auditors consider necessary for related party transactions? (3.11)

8 What kinds of transactions should the auditors be alert to as they may indicate the existence of related parties? (3.12)

9 What types of information may indicate non-compliance with laws and regulations? (4.5)

10 What are the five criminal offences that relate to money laundering? (4.14)

11 How can fraud be defined? (5.3)

12 Give five examples of conditions which may increase the risk of fraud and error. (5.5)

Question to try	Level	Marks	Time
11	Exam	25	45 mins

Chapter 12

AUDIT REPORTING AND CURRENT ISSUES

Chapter topic list	Syllabus reference
1 Statutory requirements	5(c), 6(a)
2 SAS 600 *Auditors' reports on financial statements*	5(c), 6(a)
3 Qualifications in audit reports	5(c), 6(a)
4 Reporting inherent uncertainty	5(c), 6(a)
5 The audit report as a means of communication	5(c), 6(a)
6 Legal liability of the auditor	5(d), (h), 6(a)
7 Summary financial statements	5(c)
8 Reporting to regulators	5(c), (d)
9 Quality control	5(a)
10 The changing role of the auditor	6(a)

Introduction

The importance of the audit report is reflected in the fact that it is governed not only by an auditing standard (SAS 600), but also by statute, in the form of the Companies Act 1985. These statutory requirements are discussed in Section 1.

The audit report is the means by which the auditors express their opinion on the **truth** and **fairness** of a company's financial statements for the benefit principally of the shareholders, but also for other users. Statute has consistently recognised its importance by requiring that certain mandatory statements appear in the report. SAS 600 was the first step taken by the APB towards closing the 'expectations gap' which was defined in an earlier consultative paper as: 'the difference between the apparent public perceptions of the responsibilities of auditors on the one hand (hence the assurance that their involvement provides) and the legal and professional reality on the other'.

A qualified audit report may be unpopular with clients, and discussions about audit reports are part of managing the audit relationship which is now in the syllabus for paper 10. This chapter therefore discusses how qualified reports may be avoided.

The legal liability of auditors is a controversial area.

Two of the rarer aspects of audit reporting are considered in Sections 7 and 8. These are specifically examinable in Paper 10.

We also cover quality control, revising quality control on individual assignments and also discussing wider quality control issues auditors are facing (such as total quality management). Lastly we summarise recent proposals that indicate how the role of auditors may change in the next few years.

1   STATUTORY REQUIREMENTS

1.1   The Companies Act requires the auditors to state *explicitly* (s 235) whether in the auditors' opinion the annual accounts have been properly prepared in accordance with the Act and in particular whether a **true and fair view** is given:

(a)   in the balance sheet, of the **state of the company's affairs** at the end of the financial year;

(b)   in the profit and loss account, of the **company's profit or loss** for the financial year; and

(c)   in the case of group accounts, of the state of affairs at the end of the financial year and the profit or loss for the year of the undertakings included in the consolidation, so far as concerns members of the company.

1.2   In addition certain requirements are reported on by exception; the auditor only has to report if they have not been met. The following are matters with which the auditors *imply* satisfaction in an unqualified report under s 237 of the Companies Act 1985.

(a)   **Proper accounting records** have been kept and proper returns adequate for the audit received from branches not visited.

(b)   The **accounts** are in **agreement** with the **accounting records** and returns.

(c)   **All information** and **explanations** have been **received** as the auditors think necessary and they have had access at all times to the company's books, accounts and vouchers.

(d)   **Details** of **directors' emoluments** and other benefits, and particulars of higher paid employees have been correctly **disclosed** in the financial statements.

(e)   **Particulars of loans** and other **transactions** in favour of **directors** and others have been correctly **disclosed** in the financial statements.

(f)   The **information** given in the **directors' report** is **consistent** with the **accounts**.

Directors' emoluments

1.3   The auditors should include in their report the required disclosure particulars of directors' emoluments and transactions with directors, if these requirements have not been complied with in the accounts (s 237). This means that the auditors will carry out various procedures to ensure that they are aware of all such emoluments and transactions by reference to directors' service contracts, board minutes, cash book payments and so on. Benefits received in kind may be particularly hard to identify. See Chapter 11 for further details.

2   SAS 600 AUDITORS' REPORTS ON FINANCIAL STATEMENTS

SAS 600.1

Auditors' reports on financial statements should contain a clear expression of opinion, based on review and assessment of the conclusions drawn from evidence obtained in the course of the audit.

2.1   The auditors' report should be placed before the financial statements. The directors' responsibilities statement (explained later) should be placed before the auditors' report.

2.2   The SAS makes an important statement about the nature of the assurance provided by the audit report.

> 'The view given in financial statements is derived from a combination of fact and judgement, and consequently cannot be characterised as either "absolute" or "correct". When reporting on financial statements, therefore, auditors provide a level of assurance which is reasonable in that context but, equally, cannot be absolute. Consequently it is important that the reader of financial statements is made aware of the context in which the auditors' report is given.'

Basic elements of the auditors' report

SAS 600.2

Auditors' reports on financial statements should include the following matters:

(a)   a title identifying the person or persons to whom the report is addressed;

(b)   an introductory paragraph identifying the financial statements audited;

(c)   separate sections, appropriately headed, dealing with:

    (i)   respective responsibilities of directors (or equivalent persons) and auditors;
    (ii)   the basis of the auditors' opinion;
    (iii)   the auditors' opinion on the financial statements;

(d)   the manuscript or printed signature of the auditors; and

(e)   the date of the auditors' report.

2.3   The following is given as an example of an unqualified audit report in an appendix to the SAS.

Example 1. Unqualified opinion: company incorporated in Great Britain

AUDITORS' REPORT TO THE SHAREHOLDERS OF XYZ PLC

We have audited the financial statements on pages ... to ... which have been prepared under the historical cost convention (as modified by the revaluation of certain fixed assets) and the accounting policies set out on page ....

Respective responsibilities of directors and auditors
As described on page ... the company's directors are responsible for the preparation of financial statements. It is our responsibility to form an independent opinion, based on our audit, on those statements and to report our opinion to you.

Basis of opinion
We conducted our audit in accordance with Auditing Standards issued by the Auditing Practices Board. An audit includes examination, on a test basis, of evidence relevant to the amounts and disclosures in the financial statements. It also includes an assessment of the significant estimates and judgements made by the directors in the preparation of the financial statements, and of whether the accounting policies are appropriate to the company's circumstances, consistently applied and adequately disclosed.

We planned and performed our audit so as to obtain all the information and explanations which we considered necessary in order to provide us with sufficient evidence to give reasonable assurance that the financial statements are free from material misstatement, whether caused by fraud or other irregularity or error. In forming our opinion we also evaluated the overall adequacy of the presentation of information in the financial statements.

Opinion
In our opinion the financial statements give a true and fair view of the state of the company's affairs as at 31 December 19.. and of its profit (loss) for the year then ended and have been properly prepared in accordance with the Companies Act 1985.

Registered auditors   *Address*

Date

---

* A reference to the convention draws attention to the fact that the values reflected in the financial statements are not current but historical and, where appropriate, to the fact that there is a mixture of past and recent values.

2.4   The report recommends the use of standard format as an aid to the reader, including headings for each section, for example 'Qualified opinion'. The title and addressee and the introductory paragraph are fairly self explanatory. You may have noticed that the audit report does not refer to the company's cash flow statement in the opinion paragraph. This is discussed in the next section.

Statements of responsibility and basic opinion

SAS 600.3

(a)   Auditors should distinguish between their responsibilities and those of the directors by including in their report:

   (i)   a statement that the financial statements are the responsibility of the reporting entity's directors;

   (ii)   a reference to a description of those responsibilities when set out elsewhere in the financial statements or accompanying information; and

   (iii)   a statement that the auditors' responsibility is to express an opinion on the financial statements.

(b)   Where the financial statements or accompanying information (for example the directors' report) do not include an adequate description of directors' relevant responsibilities the auditors' report should include a description of those responsibilities.

Example wording of a description of the directors' responsibilities for inclusion in a company's financial statements

2.5   A description of the directors' responsibilities is given in an example in an appendix. It can be produced by the directors or included by the auditors in their report.

Company law requires the directors to prepare financial statements for each financial year which give a true and fair view of the state of affairs of the company and of the profit or loss of the company for that period. In preparing those financial statements, the directors are required to:

(a)   select suitable accounting policies and then apply them consistently;

(b)   make judgements and estimates that are reasonable and prudent;

(c)   state whether applicable accounting standards have been followed, subject to any material departures disclosed and explained in the financial statements (large companies only);

(d)   prepare the financial statements on the going concern basis unless it is inappropriate to presume that the company will continue in business (if not separate statement on going concern is made by the directors).

The directors are responsible for keeping proper accounting records which disclose with reasonable accuracy at any time the financial position of the company and to enable them to ensure that the financial statements comply with the Companies Act 1985. They are also responsible for safeguarding the assets of the company and hence for taking reasonable steps for the prevention and detection of fraud and other irregularities.

This wording can be adapted to suit the specific situation.

Explanation of auditors' opinion

> **SAS 600.4**
>
> Auditors should explain the basis of their opinion by including in their report:
>
> (a) a statement as to their compliance or otherwise with Auditing Standards, together with the reasons for any departure therefrom;
>
> (b) a statement that the audit process includes:
>
>   (i) examining, on a test basis, evidence relevant to the amounts and disclosures in the financial statements;
>
>   (ii) assessing the significant estimates and judgements made by the reporting entity's directors in preparing the financial statements;
>
>   (iii) considering whether the accounting policies are appropriate to the reporting entity's circumstances, consistently applied and adequately disclosed;
>
> (c) a statement that they planned and performed the audit so as to obtain reasonable assurance that the financial statements are free from material misstatement, whether caused by fraud or other irregularity or error, and that they have evaluated the overall presentation of the financial statements. (SAS 600.4)

2.6 In some exceptional circumstances, a departure from auditing standards may be appropriate to fulfil the objectives of a specific audit more effectively. If this is the case, the auditors should explain the reasons for that departure in their report. Other than in such exceptional and justifiable circumstances, a departure from an auditing standard is a limitation on the scope of work undertaken by the auditors (see later).

Expression of opinion

> **SAS 600.5**
>
> An auditors' report should contain a clear expression of opinion on the financial statements and on any further matters required by statute or other requirements applicable to the particular engagement.

2.7 An unqualified opinion on financial statements is expressed when in the auditors' judgement they give a true and fair view (where relevant) and have been prepared in accordance with relevant accounting or other requirements. This judgement entails concluding whether *inter alia*:

(a) the financial statements have been prepared using **appropriate consistently applied accounting policies**;

(b) the financial statements have been **prepared** in accordance with **relevant legislation, regulations** or **applicable accounting standards** (and that any departures are justified and adequately explained in the financial statements); and

(c) there is **adequate disclosure** of all information relevant to the proper understanding of the financial statements.

Date and signature of the auditors' report

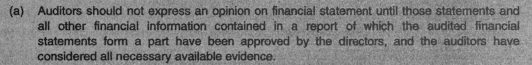

SAS 600.9

(a) Auditors should not express an opinion on financial statement until those statements and all other financial information contained in a report of which the audited financial statements form a part have been approved by the directors, and the auditors have considered all necessary available evidence.

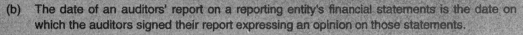

(b) The date of an auditors' report on a reporting entity's financial statements is the date on which the auditors signed their report expressing an opinion on those statements.

2.8 The date of the auditors' report is, therefore, the date on which, following:

(a) receipt of the financial statements and accompanying documents in the form approved by the directors for release;

(b) review of all documents which they are required to consider in addition to the financial statements (for example the directors' report, chairman's statement or other review of an entity's affairs which will accompany the financial statements); and

(c) completion of all procedures necessary to form an opinion on the financial statements (and any other opinions required by law or regulation) including a review of post balance sheet events;

the auditors sign their report expressing an opinion on the financial statements for distribution with those statements.

2.9 If the date on which the auditors sign the report is later than that on which the directors approve the financial statements, then the auditors must check that the post balance sheet event review has been carried out up to the date they sign their report and that the directors would also have approved the financial statements on that date.

Forming an opinion on financial statements

2.10 Appendix 1 of the SAS considers the process of forming an audit opinion using the flowchart shown on the next page. The flowchart is drawn up on the basis that the directors make no further amendments to the financial statements following the audit.

2.11 The principal matters which auditors consider in forming an opinion may be expressed in three questions.

(a) Have they **completed all procedures necessary** to meet auditing standards and to obtain all the information and explanations necessary for their audit?

(b) Have the financial statements been **prepared in accordance** with the **applicable accounting requirements**?

(c) Do the financial statements, as prepared by the directors, give **a true and fair view**?

Note. Requirements are referred to in terms of generally accepted accounting principles.

FORMING AN OPINION ON FINANCIAL STATEMENTS

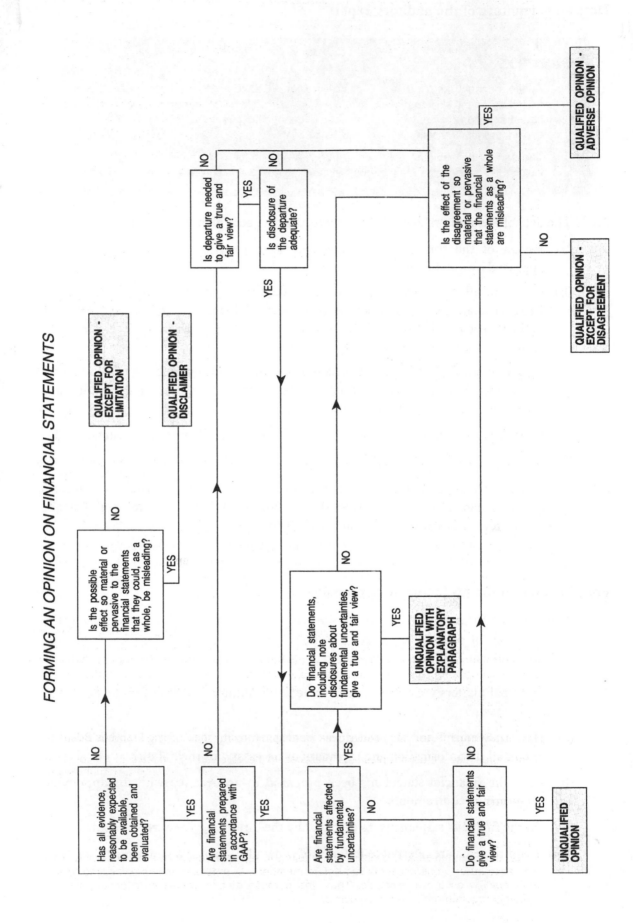

Question 1

The following is a series of extracts from an unqualified audit report which has been signed by the auditors of Kiln Ltd.

AUDITORS' REPORT TO THE SHAREHOLDERS OF KILN LIMITED

We have•audited *the financial statements on pages .... to ....* which have been prepared under the historical cost convention.

We have conducted our audit *in accordance with Auditing Standards* issued by the Auditing Practices Board. An audit includes examination on a test basis of evidence relevant to the amounts and disclosures in the financial statements.

In our opinion the financial statements give a true and fair view of the state of the company's affairs as at 31 December 1993 and of its profit for the year then ended and have been properly prepared in accordance with the Companies Act 1985.

Required

Explain the purpose and meaning of the following phrases taken from the above extracts of an unqualified audit report.

(a)   '... the financial statements on pages .... to ....'
(b)   '... in accordance with Auditing Standards.'
(c)   'In our opinion ...'

Answer

(a)   *'...the financial statements on pages 8 to 20...'*

   Purpose
   The purpose of this phrase is to make it clear to the reader of an audit report the part of a company's annual report upon which the auditors are reporting their opinion.

   Meaning
   An annual report may include documents such as a chairman's report, employee report, five year summary and other voluntary information. However, under the Companies Act, only the profit and loss account, balance sheet and associated notes are required to be audited in true and fair terms. FRS 1 requires a cash flow statement and FRS 3 requires a statement of total recognised gains and losses which, under auditing standards, is audited in true and fair terms. Thus the page references (for instance, 8 to 20) cover only the profit and loss account, balance sheet, notes to the accounts, cash flow statement and statement of total recognised gains and losses. The directors' report, although examined and reported on by exception if it contains inconsistencies, is not included in these page references.

(b)   *'...in accordance with Auditing Standards...'*

   Purpose
   This phrase is included in order to confirm to the reader that best practice, as laid down in Auditing Standards, has been adopted by the auditors in both carrying out their audit and in drafting their audit opinion. This means that the reader can be assured that the audit has been properly conducted, and that should he or she wish to discover what such standards are, or what certain key phrases mean, he or she can have recourse to Auditing Standards to explain such matters.

   Meaning
   Auditing Standards are those auditing standards prepared by the Auditing Practices Board.

   These prescribe the principles and practices to be followed by auditors in the planning, designing and carrying out various aspects of their audit work, the content of audit reports, both qualified and unqualified and so on. Members are expected to follow all of these standards.

(c)   *'In our opinion ...'*

   Purpose
   Under the Companies Act, auditors are required to report on every balance sheet, profit and loss account or group accounts laid before members. In reporting, they are required to state their *opinion* on those accounts. Thus, the purpose of this phrase is to comply with the statutory requirement to report an opinion.

   Meaning
   An audit report is an expression of opinion by suitably qualified auditors as to whether the financial statements give a true and fair view, and have been properly prepared in accordance with the Companies Act. *It is not a certificate*; rather it is a statement of whether or not, in the professional judgement of the auditors, the financial statements give a true and fair view.

3   QUALIFICATIONS IN AUDIT REPORTS

3.1   Prior to the introduction of auditing standards, qualified audit reports were often criticised as failing to convey the meaning intended.

The standard on audit reports aimed:

(a)   to outlaw the use of ambiguous ways of qualifying;

(b)   to categories the circumstances giving rise to qualification;

(c)   to prescribe suggested wording and format for different categories of qualification;

(d)   to introduce a distinction between material and fundamental problems;

(e)   to promote better drafting by using non-technical language and clear presentation.

The qualification 'matrix'

3.2   SAS 600 gives the circumstances in which each sort of qualification would be appropriate. Where the auditors are unable to report affirmatively on the matters contained in the paragraphs about which they have reservations, they should give:

(a)   a full explanation of the reasons for the qualification;

(b)   whenever possible, a quantification of its effect on the financial statements. Where appropriate, reference should be made to non-compliance with relevant legislation and other requirements.

3.3   The standard stresses the fact that **a qualified audit report should leave the reader in no doubt as to its meaning and its implications for an understanding of the financial statements**. In order to promote a more consistent understanding of qualified audit reports, the APB recommends that the forms of qualification described in the standard should be used unless, in the auditors' opinion, to do so would fail to convey clearly the intended meaning.

3.4   The APB takes the view that the nature of the circumstances giving rise to a qualification of the auditor's opinion will generally fall into one of two categories:

(a)   where there is a **limitation in the scope of work** which prevents the auditors from forming an opinion on a matter (uncertainty - see SAS 600.7); or

(b)   where the auditors are able to form an opinion on a matter but this **conflicts** with the view given by the financial statements (disagreement - see SAS 600.8).

3.5   Either case, uncertainty or disagreement, may give rise to alternative forms of qualification. This is because the uncertainty or disagreement can be:

(a)   material but not fundamental; or

(b)   of fundamental importance to the overall true and fair view.

The standard requires that the following forms of qualification should be used in the different circumstances outlined below.

QUALIFICATION MATRIX

Nature of circumstances	Material but not fundamental	Fundamental
Limitation in scope	Except for .. might	Disclaimer of opinion
Disagreement	Except for ...	Adverse opinion

Except for . . . might	Auditors disclaim an opinion on a particular aspect of the accounts which is not considered fundamental.
Disclaimer of opinion	Auditors state they are unable to form an opinion on truth and fairness.
Except for	Auditors express an adverse opinion on a particular aspect of the accounts which is not considered fundamental.
Adverse opinion	Auditors state the accounts do not give a true and fair view.

Limitations in the scope of an audit

3.6 One source of uncertainties is **limitations in the scope of the audit**. Scope limitations will arise where the auditor is unable for any reason to obtain all the information and explanations which he considers necessary for the purpose of his audit, arising from:

(a) absence of proper accounting records;

(b) an inability to carry out audit procedures considered necessary as, for example, where the auditor is unable to obtain satisfactory evidence of the existence or ownership of material assets.

SAS 600.7

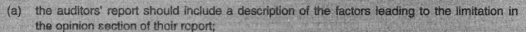

When there has been a limitation on the scope of the auditors' work that prevents them from obtaining sufficient evidence to express an unqualified opinion:

(a) the auditors' report should include a description of the factors leading to the limitation in the opinion section of their report;

(b) the auditors should issue a disclaimer of opinion when the possible effect of a limitation on scope is so material or pervasive that they are unable to express an opinion on the financial statements;

(c) a qualified opinion should be issued when the effect of the limitation is not as material or pervasive as to require a disclaimer, and the wording of the opinion should indicate that it is qualified as to the possible adjustments to the financial statements that might have been determined to be necessary had the limitation not existed.

3.7 When giving this type of qualified opinion, auditors should assess:

(a) the **quantity and type of evidence** which may reasonably be expected to be available to support the figure or disclosure in the financial statements;

(b) the **possible effect** on the financial statements of the matter for which insufficient evidence is available.

3.8　SAS 600 gives the following examples.

Example 8. Qualified opinion: limitation on the auditors' work

(Basis of opinion: excerpt)

.... or error. However, the evidence available to us was limited because £... of the company's recorded turnover comprises cash sales, over which there was no system of control on which we could rely for the purposes of our audit. There were no other satisfactory audit procedures that we could adopt to confirm that cash sales were properly recorded.

In forming our opinion we also evaluated the overall adequacy of the presentation of information in the financial statements.

Qualified opinion arising from limitation in audit scope

Except for any adjustments that might have been found to be necessary had we been able to obtain sufficient evidence concerning cash sales, in our opinion the financial statements give a true and fair view of the state of the company's affairs as at 31 December 19.. and of its profit (loss) for the year then ended and have been properly prepared in accordance with the Companies Act 1985.

In respect alone of the limitation on our work relating to cash sales:

(a)　we have not obtained all the information and explanations that we considered necessary for the purpose of our audit; and

(b)　we were unable to determine whether proper accounting records had been maintained.

Example 9. Disclaimer of opinion

(Basis of opinion: excerpt)

.... or error. However, the evidence available to us was limited because we were appointed auditors on (date) and in consequence we were unable to carry out auditing procedures necessary to obtain adequate assurance regarding the quantities and condition of stock and work in progress, appearing in the balance sheet at £... . Any adjustment to this figure would have a consequential significant effect on the profit for the year.

In forming our opinion we also evaluated the overall adequacy of the presentation of information in the financial statements.

Opinion: disclaimer on view given by financial statements

Because of the possible effect of the limitation in evidence available to us, we are unable to form an opinion as to whether the financial statements give a true and fair view of the state of the company's affairs as at 31 December 19.. or of its profit (loss) for the year then ended. In all other respects, in our opinion the financial statements have been properly prepared in accordance with the Companies Act 1985.

In respect of the limitation on our work relating to stock and work-in-progress:

(a)　we have not obtained all the information and explanations that we considered necessary for the purpose of our audit; and

(b)　we were unable to determine whether proper accounting records had been maintained.

Note. Because of the length of the audit report, we have only shown those parts of each qualified report which differ from the unqualified report shown in Section 2.

Circumstances giving rise to disagreements

3.9　The explanatory notes suggest that circumstances giving rise to disagreement include the following.

(a)　**Inappropriate accounting policies** (for a limited company this could mean failure to comply with the accounting requirements of the Companies Act 1985, and/or SSAPs or FRSs or additional Stock Exchange disclosures).

(b)　**Disagreement** as to the **facts or amounts** included in the financial statements.

(c) **Disagreement** as to the **manner or extent of disclosure** of facts or amounts in the financial statements.

(d) **Failure to comply** with **relevant legislation** or **other requirements**.

SAS 600.8

Where the auditors disagree with the accounting treatment or disclosure of a matter in the financial statements, and in the auditors' opinion the effect of that disagreement is material to the financial statements:

(a) the auditors should include in the opinion section of their report:

  (i) a description of all substantive factors giving rise to the disagreement;
  (ii) their implications for the financial statements;
  (iii) whenever practicable, a quantification of the effect on the financial statements;

(b) when the auditors conclude that the effect of the matter giving rise to disagreement is so material or pervasive that the financial statements are seriously misleading, they should issue an adverse opinion;

(c) in the case of other material disagreements, the auditors should issue a qualified opinion indicating that it is expressed except for the effects of the matter giving rise to the disagreement.

Example 7. Qualified opinion: disagreement

Qualified opinion arising from disagreement about accounting treatment

Included in the debtors shown on the balance sheet is an amount of £Y due from a company which has ceased trading. XYZ plc has no security for this debt. In our opinion the company is unlikely to receive any payment and full provision of £Y should have been made, reducing profit before tax and net assets by that amount.

Except for the absence of this provision, in our opinion the financial statements give a true and fair view of the state of the company's affairs as at 31 December 19.. and of its profit (loss) for the year then ended and have been properly prepared in accordance with the Companies Act 1985.

Example 10. Adverse opinion

Adverse opinion

As more fully explained in note ... no provision has been made for losses expected to arise on certain long-term contracts currently in progress, as the directors consider that such losses should be off-set against amounts recoverable on other long-term contracts. In our opinion, provision should be made for foreseeable losses on individual contracts as required by Statement of Standard Accounting Practice 9. If losses had been so recognised the effect would have been to reduce the profit before and after tax for the year and the contract work in progress at 31 December 19.. by £.. .

In view of the effect of the failure to provide for the losses referred to above, in our opinion the financial statements do not give a true and fair view of the state of the company's affairs as at 31 December 19.. and of its profit (loss) for the year then ended. In all other respects, in our opinion the financial statements have been properly prepared in accordance with the Companies Act 1985.

Avoiding qualifications

3.10 Some of the audit qualifications shown above could not be avoided by the companies concerned. A disclaimer of opinion, by its very nature, precludes any negotiation because nobody knows the necessary information. An adverse opinion would also imply that the situation has reached a stage where no action could be taken to remedy matters. In the case of the material but not fundamental qualifications, however, the company and the auditors might be able to adjust matters through negotiation so that a qualification can be avoided.

3.11 A qualification may be avoided just through the **actions** of the **directors** to correct the situation which caused the qualification. For example, Titaghur plc (manufacturer of jute products in India) received a clean auditors' report on its accounts for the year ended 31 March 1992 after changing its system of accounting and reporting. This was a big improvement on the situation in 1989/90 when the accounts had a full page of audit qualifications. The chairman of the company commented that the substantial changes were made 'all to help in the cause of a clean auditors' report'.

3.12 A clean auditors' report is very important to some companies, in particular when a qualification would breach loan covenants or cause great concern to institutional investors. A qualification can have a damaging effect on a company's reputation, its share price and even its ability to carry on trading.

3.13 A qualification is quite frequently the result of a **failure in negotiations** between the company and its auditors. Almost all other problems are ironed out as the audit progresses. When a qualification is first suggested as an option by the auditors, then the company might be able to negotiate a compromise. This is not likely to be possible for a straightforward disagreement. For example, if the auditors wish to qualify the accounts because a material debt they consider irrecoverable has not been provided for, then the qualification is unlikely to be avoided unless the company makes the provision.

3.14 Compromises might be reached in more controversial areas. For example, a company might decide to capitalise its internally generated brand names one year. While this practice is currently outlawed, many companies have carried out the same exercises and avoided qualification of their accounts. The reasoning has been that attributing value to such brands gives a true and fair view, while attributing no value does not. The first reaction of the auditors might be to threaten a qualification. However, the company might persuade the auditors that a qualification is unnecessary using the following arguments.

(a) An independent specialist has valued all the brands on a consistent `and` prudent basis.

(b) All brands will be amortised, again on a prudent basis.

(c) Brand values will be reviewed yearly, and any diminution in value will be written off immediately.

3.15 The company may persuade the auditors that the accounts will show a true and fair view and therefore a qualification will be avoided. Keep your eye on the accountancy press for this type of situation.

4   REPORTING INHERENT UNCERTAINTY

Inherent and fundamental uncertainty

KEY TERMS

An **inherent uncertainty** is an uncertainty whose resolution is dependent upon uncertain future events outside the control of the reporting entity's directors at the date the financial statements are approved.

> A **fundamental uncertainty** is an inherent uncertainty where the magnitude of its potential impact is so great that, without clear disclosure of the nature and implications of the uncertainty, the view given by the financial statements would be seriously misleading.

SAS 600.6

(a) In forming their opinion on financial statements, auditors should consider whether the view given by the financial statements could be affected by inherent uncertainties which, in their opinion, are fundamental.

(b) When an inherent uncertainty exists which:

   (i)   in the auditors' opinion is fundamental; and

   (ii) is adequately accounted for and disclosed in the financial statements;

the auditors should include an explanatory paragraph referring to the fundamental uncertainty in the section of their report setting out the basis of their opinion.

(c) When adding an explanatory paragraph, auditors should use words which clearly indicate that their opinion on the financial statements is not qualified in respect of its concepts.

4.1 The following points are relevant.

(a) Inherent uncertainties about the outcome of future events frequently affect, to some degree, a wide range of components of the financial statements at the date they are approved.

(b) In forming an opinion, auditors take into account:

   (i)   the **appropriateness** of the **accounting policies**;

   (ii) the **adequacy** of the **accounting treatment**;

   (iii) estimates and disclosures of inherent uncertainties in the light of evidence available at the date they express their opinion.

(c) Inherent uncertainties are regarded as fundamental when they involve a significant level of concern about the validity of the going concern basis or other matters whose potential effect on the fundamental statements is unusually great. A common example of a fundamental uncertainty is the outcome of major litigation.

4.2 The auditor will need to consider:

(a) the **possibility** that the **estimate** included in the accounts may be **subject to change**;

(c) the **possible range of values** it may take;

(b) the **consequences** of that range of potential values on the view shown in the financial statements.

> **Example 4. Unqualified opinion with explanatory paragraph describing a fundamental uncertainty**.
>
> *Fundamental uncertainty* (insert just before opinion paragraph)
>
> In forming our opinion, we have considered the adequacy of the disclosures made in the financial statements concerning the possible outcome to litigation against B Limited, a subsidiary undertaking of the company, for an alleged breach of environmental regulations. The future settlement of this litigation could result in additional liabilities and the closure of B Limited's business, whose net assets included in the consolidated balance sheet total £... and whose profit before tax for the year is £... . Details of the circumstances relating to this fundamental uncertainty are described in note .... . Our opinion is not qualified in this respect.

Question 2

During the course of your audit of the fixed assets of Eastern Engineering plc at 31 March 19X4 two problems have arisen.

(i)   The calculations of the cost of direct labour incurred on assets in course of construction by the company's employees have been accidentally destroyed for the early part of the year. The direct labour cost involved is £10,000.

(ii)   The company has received a government grant of £25,000 towards the cost of plant and equipment acquired during the year and expected to last for ten years. The grant has been credited in full to the profit and loss account as exceptional income.

(iii)   Other relevant financial information is as follows.

	£
Profit before tax	100,000
Fixed asset additions	133,000
Assets constructed by company	34,000
Fixed asset at net book value	666,667

Required

(a)   List the general forms of qualification available to auditors in drafting their report and state the circumstances in which each is appropriate.

(b)   State whether you feel that a qualified audit report would be necessary for each of the two circumstances outlined above, giving reasons in each case.

(c)   On the assumption that you decide that a qualified audit report is necessary with respect to the treatment of the government grant, draft the section of the report describing the matter (the whole report is not required).

(d)   Outline the auditors' general responsibility with regard to the statement in the directors' report concerning the valuation of land and buildings.

Answer

(a)   SAS 600 *Auditors' report on financial statements* suggests that the auditors may need to qualify their audit opinion under one of two main circumstances:

(i)   limitation in scope of the auditors' examination; and

(ii)   disagreement with the treatment or disclosure of a matter in the financial statements (including inherent uncertainties).

For both circumstances there can be two 'levels' of qualified opinion:

(i)   *material but not fundamental,* where the circumstances prompting the uncertainty or disagreement is material but confined to one particular aspect of the financial statements, so that it does not affect their overall value to any potential user;

(ii)   the more serious qualification where the extent of the uncertainty or disagreement is such that it will be *fundamental* to the overall view shown by the financial statements, ie the financial statements are or could be misleading.

The general form of qualification appropriate to each potential situation may be seen by the following table.

	Material but not	
Circumstance	fundamental	Fundamental
Limitation of scope	Except for ... might	Disclaimer of opinion
Disagreement	Except for ...	Adverse opinion

(b) Whether a qualification of the audit opinion would be required in relation to either of the two circumstances described in the question would depend on whether or not the auditors considered either of them to be material. An item is likely to be considered as material in the context of a company's financial statements if its omission, misstatement or non-disclosure would prevent a proper understanding of those statements on the part of a potential user. Whilst for some audit purposes materiality will be considered in absolute terms, more often than not it will be considered as a relative term.

(i) *Loss of records relating to direct labour costs for assets in the course of construction*

The loss of records supporting one of the asset figures in the balance sheet would cause a limitation in scope of the auditors' work. The £10,000, which is the value covered by the lost records, represents 29.4% of the expenditure incurred during the year on assets in course of construction but only 6% of total additions to fixed assets during the year and 1.5% of the year end net book value for fixed assets. The total amount of £10,000 represents 10% of pre-tax profit but, as in relation to asset values, the real consideration by the auditors should be the materiality of any over- or under-statement of assets resulting from error in arriving at the £10,000 rather than the total figure itself.

Provided there are no suspicious circumstances surrounding the loss of these records and the total figure for additions to assets in the course of construction seems reasonable in the light of other audit evidence obtained, then it is unlikely that this matter would be seen as sufficiently material to merit any qualification of the audit opinion. If other records have been lost as well, however, it may be necessary for the auditors to comment on the directors' failure to maintain proper books and records.

(ii) *Government grant credited in total to profit and loss account*

The situation here is one of disagreement, since best accounting practice, as laid down by SSAP 4, requires that capital-based grants should be credited to the profit and loss account over the useful life of the asset to which they relate.

This departure from SSAP 4 does not seem to be justifiable and would be material to the reported pre-tax profits for the year, representing as it does 22.5% of that figure.

Whilst this overstatement of profit (and corresponding understatement of undistributable reserves) would be material to the financial statements, it is not likely to be seen as fundamental and therefore an 'except for' qualified opinion would be appropriate.

(c) *Qualified audit report extract*

'As explained in note ... government grants in respect of new plant and equipment have been credited in full to profits instead of being spread over the lives of the relevant assets as required by Statement of Standard Accounting Practice 4; the effect of so doing has been to increase profits before and after tax for the year by £22,500.

Except for ...'

(d) The auditors' general responsibility with regard to the statement in the directors' report concerning the valuation of land and buildings is to satisfy themselves that this is consistent with the treatment and disclosure of this item in the audited financial statements. If the auditors are not satisfied on the question of consistency then an appropriate opinion will be required following their audit report.

---

5 THE AUDIT REPORT AS A MEANS OF COMMUNICATION

5.1 We saw in an earlier chapter that the audit report could convey a great deal of information to the reader of financial statement. Now that we have examined the audit report in more detail, we can mention the topic again.

5.2 Unqualified audit reports may not appear to give a great deal of information. The report says a lot, however, by implication.

5.3 The real problem here is that, unfortunately, most users do not know that this is what an unqualified audit report tells them.

5.4 This difference between the actual and the public perception is part of what is called the 'expectation gap', which we have already discussed. The question remains: how can we make the *meaning* of an unqualified audit report clear to the user? The Auditing Practises Board (APB) came up with SAS 600, as we saw in the earlier sections of this chapter.

5.5 The APB made it clear that the new audit report was to be seen as a step towards closing the 'expectation gap' which was defined in an earlier consultative paper as 'the difference between the apparent public perceptions of the responsibilities of auditors on the one hand (and hence the assurance that their involvement provides) and the legal and professional reality on the other'.

5.6 The APB stressed that the above definition is not definitive and that the expectation gap is not a 'static phenomenon'. However, the Board has addressed specific issues.

(a) **Misunderstandings of the nature of audited financial statements**, for example:

(i) that the balance sheet provides a fair valuation of the reporting entity;

(ii) that the amounts in the financial statement are stated precisely; and

(iii) that the audited financial statement will guarantee that the entity concerned will continue to exist.

(b) **Misunderstanding as to the type and extent of work undertaken by auditors.**

(c) **Misunderstanding about the level of assurance provided by auditors,** for example:

(i) that an unqualified auditors' report means that no frauds have occurred in the period;

(ii) that the auditors provide absolute assurance that the figures in the financial statements are correct (ignoring the concept of materiality and the problems of estimation).

5.7 Note that the Cadbury Report *The Financial Aspects of Corporate Governance* also recommends many of the suggestions made in SAS 600, particularly the statement of both directors' and auditors' responsibilities.

5.8 The new audit report does not refer to the cash flow statement. This has already caused some controversy and indeed there was a dissenting opinion in the SAS by one member of the APB on this issue. Some of the larger auditing firms have said that they will still include the cash flow reference in audit reports. The APB is criticised for not supporting the ASB, which sees the cash flow statement as extremely important.

6 LEGAL LIABILITY OF THE AUDITOR   12/94, 12/95, 6/97

6.1 The current legal position in relation to auditor liability is still based on the *Caparo* case.

Caparo Industries plc v Dickman & Others 1990
The facts as pleaded were that in 1984 Caparo Industries purchased 100,000 Fidelity shares in the open market. On June 12 1984, the date on which the accounts (audited by Touche Ross) were published, they purchased a further 50,000 shares. Relying on information in the accounts, further shares were acquired. On September 4, Caparo made a bid for the remainder and by October had acquired control of Fidelity. Caparo alleged that the accounts on which they had relied were misleading in that an apparent pre-tax profit of some £1.3 million should in fact have been shown as a loss of over

£400,000. The plaintiffs argued that Touche owed a duty of care to investors and potential investors.

Held: (by the House of Lords)

(a)   The auditors of a public company's accounts owed **no duty of care** to members of the public at large who relied upon the accounts in deciding to buy shares in the company.

(b)   As a purchaser of further shares, while relying upon the auditors' report, a **shareholder stood** in the **same position** as any other investing member of the public to whom the auditors owed no duty.

(c)   The purpose of the audit was simply that of fulfilling the statutory requirements of the Companies Act 1985.

(d)   There was nothing in the statutory duties of company auditors to suggest that they were intended to protect the interests of investors in the market. In particular, there was no reason why any special relationship should be held to arise simply from the fact that the affairs of the company rendered it susceptible to a takeover bid.

6.2   In its report *The Financial Aspects of Corporate Governance*, the Cadbury Committee gave an opinion on the current situation as reflected in the *Caparo* ruling. It felt that *Caparo* did not lessen auditors' duty to use skill and care because auditors are still fully liable in negligence to the companies they audit and their shareholders collectively. Given the number of different users of accounts, it was impossible for the House of Lords to have broadened the boundaries of the auditors' legal duty of care.

Proximity

6.3   The conclusions must be that the decision in *Caparo v Dickman* has considerably narrowed the auditors' potential liability to third parties and that the case could have far-reaching implications for the idea of there being various classes of 'user groups' who may make use of audited accounts. The judgement would appear to imply that members of various such user groups, which could include creditors, potential investors or others, will not be able to sue the auditors for negligence by virtue of their placing reliance on audited annual accounts.

6.4   In *James McNaughton Paper Group Ltd v Hicks Anderson & Co 1990*, Lord Justice Neill set out the following position in the light of Caparo and earlier cases which is a useful summary of the current law:

'(a)   that in England a restrictive approach was now adopted to any extension of the scope of the duty of care beyond the person directly intended by the maker of the statement to act upon it; and

(b)   that in deciding whether a duty of care existed in any particular case it was necessary to take all the circumstances into account; but

(c)   that, notwithstanding (b), it was possible to identify certain matters which were likely to be of importance in most cases in reaching a decision as to whether or not a duty existed.'

6.5   Future cases may shed further light on this issue. As things stand, however, the 'certain matters' referred to in the *McNaughton Paper* case would appear to be the following.

(a)   The purpose for which the statement (advice or audit report) was made.

(b) The purpose for which the statement was communicated. (Presumably, in the case of a company audit report, its statutory purpose would be considered to be of importance.)

(c) The relationship between the adviser (the auditor), the advisee (the report's recipient) and any relevant third party. Where the statement had been prepared or made in the first instance to or for the benefit of someone other than the advisee it would be necessary to consider the relationship between the parties.

(d) The size of any class to which the advisee belonged.

(e) The state of the knowledge of the adviser. In this context, knowledge includes not only actual knowledge but also such knowledge as would be attributed to a reasonable person in the circumstances in which the adviser had been placed. Whether the adviser had known that the advisee would rely on the statement without obtaining independent advice would also need to be considered.

6.6 This case law has raised some problems. In spite of the Caparo judgement, the commercial reality is that creditors and investors (especially institutional ones) *do* use audited accounts. S 241 CA 1985 requires a company to file accounts with the Registrar. Why is this a statutory requirement? It is surely because the public, including creditors and potential investors, have a need for a credible and independent view of the company's performance and position.

6.7 It would be unjust if auditors, who have secondary responsibility for financial statements being prepared negligently, bore the full responsibility for losses arising from such negligence just because the are insured. It would also be unjust if the auditors could be sued by all and sundry. While the profession has generally welcomed *Caparo*, two obvious problems are raised by decision.

(a) Is a restricted view of the usefulness of audited accounts in the profession's long-term interests?

(b) For private companies there will probably be an increase in the incidence of personal guarantees and warranties given by the directors to banks and suppliers.

(c) Solicitors and bankers are advising clients who are seeking to acquire companies to obtain assurance on the truth and fairness of the accounts directly from the target's auditors as in the BBH case below.

6.8 Recent developments which may impact upon the possibility of successfully suing auditors are the *BBH v ADT* case and APC Practice Note 4.

BBH v ADT

6.9 In December 1995, a High Court judge awarded electronic security group ADT £65m plus interest and costs (£40m) in damages for negligence against the former BDO Binder Hamlyn (BBH) partnership.

6.10 The firm had jointly audited the 1988/89 accounts of Britannia Security Group (BSG), which ADT acquired in 1990 for £105m, but later found to be worth only £40m. Although, under *Caparo*, auditors do not owe a duty of care in general to third parties, the judge found that BBH audit partner Martyn Bishop, who confirmed that the firm stood by BSG's accounts at a meeting with ADT in the run-up to the acquisition, had thereby taken on a contractual relationship with ADT.

6.11 During 1997 the case was settled out of court.

APC Practice Note 4

6.12   This practice note, entitled *Reliance by banks on audited financial statements*, was produced in answer to some of the controversy surrounding the auditors' liability to third parties. The practice note contains a joint statement by the APC and the Committee of London and Scottish Bankers.

6.13   The statement:

(a)   recognises that banks do place reliance on financial statements;

(b)   outlines some of the inherent limitations of financial statements (historical not predictive, presence of estimates and so on; and

(c)   considers the conditions which may affect the extent to which a bank may rely (date of reliance compared with date of accounts, should reliance require more forward looking information and so on).

6.14   The practice note ends with the following statement.

> 'The degree of reliance that should be placed by a bank on a company's audited financial statements in connection with its assessment and monitoring of the financial condition of that company will vary according to the particular circumstances. Therefore, it is preferable for the auditor, the bank and the borrower to have a common understanding of the context in which the bank is using the company's audited financial statements.
>
> Whether this understanding of the bank's position extends to a legal duty of care by the auditor to the bank can only be determined by an examination of the facts of each individual case.'

6.15   In certain circumstances the duty of care owed by auditors to the company may extend to the directors. In *Coulthard and others v Neville Russell 1997*, the Court of Appeal held that in principle auditors owed a duty of care to advise directors that a proposed transaction might breach the financial assistance provisions of the Companies Act. As auditors often do advise on the treatment of specific items in the accounts, the duty to advise about transactions could arise quite often.

Limited liability on audits

6.16   In recent years the large accountancy firms have been considering ways in which their liability can be limited. KPMG incorporated their audit practice, but this option is unattractive to other firms because of the tax implications.

6.17   Other firms have considered becoming limited liability partnerships, either in the UK under proposed changes to the UK partnership law regime, or in Jersey or in Delaware in the United States. Under the Jersey limited liability regime, partnerships would provide a bond of £5 million. Claims could be made against:

(a)   the partnership's Professional Indemnity Insurance;

(b)   the *partnership's* assets (not those of the individual partners);

(c)   the £5 million bond;

(d)   the assets of the partner who signed the audit report. The assets of the other partners could not be touched.

6.18   Critics have argued that a limited liability partnership regime will reduce the time auditors spend on audits and hence the reliability of the audit report. However limitations on the amount cover PII policies give and limitations on the personal resources of partners mean that there are limits to how much even an unlimited partnership will be able to contribute in the event of a very large settlement against it.

6.19   The recent merger negotiations between various of the Big Six firms have meant that the firms involved have deferred decisions about limitation of liability. However Ernst and Young recently (at the time of writing) announced they were still considering registering as a partnership in Jersey. The issue therefore remains topical, and you should look out for news of further developments.

Avoiding or disclaiming liability to third parties: non-statutory work

6.20   The cases above suggest that a duty of care to a third party may arise when an accountant does not know that his work will be relied upon by a third party, but only knows that it is work of a kind which is liable in the ordinary course of events to be relied upon by a third party.

6.21   Conversely, an accountant may sometimes be informed, before he carries out certain work, that a third party will rely upon the results. An example is a report upon the business of a client which the accountant has been instructed to prepare for the purpose of being shown to a potential purchaser or potential creditor of that business. In such a case an accountant should assume that he will be held to owe the same duty to the third party as to his client.

6.22   One way that the accountant may seek to avoid liability to third parties is to limit access to his work or reports. Another approach might be to include a **disclaimer of liability** in the relevant documents or reports. To obtain guidance on both these possibilities we can return to the ethical statement *Professional liability of accountants and auditors*.

(a)   When publishing documents generally an accountant may find it advantageous to include in the document a clause **disclaiming liability**. For example:

'While every care has been taken in the preparation of this document, it may contain errors for which we cannot be held responsible.'

(b)   When submitting unaudited accounts or other unaudited financial statements or reports to the client, an accountant should ensure that any **special purpose** for which the statements or reports have been prepared is **recorded** on their face, and in appropriate cases should introduce a clause recording that the report or **statement** is **confidential** and has been prepared solely for the private use of the client. For example:

'This report (statement) has been prepared for the private use of X (the client) only and on condition that it must not be disclosed to any other person without the written consent of Y (the accountant).'

(c)   There are areas of professional work (for example when acting as an auditor under the Companies Act), where it is not possible for liability to be limited or excluded. There are other areas of professional work (for example when preparing reports on a business for the purpose of being submitted to a potential purchaser) where although such a limitation or exclusion may be included, its effectiveness will depend on the view which a court may subsequently form of its reasonableness.

6.23   The case of *Omega Trust Co Ltd v Wright Son & Pepper 1997* appears to give legal backing to disclaimers. In this case (which related to surveyors but the facts of which can be applied to accountants) the court held that the surveyor was entitled to know who his client was and to whom his duty was held. He was entitled to refuse liability to an unknown lender or any known lender with whom he had not agreed.

Prospective financial information

6.24   One type of non-audit service which accountants are increasingly being asked to provide is reporting on **prospective financial information**. Prospective financial information includes profit forecasts, estimates and projections, and hypothetical illustrations which are sometimes used in start-up situations.

6.25   In April 1998 the Auditing Practices Board issued a discussion paper on *Prospective Financial Information*. The discussion paper considers a number of issues including whether accountants should be required to report explicitly on whether assumptions made when the information was prepared are reasonable. The paper also considers whether accountants should report on whether the forecast is likely to be achieved; this option is not favoured by the APB.

6.26   The paper also considers the question of **liability.** The APB sees this as tied in with what the subject is of the accountant's report. The paper raises the possibility that reports on certain categories of information should only be given in terms that limit the accountants' liability. The paper suggests that an accountants' review with limited liability would be better than no review at all.

6.27   The paper also notes that in the USA there is "**safe harbour**" legislation relating to reports on prospective financial information. This gives protection from forward-looking statements being used as a basis for liability if certain cautionary words accompany the statements, and the plaintiffs fail to establish that those making the statement knew they were false and misleading. In other countries prospective financial information is often not published because of the **liability risks** involved.

6.28   The paper points out that increases in the information provided will reduce investors' risk, and investors are after all seeking a return from a **risk-based** investment. It may be inequitable therefore for the liability of accountants (and directors and sponsors) to increase because of efforts they are making to reduce investors' risk. This paper does though acknowledge the contrary argument, that giving protection from liability may mean that forecasts and projections are recklessly included in investment circulars.

6.29   The debate about guidance in this area and the related question of liability is likely to develop both in the United Kingdom and internationally over the next few years.

Exam focus point
Exam questions may focus on auditor responsibility for detection of fraud, and the likelihood that certain procedures will detect fraud.

Question 3
Read the financial and accountancy press on a regular basis between now and your examination and note any new cases or developments in the question of auditor liability.

7   SUMMARY FINANCIAL STATEMENTS

7.1   S 251(1) of the Companies Act 1985 provides that a listed public company may issue only summary financial statements to its members instead of the full annual accounts and directors' report. Such statements must comply with Regulations laid down by the Secretary of State.

7.2 The summary financial statements must be accompanied by a statement from the company's auditors which states that:

(a) the summary financial statements are **consistent** with the **annual accounts** and the directors' report; and

(b) the summary financial statements comply with s 251 Companies Act 1985 and the regulations made under that section (Companies (Summary Financial Statement) Regulations 1990 (SI 1990/515)).

7.3 The APC auditing guideline *The auditor's statement on the summary financial statement*, the broad principles of which are outlined below, has not yet been replaced by any APB guidance.

7.4 The auditors' procedures in relation to the summary financial statement will primarily be directed towards consideration of:

(a) whether it is consistent with the annual accounts and the directors' report; and
(b) whether it complies with the requirements of s 251 and of the Regulations.

7.5 In cases where an inconsistency is found, if discussion with management does not result in the elimination of the inconsistency, the auditors should qualify their statement under s 251(4)(b), referring to the inconsistency.

7.6 If the auditors' report on the annual accounts was qualified, or if it included a statement under s 237(2) or (3) (for example that proper accounting records were not kept), the qualified report or statement is required to be set out in full in the summary financial statement.

8   REPORTING TO REGULATORS

8.1 Auditors are required to report directly to the regulators of certain types of company, for example those regulated under the Financial Services Act 1986. The APB has produced guidance on such reporting situations in the form of SAS 620 *The auditors' right and duty to report to regulators in the financial sector*.

8.2 The following statements of auditing standards appear in SAS 620 and they summarise the approach of the APB in this area.

Auditors of regulated entities should bring information of which they have become aware in the ordinary course of performing work undertaken to fulfil their audit responsibilities to the attention of the appropriate regulator without delay when:

(a) they conclude that it is relevant to the regulator's functions having regard to such matters as may be specified in statute or any related regulations; and

(b) in their opinion there is a reasonable cause to believe it is or may be of material significance to the regulator. (SAS 620.1)

Planning

When gaining a knowledge of the business for the purpose of their audit, auditors of a regulated entity should obtain an understanding of its current activities, the scope of its authorisation and the effectiveness of its control environment. (SAS 620.2)

Supervision and control

Auditors should ensure that all staff involved in the audit of a regulated entity have an understanding of:

(a)   the provisions of applicable legislation;
(b)   the regulator's rules and any guidance issued by the regulator; and
(c)   any specific requirements which apply to the particular regulated entity;

appropriate to their role in the audit and sufficient (in the context of that role) to enable them to identify situations which may give reasonable grounds to believe that a matter should be reported to the regulator. (SAS 620.3)

Identifying matters requiring a report direct to regulators

Where an apparent breach of statutory or regulatory requirements comes to the auditors' attention, they should:

(a)   obtain such evidence as is available to assess its implications for their reporting responsibilities; and

(b)   determine whether, in their opinion, there is reasonable cause to believe that the breach is of material significance to the regulator. (SAS 620.4)

The auditors' statutory duty to report direct to regulators

When the auditors conclude, after appropriate discussion and investigations, that a matter which has come to their attention gives rise to a statutory duty to make a report, they should bring the matter to the attention of the regulator without undue delay in a form and manner which will facilitate appropriate action by the regulator. When the initial report is made orally, the auditors should make a contemporaneous written record of the oral report and should confirm the matter in writing to the regulator. (SAS 620.5)

When the matter giving rise to a statutory duty to make a report direct to a regulator casts doubt on the integrity of the directors or their competence to conduct the business of the regulated entity, the auditors should make their report to their regulator without delay and without informing the directors in advance. (SAS 620.6)

The auditors' right to report direct to regulators

When a matter comes to the auditors' attention which they conclude does not give rise to a statutory duty to report but nevertheless may be relevant to the regulator's exercise of its functions, they should:

(a)   consider whether the matter should be brought to the attention of the regulator under the terms of the appropriate legal provisions enabling auditors to report direct to the regulator; and if so

(b)   advise the directors that in their opinion the matter should be drawn to the regulators' attention.

Where the auditors are unable to obtain, within a reasonable period, adequate evidence that the directors have properly informed the regulator of the matter, they should make a report direct to the regulator without undue delay. (SAS 620.7)

Contents of a report initiated by auditors

When making or confirming in writing a report direct to a regulator, the auditors should:

(a)   state the name of the regulated entity concerned;

(b)   state the statutory power under which the report is made;

(c)   state that the report has been prepared in accordance with SAS 620 *The auditors' right and duty to report to regulators in the financial sector*;

(d)   describe the context in which the report is given;

(e)   describe the matter giving rise to the report;

> (f)   request the regulator to confirm that the report has been received;
>
> (g)   state the name of the auditors, the date of the written report and, where appropriate, the date on which an oral report was made to the regulator and the name and title of the individual to whom the oral report was made. (SAS 620.8)
>
> *Relationship with other reporting responsibilities*
>
> When issuing a report expressing an opinion on a regulated entity's financial statements or on other matters specified by legislation or a regulator, auditors:
>
> (a)   should consider whether there are consequential reporting issues affecting their opinion which arise from any report previously made direct to the regulator in the course of their appointment; and
>
> (b)   should assess whether any matters encountered in the course of their audit indicate a need for a further direct report. (SAS 620.9)

8.3   The standard is long and detailed because of the complexity of the relevant legislation and the fine line the auditors must tread between following regulatory rules on reporting and breaching client confidentiality.

8.4   As an aid to auditors, the SAS includes as an appendix a diagram showing the action required of the auditors on discovery of a breach of a regulator's requirements.

ACTION BY AUDITORS ON DISCOVERY OF A BREACH OF A REGULATOR'S REQUIREMENTS

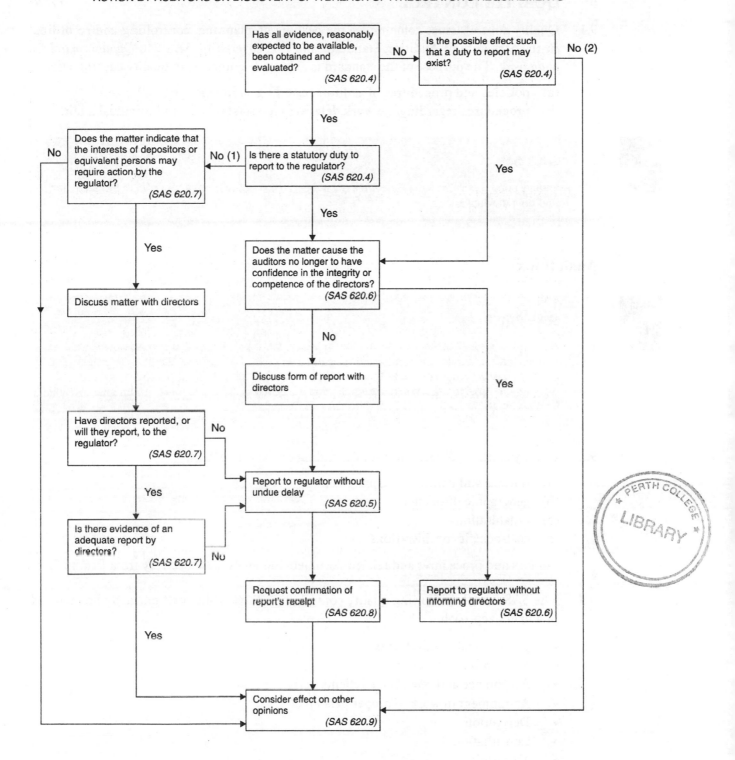

Notes

(1) This route would be followed only when a distinct right to report to the regulator exists. Otherwise, where no duty to report exists, auditors would next consider effect on other opinions.

(2) Where the auditors consider that a distinct right to report to the regulator exists, they would next consider the question marked (1)

9   QUALITY CONTROL   12/94

9.1   Quality control issues come under the heading of 'planning, controlling and recording' in the Structure of Auditing Standards and it is covered by SAS 240 *Quality control for audit work*. The purpose of the standard is to provide guidance on quality control over:

(a)   **policies** and **procedures** of auditors regarding audit work generally; and

(b)   **procedures** regarding the **work delegated to assistants** on an individual audit.

SAS 240.1

Quality control policies and procedures should be implemented both at the level of the audit firm and on individual audits.

Audit firms

SAS 240.2

Audit firms should establish and monitor quality control policies and procedures designed to ensure that all audits are conducted in accordance with the Auditing Standards contained in SASs and should communicate those policies and procedures to their personnel in a manner designed to provide reasonable assurance that the policies and procedures are understood and implemented.

9.2   Quality control policies will vary depending on factors such as:

(a)   the size and nature of the practice;

(b)   geographic dispersion;

(c)   organisation;

(d)   cost-benefit considerations.

Policies and procedures and related documentation will therefore vary from firm to firm.

9.3   The SAS lists the following quality control procedures which will normally be included in a firm's approach.

- Professional requirements
- Skills and competence
- Acceptance and retention of clients
- Assignment of work to proper personnel
- Delegation
- Consultation
- Monitoring

Individual audits

> ### SAS 240.3
>
> For each audit, the audit engagement partner should apply quality control procedures appropriate to the particular audit which ensure compliance with Auditing Standards.
>
> ### SAS 240.4
>
> Any work delegated to assistants should be directed, supervised and reviewed in a manner which provides reasonable assurance that such work is performed competently.

9.4   The SAS goes on to look at direction, supervision and review of assistants' work in turn.

Direction

9.5   This will involve informing assistants of:

    (a)   **their responsibilities** and the objectives of the procedures they are to perform;

    (b)   matters such as:

        (i)   the **nature** of the **entity's business**; and

        (ii)   **possible accounting or auditing problems,** which may affect the procedures they are carrying out.

9.6   Directions are communicated orally, both informally and at briefing meetings and via audit manuals, checklists and of course the audit programme and overall audit plan.

Supervision

9.7   Supervision is closely related to both direction and review and may involve elements of both. Personnel with supervisory duties will perform the following functions during an audit.

    (a)   Monitor the progress of the audit to consider whether assistants:

        (i)   have the **necessary skills and competence** to carry out their assigned tasks;

        (ii)   **understand the audit directions**; and

        (iii)   **are carrying out** the work in accordance with the overall audit plan and the audit programme.

    (b)   Become informed of and **address significant accounting and auditing questions** raised during the audit, by assessing their significance and modifying the overall audit plan and the audit programme as appropriate.

    (c)   **Resolve any differences of professional judgement** between personnel and consider the level of consultation that is appropriate.

Review

9.8   Work performed by each assistant should be reviewed by personnel of appropriate experience to consider whether:

    (a)   the work has been **performed** in **accordance with the audit programme**;

    (b)   the work performed and the results obtained have been **adequately documented**;

(c)   any **significant matters** have been **resolved** or are reflected in audit conclusions;

(d)   the **objectives** of the audit procedures have been **achieved**; and

(e)   the **conclusions** expressed are **consistent** with the results of the work performed and support the audit opinion.

9.9   The following should be reviewed on a timely basis.

(a)   The **overall audit plan** and the **audit programme**.

(b)   The **assessments of inherent and control risks**, including the results of tests of control and the modifications, if any, made to the overall audit plan and the audit programme as a result thereof.

(c)   The **documentation obtained from substantive procedures** and the conclusions drawn therefrom including the results of consultations.

(d)   The **financial statements**, proposed audit adjustments and the proposed auditors' report.

9.10   In some cases, particular in large complex audits, personnel not involved in the audit may be asked to review some or all of the audit work, the auditors' report etc. This is sometimes called a **peer review**.

Review of audit working papers: practical points

9.11   Throughout the audit, a system of review of all working papers will be used. In the case of a large audit, the work of assistants will be reviewed by the supervisor(s). In turn, the audit manager will review the work of the supervisor and at least some, if not all, of the work performed by the assistants. The overall and final review will be undertaken by the audit engagement partner.

9.12   Each working paper should be initialled (or signed) and dated by the person who prepared it.

9.13   After the supervisor has reviewed the work of the assistants there will usually be (in larger audit firms):

(a)   a **manager review**, which will cover some of the assistants' work and an overall review of the audit work; and then

(b)   an **engagement partner review**, which will look at the manager's review, any controversial areas of the audit, the auditors' report etc.

9.14   Many firms have a further review stage in the audit process, referred to as the **debriefing meeting**. This meeting is timed to take place as soon as practicable after completion of the audit. Its purpose is to review the conduct of the audit as a whole with the objective of improving performance of individuals and conduct of future audits and more specifically to develop the initial plan for the following year's audit.

ISO 9000

9.15   ISO 9000 is a British Standard accreditation. It was originally designed for manufacturing industries (particularly defence contractors), but by gearing it towards service industries by rewriting the standard, it may be applied to accountancy firms. The ISO 9000 sets rigorous standards of management which are enforced by random checks and audits. It covers all aspects of practice management from staff training through to complaint procedures.

9.16 To date very few auditing firms have taken on the task of meeting ISO 9000, and even fewer have attained it. It has been pointed out however that with audit regulation (discussed above), most firms are probably well on the way to meeting the standards demanded by ISO 9000. It might be said that being monitored and approved by an independent quality assessor, as required by ISO 9000, can only enhance a firm's reputation.

9.17 The ICAEW has said that it intends to develop a variant of ISO 9000 to make it directly relevant to accountancy firms. It has been suggested that acquisition of this quality kite mark might be necessary to obtain work from certain clients, particularly in the public sector and in Europe. Consequently many firms may be pressurised into obtaining ISO 9000 at some considerable cost.

9.18 At present, the value of ISO 9000 is seen as a way of measuring the quality required for monitoring visits, or even the success of a Total Quality Management (TQM) initiative.

Total Quality Management (TQM)

9.19 TQM is also a phenomenon that originated in the manufacturing sector. TQM has been described as:

> 'the process of applying total quality to the management of all resources and relationships within the firm as the means of developing and sustaining a culture of continuous improvement which focuses on meeting customers' expectations'.
>
> (Kim West, *Accountancy*, January 1992)

9.20 TQM is a 'philosophical approach to achieving quality'. TQM is different from ISO 9000 because it is not defined in hard rules and principles; rather, it relates to systems, operations and relationships. It is based on the principle of always finding better and more efficient ways of doing things, and it seeks to achieve a shift in attitudes which enables partners and staff to question their role within the firm and to consider how that role should be adapted to meet the client's constantly changing needs. ISO 9000, in comparison, is based on consistency.

9.21 There have been other developments which affect the concept of audit quality, but these are discussed in a later section, partly because their proposals have not yet been implemented. These matters are therefore discussed under 'current issues'.

10 THE CHANGING ROLE OF THE AUDITOR

10.1 We have already examined many of the ways in which the auditors role has changed over the last few years. This section indicates the changes that may occur over the next few years.

Expectations gap

10.2 Many of the recent developments of the auditor's role involve attempts to bridge the 'expectations gap' by the APB and other relevant bodies. In two articles in the *Students' Newsletter* (May and June 1996) 'Bridging the audit reporting expectations gap' Dr Karl V Roberts describes three main views of the expectations gap.

(a) **Reporting gap:** the profession's and public's view of what the auditors should be reporting are different. This is the responsibility of a regulatory authority, which is why the APB has produced the documents discussed below.

(b) **Performance gap:** auditors perform below existing standards. This is the responsibility of the professional bodies (ACCA, ICAEW) and audit firms.

(c) **Liability gap:** the profession's and the public's view of to whom the auditors are liable are different. This is the responsibility of the regulatory authority and the legal system.

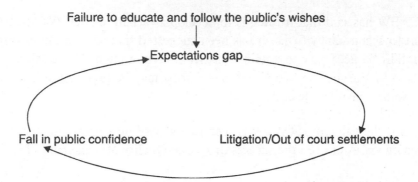

10.3 Although these articles are concerned with the international situation regarding auditor litigation, they provide a useful summary of the problems involved in reducing the expectations gap, which Dr Roberts describes as a 'vicious circle', as shown below.

10.4 The articles look at the auditors' liability for fraud (with which you should be familiar) and several recent US cases are described. An appendix to the first article gives a useful summary of the audit reporting expectations gap.

THE AUDIT REPORTING EXPECTATIONS GAP		
The audit profession		*The public*
1	Shareholders appoint auditor	Management appoint auditor
2	Auditor reports and is liable to shareholders	Auditor reports and is liable to interested parties
3	Management prepares financial statements	Auditor prepares financial statements
4	Examination of financial statements	Ensure CA 1985 requirements are met
5	Ensure financial statements give a true and fair view	Guarantee financial statements as correct
6	Base opinion on past evidence	Base opinion on future estimates
7	Provide opinion	Guarantee existence in future
8	Sample of transactions are tested	Every transaction is tested
9	Reasonable standards must be followed	Fraud detection
10	Audit standards must be followed	Same procedure is followed
11	Only judge management when they have the financial statements	Judge management at all times
12	Voluntary advice given	Statutory advice given

10.5 At the end of the second article, Dr Roberts proposes various recommendations (with which you may not necessarily agree) and these are summarised as follows.

	THE AUDIT REPORTING EXPECTATIONS GAP RECONCILIATION	
	The audit profession and the public's expectations	
1	Independent body appoints auditor	Change authority
2	Auditor reports and is liable to shareholders	Educate public
3 .	Management prepares financial statements	Educate public
4	Examination of financial statements	Educate public
5	Ensure financial statements give a true and fair view	Educate public
6	Base opinion on future estimates	Change objectives
7	Provide opinion	Educate public
8	Sample transactions are tested	Educate public
9	Fraud detection	Change objectives
10	Audit standards must be followed	Educate public
11	Only judge management when they have manipulated the financial statements	Educate public
12	Voluntary advice given	Educate public

10.6 You should come up with your own conclusions about how the expectations gap should be closed so that you can discuss the issues *and* express an opinion in the exam.

APB *The audit agenda - next steps*

10.7 In February 1996 the APB published *The Audit Agenda - Next Steps,* the follow up to previous discussion documents *The Audit Agenda* and *The Future Development of Auditing.* At the same time the APB published an audit research agenda, listing preferred topics for academic study, and an auditor's code, which breaks new ground by setting out nine fundamental principles as a guide for the conduct of auditors.

10.8 This is a difficult time for the APB as the CCAB bodies are reviewing its future role. The rationale behind the *Next Steps* document seems to have been primarily to strengthen audit objectivity. This is the factor behind the APB's decision to press ahead with its proposal that an audit partner signs the audit report in his or her own name, rather than that of the firm.

10.9 Other issues tackled by the document include fraud, and auditor liability and litigation. The APB wants auditors to cap liabilities arising from reporting beyond the call of statutory duty. In other words, the APB wishes to expand the work of auditors, but this can only take place with protection from subsequent unlimited claims.

10.10 The research programme reflects the key concerns in *Next Steps,* namely:

(a) the auditors' responsibilities in relation to fraud and breaches of law and regulations;

(b) the culture in the auditing firm and its effect on the conduct of the audit;

(c) preserving auditors' objectivity through reinforcing the professional ethics of auditors and by the involvement of the audit committee in the appointment of auditors; and

(d) litigation and audit liability.

10.11 These proposals, summarised below, appear to be a bid by the APB to remain in existence now that its main job of revising auditing standards is complete. Watch the accountancy press for details.

10.12 Here is a summary of the *Next Step* proposals.

(a)   The APB has drawn up an *Auditors' Code* setting out nine key principles to guide conduct (see below).

(b)   Auditing standards are to be amended so that partners sign audit reports in their own names.

(c)   The APB is to develop guidance on:

    (i)   application of auditing standards to owner-managed businesses; and
    (ii)   better communication between auditors and audit committees.

(d)   Listed company auditors are to report to boards on adequacy of controls for deterring fraud.

(e)   A fraud task force will be set up to identify factors increasing the risk of fraud.

(f)   Auditors are to report on the quality of financial reports to boards of directors.

(g)   A working party will be set up to review techniques for ensuring audit quality.

(h)   Publication of the APB's *Audit Research Agenda*.

(i)   The APB is to consult with the Stock Exchange on:

    (i)   differentiating the scope of listed company audits (ie compared to small businesses);

    (ii)   the extent of auditors' involvement in interims and preliminary announcements; and

    (iii)   amending listing rules to enhance the role of audit committees.

(j)   There is no plan on reporting for secondary or tertiary stakeholders.

(k)   There is no obligation for companies to commission forensic audits.

10.13 The new *Auditors' Code* contains nine fundamental principles of auditing. It is the first time that a code of this nature has been suggested (although individual bodies, like the ACCA, do have their own ethical rules for auditors).

THE AUDITORS' CODE

The nine fundamental principles of independent auditing

ACCOUNTABILITY

Auditors act in the interest of primary stakeholders, whilst having regard to the wider public interest. The identity of primary stakeholders is determined by reference to the statute or agreement requiring an audit: in the case of companies, the primary stakeholder is the general body of shareholders.

INTEGRITY

Auditors act with integrity, fulfilling their responsibilities with honesty, fairness and truthfulness. Confidential information obtained in the course of the audit is disclosed only when required in the public interest, or by operation of law.

OBJECTIVITY AND INDEPENDENCE

Auditors are objective. They express opinions independently of the entity and its directors.

COMPETENCE

Auditors act with professional skill, derived from their qualification, training and practical experience. This demands an understanding of financial reporting and business issues, together with expertise in accumulating and assessing the evidence necessary to form an opinion.

RIGOUR

Auditors approach their work with thoroughness and with an attitude of professional scepticism. They assess critically the information and explanations obtained in the course of their work and such additional evidence as they consider necessary for the purposes of their audit.

JUDGEMENT

Auditors apply professional judgement taking account of materiality in the context of the matters on which they are reporting.

CLEAR COMMUNICATION

Auditors' reports contain clear expressions of opinion and set out information necessary for a proper understanding of that opinion.

ASSOCIATION

Auditors allow their reports to be included in documents containing other information only if they consider that the additional information is not in conflict with the matters covered by their report and they have no cause to believe it to be misleading.

PROVIDING VALUE

Auditors add to the reliability and quality of financial reporting; they provide to directors and officers constructive observations arising from the audit process; and thereby contribute to the effective operation of business, capital markets and the public sector.

10.14 Other future developments include further guidance on computerisation and APB review of existing Auditing Standards.

Chapter roundup

- The Companies Act requires **specific reference** in the audit report to:

  o   the truth and fairness of the state of the company's affairs at the period-end;

  o   the truth and fairness of the profit or loss;

  o   whether the accounts have been properly prepared in accordance with the Companies Act.

- The Companies Act requires certain other matters to be reported on by **exception**:

- SAS 600 *Auditors' report on financial statements* radically altered the form of both unqualified and qualified audit reports.

- The examples of **qualification** are given only as an indication of what is required. Each case will be different and will require different disclosures.

- Auditors may qualify their audit opinion on the grounds of **uncertainty or limitation of scope**; these may be **material** or **fundamental.**

- Auditors are also concerned with the correct **treatment** and **disclosure** of **inherent** and **fundamental uncertainties**, which relate to uncertain future events. Auditors should include an **explanatory paragraph** in their audit report if **fundamental uncertainties** exist

- SAS 600 is seen as a step in closing the **'expectation gap'** and the improvement of the audit report as a means of communication.

- **Negotiations** over possible qualifications often have an important effect on the relationship between auditors and clients.

- Audit reports on **summary financial statements** and auditors' **reports to regulators** will arise only in very specific circumstances in practice.

- Auditors are unlikely to be able to **restrict liability** to clients under contract law.

- Auditors may be liable to third parties (and rarely to clients) in **tort.** However to be liable in **tort proximity** must be established and the **Caparo** case has made this difficult.

- **Proximity** *may* be established by direct assurances from the auditors on the accounts (**BBH v ADT** case).

- Major components in the **quality control** of individual audits are:

  o   direction;
  o   supervision;
  o   review.

Quick quiz

1 What are the express references in an audit report required by CA 1985? (see para 1.1)

2 What are the matters with which the auditors of a limited company imply satisfaction in an unqualified report? (1.2)

3 What are the basic elements of the auditors' report under SAS 600? (2.3)

4 Write down a description of the directors' responsibilities which should be included in the financial statements. (2.5)

5 What will the judgement of whether the financial statements show a true and fair view entail? (2.7)

6 When will a qualified opinion be issued? (3.2)

7 Sketch the qualification matrix. (3.5)

8 What is the effect of a limitation of scope on the audit report? (3.6)

9 What should the auditors consider when determining whether an uncertainty is fundamental? (4.2)

10 Summarise the effect of the *Caparo* decision. (6.1)

11 How has the BBH/ADT judgement (as it currently stands) developed audit liability case law? (6.10)

12 What must the auditors say in the statement which accompanies the summary financial statements? (7.2)

13 What will be the contents of a report to the regulator initiated by the auditors? (8.2)

14 At what two levels should quality control procedures be implemented according to SAS 240? (9.3)

15 What quality control procedures should normally be listed in a firm's approach? (9.3)

16 Define the 'expectations gap'. (10.2)

17 What are the main proposals of *The Audit Agenda - Next Steps*? (10.12)

The revision question below illustrates how the audit report may be affected by certain accounting treatments.

Question to try	Level	Marks	Time
12	Revision	n/a	36 mins

Exam question bank

Examination standard questions are indicated by mark allocations and time limits.

1 AUDITING TERMS *30 mins*

Many expressions and terms used by the auditors have a specific meaning in relation to the auditing profession.

Required

Explain what you understand by the following expressions and terms indicating the context in which they might be used.

(a) Quality of evidence
(b) Audit trail
(c) Segregation of duties
(d) Not material
(e) Ethical

2 BEVIS MARKS *25 mins*

The directors of Bevis Marks Ltd, a newly formed company, have asked you to accept the position of auditor to the company. Their letter states:

'The directors will determine your rights and duties. In general, these duties will conform with the requirements of current company legislation, however, in the event of conflict or exclusion we will indemnify you against any action. The directors also reserve the right to dismiss you without having to inform you of the reasons.'

Required

(a) Briefly state what you understand to be the duties of auditors and indicate those adverse matters which may need to be referred to in the report to the members.

(b) Outline the rights of auditors under the Companies Act 1985.

3 LAMBLEY PRODUCTS *45 mins*

You are the manager responsible for the audit of Lambley Products plc which has a turnover of about £15 million. The company has been audited by your firm for a number of years and this is the second year you have been responsible as manager for the audit. Because of your responsibilities for other audits you are only proposing to make periodic visits to the company during the course of the audit and you will not be concerned with any of the detailed audit work.

Required

(a) Detail the matters you would consider and the work you would perform (including what you would record) in planning the audit prior to commencement of the detailed audit work.

(b) Describe the ways in which you would control the audit from the commencement of work by the audit staff to the final review of the audit by the partner immediately prior to him signing the audit report.

4 THIRD PARTY EVIDENCE (20 marks) *36 mins*

In carrying out an audit, the auditors must consider the reliability of audit evidence.

You are carrying out the audit of Hilton Engineering plc which has a turnover of about £15 million. The company's properties comprise a number of factories, which are within about 5 miles (8 kilometres) of each other.

Consider, in relation to evidence from third parties:

(a) the reliability of the evidence; and

(b) where there are differences between the balance stated by the third party and the company's records, the audit procedures you would carry out to check the reasons for the difference.

You should consider these matters for the following sources of third party evidence:

(a) matters confirmed in the letter the auditors receive direct from the bank;

(b)   the replies to a debtors' circularisation;

(c)   valuation of the company's properties by a valuer. The valuation is to be incorporated in the company's accounts.

5   FEES AND INDEPENDENCE (20 marks)   *36 mins*

'I believe that auditors can never be independent, as their audit fee is paid by the firm they are auditing. Effectively, the directors decide who will be the auditors, as:

(i)   with director-controlled companies the directors and their families own the majority of the shares, so they can change the auditor and appoint one who is acceptable to them;

(ii)   even in public companies, the shareholders usually accept any change of auditor suggested by the directors.'

You are required critically to discuss this statement, and in particular:

(a)   the statement that:

(1)   auditors are paid by the firm they are auditing; and
(2)   the points raised in parts (i) and (ii) above; and

(b)   to come to a conclusion on whether you consider auditors can be independent.

6   MONETARY UNIT SAMPLING (25 marks)   *45 mins*

(a)   You are required to explain the factors which the auditors should consider when determining the level of materiality to be employed in an audit.

(b)   You are given the following information relating to a monetary unit sampling scheme.

R Factor	0.5	1.0	1.5	2.0	2.5	3.0
Required confidence level (%)	39	63	78	86	92	95

The internal audit department of the XYZ Group plc applies the following materiality limits in relation to the turnover of group operating units.

Range of turnover	*Materiality limit*
£'000	%
0 - 50	4.0
50 - 100	3.0
100 - 200	2.0
200 - 500	1.5
500 - 1,500	1.0
1,500 - 3,000	0.5

Note. The materiality limit values are used in determining the monetary precision required.

You are required to make use of the information given above in explaining, for a monetary unit sampling scheme:

(i)   what considerations would apply in choosing the confidence levels;
(ii)   how the internal auditors would have set the materiality limits;
(iii)   how the sample size would be determined.

(c)   Using your answers to (a) and (b), you are required to discuss the view that the objectivity of analysis attributed to the employment of statistical sampling in auditing is seriously diminished by a lack of precision in the concept of materiality.

7   ANALYTICAL PROCEDURES (15 marks)   *27 mins*

It is now recognised that the performance of analytical procedures on the information contained a set of financial statements is an essential part of any audit. You are required to describe the considerations that the auditors should bear in mind when conducting such procedures indicating the specific tests that they might adopt and the contents of their working papers dealing with this part of the audit.

8   JEYES TEXTILES   *36 mins*

Jeyes Textiles Ltd is a small company which manufactures sportswear for retail stores. It has recently purchased a PC to process accounting data. The company has a full time bookkeeper, Mrs Rodgers, who is responsible for maintaining the sales ledger, purchase ledger, cash book and payroll. She is assisted by a part-time bookkeeper, Miss Smith, who also deputises when Mrs Rodgers is ill or on holiday. The managing director, Mr Jeyes, is concerned that when the sales system is transferred on to the computer he will not be able to check the bookkeeper's work as effectively as with the manual system. He has asked you to advise him on the controls which could be exercised to minimise the risk of fraud and error in the new computerise system.

With the new computerised system Mr Jeyes will continue to authorise the despatch of goods, and sales invoices will continue to be prepared manually by the despatch department from pre-numbered advice note/invoice sets (these invoices are priced by the accounts department).

A sales ledger program has been purchased from a software supplier, and no-one in the company has any knowledge of experience of programming computers. The computer allows posting of invoices, credit notes, cash and discount, debit and credit adjustments. Data must be input in batches and the computer checks a manually calculated batch control total with the total value of items accepted by the computer. At the end of each run the computer also prints an analysis of invoice expenses for posting to the nominal ledger. At the end of each month the computer produces:

(a)   statements for customers;

(b)   an age analysis of debtors;

(c)   a summary day book, giving the opening balance, the total of each batch processed and the closing balance for the month.

The managing director has some accounting knowledge and can check the sales ledger control account and bank reconciliation which is prepared monthly by Mrs Rodgers.

Required

(a)   Describe the controls which should be exercised in the computerised sales system:

    (i)   over standing data files and transaction files, which are stored on disks;
    (ii)   over input of transactions into the system;
    (iii)   by the managing director on a monthly basis.

(b)   List and briefly describe the audit tests you would carry out on the computerised sales system at the interim and final audits.

Note. You are only required to describe the checks of the system from receipt by the accounts department of unpriced sales invoices from the despatch department. You are not required to consider the use of test packs and computer audit programs in testing the system.

9   BINGHAM ENGINEERING (25 marks)   *45 mins*

You are auditing the accounts of Bingham Engineering Ltd for the year ended 31 March 19X7, which is experiencing going concern problems.

The company prepares monthly, as well as annual accounts and its accountant has supplied you with the following forecasts to enable you to assess whether the company will be a going concern. The forecasts have been prepared on a monthly basis for the year to 31 March 19X8, and are:

(a)   capital expenditure/disposal forecast;
(b)   profit forecast;
(c)   cash flow forecast.

The capital expenditure/disposal forecast and profit forecast have been used to prepare the cash flow forecast.

Required

(a)   Briefly describe what you understand by the term 'going concern' and state the minimum period you would expect the company to continue in business for it to be considered a going concern.   (3 marks)

(b)   List the factors which may indicate that a company is not a going concern and briefly describe why each of these factors indicates going concern problems.   (9 marks)

(c)   Describe the work you would perform to verify that the value of items in the following forecasts, prepared by the company's accountant, are reasonable:

(i)   capital expenditure/disposal forecast;
(ii)   profit forecast;
(iii)   cash flow forecast.   (10 marks)

(d)   Briefly describe the further work, in addition to that described in (b) and (c) above, you would perform to enable you to determine whether the company is a going concern.   (3 marks)

10   DISPOSAL OF A SUBSIDIARY (20 marks)   *36 mins*

You are auditing the accounts of Hyson plc for the year ended 31 August 19X6. The group comprises Hyson plc and its wholly owned subsidiary Green Ltd and the main activities of both companies are the manufacture and sale of household textiles. During the year under review Green Ltd made a substantial trading loss and the board of directors of Hyson plc has decided to sell the subsidiary. A suitable buyer has been found and the sale was legally completed on 5 September 19X6.

A summary draft profit and loss account for the year ended 31 August 19X6 has been prepared (shown below), which divided the group profit between continuing activities (those of Hyson plc) and discontinued activities (those of Green Ltd).

	Continuing operations £'000	Discontinuing operations £'000	Total £'000
Turnover	25,700	10,000	35,700
Profit(loss) on ordinary activities	1,300	(1,000)	300
Exceptional item: loss and disposal of discontinued operations (note 1)			(1,000)
Profit before taxation			(700)
Taxation (note 2)			200
			(500)
Dividend			(500)
Transfer (from) reserves			(1,000)

Notes to the accounts (extract)

1   *Exceptional item: provision for loss and disposal of subsidiary*

	£'000	£'000
Net assets of Green Ltd at 31 August 19X6		1,800
Capital arising on acquisition	300	
Cash proceeds	500	
Loss on disposal		800
		1,000

2   *Taxation*

	£'000	£'000
Group tax charge (ex Green)	(700)	
Green tax credit	450	
		(250)
Group relief receivable re sale of subsidiary		450
Tax credit for year		200

The results of Green Ltd, included above, have been obtained from the company's management accounts. No audited accounts of Green Ltd are available as Green's new owners have a different year end from Hyson plc and Hyson plc no longer has control over Green Ltd.

You have approached Green Ltd and, in view of the change in ownership, they have said that they are not prepared to allow you to carry out an audit of their accounts or to answer questions on the management accounts to 31 August 19X6. However, the directors of Hyson plc are prepared to give you as much information about the preparation of Green Ltd's accounts as they are able.

Required

Assuming that the results of Green Ltd for the year ended 31 August 19X6 are consolidated into accounts of Hyson plc, describe the audit work you would perform and the matters you would consider in relation to the *profit and loss account* of Green Ltd which is included in the group accounts of Hyson plc as shown in the schedule above. Your answer should include consideration of:

(a) the factors you would take into account in deciding whether the results of Green Ltd are sufficiently reliable to be included in the group accounts and receive an unqualified audit report;   (7 marks)

(b) the factors that would influence the level of materiality (or acceptable error) you would accept in the results of Green Ltd which are included in the group profit and loss account; and(7 marks)

(c) how you would audit the items in note 1 to the accounts: 'provision for loss on disposal of subsidiary'.   (6 marks)

Note. You should assume that the disposal of Green Ltd is an adjusting event for the purposes of SSAP 17 *Accounting for post balance sheet events.*

11   RIPLEY MANUFACTURING (25 marks)   *45 mins*

Your firm has recently been appointed auditor of Ripley Manufacturing plc. The company is quoted on the London Stock Exchange and the directors own less than 5% of the company's shares.

You have been asked by the senior in charge of the audit to carry out work in relation to directors' transactions with the company, which are required to be disclosed in the company's annual accounts.

Required

(a) List and briefly describe the work you would carry out to check if the company has made any loans or quasi-loans to a director, or entered into any guarantees in connection with a loan to a director.   (7 marks)

(b) List and briefly describe the work you would carry out to check if there are any:

   (i)   directors' service agreements with the company;

   (ii)   options granted by the company to enable directors to purchase shares in the company at a fixed price at a future date.   (5 marks)

(c) List and briefly describe the investigations you would carry out to determine whether any director has had a material interest in a contract with the company (other than those described in part (b) above).   (6 marks)

(d) List and describe the work you would carry out and the matters you would consider if your investigations revealed that Ripley Manufacturing plc had purchased all the shares in Lowdham Engineering plc for £4,000,000. One of the directors of Ripley Manufacturing plc owns 50% of the shares of Lowdham Engineering plc.   (4 marks)

(e) A partner of your firm has asked your advice on another transaction, in which Ilkeston Electrical Ltd purchased all the shares in Nuthall Distributors Ltd for £40,000. Nuthall Distributors Ltd was owned by the two directors of Ilkeston Electrical Ltd, and all the shares in Ilkeston Electrical Ltd are owned by these two directors and their families. You are required to list and describe the work you would carry out and the matters you would consider in relation to the purchase of Nuthall Distributors Ltd by Ilkeston Electrical Ltd.

(3 marks)

12   WISEGUYS NATIONAL BAKERIES   *36 mins*

You firm acts as auditors of Wiseguys National Bakeries Ltd. The finance director has prepared the financial statements of the company for the year ended 31 December 19X3 which show a pre-tax profit of £450,000. You have been advised that the board of directors has approved the financial statements and decided that no amendments should be made thereto.

As partner responsible for the audit, you have noted the following matters during your review of the financial statements and the audit working papers.

(a) The freehold property which was included in cost in previous years' balance sheets has now been restated at a professional valuation of £1,250,000 carried out during the year. You are satisfied with the valuation, the relevant figures have been adjusted and the necessary information disclosed in the notes to the accounts.

(b) As in previous years, the directors have been unwilling to obtain an independent valuer's report to support the value of trade marks which have been included in the balance sheet at £800,000 ever since they were valued by the directors in 19X0.

(c) An amount of £45,000 due from a customer in respect of sales during the year is included in debtors but, from information made available to you, you conclude that no part of this debt will be recovered. No provision has been made against this amount.

(d) The financial statements do not disclose the fact that a director was indebted to the company for an amount of £22,000 during the period of six weeks commencing 1 February 19X3.

(e) A substantial claim was lodged against the company arising from a major breach of contract and alleged damage to a customer's business. No provision has been made for legal costs or compensation payable as it is not possible to determine with reasonable accuracy the amounts, if any, which may become payable. A satisfactory explanation of the circumstances is given in the notes to the accounts.

Required

Write a letter to the directors explaining how you propose to deal with the above matters in your audit report.

Exam answer bank

1   AUDITING TERMS

> *Tutorial note.* You must have a good understanding of all of these topics.

(a)   *Quality of evidence*

SAS 400 *Audit evidence* states that auditors should obtain sufficient appropriate audit evidence to be able to draw reasonable conclusions on which to base the audit opinion.

The quality of evidence is perhaps to be seen as synonymous with its reliability. Generally speaking, the auditors will always regard documentary evidence as being more reliable than oral evidence, not least because it is easier to substantiate it at a later date. Documentary evidence can itself take a variety of forms and be obtained from a number of different sources, some of which will be seen as more reliable than others. The four main types of documentary audit evidence in their ascending order of comparative reliability may be seen as:

(i)   that which is both originated and forms part of the records maintained by the client's staff;

(ii)   that which originates outside the business but then forms part of the records maintained by the client's staff;

(iii)   that which the auditors obtain direct from third parties; and

(iv)   that which the auditors themselves generate as a result of their own tests and enquiries.

(b)   *Audit trail*

Audit trail is an expression used to describe the ability to trace a transaction through its various stages in the processing cycle and gain evidence of the controls which form part of the system being exercised at each stage.

The loss of audit trail, very commonly associated with computer systems where there is often no visible evidence available of the working of programmed controls, is very significant to the auditor.

Where there is a loss of audit trail, the auditors should seek alternative audit evidence in order that he may be satisfied as to the reliability of the company's systems and the results generated by them.

(c)   *Segregation of duties*

Segregation of duties is a vital part of any system of internal control and is often referred to as a system of internal check. In an effective system of internal control, no one person should have complete responsibility for all aspects of a transaction and whenever possible the work of one person should be independently reviewed by another.

If a company's systems do not allow for an effective segregation of duties, then it will mean that there is a much greater chance of errors, whether clerical or fraudulent, going undetected. Such a situation would mean that the auditors would be less able to place reliance on the company's internal control systems and would therefore need to carry out an extended programme of substantive testing in order to arrive at their audit opinion; in extreme cases it might be necessary for them to disclaim an opinion.

(d)   *Not material*

Generally speaking, transactions or other events will be seen as material in the context of an enterprise's financial statements if their omission, misstatement or non-disclosure prevents a proper understanding of these statements on the part of a potential user.

Auditors are responsible for forming an opinion on the truth and fairness of the financial statements on which they report, in order to lend some credibility to these statements which will have been prepared by the management of the enterprise.

In order to form an opinion on truth and fairness, the auditors will need to exercise their professional judgement and experience in relation to the question of materiality. Auditors should assess materiality not merely in monetary terms but also in the overall context of the company's financial statements, statutory requirements and recognised best accounting and auditing practice.

(e) *Ethical*

To talk about what is ethical for auditors to do would be to talk about what it would be reasonable, right and proper for them to do in the light of what is expected of people with their professional standing, both in terms of the requirements of the profession and the expectation of the general public.

All members and students of the Association, are expected to follow, at all times, the recommendations of the *Rules of Professional Conduct* which deals with all important matters of professional ethics such as confidentiality, independence, dealing with clients' moneys, advertising and publicity and so on.

If an auditor was found to have been in breach of the *Rules of Professional Conduct*, then he or she would be liable to disciplinary proceedings by the Association, whose ultimate sanction would be to exclude the auditor from membership.

2   BEVIS MARKS

(a) The duties of the auditors of a limited company are laid down by the Companies Act 1985. An audit involves the independent examination of, and an expression of an opinion on, the financial statements of an enterprise.

There are two matters which the auditors must consider and must refer to explicitly in their audit report even where their findings are satisfactory.

(i) They must consider and state whether the accounts have been properly prepared in accordance with the Companies Act 1985.

(ii) They must consider and state their opinion on whether the balance sheet shows a true and fair view of the company's affairs at the end of the period and whether the profit and loss account shows a true and fair view of the results of the period.

The auditors must also report 'by exception' if their findings are adverse on the following:

- whether proper accounting records have been kept;
- whether proper returns adequate for the audit have been received from branches not visited by the auditors;
- whether the accounts are in agreement with the accounting records;
- whether they have received all the information and explanations required for their audit;
- whether the directors' report is consistent with the accounts.

The auditors are also required to include certain items of information in their report if the accounts fail to do so. These include details of directors' emoluments and other benefits, and of loans and other transactions in favour of directors and others.

The auditors should ensure that the accounts comply with Statements of Standard Accounting Practice (SSAPs) and Financial Reporting Standards (FRSs), and should conduct their audit in accordance with auditing standards.

The directors cannot restrict the scope of the auditors' work, although they may extend it. They cannot indemnify the auditors against claims arising from a failure to perform the duties of the auditors under the Companies Act 1985.

(b) The auditors have the following rights under the Companies Act 1985:

(i) a right of access at all times to the books, accounts and vouchers of the company;

(ii) a right to all such information and explanations as they think necessary for the performance of their duties;

(iii) a right to attend any general meetings and to receive all notices and communications relating to such meetings which any member of the company is entitled to receive;

(iv) a right to speak at general meetings on any part of the business that concerns them as auditors;

(v) a right to be informed of any proposal to dismiss or replace them as auditors.

3   LAMBLEY PRODUCTS

> *Tutorial note.* Remember that SAS 240 emphasises the importance of quality control on individual audits.

(a)   As the manager responsible for the audit of Lambley Products plc, the matters to be considered and the work to be performed in planning the audit prior to the commencement of the detailed audit work would include the following.

(i)   Consultation with management to ascertain whether there have been any significant changes, since the occasion of the last audit, in the characteristics of the company's business. In particular, consideration should be given to the following:

(1)   the economic climate of the industry;
(2)   factors affecting the industry;
(3)   the position of the company within the industry;
(4)   the company's main competitors;
(5)   the company's marketing methods and methods of distribution;
(6)   the production functions;
(7)   labour relations.

(ii)   Consultations should also take place with management to ascertain whether there have been any significant changes in the structure of the organisation. In particular, consideration should be given to:

(1)   the organisation chart of the company showing the names, responsibilities and authority limits of the company's officials;

(2)   the location of the main operating, accounting and custodian centres;

(3)   the existence or otherwise of an internal audit department;

(4)   the flow of documentation including budgets and reports.

(5)   the accounting and ancillary records.

(iii)   A review of the continuing relevance of matters raised during previous audits and in particular ascertaining what steps management have taken to implement recommendations previously made by the auditor.

(iv)   Review any interim and management accounts which may be available and discussing with management the implications of any significant changes which had not been anticipated, and/or expected changes which have failed to materialise.

(v)   An assessment of the effects on the enterprise's financial statements of any changes in legislation or accounting practice.

(vi)   Preparation of a time budget showing the dates of all the significant stages of the audit work. For example, it will be necessary to ascertain when management want the accounts finalised, the locations and dates when stock counts will be taken etc.

(vii)   Ensure that the required numbers of suitably experienced staff will be available at the times required and making arrangements to ensure that all staff are properly briefed as to the nature of the client's business and the scope of the audit work to be carried out.

(viii)   Establishing any critical areas to which particular attention will need to be paid. Experience gained from the previous audit should help in identifying those parts of the audit which are likely to cause problems requiring professional judgement to resolve.

(ix)   Consult with the internal auditors, if any, in order to establish to what extent their work can be of assistance to the external audit.

The details of the audit manager's planning should be recorded in the following way.

(i)   Matters of continuing importance affecting the company or the audit should be kept in a separate permanent audit file, for example details of changes in the company's procedures, organisation etc.

(ii)   Matters of particular concern to the current year's audit should be noted and held in the 'current file', for example audit timetable, and details of potential problem areas.

Full details of the specific requirements for the current year's audit should be noted in an 'audit planning memorandum' copies of which, after discussion with and agreement by the partner responsible for the audit of Lambley Products plc, should be made available to all members of audit staff assigned to the current audit.

(b)   So far as control of the audit of Lambley Products plc is concerned there should be during the course of the audit, a continuing process of monitoring the quality of work. The main areas to be considered would be as follows.

    (i)   *General control procedures*

        (1)   Allocate work to members of staff having a suitable degree of experience.

        (2)   Ensure that all members of the audit team clearly understand their responsibilities, especially those relating to the supervision of the work of others.

        (3)   Ensure that the working papers are adequate to enable achieved performance to be assessed against that expected.

    (ii)   *Control during the audit*

    All work performed on the audit must be reviewed by more senior members of the firm (it is normal practice to find the review evidenced by the initials of the person carrying it out).

The audit manager should pay regular visits to the audit throughout its various stages, but particular attention should be paid to the final stages of the audit. It is at this time that pressures are greatest and, consequently, control is most needed. It may be found that the use of audit completion check lists, with sections for completion by the senior in charge, the manager and partner, will help to ensure that all significant aspects of the firm's procedures have been observed.

4   THIRD PARTY EVIDENCE

Tutorial note. You may have to apply the principles described in this question to other situations - in December 1996 there was a question about audit evidence on the Internet. Remember the key points

(a)   Third party confirmation that has unquestionably come from the third party is very strong evidence.

(b)   Auditors must investigate:

    (i)   incomplete replies from third parties;
    (ii)   differences between third party confirmations and the client's records.

(c)   Care must be taken when choosing samples of items to be confirmed (for example when circularising debtors) to choose a sample that will fulfil the objectives of the test. (This may involve selecting certain items as key items, for example long-outstanding or large balances).

(d)   Auditors should be aware of the limitations of third party evidence, for example in matters of opinion (valuation by an expert) or because the evidence provides assurance in meeting some but not other audit objectives (for example a debtors' circularisation confirms that the money is owed, it does not confirm that the money will be paid).

(a)   The auditors can normally regard the bank report as correct and complete third party evidence, but must ensure that the report is received direct from the bank. The auditors must check that the bank has answered all questions and that their answers agree with details already recorded on audit working papers. Any new information, eg accounts or arrangements not shown in the firm's books and papers, and any discrepancies, must be followed up and rigorously investigated.

The bank report provides the following evidence.

(i)   Confirms the balances on the company's bank accounts

(ii)   Gives details of any balances secured and the nature of the security

(iii)   Details of assets and documents held, eg deeds, share certificates, bonds, bills of exchange etc

(iv)   Details of overdraft and loan facilities and terms

(v)   Contingencies, eg guarantees, bills, indemnities etc

Differences between the details stated by the bank and the company's records must be explained, because they are uncommon. Bank account balances given in the report should be agreed with the bank statements held by the company and any discrepancies should be traced to see if they originated at the bank or within the company. Bank statements corrupted by company employees give strong *prima facie* evidence of fraud.

Where the bank statement balance differs from the balance in the company's cash book it must be checked to confirm that it arises from timing differences on bank reconciliation. Permanent differences will probably require the company's cash balance or balance of debtors or creditors to be amended. Errors that appear to originate with the bank, eg missing entries or items wrongly appearing in the company's accounts, must be corrected after agreement between the parties.

The auditors must pay particular attention to accounts opened or closed, special-purpose accounts, set-off arrangements, accrued interest and charges and uncleared lodgements and cheques at the year end. Delays in clearing lodgements and cheques after the year end must be explained in case they arise from items posted in the wrong year or items held over to facilitate teeming and lading or window dressing.

Details of security for loans and overdrafts and charges on the assets of the company must be adequately disclosed. The auditors should check the physical existence of property deeds, share certificates and other documents held by the bank and agree their details with the company's records. The matching up of information provided by the bank with the company's records will both locate differences and help the auditors assess the reliability of both sets of evidence.

(b)   Replies from debtors circularised are reliable evidence in that they come from a third party and are not passed through or generated by the client's accounting system. However the auditors must take several precautions. They must ensure that all circularisation requests show the audit firm as the return address in case of non-delivery, and include the firm's stamped self-addressed envelope. The auditors must mail the letters personally. This must not be left to the client or pass through their mail room.

Replies received from debtors may be unreliable for several reasons.

(i)   Delays within the debtors organisation in processing through to their purchase ledger may mean that the ledger balance excludes invoices sent by the company close to the year end.

(ii)   The debtor may confirm the balance specified without checking their purchase ledger balance. The customer's purchase ledger clerk may not bother as no duty of care is owed to either the audit firm or the client. This considerably reduces the value of replies as evidence to be relied upon. Where the auditors suspect this has happened the balance must be verified by alternative means

(iii)   Some debtors do not bother to reply or say they cannot confirm the balance due to or from the firm. In these cases the auditors should recontact the debtor to try to get confirmation of selected invoices and details of recent payments.

Where the debtors do not agree the balance they should state the balance according to their records and suggest reasons for the difference. The auditors must reconcile the two figures by explaining the difference and taking appropriate action. The difference may be due to several causes.

(i)   Goods may be in transit or at the customers premises but unprocessed. If the invoice is sent separately it may be that the customer has processed the delivery note but is awaiting the invoice. It is important that the auditors check that goods and invoices were sent before the year end and assess how long both have been in the customers hands. A long period may indicate that a credit note may have to be issued on return of faulty or incorrect goods.

(ii)   A credit note may be in transit or goods may be in transit back to the client.

(iii)   Cash may be in transit in payment of certain invoices. The auditors can confirm this by locating the receipt in the debtors account in the sales ledger after the year end. However this may be a problem if the settlement period is long.

The auditors must pay particular attention to cut-off aspects of invoices and credit notes in transit. Reliability of the debtors circularisation may be improved in several ways. The auditors can review the previous year's audit file for problems and evidence of lack of reliability. A different sample may be chosen for the current year's circularisation and debtors not replying may be investigated if their account at the company shows suspicious entries, or a lack of certain entries. This may be evidence of collusion to misappropriate goods or cash drawn in payment. Old balances and high value items that are not confirmed may need to be the subject of a provision for doubtful debts.

(c) Land and buildings are often included in the balance sheet at a valuation rather than at cost, and in the case of investment properties this is required by SSAP 19. The reliability of the third party valuation and the scope of the audit work to be undertaken depends upon the following factors.

(i) The technical qualifications, reputation and independence of the valuer.

(ii) The experience of the valuer in valuing similar properties as evidenced by the accuracy of past valuations.

(iii) The basis of valuation adopted and the assumptions made, which should be consistent with those used in previous years where relevant, eg on annual revaluation and no material change of use. The brought forward value in the accounts should be checked as correct.

(iv) The size of the change in value since the last valuation and its overall reasonableness in view of inflation since the last valuation.

(v) The valuation compared with prices for similar properties in the immediate vicinity, allowing for any differences, eg facilities and condition.

Properties are difficult to value and specialised buildings or facilities may be valued differently by different valuers. The auditors must check that the amount of the valuation is correctly incorporated into the company's accounts and that revaluation surpluses are properly accounted for.

5 FEES AND INDEPENDENCE

> *Tutorial note*. This question highlights the interaction of relationships with the client and independence

The statement makes a number of points, each of which can usefully be considered separately.

Approval of change in auditors

In public companies, the shareholders usually vote in favour of resolutions proposed by the directors to change the company's auditors. This concurrence between the voting of the shareholders and the resolutions put forward by directors may indicate simply that the companies concerned are being well-managed by directors who only change auditors for the best of reasons. Shareholders fully understand why the directors are proposing the change of auditors and fully concur with their view on the basis of a reasoned consideration of the decision rather than simply a blind acceptance of the directors' views. Shareholders will be made aware of controversial aspects behind the change of auditors by:

(a) the auditors exercising their right to make representations to the shareholders either directly (in writing) or at a general meeting,

(b) press publicity.

Directors who own a majority shareholding will have the power to dismiss the current auditors and appoint another. The representations which the retiring auditor is able to make at the AGM or in writing will be unlikely to have an effect since the directors control over 50% of the shares. In this situation, there may be a tendency for the auditor to avoid conflict with the directors because he does not wish to lose his office as auditor.

Reasons for change

A common reason for changing auditors is in order to take advantage of lower audit fees charged by an alternative firm. It might be argued that changing audit firm simply on grounds of the fees charged may well result in a deterioration of the quality of the audit work since audit firms will be tempted to cut corners in order to cut their fees and attract new work. Clearly, the quality of service provided by the alternative firm should be considered carefully by the directors, and they may wish to present information on this to shareholders in order to make a case for a change in auditor.

Remuneration of auditors

The Companies Act states that the remuneration of the auditors is fixed by the members of the company. In practice, the power to fix the auditors' remuneration is usually delegated by the members to the directors by means of a resolution at the AGM. In most cases, the fee is agreed between the directors and the auditors prior to beginning audit work, and the fee is only exceeded if significant unforeseen problems are encountered. It would generally be difficult to arrive at a practicable and flexible arrangement whereby the members fix the remuneration of the auditors themselves. In this case, as in many other cases where the stewardship of the company's assets is involved, the members entrust the matter to directors.

Professional pressures to maintain independence

Ultimately, maintaining independence as an auditor is a matter of professional integrity: in other words, a matter of maintaining an independent attitude of mind. However, the profession maintains guidelines which seek to promote the independence of the auditor. Firstly, the ACCA recommends that no audit fee individually should represent over 15% of the total income of the audit firm. This recommendation is most likely to affect the smaller firms; indeed the existence of this recommendation has itself precipitated the merger of audit firms so that the merged firm receives less than 15% of its income from a client who generated over 15% of the fee income of one of the firms individually.

Auditors who allow their independence to be compromised in such a way that their opinions are influenced risk being liable for negligence. However, the scope for third parties such as creditors and individual shareholders suing auditors for negligence appears to have been narrowed considerably by the ruling in the recent *Caparo* case. Such auditors also risk losing professional credibility among their colleagues, and may face the disciplinary proceedings of their professional body for cases of misconduct.

Some commentators have argued that obtaining work by quoting lower fees is bound to lead to standards being compromised. However, an audit firm cannot afford to lower its standards to unacceptably low levels in order to cut costs. The firm must always consider the higher audit risk which results from lower quality audit work: this is the risk that an incorrect opinion will be given, opening the auditor to the possibility of being sued for negligence.

Conclusion

In conclusion the statement highlights the fact that the auditors are in a relatively weak position in resisting removal. In the case of public company shareholders, although it is generally the directors who propose resolutions to change the auditors, it must be remembered that shareholders in a majority are able to veto the decision to change auditors. Directors who propose changes to the auditors for the wrong reasons risk the adverse publicity which may result. In companies controlled by directors, the auditors have very limited ability to prevent their removal by the directors. However, even in this case, the auditors can remain independent if they are prepared to act with the highest professional integrity even where this means that there is likely to be conflict with the directors.

So we return again to the point that whatever commercial or regulatory factors militate for or against the position of independence adopted by the auditor, it is his or her attitude of mind which is ultimately important in ensuring the auditor's independence. If standards are not maintained, the auditors may face disciplinary action and, just as seriously, may face the possibility of a claim for negligence, as well as a loss of reputation.

6   MONETARY UNIT SAMPLING

> *Tutorial note.* The point in (c) about judgement being used to determine the materiality level and confidence level means that statistical sampling is not completely objective. However, the materiality levels and the key confidence levels figures given in the question are in line with those used by many firms.

(a)   When planning an audit the level of materiality to be applied must be determined in advance. This will enable the auditors to be more objective when any particular error is found. The level of materiality to be set for each item will depend heavily on the judgement of the auditors.

The following factors should be considered.

(i)   *The size of the error*

Both the relative and the absolute size of the error should be considered.

Relative size

Auditors commonly exercise their judgement to apply 'rules of thumb' and the size of the error is compared with, for example, the total value of assets, the total company turnover and so on. For example the following rules may be set for an error in the valuation of stock.

If the error is less than 5% of the correct stock value, it is not material.
If the error is 5% to 10% of the correct value, it may be material.
If the error is more than 10% of the correct value, it is probably material.

Absolute size

The material absolute size will depend not only on the size of the organisation but also on the item being considered. For example a difference on stock valuation of £50,000 may be material for a small company but not for a large company. However an error of £50,000 in the cash balances may be material for both companies because of the risk of embezzlement.

(ii)   *The nature of the error*

This relates to non-quantifiable criteria by which an error may be judged material regardless of its size. The situation described earlier of a discrepancy on cash would be an example of an error which is of a highly sensitive nature and is therefore material. Auditors also take into account the nature of the error when considering sensitive disclosures in the accounts (for instance loans to directors).

(b)   (i)   The confidence level is the degree of probability that the sample taken will represent the true condition of the whole population under examination. For example the auditors may be prepared to accept a risk of 5% that an error which is not material in a sample may be material for the whole population. This means that the auditors want to be 95% confident that the error is not material.

In setting the confidence levels the auditors have to consider the fact that although the risk of drawing incorrect conclusions reduces with larger samples, the cost is also higher. There has to be a trade off between the cost of an audit and the risk of incorrect conclusions being drawn.

The level of confidence to be set will depend on the following.

(1)   Whether the audit is being conducted purely through substantive tests or through analytical procedures.

(2)   If a systems approach is being adopted, the level of confidence will depend on the auditors' judgement of the effectiveness of the relevant internal controls and the quality of the system. For example if the auditors are very confident about the internal controls established by management they are likely to set a low confidence level, perhaps 63%. Conversely if auditors feel that internal control is weak then they will set a high confidence level of say, 95%, so that they minimise the chance of forming an incorrect opinion of the accounts (the lower the risk that the results from statistical sampling fail to indicate a material error in the population).

(ii)   The setting of the materiality limits will depend on the auditors' judgement and on the factors discussed in part (a).

In the example given, as regards the size of the error, the auditors are combining the need to consider the relative size and the absolute size: in the table the percentage materiality limit reduces as the absolute range of turnover increases.

(iii)   Monetary unit sampling enables a sample size to be determined that will give the auditors sufficient confidence that material error does not exist in the population.

The sample size will depend on the confidence level required and the monetary precision or materiality limit to be applied.

For example if an operating unit has a turnover of £150,000 a materiality limit of 2% applies, or £3,000. For a required confidence level of say, 95% the R factor or basic precision factor is 3.0. The average sample internal is determined as follows.

Average sample internal $= \dfrac{\text{Monetary precision}}{\text{Basic precision factor}}$

$$= \frac{£3,000}{3.0} = £1,000$$

A sample taken from a population of £150,000, using intervals of £1,000, will result in a sample size of 150.

(c)   Statistical sampling is designed to produce the 'correct' sample size for auditing purposes. The statistical analysis involved means that the auditors have some objective guidance as to the appropriate sample size.

However while the sample size is to an extent objective, as outlined in (b), its determination still depends partly on the subjective judgement of the auditors in establishing the correct confidence level and the monetary precision to be applied.

The discussion in part (a) confirms that there is a lack of precision in the concept of materiality. However, as long as the authors and users of audit reports are aware of the limitations of the concept of materiality, the limits set do at least give a predetermined yardstick against which errors can be judged.

7   ANALYTICAL PROCEDURES

Tutorial note. Note the different elements this answer brings in.

(a)   The comparisons that may be made

(b)   The ratios etc that may be calculated

(c)   The fact that analytical procedures can use financial and non-financial information

(d)   The recording of analytical information on the current year file, and also on the permanent file as a source of information for future years.

In addition the answer emphasises the importance of investigating material variations identified by analytical procedures.

The purpose of analytical procedures is to ensure that account items are consistent with each other, with known trends and with the auditors' knowledge of the enterprise's business. Any apparent inconsistencies could indicate areas in which significant omissions, errors or irregularities have occurred which have not been detected by other audit tests.

The auditors needs to exercise skill, imagination and judgement in recognising the matters to be examined in an analytical procedures and in interpreting the results obtained. The exact procedures carried out will depend on the particular activities of the enterprise and on the position of the industry in which it operates, but some of the comparisons made as part of a review might include:

(a)   a comparison with individual amounts within the accounts with other related amounts;

(b)   comparisons of amounts in the financial accounts with previous years, and of the results on a month by month basis;

(c)   comparisons of amounts in the financial accounts with management accounts and budgets;

(d)   comparisons of the results of any different operating units within the company.

In many cases, comparisons can be made more meaningful by calculating suitable ratios. These may be based on financial data or on non-financial information such as production and employment statistics. In particular, the use of ratios will enable the auditors to compare different companies in the same industry. Some examples of statistics and ratios that should be examined for a manufacturing company will include:

(a)   contribution as a percentage of sales;
(b)   total contribution per product;
(c)   stock as a percentage of cost of sales;
(d)   debtors' turnover;

(e)   creditors' turnover;

(f)   debtors' provisions as a percentage of debtors;

(g)   warranty claim provisions as a percentage of sales;

(h)   obsolescence and other stock provisions as a percentage of stocks.

As a result of the comparisons carried out as part of the review the auditors may discover unexpected variations or find that they fail to discover expected variations. Many of these anomalies will need further investigation, although some will be explained as a result of detailed work already performed.

The auditors must ensure that the completed results of their analytical procedures are contained in their working papers. The documentation might include:

(a)   the audit programme for the review work;

(b)   a summary of all significant figures and relationships for the accounting period;

(c)   a summary of comparisons made with budgets and with previous years;

(d)   details of all material variations examined;

(e)   details of the results of any further investigations into such variations;

(f)   the conclusions reached by the audit staff;

(g)   any information brought to light that might be useful in planning subsequent audits.

It will also be necessary for the auditors to maintain a record of ratios and other statistics from past years and other businesses. This may involve a considerable amount of initial research when analytical procedures are first performed but subsequently should be a fairly straightforward updating procedure.

Analytical procedures are an essential part of an audit, but they are not a replacement for other audit work. Suitable comparisons of key figures should be made and any unexpected results investigated. Such analysis should not only be carried out when the final accounts are available, but also throughout the audit as an aid to planning the work and directing attention to the most critical areas. A proper review requires a considerable amount of skill and judgement and should therefore always be carried out by a suitably experienced member of the audit team.

8   JEYES TEXTILES

> *Tutorial note.* Standing data files are very important in computerised systems, and proper maintenance and reconstruction controls are vital.

(a)   The controls which should be exercised in the computerised sales system of Jeyes Textiles Ltd, in the three areas referred to in the question, would be as follows.

(i)   *Standing data files and transaction files*

(1)   The company should ensure that there is an adequate reconstruction control facility over the disk files, on which these records are maintained, by instituting a 'generation cycle' (more commonly know as 'grandfather, father, son' cycle).

(2)   There should be regular checks on the accuracy of the standing data (eg customer credit limits). This can be simply, but effectively, carried out by periodically having a full print-out of the standing data which will then be checked by an independent official against the manual records which should still be maintained by the company.

(ii)   *Input transactions.*

The company should institute a system whereby transactions are grouped in convenient sized batches over which a control total is established and the details of which are entered in a batch register.

The person responsible for establishing batch control totals and maintaining the batch register (Miss Smith) should be someone other than the person responsible for inputting the data to the computer (Mrs Rodgers). Any differences between the control total and the total recorded as input to the computer, should be fully investigated by the managing director (Mr Jeyes).

(iii)   *Monthly checks by the managing director.*

The checks carried out each month by Mr Jeyes should include the following.

(1) Checking fully the details (cash book postings, journal entries, and so on) on the sales ledger control account maintained by Mrs Rodgers and agreeing the closing balance to the list of balances printed out by the computer. Any differences should be fully investigated.

(2) Checking the bank reconciliation statement. Particular care should be taken to ensure that there is not undue delay in the banking of monies received.

(3) Reviewing the aged analysis of debtor balances and investigating further any old uncleared balances/items.

(4) Checking the batch register to the computer sales day book to ensure that all batches have been properly dealt with.

(5) Testing a random sample of invoices to ensure that the goods in question had been properly priced and that the details were properly recorded in the books.

(b) The audit test which should be carried out on the computerised sales system at the interim and final audits would be as follows.

Interim audit work

(i) Select a sample of items from the goods despatched records and check:

    (1) with customer's orders;

    (2) with sales invoices:

- quantities;
- prices charged with price lists;
- proper treatment of discounts;
- calculations and additions;
- checking entries in computer sales day book;
- checking postings to sales ledger;

    (3) entries in stock records.

(ii) Select a sample of credit notes and check:

    (1) with correspondence and/or other supporting evidence;

    (2) approval by Mr Jeyes:

- entries in goods returned and stock records;
- entries in day book;
- postings to sales ledger.

(iii) Test numerical sequence of despatch notes and enquire into any missing numbers.

(iv) Test numerical sequence of invoices and credit notes, enquiring into any missing numbers and inspecting copies of those cancelled.

(v) In relation to the sales day book:

    (1) test check entries with both invoices and credit notes;
    (2) test check additions, cross casts and posting to nominal ledger and control account;
    (3) test check postings to sales ledger.

(vi) In relation to the sales ledger, select a sample of accounts and:

    (1) test check entries back to books of prime entry;
    (2) test check additions and balances carried down;
    (3) note and enquire into contra entries;
    (4) ensure that control account balancing has been regularly carried out.

(vii) Write conclusions covering any errors or weaknesses discovered during the above tests and noting any possible management letter points.

Final audit work

(i) If interim audit occurred prior to the year-end, extend samples chosen so that they cover the whole year.

(ii) Test check that sales ledger balances have been correctly extracted.

(iii) Verify that the sales ledger control account agrees with the schedule of balances extracted from the sales ledger.

    (iv)   Test check that sales ledger balances have been properly identified with unpaid invoices.

    (v)   Check casting of schedule of sales ledger balances.

    (vi)   Consider circularisation of debtors (if not done at the interim).

    (vii)   Verify that adequate provision has been made for bad and doubtful debts.

    (viii)   Check cut-off procedures have been properly applied.

9   BINGHAM ENGINEERING

Tutorial note. This question emphasises a number of important points about auditing going concern.

In (a) the auditors should expect the directors to consider a period not less than 12 months after the date the accounts are signed; consideration of a shorter period should be noted in the financial statements or audit report.

The answer to (b) goes beyond listing the possible indications of going concern problems by pointing out that some are more important than others, and most of the signs are less worrying if the business has ready sources of finance.

In (c) checking the assumptions of each forecast is important, and also checking whether the forecasts are consistent with each other. Direct confirmation of future finance is very desirable audit evidence.

(a)   The 'going concern' concept assumes that the accounts are drawn up on the basis that the business will continue to exist as a viable commercial entity, without any need for any significant curtailment in its present level of activity for the 'foreseeable future'.

When forming his opinion at the conclusion of the post balance sheet period the auditor should have regard to the term 'foreseeable future' identified in SSAP 2 in the context of going concern. While the foreseeable future must be judged in relation to specific circumstances, the auditors should normally expect the directors to have considered information which relates to a minimum of 12 months following the date of approval of the financial statements.

(b)   The most common factors indicating that a company may not be regarded as a going concern are as follows.

    (i)   Adverse financial figures or ratios:

        (1)   recurring operating losses;
        (2)   financing to a considerable extent out of overdue suppliers and other creditors;
        (3)   heavy dependence on short-term finance for long-term needs;
        (4)   working capital deficiencies;
        (5)   low liquidity rates;
        (6)   over-gearing, in the form of high or increasing debt to equity ratios;
        (7)   under capitalisation, particularly if there is a deficiency of share capital and reserves.

    (ii)   Borrowing in excess of limits imposed by debenture trust deeds.
    (iii)   Defaults on loans or similar agreements.
    (iv)   Dividends in arrears.
    (v)   Restrictions placed on usual trade terms.
    (vi)   Excessive or obsolete stock.
    (vii)   Long overdue debtors.
    (viii)   Non-compliance with statutory capital requirements.
    (ix)   Deterioration of relationship with bankers.
    (x)   Necessity of seeking new sources or methods of obtaining finance.
    (xi)   The continuing use of old fixed assets because there are not funds available to replace them.
    (xii)   The size and content of the order book.
    (xiii)   Potential losses on long-term contracts.

Other factors, not necessarily suggesting inability to meet debts, may be internal or external matters.

(i)   *Internal matters*

    (1)   Loss of key management or staff.

    (2)   Significantly increasing stock levels.

    (3)   Work stoppages or other labour difficulties.

    (4)   Substantial dependence upon the success of a particular project or particular asset.

    (5)   Excessive reliance on the success of a new product.

    (6)   Uneconomic long-term commitments.

(ii)   *External matters*

    (1)   Legal proceedings or similar matters that may jeopardise a company's ability to continue in business.

    (2)   Loss of a key franchise or patent.

    (3)   Loss of a principal supplier or customer.

    (4)   The undue influence of a market dominant competitor.

    (5)   Political risks.

    (6)   Technical developments which render a key product obsolete.

    (7)   Frequent financial failures of enterprises in the same industry.

The indications above vary in importance and some may only have significance as audit evidence when viewed in conjunction with others.

The significance of the indications above may diminish because they are matched by audit evidence indicating that there are mitigating factors. Indications that the business may be having to sell fixed assets to meet present cash demands may be mitigated by the possibility of obtaining new sources of finance or of renewing and expanding loan finance. Indications of problems that raise questions about the continuation of the business without suggesting inability to meet debts may be mitigated by factors relating to the enterprise's capacity to adopt alternative courses of action, for example, the likelihood of finding alternative sales markets where a principal customer is lost.

(c)   (i)   Under the present circumstances of the company, it is unlikely that the capital expenditure/disposal forecast will contain many items of capital expenditure because of the adverse effect that this would have on the company's cash flow. For such items as there are, the auditor should check that the quoted costs are reasonable, with any large value items being checked against price lists etc. Enquiries should be made of management as to whether there are any proposed items of capital expenditure not included in the forecast.

    In relation to any intended disposals of fixed assets, the auditors should:

    (1)   check whether the proceeds of sale appear to be reasonable with particular care being taken to see that any estimates are arrived at on a prudent basis; and

    (2)   consider whether the estimates of the timing of the receipt of sale proceeds appear to be reasonable and, once again, arrived at on a prudent basis.

(ii)   The audit work required in relation to the profit forecast would be as follows.

    (1)   Check that the level of projected sales is reasonable, being similar to the previous year and consistent with current market conditions and the confirmed orders received from the company's customers.

    (2)   Consider whether the gross profit margin appears reasonable in the light of the company's recent experiences and there has been consistency in the recognition of those items affecting the calculation of this key ratio.

    (3)   Compare the level of profit and loss account items to the previous year, investigating carefully any areas of significant change. Any projected savings in expenditure must be justified and the auditor should take particular care to see that proper provision has been made for all bank charges and interest.

    (4)   All castings and extensions in the profit forecast should be checked and comparison made with common items dealt with in the other two forecasts.

(iii)   The cash flow forecast which is based on the above two forecasts should be checked in the following way.

    (1)   The opening balance should be checked to the draft financial statements and the company's cash book. For the expired period of the forecast, the month end balance should also be checked to the cash book.

(2)   All receipts and payments for the elapsed period of the forecast should be checked against supporting documentation.

(3)   The reasonableness of the timing of future receipts and payments should be considered in the light of the normal period of credit taken by customers and extended by suppliers, due date for payment of PAYE, VAT etc.

(4)   The consistency of items in the cash flow forecast with the other two forecasts should be considered, as well as consistency and accuracy of forecasts in previous years.

(5)   All castings and extensions in the forecast should be checked.

(d)   The reasonableness of the three forecasts referred to above and the willingness of the company's bankers and other creditors to supply the required funds will be the main factors to consider in assessing whether the company is a going concern.

If the work already carried out suggests that the forecasts are reasonable, then with the permission of the client, some direct confirmation of the future 'co-operation' of the bank and major suppliers should be sought. Such co-operation is more likely to be forthcoming if the company is forecast to make profits rather than losses and consideration should also be given to any security held by the various creditors and the chances of any single creditor precipitating a crisis by seeking to invoke his own security.

10   DISPOSAL OF A SUBSIDIARY

Tutorial note. The situation in this question of only being able to consolidate and audit draft figures of a subsidiary that has been sold happens a lot in practice.

(a)   *Availability and reliability of information*

Since no direct communication with subsidiary company management is possible, and audit results are not available, the auditors should consider the results of Green Ltd in the light of:

(i)   the reliability of management accounts in previous years;

(ii)   any evidence that this year's management accounts have been prepared on a basis consistent with that applied in earlier years;

(iii)   the amount of information and explanations which the management of Hyson plc are able to provide from their knowledge acquired whilst still in control of Green Ltd;

(iv)   any audit work carried out on an interim visit and the extent to which useful audit evidence may be obtained by reviewing the work of Hyson plc's internal auditors on the accounts of Green Ltd in respect on the year ended 31 August 19X6;

(v)   any year-end audit work, such as attendance at stocktake and debtor circularisation, carried out before control of Green Ltd was lost.

(b)   *Materiality level (or acceptable error) in relation to Green Ltd's results*

There is no reason to suppose that the reported turnover of Green Ltd is incorrect: the main question mark would be against the extent of the pre-tax loss. The reliability of the figure for the reported loss would be very much dependent on the matters considered in (a) above.

Under the circumstances prevailing, over or understatement of the pre-tax loss would be offset by a corresponding decrease in the exceptional item, loss on sales of subsidiary. In the light of this compensating effect, the auditors of Hyson plc would be able to accept a higher level of error than would have been the case if the group structure had continued as before.

(c)   *Audit of provision for loss on disposal of subsidiary*

The auditors of Hyson plc should check the loss arising on the disposal of its subsidiary Green Ltd as follows.

(i)   Verify that the capital reserve arising on acquisition is the same figure as used in previous years' consolidation working papers.

(ii)   Check the group tax relief against any computation available and confirm that Hyson plc is in fact entitled to such relief in the light of the changed circumstances of the group.

(iii)   The cash proceeds should be vouched to any agreement in relation to the sale of Green Ltd and agreed to any post balance sheet receipts.

(iv)   Check that disclosure of the provision and any other matters related to the sale are in accordance with FRS 3 *Reporting financial performance*.

11   RIPLEY MANUFACTURING

Tutorial note. This question covers several types of transaction with directors. For every type of transaction the general procedures are similar.

(a)   Enquiry of and confirmation from directors of emoluments or transactions

(b)   Examination of direct sources of evidence (service agreements, the company's articles to check whether approval was needed)

(c)   Examination of other sources of evidence for undisclosed transactions (general ledger, board minutes)

(d)   Alertness throughout the audit for any transactions that appear to be unusual (see (c) (vi)

Note the auditors should be particularly concerned with whether or not transactions are at arms-length; inter alia transactions that appear unduly favourable to the interests of the directors may be a sign of lack of management integrity which would impact on the whole audit.

(a)   In order to determine whether a company had made any loans or quasi-loans to any of its directors, auditors should:

(i)   review the nominal ledger or its equivalent to determine whether any loans to directors were recorded or whether any of the directors' current accounts with the company were overdrawn;

(ii)   determine, by direct enquiry from both the directors themselves and from the company secretary, whether any loans to directors had been entered into;

(iii)   check with both the company secretary and with the directors whether any mortgages had been entered into on favourable terms;

(iv)   obtain from each director confirmation in writing of his answers to (ii) and (iii);

(v)   examine directors' expense claims to determine whether company credit cards were being used for private expenditure (which would constitute a form of quasi-loan if reimbursement of the company were delayed).

In the case of guarantees, the audit work to be carried out would be broadly similar, though auditors should also check whether bank confirmations received included any mention of guarantees made by the company with respect to a loan to any of the directors. (Where a guarantee had been given to a bank other than one of the company's own banks, this would be very difficult to detect unless the company disclosed the information of its own volition.)

Where any loans, quasi-loans or guarantees were discovered during the course of the audit it would be necessary to check whether disclosure was required under the 1985 Companies Act.

(b)   (i)   In order to determine whether there are any service agreements between the directors of Ripley Manufacturing plc and the company, the best course of action would be:

(1)   to ask the company secretary and the directors whether there are any service agreements with the company;

(2)   to inspect the previous years' accounts to see if there had been any disclosure of service agreements in the past;

(3)   to check the board minutes for any evidence of service agreements;

(4)   to check the documentation of any service agreements found, to ensure that the treatment in the accounts is the correct one.

(ii)   The audit work required to test whether any options to purchase shares had been granted by the company to the directors would be broadly similar to that above. In addition, auditors should review the company's articles of association in order to determine whether the approval of the members was required for such transactions. If members' approval was found to be necessary, it would be necessary to confirm that any share option arrangements had indeed been approved.

(c) A director is most likely to have a material interest in a contract where he is a director of one company and a substantial shareholder in another. Unless the director concerned is frank about his interests, it may be difficult for the auditor to discover them. The following steps are likely to prove the most productive:

(i) checking with the directors themselves and with the company secretary whether there are any material interests;

(ii) comparing major suppliers or customers with known directors' interest (obtained from the annual return and by direct enquiry) to determine whether any names appear on both lists;

(iii) checking to see whether there are any contracts between the company and another company owned by a close relative of a director, or with a partnership involving a director;

(iv) where material contracts have been uncovered in which one or more directors have an interest, checking that the transaction involved has been conducted at arm's length;

(v) checking whether any property leased by Ripley Manufacturing plc was owned by one or more of its directors since here too a disclosable interest could have arisen.

(vi) Reviewing accounting records for indications of transactions with directors. SAS 460 lists several types of transaction or arrangement, the unusual features of which mean director involvement is possible.

(1) Transactions which have abnormal terms of trade
(2) Transactions which appear to lack a logical business reason
(3) Transactions where substance differs from form
(4) Transactions processed or approved in a non-routine manner
(5) Unusual transactions around the year-end

(d) The problem in these circumstances is that, because one of the directors of Ripley Manufacturing plc owned 50% of Lowdham Engineering plc's issued share capital, Lowdham Engineering may have been purchased for more than it was worth, with an obvious benefit to the director concerned. To ensure that this has been an arm's length transaction, the following matters should be considered.

(i) It will be necessary to consider whether the price paid for Lowdham Engineering plc was a reasonable one, based on the current value of its assets, together with its profits and the expectation of future profits. To do this, it will be necessary to obtain a set of Lowdham Engineering's annul accounts and to take a view on the valuation of its fixed assets (if the price paid for the company included a significant amount in respect of revalued fixed assets, that revaluation should be supported by the report of a qualified valuer).

(ii) An inspection of Ripley Manufacturing plc's articles of association and its minutes should be made to check whether all necessary approvals have been obtained from the shareholders (it may be, of course, that none are required).

(iii) Check whether the purchase of Lowdham Engineering plc has been properly disclosed in the annual accounts of Ripley Manufacturing.

(e) Since the shares of both Ilkeston Electrical and Nuthall Distributors are owned by the same directors and their families, only the Inland Revenue would be likely to query the transaction since it has taken place between connected parties. It is possible that creditors of Ilkeston Electrical Ltd could be interested if that company were having going concern problems.

Obviously the transaction would have to be properly disclosed in the accounts of Ilkeston Electrical and would result in Nuthall Distributors becoming its subsidiary. It would also be necessary to check the articles of association to see whether the approval of ordinary members was required and, if so, whether it had been received.

12   **WISEGUYS NATIONAL BAKERIES**

Tutorial note. The key point in this question is a clear explanation of the consequences on the audit report of each problem. Note that the auditor hints in the second-last paragraph that the directors may wish to amend the accounts, but also makes it clear that it is up to the directors to make this decision.

S J Bishop & Co
Castle House, 67-70 Knights Road
London EC1

Mr N King
Finance Director
Wiseguys National Bakeries Ltd
Wiseguys House
Woodley Industrial Estate
Woodley, Beds

28 February 19X4

Dear Mr King,

Financial Statements: year ended 31 December 19X3

Thank you for your letter dated 21 January 19X4 and copy of the minutes of your board meeting at which the above financial statements were approved. We note also that it was resolved that no amendments should be made to the statements as approved.

We must, nevertheless, point out that there are certain matters which we have noted during our review of the financial statements and, subject to further discussion, these may well require suitable reference in our audit report when this is finalised in due course. These matters are accordingly listed below.

1   *Freehold property*

In past years this property has been shown in the statement at its original cost, whereas it is now restated at £1,250,000 as professionally valued during the year. We are satisfied as to the basis of the revaluation, adjustment to and disclosure within the financial statements. As a result no further reference to the property revaluation will be required in our audit report.

2   *Value of trade marks*

In view of the materiality of the valuation originally attributed to trade marks by the directors in 19X7, and the practical problem of obtaining relevant, reliable and sufficient audit evidence to verify this value, we are obliged as in previous years to note our limitation in audit scope in this regard. This will be referred to in the basis of opinion paragraph of our report, in which we shall state that:

(a)   the trade marks were valued by the directors at £800,000 in 19X0 and have been included in the balance sheet as this figure;

(b)   as in previous years, we have been unable to carry out any procedures to confirm that this valuation is justified;

(c)   we are therefore uncertain as to whether the company's assets and reserves have accordingly been overstated; and

(d)   we have qualified our report in previous years on the grounds of the same uncertainty

We shall follow this by saying that, except for any adjustments that might have been found to be necessary had we been provided with satisfactory information and explanations regarding revalued trade marks, a true and fair view is given of the state of the company's affairs.

3   *Doubtful debt provision*

It is our belief that no part of the debt of £45,000 due from XYZ Ltd will be recovered by the company. Since the financial statements which the directors have approved include no provisions against this debt, it will be necessary for us to state that:

(a)   no provision has been made against an amount of £45,000 owing by the customer;

(b)   we believe such amount to be irrecoverable; and

(c)   except for the failure to make such provision, in our opinion a true and fair view of the state of the company's affairs and its results is given by the financial statements.

4   *Loan to a director*

Since the director's indebtedness of £22,000, which subsisted during a six week period, has not been disclosed in the financial statements in accordance with the provisions of the Companies Act 1985, we are obliged under the Act to include in our report a statement giving the required particulars.

The particulars include:

(a)   the name of the director;
(b)   the fact of his indebtedness; and
(c)   the amount due (including any interest) ie £22,000.

5   *Alleged breach of contract*

Because of the potential materiality of the uncertainty concerning the amount of compensation (possibly including costs) which it appears will be payable following the major breach of your contract with LMBN Ltd, we feel it will be necessary for our report to refer to the explanatory note in the financial statements in which this contingent liability is disclosed under a fundamental uncertainty paragraph.

This paragraph simply draws closer attention to this matter. It is not a qualification of our opinion.

Should you and your co-directors wish to discuss these matters further, please do not hesitate to contact us. If it is believed that, in the light of the above comments, amendments to the accounts should be made, it will, of course, be necessary for the board to re-approve the amended financial statements.

However, should the board still consider that no amendments are to be made, it will be necessary for us to draft our audit report incorporating the various matters referred to in this letter. A copy of the proposed report will be forwarded for your information.

Yours sincerely

For S J Bishop & Co.

Lecturers'
question bank

Examination style questions are indicated by mark allocations and time limits.

1   JARNDYCE

(a)   State who can be appointed as auditor of a limited company.

(b)   For some years your firm has been auditor to Jarndyce Ltd. Recently the directors who were also the major shareholders have sold their shares to a large multinational company. It is that company's policy to appoint its own auditors to all the subsidiary companies and your firm has been asked to resign.

   Required

   (i)   How may auditors resign their office?

   (ii)   Describe briefly the powers given to a resigning auditor to ensure that the members of a company are aware of any special reasons surrounding his resignation.

2   KEELE CONSTRUCTION (25 marks)   *45 mins*

Keele Construction plc undertakes long-term contracts, which include industrial buildings, offices and roads. You have been asked to audit the long-term contracts, as shown in the company's accounts at 30 September 19X9. At the year end the company has three fixed price long-term contracts in progress, as follows.

	Hawthorne	*Lindsey*	*Barnes*
	£'000	£'000	£'000
Direct costs to date	480	2,080	3,360
Cost of work completed	0	1,800	3,200
Additional direct costs to completion	1,200	320	640
Contract price	1,900	2,800	3,500
Progress payments received	300	2,000	3,100

Direct costs include:

(a)   design costs, and expenses incurred on the site including labour costs, materials and other expenses directly incurred by the site (for example costs of leasing machinery, vehicles and portable buildings, transport costs, stationery and telephone expenses);

(b)   labour costs which are allocated to the project from the payroll;

(c)   other expenses are charged from purchase invoices;

(d)   attributable overheads which comprise expenses incurred by the head office which are directly attributable to the project. Attributable overheads have been included at 60% of the cost of the items in (a), (b) and (c) above.

The additional direct costs to completion are the estimated further costs required to complete the contract, in addition to the direct costs incurred up to the balance sheet date.

The statement of accounting policy for long-term contract work in progress in the company's accounts is in accordance with SSAP 9 *Stocks and long-term contracts*.

The value of work completed is calculated as:

$$\frac{\text{Cost of work completed}}{\text{Estimated costs to completion}} \times \text{Contract price}$$

The estimated costs to completion is the sum of the actual direct costs to date and the additional direct costs to completion.

The company's accounting policy on attributable profit and foreseeable losses for long term contract work in progress is as follows.

(a)   Full provision is made for any foreseeable losses.

(b)   Attributable profit is taken as the product of:

   (i)   the total profit currently estimated to arise over the duration of the contract; and

   (ii)   the ratio of the value of work completed to the contract price. No attributable profit is included until the outcome of the contract can be assessed with reasonable certainty.

Required

(a) For each of the three long-term contracts, Hawthorne, Lindsey and Barnes, state:

    (i) the value of work completed and the attributable profit or foreseeable loss which should be included in the profit and loss account; and

    (ii) the values of the items which should appear in the balance sheet at 30 September 19X9, and how these items should be disclosed in the accounts.

You should include appropriate workings and explanation of the figures to support your answer.
(9 marks)

(b) List the checks and describe the audit work you would perform to verify that the long-term contract work in progress has been correctly stated in the company's accounts. Your answer should include a description of the audit tests you would perform in checking:

    (i) direct costs incurred to the balance sheet date;
    (ii) attributable overheads;
    (iii) estimated costs to completion;
    (iv) the addition of attributable profit or deduction of foreseeable loss;
    (v) the correct presentation of the long-term contract work in progress in the accounts.
(16 marks)

3 MAGDALA WHOLESALERS (25 marks)   *45 mins*

Magdala Wholesalers plc are wholesalers of electrical goods and they currently operate a manual stock control system. Following representations by the manager of the stock control department, the directors have agreed that a computerised stock control system should be introduced. Because of the specialised nature of the company's business, it has been decided that the computer programs for this new system should be written by the systems analysts and programmers from the company's own data processing department. It is the company's policy to have all programs checked for correct operation by a separate section of testers within the data processing department.

Required

(a) List and briefly describe the stages you would expect to see in operation from the initial proposal for the development of the stock control system to live running of the system by the user department.
(10 marks)

(b) Describe the checks you would perform to verify that proper controls have been exercised over the development of the new computerised stock control system.
(9 marks)

(c) Explain the reasons why it should not normally be necessary for the auditors of Magdala Wholesalers plc to check the detailed listings of the program instructions. Your answer should describe the controls which the auditors should check and the alternative procedures they could use which would make checking of the program instructions unnecessary.
(6 marks)

4 AUDIT RISK

Audit risk is a combination of the risk that the financial statements being audited may contain material errors and that these errors may not be detected by the auditors' testing procedures. A failure to detect such errors may leave the auditors liable for losses suffered by other parties.

Required

(a) Briefly describe what you understand by the terms 'inherent risk', 'control risk' and 'detection risk'.

(b) Explain, in the light of recent case law, what you understand to be the auditors' liability for losses suffered by other parties.

List of key terms, Cases and Index

These are the terms which we have identified throughout the text as being KEY TERMS. You should make sure that you can define what these terms mean; go back to the pages highlighted here if you need to check.

ORDER FORM

To order your ACCA books, you can phone us on 0181 740 2211, email us at publishing@bpp.co.uk, fax this form to 0181 740 1184 or cut this form out and post it to the address below.

To: BPP Publishing Ltd, Aldine House, Aldine Place,
London W12 8AW **Tel: 0181-740 2211**
Fax: 0181-740 1184

Forenames (Mr / Ms): _____ Surname:_____

Daytime delivery address: _____

_____

Post code: _____ Date of exam (month/year):_____

Please send me the following books:

	Price			Quantity			Total
	6/98 Text £	1/98 Kit £	1/98 Passcards £	Text	Kit	Passcards	£
Foundation							
The Accounting Framework	18.95	8.95	4.95	....	....	....	....
The Accounting Framework (Int'l)	18.95	8.95★		....	....		....
The Legal Framework	18.95	8.95	4.95	....	....	....	....
Management Information	18.95	8.95	4.95	....	....	....	....
The Organisational Framework	18.95	8.95	4.95	....	....	....	....
Certificate							
Information Analysis	18.95	8.95	4.95	....	....	....	....
The Audit Framework	18.95	8.95	4.95	....	....	....	....
The Audit Framework (Int'l)	18.95	8.95★		....	....		....
The Tax Framework FA 98 (7/98 Text, 8/98 P/c, 8/98 Kit)	18.95	8.95	4.95	....	....	....	....
Managerial Finance	18.95	8.95	4.95	....	....	....	....
Professional							
Information for Control and Decision Making	19.95	9.95	5.95	....	....	....	....
Accounting and Audit Practice A: Accounting	15.95	9.95	5.95	....	....	....	....
Accounting and Audit Practice A: Accounting (Int'l)	15.95	9.95★		....	....		....
Accounting and Audit Practice B: Auditing	13.95			....			....
Accounting and Audit Practice B: Auditing (Int'l)	13.95			....			....
(Kit and Passcards cover both accounting and auditing)							
Tax Planning FA 98 (7/98 Text, 8/98 P/c, 8/98 Kit)	19.95	9.95	5.95	....	....	....	....
Management and Strategy	19.95	9.95	5.95	....	....	....	....
Financial Reporting Environment	19.95	9.95	5.95	....	....	....	....
Financial Reporting Environment (Int'l)	19.95	9.95★		....	....		....
Financial Strategy	19.95	9.95	5.95	....	....	....	....

Postage and packaging:

UK: Texts £3.00 for first plus £2.00 for each extra		....	....	....
Kits and Passcards £2.00 for first plus £1.00 for each extra		....	....	....
Europe (inc ROI & CI): Texts £5.00 for first plus £4.00 for each extra		....	....	....
Kits and Passcards £2.50 for first plus £1.00 for each extra		....	....	....
Rest of the World: Texts £20.00 for first plus £10.00 for each extra		....	....	....
Kits and Passcards £15.00 for first plus £8.00 for each extra		....	....	....

(Single Kits/Passcards are airmailed. All other parcels are sent by courier and should arrive in not more than six days.)

★ International Stream Kits will be published in Autumn 1998   Total _____

I enclose a cheque for £ _____ **or charge to Access/Visa/Switch**

Card number | | | | | | | | | | | | | | | | | | |

Start date (Switch only) _____ **Expiry date** _____ **Issue no. (Switch only)**___

Signature _____

REVIEW FORM & FREE PRIZE DRAW

All original review forms from the entire BPP range, completed with genuine comments, will be entered into one of two draws on 31 January 1999 and 31 July 1999. The names on the first four forms picked out on each occasion will be sent a cheque for £50.

Name: _____   Address: _____

_____

_____

How have you used this Text?
(Tick one box only)

☐ Home study (book only)

☐ On a course: college _____

☐ With 'correspondence' package

☐ Other _____

Why did you decide to purchase this Text?
(Tick one box only)

☐ Have used BPP Texts in the past

☐ Recommendation by friend/colleague

☐ Recommendation by a lecturer at college

☐ Saw advertising

☐ Other _____

During the past six months do you recall seeing/receiving any of the following?
(Tick as many boxes as are relevant)

☐ Our advertisement in *Students' Newsletter*

☐ Our advertisement in *Pass*

☐ Our brochure with a letter through the post

Which (if any) aspects of our advertising do you find useful?
(Tick as many boxes as are relevant)

☐ Prices and publication dates of new editions

☐ Information on Text content

☐ Facility to order books off-the-page

☐ None of the above

Your ratings, comments and suggestions would be appreciated on the following areas

	Very useful	Useful	Not useful
Introductory section (Key study steps, personal study plan etc)	☐	☐	☐
Chapter introductions	☐	☐	☐
Key terms	☐	☐	☐
Explanations	☐	☐	☐
Questions and answers	☐	☐	☐
Chapter roundups	☐	☐	☐
Quick quizzes	☐	☐	☐
Exam focus points	☐	☐	☐
Exam question bank	☐	☐	☐
Exam answer bank	☐	☐	☐
List of key terms and index	☐	☐	☐
Icons	☐	☐	☐

	Excellent	Good	Adequate	Poor
Overall opinion of this Text	☐	☐	☐	☐

Do you intend to continue using BPP Study Texts/Kits?   ☐ Yes   ☐ No

Please note any further comments and suggestions/errors on the reverse of this page.

Please return to: Edmund Hewson, BPP Publishing Ltd, FREEPOST, London, W12 8BR

REVIEW FORM & FREE PRIZE DRAW (continued)

Please note any further comments and suggestions/errors below

FREE PRIZE DRAW RULES

1 Closing date for 31 January 1999 draw is 31 December 1998. Closing date for 31 July 1999 draw is 30 June 1999.

2 Restricted to entries with UK and Eire addresses only. BPP employees, their families and business associates are excluded.

3 No purchase necessary. Entry forms are available upon request from BPP Publishing. No more than one entry per title, per person. Draw restricted to persons aged 16 and over.

4 Winners will be notified by post and receive their cheques not later than 6 weeks after the relevant draw date. Lists of winners will be published in BPP's *focus* newsletter following the relevant draw.

5 The decision of the promoter in all matters is final and binding. No correspondence will be entered into.

PERTH COLLEGE
★ ★
LIBRARY